4/86

VAX
COBOL

VAX
COBOL

Stephen M. Samuels

Reston Publishing Company, Inc.
A Prentice-Hall Company
Reston, Virginia

Library of Congress Cataloging in Publication Data

Samuels, Stephen Michael.
  VAX COBOL.

  1. VAX-11 (Computer)—Programming. 2. COBOL
(Computer program language) I. Title.
QA76.8.V37S26 1985   001.64'2   84-22344
ISBN 0-8359-8248-3

Interior design and production: Meridee Mucciarone

© 1985 Reston Publishing Company, Inc.
A Prentice-Hall Company
Reston, Virginia 22090

10   9   8   7   6   5   4   3   2   1

PRINTED IN THE UNITED STATES OF AMERICA

To Sharon, Michael, and Amy,
who suffered through my "terminal" illness.

Contents

Preface

This book is specifically designed for learning COBOL programming on a DEC VAX-11. It employs listings along with structured design and coding techniques as its primary educational foundation. Further, many errors of compilation and execution are presented along with these listings to aid the learning process. The main rules of COBOL syntax are presented as one progresses from chapter to chapter. Problem solving using a modular design system is emphasized; this is done by adding on portions (coded modules) to existing COBOL programs and using incremental testing techniques with each additional module.

This text was written from extensive lecture notes and problem sets used in DePaul University's Computer Career Program, an intensive 7-month career change program for students with college degrees in other academic areas. These notes and problems are also used in the introductory and advanced COBOL courses in DePaul University's Computer Science Department.

It is hoped that the use of this text will enable students to write superior programs at an accelerated rate. Specifically, students will:

a. Learn by doing from the very beginning. In the first few chapters emphasis is placed on writing simple programs and observing the wide range of syntax errors given by the compiler that inevitably come to every COBOL programmer. This has proven to be a far better approach than having the students learn all the combinations of syntax rules *before* they begin to program. By learning to code from the very beginning, and by writing program after program, the student learns new syntax rules when appropriate. [An on-line VAX with a line editor makes this not only possible but highly practical.]

b. Use structured design, code, and incremental testing techniques throughout. Rather than trying to understand complicated flowcharts, students will see and learn modular design wtih the incremental testing of added modules to programs. By writing many shorter programs, students will become familiar with most compiler errors. After editing and successfully running these programs, they will easily be able to handle more complex problems, design structure, and complicated coding techniques.

c. Write complex programs that not only update files, but also allow for on-line user input of data. Students will be able to write COBOL programs that handle screen display, cursor movement, and random updating of indexed files at the same time.

I wish to thank Dr. Helmut Epp who was not only instrumental in building a very successful Computer Science Department at DePaul University but also helped develop innovative courses of study such as the Computer Career Program and Executive Program. Special thanks go to Dr. Robert Fisher who was always there when hardware problems appeared. I also wish to thank Mrs. Beth Elderd who encouraged me to write this text and to Ms. Joyce Johnson who did all of the initial editing.

Stephen M. Samuels

1

Introduction

1.1 PURPOSE OF THIS TEXT

This book is specifically designed for learning COBOL programming on a VAX–11 Computer System. It employs listings along with structured design and coding techniques as its primary educational foundation. The main rules of the COBOL syntax, or language, are presented as one progresses from chapter to chapter. Further, many errors of compilation and execution are shown. Problem solving using a modular design system is emphasized; this is done by "adding on" portions (coded modules) to existing COBOL programs and using incremental testing techniques with each additional module. Specifically, students will:

a. "learn by doing" from the very beginning. In the first few chapters, emphasis will be placed on writing simple programs, observing and correcting a range of common syntax errors given by the COBOL compiler, correcting execution errors, and finally making additions to successfully executed programs. By learning to code from the beginning, and by writing program after program, the student learns new syntax rules where appropriate.

b. use structured design, code, and incremental testing techniques throughout this text. A basic four-module design will be presented to solve fairly simple problems. From this design, students will write short programs and become familiar with most compiler errors. After editing and successfully running these programs, more complex problems can be solved through additions to the basic modular design structure. Incremental testing of these modules is stressed throughout this text.

c. use advanced coding techniques for on-line processing, which includes the management of random files along with screen cursor movement techniques.

1.2 THE VAX–11 COMPUTER SYSTEM

Digital Equipment Corporation (DEC) is the manufacturer of the VAX–11 machine, a general purpose digital computer. It is similar in its instruction set to the PDP–11 but has extended addressing capabilities. The name VAX means Virtual Address eXtension. There are two popular models currently used throughout the industry, the VAX–11/750 and the VAX–11/780, the latter being the larger of the two. Figure 1–1 displays these two models.

A computer system is normally made up of a central processing unit (CPU), storage devices, input/output devices, and printers. A CPU is quite similar to a very fancy calculator with a large amount of memory or primary storage. Input devices feed information to the CPU while output devices receive information from the CPU. Some devices (terminals, for example) do both. The CPU is capable of processing large amounts of information or data. There is a need for secondary storage devices, such as disk units and tape drives. These devices can hold much more information than the CPU's main memory can. These data are stored on disks and tapes, just as music or video can be stored on records and tapes. The number of disk, tape, and terminal units that are connected to (or "interface" with) a particular VAX–11 can vary.

Finally, no computer system is complete without an operating system, which is a series of programs (software) to enable the processor, disk and tape drives, and terminals (hardware) to function. To control allocation of memory, input/output operations, system subroutines, etc., VAX–11 comes with an operating system called Virtual Management System (VMS). From time to time the operating system is upgraded, hence when one "logs on" with a terminal, a message usually appears that says:

Welcome to VAX/VMS Version 3.1

The number 3.1 represents the current edition or update of the operating system. The logon procedure is discussed in full in the next chapter. Any computer can be represented as diagrammed in Figure 1–2.

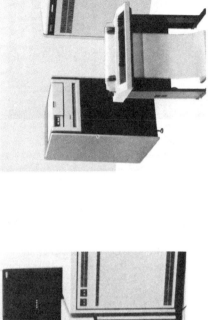

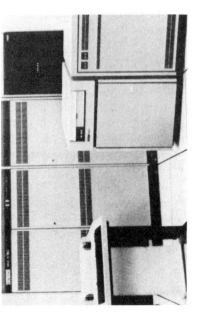

VAX-11/780 RM05/TU77 System

SV-AXDBD-CA(CD)

Components

- 2 MB (64K chip) ECC MOS memory
- REM05 disk subsystem (MBA and single-ported 256 MB RM05 disk drive) for use as the system device in a freestanding, 36 in (91.4 cm) high cabinet and one 36 in (91.4 cm) high utility cabinet housing the RM05 drive adapter
- TEU77 tape subsystem (MBA and 125 in/sec, 800/1600 bits/in tape transport) for use as the backup/load device in a freestanding 60 in (152.4 cm) high H9602 cabinet
- DZ11-A 8-line asynchronous multiplexer

VAX-11/750 RM03/TS11 System

SV-BXTAB-CA(CD)

Components

- 2 MB (64K chip) ECC MOS memory
- RGM03 disk subsystem (MBA and single-ported 67 MB RM03 disk drive) for use as the system device in a freestanding, 39 in (99 cm) high H969 cabinet
- TS11 tape subsystem (UNIBUS controller and 45 in/sec, 1600 bits/in tape transport) for use as the backup/load device in a bolt-on, 60 in (152.4 cm) high H9646 cabinet
- DZ11-A 8-line asynchronous multiplexer

Figure 1-1 Reprinted with permission of Digital Equipment Corporation. From *Vax Systems & Options Catalog*, April–June, 1983.

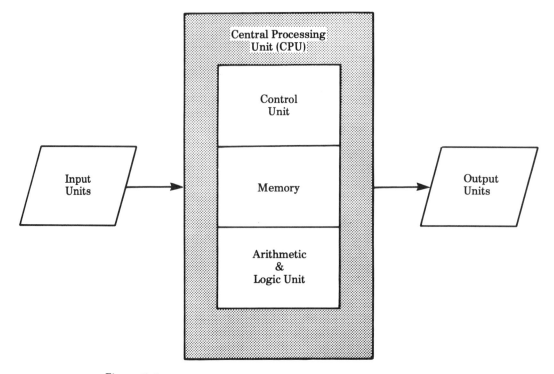

Figure 1-2

1.3 COMPUTER PROGRAMMING

Since computer systems have a large amount of storage capability, it is possible to store instructions. These instructions, then, tell the CPU what to do with data. But the instructions not only have to be correct, they have to be in a specific order. The job of a computer programmer is to write these explicit, ordered instructions so that a computer system can do a required task or tasks. To do this, the programmer must learn how to provide algorithms (solutions to problems), code these algorithms using an acceptable computer programming language (a computer program), and enter this computer program into a computer system. If everything goes well, the task is completed correctly. This task is the processing of data in a rapid and efficient or error-free way. In most cases the task is the process of receiving input, manipulating it in some way, and producing output. A good payroll program, for example, should make the computer system enter a file containing records that may each have a name, hours worked, and rate, and produce payroll checks for each employee.

But computer programming is not a mysterious art practiced only by highly trained specialists after years of study and programming. Using a suitable computer programming language like COBOL, a person with no previous programming experience can write useful programs right from the beginning. Learning a computer language is like learning English. One need not know the entire dictionary before writing a letter. One need not know the entire COBOL language or syntax before writing a computer program. The language is learned by writing program after program after program.

It is possible to use a computer system without writing any programs. Many computer users do not write their own programs. However, to a user who writes programs, the potential use of a computer is limited only by the user's ingenuity and expertise in combining basic operations to achieve more complex goals.

1.4 COBOL

COBOL stands for COmmon Business Oriented Language. It was developed in 1959 by a committee of large computer users named the COnference of DAta SYstems Language (CODASYL). The users were employed by many different computer manufacturers, such as IBM, RCA, Honeywell, and Sperry Rand, along with the Department of Defense. Before this language was developed, one had to write programs in the machine language of the computer purchased. The cost of reprogramming, when buying new computers, was staggering. COBOL, with only slight modifications, could run on practically all large computer systems. In 1968, ANSI (American National Standards Institute) approved a standard COBOL language, ANSI COBOL. Since that time there have been standard revisions to the language. It is by far the most popular computer language used today in the business community.

To run COBOL programs, a computer operating system, like VAX/VMS, includes a COBOL compiler or translator. Each computer, whether manufactured by DEC, IBM, Honeywell, etc., operates only on its own machine instructions. The COBOL programs you will write need to be translated into the system's machine language. For example, if you only understood German, you would need a translator to change this text into German. However, you needn't have to worry because your VAX should have a COBOL compiler as part of its operating system.

The advantages of COBOL as a method to write computer programs are as follows:

1. It is a standard language. All COBOL compilers should conform to this standard.

2. It is an English-type language. It is much easier to understand the instructions in this language than in machine-level languages.

3. It is widely used and available. The business community has invested millions of dollars in COBOL programs and thousands of programmers are

trained to use COBOL. And since the majority of business computer programs are written in COBOL, this language will be around for quite some time.

4. It is self-documenting. Even lengthy COBOL programs, if well-written, are easy to follow since the program itself can be used as part of the documentation.

5. It employs excellent file-handling techniques and can process the large amounts of data normally required for business applications.

6. It is easier to learn and write programs in COBOL than machine language or other high-level computer languages like FORTRAN, PL1, or ALGOL.

There are some disadvantages to this language that must be mentioned:

1. The COBOL programs are very wordy. Many of these programs could be written with fewer instructions in other languages.

2. Some of the newer programming languages, like PL1 and Pascal, have features and modern programming techniques not available in COBOL. COBOL and FORTRAN are the oldest high-level computer programming languages. [The term high-level means that instructions written in these languages have to be translated to a low-level machine language.]

3. Programs written in the computer system's own machine language or in some sort of low-level pseudo-language (Assembler) need little or no translation (compilation). Good machine-level programs, although very difficult for others to understand, are more efficient in execution than COBOL programs that do similar things.

1.5 STEPS INVOLVED IN PROCESSING COMPUTER PROGRAMS IN COBOL

Before one writes a program, there should be a specific problem or task that needs to be figured out. An algorithm should be developed first. This may consist of using symbols or flowcharts, modular design techniques, or pseudocode (English statements) that show how a specific problem or task should be solved in a stepwise fashion. Then this algorithm is coded in a computer language, like COBOL, and entered into the computer system via some input device, terminal (on-line) or card-reader (batch mode). The compiler is then "called" to translate the instructions into machine language instructions. If the compiler detects serious errors, then there is no translation and the programmer is informed of these errors. The errors must be corrected before any translation takes place. Once translation takes place, execution of the program can commence. Output is produced or there may be an error in ex-

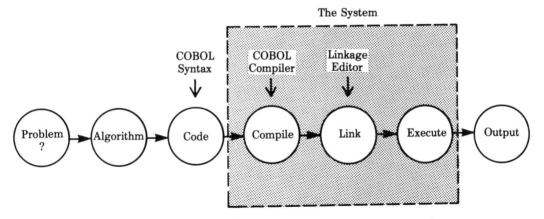

Figure 1-3

ecution. If the latter occurs, the programmer must again adjust the program so that it not only compiles correctly but executes correctly.

A COBOL program, then, is really "read" twice by the computer system—once for compilation and once for execution. The entire process can be represented schematically in Figure 1-3.

1.6   HOW TO USE THIS TEXTBOOK

It is strongly suggested that an attempt be made to answer all questions that appear in each chapter. If one really wants to learn how to write COBOL programs on a VAX-11, most of the programming problems associated with each chapter should be coded and entered via a terminal that interfaces with a VAX-11. The programming problems that have a "*" next to the number should also be attempted, although some are rather difficult. You cannot learn to play bridge or play the piano just by reading a book. Practice makes perfect! Attempt to use the modular designs and listings in each chapter as a "template." All listings are programs that were entered into a VAX-11 system and were all compiled and executed.

Introducing the VAX Editor

Before you can learn how to write COBOL programs, you need to be able to get onto the computer. It is assumed that you will be using a cathode ray tube terminal (CRT), illustrated in Figure 2–1, and that you have authority to be a user of the VAX; in other words, you have a legitimate Username and Password. It is not the intent of this chapter to describe, in detail, how a terminal accesses your VAX since there are a variety of communication networks.

2.1 LOGGING ON

To log on:

1. Turn on the terminal and wait a moment (some terminals require a longer "warm-up" time than others).

2. Press the ⟨ret⟩ (return key) once or twice to allow the VAX to recognize your terminal. When it is ready, you will see the following displayed on your terminal:

USERNAME:

3. Enter the username that was given to you and press the ⟨ret⟩. The VAX will now respond with:

Figure 2-1 Reprinted with permission of C. Itoh Electronics, Inc. From *Users Manual for Video Terminals Model CIT-101* © 1981.

PASSWORD:

4. Enter the password you were also given. Notice that when you enter the password it is not displayed ("echoed") on the screen. This is for your protection. Press the 〈ret〉 key. If you correctly entered your password VAX will respond by displaying:

WELCOME TO VAX/VMS VERSION 3.4

[messages of general interest, bulletins or maintenance schedules etc.]

$

The dollar sign, the VAX DCL prompt, indicates that your logon procedure was successful. You can now start using the Digital Command Language (DCL) which will allow you to use the Editor (EDT). The Editor will allow you to enter information, specifically COBOL programs. [Some VAX systems require EDIT.]

5. If you keyed in the wrong username and correct password, or the correct username and wrong password, the system will respond by displaying an error message such as:

"User authorization failure"

Your logon procedure was not successful and you will have to do steps 1–4 again. You should not be upset if this happens because it happens to almost everyone at one time or another!

If you have had enough for one day, you can go to the end of this chapter to learn the logout procedure; otherwise, let's continue.

2.2 DIGITAL COMMAND LANGUAGE

The Digital Command Language (DCL) allows the user to communicate with the operating system's (VMS) control program. DCL commands allow the user to create, delete, and manipulate files. They also allow for the use of compilers, control of executing processes, and other miscellaneous abilities. With the "$" appearing before you on the CRT, you now have access to your directory, a continuous area of specific size on a disk pack unit. To see what is in your directory, key in the following after the "$":

DIR⟨ret⟩

You will get the following response:

No files found

This means that your directory is empty. There are no files in it. Before learning how to create, manipulate, and delete files, you should try a few other DCL commands. Try this:

SHOW TIME⟨ret⟩

You will get the current date and time. Remember that the "$" prompt means that you are at the "command" level. Anything you enter after the "$" means that you want to invoke a particular DCL command. If you misspell a command you will get an appropriate message and get the "$" back. Try making a mistake. Try keying in $DAR or $SHOW TIEMPO. There is no DAR command and the VAX does not understand Spanish!

If you want to find out what kind of terminal you are using do the following:

SHOW TERMINAL

You will get a response telling you that the terminal is a VT100, VT52, or Terminal Type Unknown.

One useful DCL command allows the user to change his/her password.

Someone else gave you your Password. If you want to change it, do the following:

SET PASSWORD⟨ret⟩
Old Password:(you type in your current password—then ⟨ret⟩)
New Password:(you type in your new password—then ⟨ret⟩)
Verification:(you type in the new password again—then ⟨ret⟩)
$

Try to pick a Password that you can easily remember!

There are many other DCL commands one can invoke; you will be using some of them after you create files with the VAX Editor.

If you need help on any of the many DCL functions, type, "HELP" after the prompt ($). You will see a list of features. Type "HELP" and the feature name (or: TOPIC) to receive more information on that feature (TOPIC). For example:

HELP COBOL⟨ret⟩

This will give you more information about the COBOL compiler feature and will lead you to additional features for which you can request help.

The most important DCL command is the EDT command, which invokes the Editor; EDT enables you to create and modify files.

2.3   EDITOR

To invoke the Editor, use the following at the prompt ($):

EDT [filename.filetype]

where filename can be up to 9 alphanumeric characters and filetype can be up to 3 alphanumeric characters.
Some examples are:

a. PRGRAM1.COB

b. TRANSFERS.DAT

c. ROSTER.O

d. INVENT345.TXT

The best way to learn the Editor is to log on and use the rest of this chapter as a manual to help you create and manipulate a file. Let's start by creating a file that is, in fact, words to a song. Invoke the Editor by:

$EDT CASABLANC.LIB⟨ret⟩   (where the $ was already present, of course)
Input file does not exist   —system response
[EOB]   —system response
*   —system response

Notice that the system told you that:

a. The file was not present in your directory.

b. In this case the end-of-buffer designator [EOB] is the only output.

c. You are now in the edit mode of the Editor (* prompt).

There are two modes to the Editor, the edit mode and the input mode. The edit mode always has the "*" as a prompt. In the edit mode one can use commands to delete lines, move lines, and change or replace lines. However, since we do not have any lines in CASABLANC.LIB we need to use the input mode of the Editor. Entering "I" after the "*" prompt and pressing the return key sets the Editor in the input mode. The cursor moves over 16 spaces and one can now enter in lines of the song like this:

    *I

            YOU MUST REMEMBER THIS⟨ret⟩
            A KISS IS STILL A KISS⟨ret⟩
            A SIGH IS JUST A SIGH.⟨ret⟩
            THE FUNDAMENTAL THINGS APPLY⟨ret⟩
            AS TIME GOES BY.⟨ret⟩

If you are up to this point, the cursor is under "AS" waiting for another line to be added. But you have put in enough information and want to save what you have. You must now leave the input mode and reenter the edit mode. Instead of entering another line, hold the control (CTRL) key and press Z. You have just entered a CONTROL_ Z, character, which causes an exit from the input mode and returns you to the edit mode of the Editor. Entering "EX" (or "exit") at the "*" and pressing the return key "saves" this file in your directory. The whole process should look like this:

            $EDT CASABLANC.LIB
            Input file does not exist
            [EOB]
            *I

                    YOU MUST REMEMBER THIS
                    A KISS IS STILL A KISS
                    A SIGH IS JUST A SIGH.
                    THE FUNDAMENTAL THINGS APPLY
                    AS TIME GOES BY.

```
                              ^Z
        *EX
        UD2:[SAMUELS]CASABLANC.LIB;1 5 lines
        $
```

The last line before the DCL prompt ($) needs some explanation. By entering
"EX" in the edit mode of the Editor, VAX saved this file of 5 lines in my directory, which is on disk pack unit "UD2." The "1" after the ";" in CASA-
BLANC.LIB shows that it is version #1. Your disk pack unit and directory
name will be different. To prove that this file is in your directory, enter:

```
              $DIR

              Directory [SAMUELS]

              CASABLANC.LIB;1
```

VAX tells you that you have one file in your directory. If you haven't gotten
this far, kindly get there by trying again. It may be a little frustrating at the
beginning; however, it makes no sense to begin writing COBOL programs
until you become comfortable with the Editor. Enter another file in your directory like so:

```
        $EDT FUN.TXT
        Input file does not exist
        [EOB]
        *I
                        I THINK I AM
                        GOING TO LIKE
                        THE EDITOR. IT
                        IS SO MUCH FUN
                        AND EASY TO USE.
                        I AM HAVING THE TIME
                        OF MY LIFE.
                        ^Z
        *EX
        UD2:[SAMUELS]FUN.TXT;1 7 lines
        $DIR
        Directory [SAMUELS]
        CASABLANC.LIB;1   FUN.TXT;1
        $
```

If you have the above two files in your directory, you have been able to get
into and out of the input mode of the Editor. You have also learned the first
edit mode command of the Editor, "ex." Upper and lower case commands
work!

Schematically, what has happened is as shown in Figure 2–2.

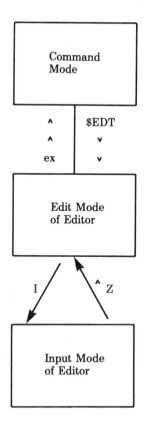

Figure 2–2

You can use the $TYPE command to "see" your file. Use:

$TYPE CASABLANC.LIB⟨ret⟩
YOU MUST REMEMBER THIS
A KISS IS STILL A KISS
A SIGH IS JUST A SIGH.
THE FUNDAMENTAL THINGS APPLY
AS TIME GOES BY.

Try this for the other file—FUN.TXT.

2.4 EDIT MODE COMMANDS

It is time to learn some of the other edit commands. These commands, of course, are used in the edit mode of the Editor. The most common ones we will use for now are:

*d	(delete a line)
*s/string1/string2	(substitute one part of a line with another)
*t w	(list the entire file in the edit mode)
*4	(lists line #4 of the file—*5 would show line #5 and so on)
*quit	(ignore all current edits and leave editor without saving the file)

We will attempt to change the second file created, FUN.TXT. Invoke the Editor on this file and watch what happens:

$EDT FUN.TXT⟨ret⟩
      1   I THINK I AM
   *

Notice that the Editor found the file and lists the first line. It would do the same with CASABLANC.LIB also. We will exit this file by using the "quit" command. If we enter the word "quit" after the "*" and press the return key, the "$" prompt appears. No current file is saved. Try this!

Now watch how we change FUN.TXT and save the current modified file:

```
$EDT FUN.TXT⟨ret⟩
        1              I THINK I AM
*t w⟨ret⟩
        1              I THINK I AM
        2              GOING TO LIKE
        3              THE EDITOR. IT
        4              IS SO MUCH FUN
        5              AND. EASY TO USE.
        6              I AM HAVING THE TIME
        7              OF MY LIFE.
[EOB]
*5⟨ret⟩
        5              AND EASY TO USE.
*D⟨ret⟩
1 line deleted
        6              I AM HAVING THE
*4⟨ret⟩
        4              IS SO MUCH FUN
*S/FUN/WORK.⟨ret⟩
                       IS SO MUCH WORK.
*2
        2              GOING TO LIKE
*S/LIKE/HATE⟨ret⟩
                       GOING TO HATE
```

```
*6
     6                    I AM HAVING THE
*S/AM/AM NOT⟨ret⟩
     6                    I AM NOT HAVING THE
*T W⟨ret⟩
     1                    I THINK I AM
     2                    GOING TO HATE
     3                    THE EDITOR. IT
     4                    IS SO MUCH WORK.
     6                    I AM NOT HAVING THE TIME
     7                    OF MY LIFE.
[EOB]
*EX⟨ret⟩
UD2:[SAMUELS]FUN.TXT;2 6 lines
$DIR⟨ret⟩

Directory [SAMUELS]

CASABLANC.LIB;1   FUN.TXT;2   FUN.TXT;1
$
```

Well, there were some changes made to FUN.TXT. The "t w" (type whole) edit command was used to list the entire file with line numbers. The Editor was then asked to list line 5 ("5" command) and then that line was deleted with the "d" command. Line 6 was then automatically listed. Line 4 was listed so that the change command "S/FUN/WORK." appropriately changed line. The same procedure applies for line #2 and line #6. Finally, the file was saved with the "ex" command and now two versions of FUN.TXT are listed in the directory. Actually, if we had made all the above changes and used "quit" to exit the Editor rather than "ex", then none of the changes would have taken place and only the original version of FUN.TXT would have remained in the directory.

In most cases it is necessary to keep only the latest version in your directory. The $PUR command comes in mighty handy. Watch!

```
               $PUR FUN.TXT
               $DIR


               Directory [SAMUELS]


                · CASABLANC.LIB;1   FUN.TXT;2
```

The version number is NOT necessary in the "PUR" command. This is a relatively safe command because if there is only one version of a particular file, it will not be purged. Attempting to purge FUN.TXT when there is only one version of FUN.TXT remaining results in an error message. Try it for yourself.

Let us try some more edit commands:

*t #:#   (lists the lines between numbers, including the num-
                        bered lines themselves)
*i   (inserts line(s) ABOVE the listed line—you have seen
                        this command before—you need a CONTROL_Z char-
                        acter to get out)

[NOTE: *I END enables one to insert lines at the bottom of a file]

*+#   (adds a # to the current line and lists it)
*−#   (subtracts a # from the current line and lists it)
*res   (resequences the line numbers—this is done automati-
                        cally when one exits from the Editor with the "ex"
                        command)
*r   (replaces the current line and then enters the input, or
                        insert mode)
*move #:# to #   (moves lines from one place to another)

We will try to illustrate the above commands by modifying FUN.TXT again:

```
$EDT FAN.TXT⟨ret⟩
Input file does not exist
[EOB]
*quit⟨ret⟩
$EDT FUN.TXT⟨ret⟩
        1                   I THINK I AM
*t 5:6⟨ret⟩
        5                   I AM NOT HAVING THE TIME
        6                   OF MY LIFE.
*−2⟨ret⟩
        3                   THE EDITOR. IT
*i⟨ret⟩
                            LOOKING AT TERMINALS,
                            PROGRAMMING, AND
                            ˆZ
*t w⟨ret⟩
        1                   I THINK I AM
        2                   GOING TO HATE
        2.1                 LOOKING AT TERMINALS,
        2.2                 PROGRAMMING, AND
        3                   THE EDITOR. IT
        4                   IS SO MUCH WORK.
        5                   I AM NOT HAVING THE TIME
```

```
        6                   OF MY LIFE
[EOB]
*1⟨ret⟩
        1                   I THINK I AM
*r⟨ret⟩
1line deleted
                            WE ALL ARE
                            ^Z
*RES⟨ret⟩
8 lines resequenced
*t w⟨ret⟩
        1                   WE ALL ARE
        2                   GOING TO HATE
        3                   LOOKING AT TERMINALS,
        4                   PROGRAMMING, AND
        5                   THE EDITOR. IT
        6                   IS SO MUCH WORK.
        7                   I AM NOT HAVING THE TIME
        8                   OF MY LIFE.
[EOB]
*move 7:8 to 1⟨ret⟩
2 lines moved
*res⟨ret⟩
8 lines resequenced
*ex⟨ret⟩
UD2:[SAMUELS]FUN.TXT;3 8 lines
$TYPE FUN.TXT⟨ret⟩
I AM NOT HAVING THE TIME
OF MY LIFE.
WE ALL ARE
GOING TO HATE
LOOKING AT TERMINALS,
PROGRAMMING, AND
THE EDITOR. IT
IS SO MUCH WORK.
$PUR FUN.TXT
$DIR⟨ret⟩
Directory [SAMUELS]
CASABLANC.LIB;1   FUN.TXT;3
```

An initial attempt was made to edit FAN.TXT instead of FUN.TXT. Since the Editor could not find FAN.TXT, the message "Input file does not exist" was displayed. To exit from the Editor without saving this file, the "quit" command was used.

After successfully invoking the Editor on FUN.TXT, line 1 was displayed. Then lines 5 and 6 were listed with the "t 5:6" command. This put the Editor pointer on line 5 so that the "−2" command listed line 3. With the "i" command two lines were inserted (input mode). The CONTROL_Z character exits from the input mode and back to the edit mode. IT IS IMPORTANT TO NOTE THAT LINES ARE ALWAYS INSERTED ABOVE THE LINE THAT IS LISTED. Notice that the lines inserted are not whole numbers but are decimal additions to line 2. Line 1 is displayed after the "1" command is used. The "r" command deletes this line and the input mode is automatically entered. The line "WE ALL ARE" is inserted above line #1. CONTROL_Z exits the input mode and the edit mode is entered again. From there all 8 lines are resequenced with the "res" command and the "t w" command proves that point. Two lines are moved with the "move 7:8 to 1" command. The Editor is exited and the file is saved with the "ex" command. It is listed outside of the Editor with the "$TYPE" DCL command. Only the latest version is kept with the "PUR FUN.TXT" DCL command. The contents of the directory are again displayed with the "DIR" DCL command.

2.5   THE $DELETE AND $LO COMMAND

One can get rid of an entire file by using the "DELETE" DCL command; either the version number or wild card (* = all versions) must be used:

$DELETE FUN.TXT;3   (or $DELETE FUN.TXT;*)
$DIR

Directory [SAMUELS]

CASABLANC.LIB;1

Say goodbye to FUN.TXT. Goodbye!
Practice makes perfect. Try doing the Editor problems listed at the end of this chapter.
The easiest DCL command of all is "LO." This is how you "disconnect" from VAX. Try this:

$LO⟨ret⟩

You'll get a message that you just logged off. In order to have more fun (you've got to be kidding!) on the VAX you will have to try your logon procedure again. Did you forget your Password?

SUMMARY

1. You have learned how to log on to the VAX.

2. You have learned the following DCL commands:

$DIR
$SHOW TIME
$SHOW TERMINAL
$SET PASSWORD
$EDT
$TYPE
$DELETE
$LO
$PUR

3. You have learned the following edit commands:

*i
*i end
*ex
*quit
*t w
*d
*r
*s/string1/string2
*t #:#
*move #:# to #
* #
*+#
*−#
*res

EDITOR PROBLEMS

1. Put the following file in your directory:

TO BE OR NOT TO BE:–
THAT IS THE QUESTION:
WHETHER 'TIS NOBLER IN THE MIND
TO SUFFER THE SLINGS AND ARROWS
OF OUTRAGEOUS FORTUNE,
OR TO TAKE ARMS AGAINST A
SEA OF TROUBLES, AND BY OPPOSING

END THEM?—TO DIE,—TO SLEEP,

2. Shakespeare will never forgive us but modify the above through the use of as many editor commands possible to get:

TO BE OR NOT TO BE:–
THAT IS THE QUESTION:
I FIND SHAKESPEARE FASCINATING
AND EASY TO LEARN ON THE TERMINAL.
TO ENJOY THE SLINGS AND ARROWS
OF OUTRAGEOUS FORTUNE,
OR TO TAKE MANY ARMS AGAINST A
HOARD OF COBOL PROGRAMS, AND BY REFUSING TO CODE
END THEM?—TO DIE,—TO SLEEP,
GOODLUCK TO ALL
AND TO ALL A GOOD NIGHT.

3

The First COBOL Program

3.1 PUTTING A COBOL PROGRAM INTO A DIRECTORY

Now that you have become somewhat familiar with the line editor, the command mode, and the files in your directory, it is about time to put in the first COBOL program. You create a COBOL file just like any other file. You must get into the Editor and "insert" each line.

As before you will also see the following:

a. ⟨ret⟩ : use the RETURN key

b. ˆZ : [CTRL_Z]—gets one out of the input mode of the Editor and into the edit mode of the Editor

c. (Editor response) : what the Editor puts on the CRT after certain edit commands

You should now enter the following into a file called FIRSTSHOT.COB:

```
$EDT FIRSTSHOT.COB⟨ret⟩
Input file does not exist (Editor response)
*I
        IDENTIFICATION DIVISION.⟨ret⟩
        PROGRAM-ID. FIRSTTRY.⟨ret⟩
```

```
AUTHOR. SAMUELS.⟨ret⟩
ENVIRONMENT DIVISION.⟨ret⟩
INPUT-OUTPUT SECTION.⟨ret⟩
FILE-CONTROL.⟨ret⟩
    SELECT INFILE ASSIGN TO INSTUFF.⟨ret⟩
    SELECT OUTFILE ASSIGN TO OUTSTUFF.⟨ret⟩
DATA DIVISION.⟨ret⟩
FILE SECTION.⟨ret⟩
FD  INFILE⟨ret⟩
    DATA RECORD IS INREC.⟨ret⟩
01  INREC.⟨ret⟩
    02  NAME-IN          PIC X(20).⟨ret⟩
    02  ADDR-IN          PIC X(30).⟨ret⟩
    02  PHONE-IN         PIC X(8).⟨ret⟩
FD  OUTFILE⟨ret⟩
    DATA RECORD IS OUTREC.⟨ret⟩
01  OUTREC.⟨ret⟩
    02 PHONE-OUT         PIC X(8).⟨ret⟩
    02 FILLER            PIC X(10).⟨ret⟩
    02 ADDR-OUT          PIC X(30).⟨ret⟩
    02 FILLER            PIC X(10).⟨ret⟩
    02 NAME-OUT          PIC X(20).⟨ret⟩
WORKING-STORAGE SECTION.⟨ret⟩
01  END-IT-ALL                   PIC XXX VALUE SPACES.⟨ret⟩
PROCEDURE DIVISION.⟨ret⟩
BEGIN.⟨ret⟩
    PERFORM 100-START.⟨ret⟩
    PERFORM 200-LOOPS UNTIL END-IT-ALL = "YES".⟨ret⟩
    PERFORM 300-END.⟨ret⟩
100-START.⟨ret⟩
    OPEN INPUT INFILE OUTPUT OUTFILE.⟨ret⟩
    READ INFILE AT END MOVE "YES" TO END-IT-ALL.⟨ret⟩
200-LOOPS.⟨ret⟩
    MOVE SPACES TO OUTREC.⟨ret⟩
    MOVE NAME-IN TO NAME-OUT.⟨ret⟩
    MOVE ADDR-IN TO ADDR-OUT.⟨ret⟩
    MOVE PHONE-IN TO PHONE-OUT.⟨ret⟩
    WRITE OUTREC.⟨ret⟩
    READ INFILE AT END MOVE "YES" TO END-IT-ALL.⟨ret⟩
300-END.⟨ret⟩
    CLOSE INFILE OUTFILE.⟨ret⟩
    STOP RUN.
    ˆZ
*ex⟨ret⟩
UD2:[SAMUELS]FIRSTSHOT.COB;1 44 lines        (Editor response)
```

$ (editor response—you are now in command mode)

If you "look into" your directory by using the following command:

$DIR⟨ret⟩

you should see FIRSTSHOT.COB;1 among the rest of your files. You can "type" the whole file by using:

$TYPE FIRSTSHOT.COB⟨ret⟩

As was stated in the previous chapter, you do NOT need the version number.

3.2 OVERVIEW OF A COBOL PROGRAM

At this time it is necessary to explain the above COBOL program. It probably doesn't make too much sense to you at the moment.

1. There are two margins in every COBOL program—the A-Margin and the B-Margin. The A-Margin starts in the first column of the input mode of the Editor. You noticed that when you used the "I" command in the Editor, the cursor came out 15 columns from the "*." This is, essentially, the A-Margin. Things like IDENTIFICATION DIVISION, FD, WORKING-STOR-AGE start in this margin. Other codes like 02, PERFORM, SELECT start in the B-margin (4 columns past the A-Margin). Just remember that the A-Margin is column 1 and the B-Margin is column 5. [Most textbooks and coding forms use column 8 and column 12 for IBM systems.] DO NOT SPACE OVER 8 COLUMNS IN THE INPUT MODE OF THE EDITOR. IT AUTOMATICALLY STARTS IN THE A-MARGIN! Did you hit the space bar 4 times to get to the B-Margin? Check your COBOL file with the above.

2. There are four divisions in every COBOL program.

a. The IDENTIFICATION DIVISION contains the program name, author's name, and other identifying information such as date written, date compiled, and installation name. See Appendix D for VAX REFERENCE FORMAT for the IDENTIFICATION DIVISION and other COBOL format code.

b. The ENVIRONMENT DIVISION has two sections: CONFIGURA-TION SECTION and INPUT-OUTPUT SECTION. The CONFIGURA-TION SECTION (which contains information on which computer compiled the program and which computer executed the program—usually the same) is absent from the above program. We will include it in later chapters. The INPUT-OUTPUT SECTION assigns logical names to external files located in your directory. On large systems with many tape, disk, card, and printer devices, this section, along with the appropriate job control information, specifies the I/O devices used by the program.

c. The DATA DIVISION describes data. It specifies record formats, data types, and all other storage areas. It can have up to four sections; however, in the first half of this text only the FILE SECTION and WORKING-STORAGE will be used.

d. The PROCEDURE DIVISION contains the logic of the entire program. It instructs the computer to solve problems by "performing" certain paragraphs to do such things as "open" files, "read" a file, "move" data fields, "write" a record, and "close" files. Arithmetic statements and conditional statements are also used, although they are not present in the above program.

3.3 BASIC MODULAR DESIGN

The programs that you will see and those that you will code, compile, link, and execute all have a basic design that is shown in Figure 3–1.

All solutions (algorithms) to the problems you will see in the next few chapters start with this basic design. The explanation of each module is "pseudocode"—a simple language that explains each module (or Procedure

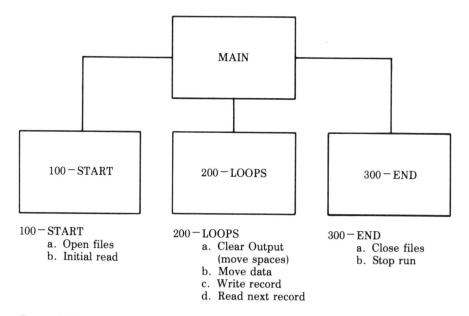

100 – START
    a. Open files
    b. Initial read

200 – LOOPS
    a. Clear Output
       (move spaces)
    b. Move data
    c. Write record
    d. Read next record

300 – END
    a. Close files
    b. Stop run

Figure 3–1

Division paragraph). Obviously, more complex problems require more complex designs. The "MAIN" module is the superordinate module. It controls the execution of the three subordinate modules. With more complex designs there are more superordinate and subordinate modules. This is top-down structured methodology you may have heard about. It employs structured code; hence the term STRUCTURED DESIGN or STRUCTURED COBOL.

3.4 EXAMINATION OF A COBOL PROGRAM—LINE BY LINE

You have a COBOL program in your directory. It is time to examine it line by line.

Line 1   IDENTIFICATION DIVISION header.

Line 2   Name of the program (FIRSTTRY).

Line 3   Author's last name.

Line 4   ENVIRONMENT DIVISION header.

Line 5   INPUT-OUTPUT SECTION header.

Line 6   FILE-CONTROL header.

Line 7   Assigns a logical name INFILE to an external file that will be found in your directory (INSTUFF.DAT). It has not been put in yet. [Some VAX systems require quotes around the external file name ("INSTUFF" for example).]

Line 8   Assigns a logical name OUTFILE to an external file that will be created when the program runs successfully. The file created is OUTSTUFF.DAT.

You need not specify the file type (.DAT) in your select statements.

Line 9   DATA DIVISION header.

Line 10   FILE SECTION header. Necessary if a COBOL program uses external files. Some COBOL programs do not use files!

Lines 11–12 File description for INFILE that was specified in the ENVIRONMENT DIVISION.

Lines 13–16 Specifies what the input record looks like—how many columns and what type used for each field.

Lines 17–18 File description for OUTFILE specified in the ENVIRONMENT DIVISION.

Lines 19–24 Specifies what the output record looks like—how many columns and what type for each field. Also notice FILLER, which is used to put more space between fields.

Line 25   WORKING-STORAGE SECTION header. This section is used in every COBOL program.

Line 26   A "switch" that is a 3-byte field initially filled with spaces.

Line 27   PROCEDURE DIVISION header.

Line 28   Paragraph name for "main" paragraph. This is required on VAX.

Line 29   A statement that transfers control to 100–START for execution of all statements in that paragraph. When execution of paragraph is over, control is passed back to the next statement after the PERFORM.

Line 30   A statement that transfers control to 200–LOOPS for execution of all statements in that paragraph until the condition END-IT-ALL = "YES." The statements in 200–LOOPS are executed over and over again until the READ statement (the last executable statement in 200–LOOPS) attempts a read when no more records are present in the file and "YES" is moved to END-IT-ALL. When this happens, the next statement after the PERFORM is executed.

Line 31   A statement that transfers control to the last paragraph (300–END). Execution of this statement ultimately stops the program execution.

Line 32   100–START paragraph name.

Line 33   OPEN statements make the input and output files (INFILE and OUTFILE) available for processing.

Line 34   Initial READ statement—reads first record of file. If no records are present a "YES" is moved to END-IT-ALL.

Line 35   200–LOOPS paragraph name.

Line 36   Move spaces to output record. Necessary to "clear" output before movement of specific data fields.

Lines 37–39   Moves data from input fields to output fields.

Line 40   Writes the output record.

Line 41   Reads a record from the file. If no more records are present a "YES" is moved to END-IT-ALL.

Line 42   300–END paragraph name.

Line 43   Opened files must be closed before termination.

Line 44   Obvious!

With practice all of the above will become clear to you. The real object of this chapter is to get your first program to run.

3.5   PUTTING A DATA FILE IN A DIRECTORY

As mentioned previously, a data file (INSTUFF.DAT) must be created in order for you to successfully run FIRSTSHOT.COB. According to the input file description, a name should occupy the first 20 columns of the record, the address the next 30 columns, and the phone number the last 8 columns.

One needs to get into the Editor again and put in data. Let's put in four records. This time it is assumed that you will use the "return" key to enter each line; i.e., we shouldn't have to show this by "⟨ret⟩" any more.

```
$EDT INSTUFF.DAT
Input file does not exist (editor response)
*I
          JOE SMITH        123 W. MADISON, CHICAGO   234-2432
          SARAH FEZZO      903 N. MAPLE, WAUKEGAN    123-4231
          PETE FLANGE      1214 CIRCLE DR., WILMETTE  310-3312
          DOREEN PLANK     12 E. CHESTNUT, CHICAGO   414-2231
          ^Z
*EX
UD2:[SAMUELS]INSTUFF.DAT;1 4 lines (Editor response)
     $ (Editor response)
```

To enter data so that they will be placed in the correct columns, enter the following as the first line of a data file:

```
123456789012345678901234567890123456789012345678901234567890
^         ^         ^         ^         ^        ^
```

Now one can enter data beneath it and delete this line after all data are entered. Example:

```
123456789012345678901234567890123456789012345678901234567890
KENT HANSEN      5677 S. ARCHER, CHICAGO       784-5323
LAURINE SLEDGE   30 S. HOLLYCOURT, HINSDALE 434-6699
     etc                    etc                  etc
```

Make sure you use the ⟨ret⟩ key after column 58 for entering data into IN-STUFF.DAT, otherwise you will wind up with records that are too large for the input file description.

3.6 · COMPILATION OF THE FIRST PROGRAM

By now you should have INSTUFF.DAT;1 and FIRSTSHOT.COB;1 in your directory. It makes no difference if a higher version is there (IN-STUFF.DAT;3 for example).

As mentioned previously, the computer does not "understand" or cannot "execute" COBOL instructions, but reads its own machine instructions. You need to "call in" the COBOL compiler to examine your program for any syntax (language) errors. If there are no major errors, it is the compiler's task to "translate" the COBOL instructions to machine instructions.

Have you checked your program with the one given above? Is everything spelled correctly? Did you space correctly (spacing for the PIC clauses is not critical; i.e., if they do not "line up" perfectly the program should still compile. ONE BLANK TO THE COMPILER IS THE SAME AS MANY BLANKS. However, did you use at least 2 spaces after the FD?). It may sound silly but ⟨ret⟩ should NOT be present; it represents the RETURN character. Enter the following in the command mode:

$COB FIRSTSHOT⟨ret⟩

YOU DO NOT NEED THE FILE TYPE. IT IS NOT NECESSARY TO USE FIRSTSHOT.COB—THE COMPILER WILL FIND THE .COB TYPE OF FIRSTSHOT!!

Wait a few seconds! If everything went okay, you should have gotten the "$" as the Editor response. If you misspelled a word, let's say ENVIRO-MENT instead of ENVIRONMENT you would have gotten the following error message:

```
        4        ENVIROMENT DIVISION
                 1
%COBOL-F-ERROR 117, (1) Invalid syntax
        5        INPUT-OUTPUT SECTION.
                 1
%COBOL-W-ERROR   297,   (1) Processing of source program resumes at
                            this point
%COBOL-E-ERROR   452,   (1) Missing  ENVIRONMENT  DIVISION
                            header assumed
%COBOL-F-ENDNOOBJ, UD2:[SAMUELS]FIRSTSHOT.COB;1 completed
                            with 3 diagnostics—object deleted
```

As you can see there is a fatal error because of a misspelled word (error 117). Error 452 states that the header was assumed so that it is a "mild" error. Programs can compile with -E- errors. The -W- error (297) is just an informational error. No translation took place according to the last line. Notice that one error (using ENVIROMENT instead of ENVIRONMENT) makes the compiler list three diagnostic messages. You'll have to get used to that since the compiler only has a certain number of error messages it can give anyway. There is a list of all compiler errors in the *VAX-II COBOL Language Reference Manual*. Only one fatal error (-F-) is necessary to cause the system to NOT produce a machine code translation of the COBOL program.

If this was the case, you must get back into the Editor and fix your program as follows:

[⟨ret⟩ assumed]

```
$EDT FIRSTSHOT.COB
        1                    IDENTIFICATION DIVISION. (Editor response)
*2
                            ENVIROMENT DIVISION. (Editor response)
*S/RO/RON
                            ENVIRONMENT DIVISION. (Editor response)
*ex
UD2:[SAMUELS]FIRSTSHOT.COB;2 44 lines (Editor response)
$ (Editor response)
```

Or, let's suppose that you had NAME-IN instead of NAME-OUT in the Data Division; that is, NAME-IN is present twice. Assume that you forgot to put in the first paragraph named BEGIN. You would get the following after $COB FIRSTSHOT:

```
    28          PERFORM 100–START.
                1
%COBOL-W-ERROR   325,   (1) Missing paragraph header
    36          MOVE NAME-IN TO NAME-OUT.
                    1            2
%COBOL-F-ERROR   337,   (1) Ambiguous reference
%COBOL-F-ERROR   349,   (2) Undefined name
%COBOL-F-ENDNOOBJ, UD2:[SAMUELS]FIRSTSHOT.COB;2 completed
with 3 diagnostics—object deleted
$
```

The compiler, in message #337, is telling you that NAME-IN is present more than one time in the Data Division. Then NAME-OUT is not present in the Data Division. The object or machine program was not produced again. Too bad!

Again, the Editor must be entered and corrections must be made as follows:

[⟨ret⟩ assumed]

```
$EDT FIRSTSHOT.COB
     1                      IDENTIFICATION DIVISION.
   *24
                               02 NAME-IN          PIC X(20).
   *S/IN/OUT
                               02 NAME-OUT         PIC X(20).
   *28
                               PERFORM 100-START.
   *I
                               BEGIN.
                               ^Z
   * 28                        PERFORM 100-START.
   *ex
   UD2:[SAMUELS]FIRSTSHOT.COB;3 44 lines.
   $
```

No matter what compiler errors you got, you must get back into the Editor and correct your program until you get the "$" after entering $COB FIRSTSHOT.

3.7   LINKING THE FIRST PROGRAM

Successful compilation puts a new file in your directory. Enter $DIR and you will see the following:

FIRSTSHOT.OBJ;1

This is the "object" or machine language translation of your program. DO NOT ATTEMPT TO TYPE OUT THIS FILE. IT WILL MAKE NO SENSE TO YOU ANYWAY!

Incidentally, you may have more than one version of your COBOL file (FIRSTSHOT.COB) and/or your data file (INSTUFF.DAT). You might want to enter $PUR to remove all versions except the last one (highest numbered).

In order to relocate (or "link") your program enter the following:

$LINK FIRSTSHOT

The linkage editor program has been called in to "look" for the .OBJ version of FIRSTSHOT. Hopefully, everything will work right and you will get the "$." The linkage editor program does some mysterious things that are of no concern to you now. However, look into your directory and you will find:

FIRSTSHOT.EXE;1

This is the executable file that can now be executed.

3.8 EXECUTING THE FIRST PROGRAM

To "run" or execute your program enter the following:

$RUN FIRSTSHOT

The system will "look" for the .EXE of FIRSTSHOT. If no data file (IN-STUFF.DAT) is present you will get the following message:

```
$RUN FIRSTSHOT
%COB-F-FILNOTFOU,file UD2:[SAMUELS]INSTUFF.DAT;
not found on OPEN
-RMS-E-ENF, file not found
%TRACE-F-TRACEBACK, symbolic stack dump follows
```

module name	routine name	line	rel PC	abs PC
			0000DF66	0000DF66
FIRSTTRY	FIRSTTRY	33	00000085	00000A85
$				

This entire stack dump informed you that it could not find the file, IN-STUFF.DAT, when it attempted to open the file with the OPEN statement that appears on line 33!

If one or more of the input records of INSTUFF.DAT is too large (more than 58 columns) you will get the following message:

```
$RUN FIRSTSHOT
%COB-F-ERRON_FIL, error on file UD2:[SAMUELS]INSTUFF.DAT;2
-RMS-W-RTB, 59 byte record too large for users buffer
%TRACE-F-TRACEBACK, symbolic stack dump follows
```

module name	routine name	line	rel PC	abs PC
			0000DF66	0000DF66
FIRSTTRY	FIRSTTRY	41	00000152	00000B52

When the directory is examined, OUTSTUFF.DAT appears. However, when the following is entered:

$TYPE OUTSTUFF.DAT

only the first two records appear as shown:

234–2432	123 W. MADISON, CHICAGO	JOE SMITH
123–4231	903 N. MAPLE, WAUKEGAN	SARAH FEZZO

Apparently the third record contained one too many characters. This caused an "overflow" in the input buffer region because the infile description called for only 58-byte records.

On the other hand, if you get the "$," you can assume that execution was successful. This output file is created in your directory:

OUTSTUFF.DAT;1

See what this output file looks like by entering $TYPE OUTSTUFF.DAT. You should get the following:

```
$TYPE OUTSTUFF.DAT
234-2432          123 W. MADISON, CHICAGO   JOE SMITH
123-4231          903 N. MAPLE, WAUKEGAN    SARAH FEZZO
310-3312          1214 CIRCLE DR., WILMETTE  PETE FLANGE
414-2231          12 E. CHESTNUT, CHICAGO    DOREEN PLANK
```

The program was successful even though the name and phone number are reversed (see INSTUFF.DAT). The program was designed to do just that—reverse these two fields. The movement of data fields will be discussed in the next chapter.

It is imperative that you go no further in this text until you successfully compile, link, and run the above program.

Every time you compile and link you produce more versions of .OBJ and .EXE. The $PUR command will remove all "old" versions but never the latest ones.

3.9   SPECIFIC INFORMATION REGARDING THE COBOL SYNTAX

Words

There are two types of words:

1. Reserved words

2. Programmer-supplied words

Reserved words are used in special ways. They must be spelled correctly and used in a prescribed manner. A complete list of reserved words can be found in appendix C. This list may vary slightly from compiler to compiler. Programmer-supplied names are used to specify paragraph names (such as 100-START, 200-LOOPS, and 300-LOOPS) and data-names (storage areas that contain data—NAME-IN, END-IT-ALL, etc.). You must adhere to the following rules in forming programmer-supplied names:

1. Letters A–Z, numbers 0–9, and the hyphen can be used.

2. There must be at least one letter.

3. Word cannot be over 30 characters.

4. Word cannot be a reserved word.

5. Word cannot begin or end with a hyphen.

Literals

These are constants (specific values), and there are two types:

1. Numeric—examples:
   43
   .07
   364.5
   +7
   −13.2

2. Non-numeric (always enclosed by "). Examples:
   "HELLO"
   "NO"
   "#3A"
   "2.6" (non-numeric because of quotes)

Symbols (arithmetic, relational, or punctuation)

The following table gives information on symbols used in COBOL:

Symbol	Type	Explanation
+	Arithmetic	addition
−	"	subtraction
*	"	multiplication
/	"	division
**	"	exponentiation
=	Relational	equal to
)	"	greater than
(	"	less than
.	Punctuation	ends a COBOL statement
,	"	delineates clauses
" "	"	encloses literals
( )	"	encloses expressions, subscripts or indexes

At least one space must precede and follow all arithmetic and relational symbols. A space cannot precede a comma but must follow it. This author never uses the comma.

COBOL Statements

These are comprised of at least one reserved word and programmer-supplied words. Examples:

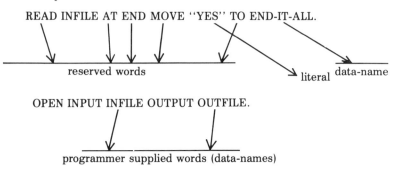

MOVE NAME-IN TO NAME-OUT.

SUMMARY

In this chapter you have learned to:

1. enter a COBOL program into your directory in the input mode of the Editor.

2. compile this program, correct any compilation errors, and compile again until a translation to machine language takes place—.OBJ type appears in the directory.

3. link this machine program.

4. execute the program.

5. COBOL words, literals, symbols, and statements.

QUESTIONS

1. List all the reserved words in the Procedure Division of the program developed in this chapter.

2. List all the programmer-supplied words in the Procedure Division of the program developed in this chapter.

3. List all the literals in the Procedure Division of the program developed in this chapter.

4. Which of the following are legal data-names?
   a. FIRST
   b. GODZILLA
   c. PAY-CLASS
   d. 12–45–N
   e. –ABBA
   f. DIVSION
   g. CODE
   h. START
   i. BEGIN HERE
   j. EMP#

5. Which are legal numeric or non-numeric literals?
   a. 34.5L
   b. "1243–SMART"
   c. 100
   d. START
   e. "45"

PROGRAMMING PROBLEMS

Wait 'til the next chapter, the chapter after that, and so on. Have you done the one for this chapter?

4

Data Movement

Well, you finally got your first program to work. If you are like most other people, it took quite a while to remove all compiler errors, errors in linking, and a stack dump or two when you attempted a run.

The problem, of course, is that you probably don't understand everything about the program, and that is to be expected at this time. You know there are four divisions in a COBOL program and the proper order in which they appear. You also know how to enter a program into your directory and use the Editor to fix compiler errors. You should also know how to compile, link, and run.

This chapter will teach you to:

1. match your data descriptions with incoming and outgoing data.

2. use proper MOVE statements in your program to get data from input to output.

3. successfully compile, link, and run these programs.

4.1 A PARTIAL SOLUTION

Let's suppose you had to write a program that would read a file containing records with the following format:

Field	Columns
Name	1–20
Employee #	21–27
Phone Number Ext.	31–34
Department	35–44

Move the above fields to an output record, and write each record to an output file. The output records have the following format:

Field	Columns
Employee #	11–17
Name	31–50
Phone Number Ext.	61–64
Department	71–80

The input records are in an external file named EMPLOYEE.DAT. The output records, after the program is run, will be in EMPREPT.DAT.

As seen in Figure 4-1, the basic modular design structure and pseudo-code are quite similar to the ones presented in the previous chapter.

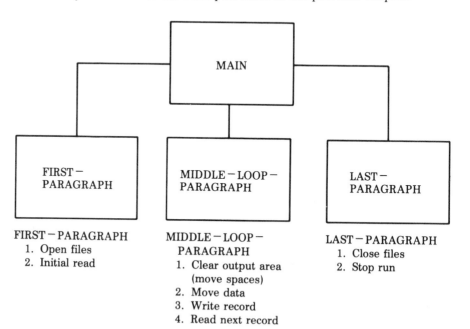

FIRST – PARAGRAPH
1. Open files
2. Initial read

MIDDLE – LOOP – PARAGRAPH
1. Clear output area (move spaces)
2. Move data
3. Write record
4. Read next record

LAST – PARAGRAPH
1. Close files
2. Stop run

Figure 4-1

We shall start programming by creating a file (actually the source code) called MOVER.COB. This is done by:

```
$EDT MOVER.COB ⟨ret⟩
input file does not exist (Editor response)
*I ⟨ret⟩
        IDENTIFICATION DIVISION.
        PROGRAM-ID. FIRST.
        AUTHOR. SAMUELS.
        ENVIRONMENT DIVISION.
        INPUT-OUTPUT SECTION.
        FILE-CONTROL.
             SELECT INFILE ASSIGN TO EMPLOYEE.
             SELECT OUTFILE ASSIGN TO EMPREPT.
        DATA DIVISION.
        FILE SECTION.
        FD   INFILE
             DATA RECORD IS INREC.
        01   INREC          PIC X(44).
        FD   OUTFILE
             DATA RECORD IS OUTREC.
        01   OUTREC         PIC X(80).
        WORKING-STORAGE SECTION.
        HERE-WE-GO.
             PERFORM FIRST-PARAGRAPH.
             PERFORM LAST-PARAGRAPH.
        FIRST-PARAGRAPH.
             OPEN INPUT IN-FILE OUTPUT OUTFILE.
        LAST-PARAGRPH.
             CLOSE INPUT INFILE OUTPUT OUTFILE.
             STOP RUN.
             ^Z

*EX ⟨ret⟩
UD2:[SAMUELS]MOVER.COB;1 25 lines (Editor response)
$              (Editor response—you are now in DEC command mode)
```

It is important to note the following:

a. The code for middle module is not present.

b. There is no "breakdown" for the input or output records. All that is known from the above code is that each input record is 44 characters (bytes) long and that each output record is 80 bytes long.

The attempt here is to show how to code in "smaller" steps. It may not be apparent now, but with much more complicated problems, you will find that the method of entering in only part of the program, compiling, linking, and running is much easier and faster. Then one can "add to" the code in small steps.

An attempt will now be made to compile this program. Use:

$COB MOVER ⟨ret⟩ (.COB is not necessary—the "hunt" for a file named
            MOVER.COB will be made even though you may have
            MOVER.DAT or MOVER.TXT etc., in your directory!)

Egad! Look what happens:

```
$COB MOVER
        2                   PROGRAM-ID. FIRST.
                                    1
%COBOL-F-ERROR    226,   (1) Missing required word
        3                   AUTHOR.          SAMUELS.
                            1
%COBOL-W-ERROR   297,   (1) Processing of source program resumes at
                        this point
%COBOL-E-ERROR     65,   (1) Missing period is assumed
       18                   HERE-WE-GO.
                            1
%COBOL-E-ERROR     66,   (1) Missing level-number—assumed same as
                        previous
%COBOL-E-ERROR     81,   (1) PICTURE clause required
       19                   PERFORM FIRST-PARAGRAPH.
                                    1
%COBOL-F-ERROR  117,   (1) Invalid syntax
       25                   STOP RUN.
                                         1
%COBOL-W-ERROR   297,   (1) Processing of source program resumes at
                        this point
%COBOL-F-ENDNOOBJ,    UD2:[SAMUELS]MOVER.COB;1    completed
                                              with 7 diagnostics
    object deleted
```

In examining the compiler errors we find:

Line 2   Only possible explanation, since everything is spelled correctly
         with correct punctuation, is that FIRST must be a reserved word—
         it cannot be used as a program name! [See Appendix]

Line 3   The result of error in line 2

Line 18   Compiler assumes that HERE-WE-GO is a data-name without a
           level number. Actually, the PROCEDURE DIVISION header is
           missing. Nice going!

Line 19   The result of error in line 18

Line 25   Tells where processing of source program continues. Not much
           help. It appears that most of the Procedure Division statements
           were not compiled!

It is necessary to get back into the Editor to:

a. change FIRST to, let's say, FIRSTX.

b. insert PROCEDURE DIVISION above line 18.

It can be done as follows:

```
        $EDT MOVER.COB ⟨ret⟩
            1        IDENTIFICATION DIVISION. (Editor response)
        *2 ⟨ret⟩
            2        PROGRAM-ID. FIRST. (Editor response)
        *S/ST/STX ⟨ret⟩
            2        PROGRAM-ID. FIRSTX. (Editor response)
        *18 ⟨ret⟩
            18       HERE-WE-GO. (Editor response)
        *I ⟨ret⟩
                     PROCEDURE DIVISION. ˆZ
                     HERE-WE-GO. (Editor response)
        *ex ⟨ret⟩
        UD2:[SAMUELS]MOVER.COB;2 26 lines
        $ (Editor response)
```

Notice that a new version, MOVER.COB;2, has been created in your directory (use $DIR ⟨ret⟩ to prove this). A $PUR command removes all "old"
versions except the last one. You can always use the $PUR command to
"clean up" your disk space of old versions of programs, data files, etc. Or,
you can purge old versions of a specific file as follows:

```
                $PUR filename.type
                example = $PUR MOVER.COB
```

Do not use the specific version number—it won't work!

It is time to try and compile the program again using:

$COB MOVER ⟨ret⟩

Oh no! More compiler errors:

```
$COB MOVER
     21                    PERFORM LAST-PARAGRAPH.
                              1
%COBOL-F-ERROR    349, (1) Undefined name
                  22 FIRST-PARAGRAPH.
%COBOL-W-ERROR    297, (1) Processing of source program resumes
                  at this point
                  OPEN INPUT IN-FILE OUTPUT OUTFILE.
     23                        1         2
%COBOL-F-ERROR    349, (1) Undefined name
%COBOL-W-ERROR    297, (2) Processing of source program resumes
                  at this point
     25           CLOSE INPUT INFILE OUTPUT OUTFILE.
                           1           2
%COBOL-F-ERROR    321, (1) Invalid statement syntax
%COBOL-W-ERROR    297, (2) Processing of source program resumes
                  at this point
%COBOL-F-ENDNOOBJ,   UD2:[SAMUELS]MOVER.COB;2 completed
                     with 6 diagnostics
—object deleted
```

An analysis of the above compiler errors is as follows:

Line 21   LAST PARAGRAPH looks okay. But it is spelled wrong in line 24. One can fix either 24 or 21.

Line 23   Should be INFILE (no dash)—see SELECT and FD statements. One must be consistent!

Line 25   Cannot use INPUT or OUTPUT on CLOSE statements—only on OPEN statements.

Once more we must get into the Editor. [This time it is assumed that you know when to return (⟨ret⟩) and what the proper Editor response is.]

```
$EDT
MOVER.COB
     1           IDENTIFICATION DIVISION.
*23
```

```
    23                 OPEN INPUT IN-FILE OUTPUT OUTFILE.
*S/IN-FILE/INFILE
    23                 OPEN INPUT INFILE OUTPUT OUTFILE.
*24
    24          PERFORM LAST-PARAGRPH.
*S/GRPH/GRAPH
    24          PERFORM LAST-PARAGRAPH.
*25
    25                 CLOSE INPUT INFILE OUTPUT OUTFILE.
*S/INPUT/
                       CLOSE INFILE OUTPUT OUTFILE
*S/OUTPUT/
                       CLOSE INFILE OUTFILE.
*EX
UD2:[SAMUELS]MOVER.COB;3 26 lines
$
```

4.2   ADDING CODE TO THE EXISTING PROGRAM

When the program is compiled again the only response is the "$." In checking our directory, no output file (EMPREPT.DAT) was created after linking and executing.

Apparently we will have to "read" the records, move the fields to the output area, and "write" the records. This is what was done in the previous chapter. We need to add some statements to the Procedure Division and Data Division.

Since a record is made up of one or more fields (in this case four fields) the compiler must know the type of each field and where it is located.

NAME is a 20-column field and can have a PIC A(20), meaning 20 alphabetic characters, or PIC X(20), meaning 20 alphanumeric characters. The author prefers the latter. EMPLOYEE NUMBER is a 7-byte (7 characters) numeric field but can be defined as PIC 9(7) or PIC X(7). Any numeric field that is used in an arithmetic calculation must have a picture type 9. But an employee number is not used numerically in this case, so we have our choice. The same for the PHONE NUMBER EXTENSION: PIC 9999, PIC 9(4), or PIC X(4) can be used. The department is a 10-byte alphabetic field so PIC X(10) will be used.

To show the compiler the arrangement of the fields for each record we need to break down the INREC (01 level) description in the above program. The 02 level will be used for this purpose. Some authors and/or manuals use 05, 10, or other numbers in place of 02.

The following represents the input file description:

```
01  INREC.
    02 NAME-IN                PIC X(20).
    02 EMPLOYEE-NUM-IN        PIC 9(7).
    02 FILLER                 PIC X(3).
    02 EXTENSION-IN           PIC X(4).
    02 DEPARTMENT-IN          PIC X(10).
```

Notice that INREC has become a group item. It represents all 44 bytes or the entire record. A FILLER is necessary because there is no field described in columns 28 through 30. Notice that the data-names describe the incoming fields pretty well. There are no reserved words except for FILLER. If one wanted to make NAME-IN a group item and have a further breakdown into last name and first name, it could be done as follows:

```
01  INREC.
    02 NAME-IN.
        03  LAST-IN           PIC X(10).
        03  FIRST-IN          PIC X(10).
    02  EMPLOYEE-NUM-IN       PIC 9(7).
    02  FILLER                PIC X(3).
    02  EXTENSION-IN          PIC X(4).
    02  DEPARTMENT-IN         PIC X(10).
```

This assumes, however, that the last name is in the first 10 columns of each record, and the first name starts in column 11.

We will not "split" the name into last and first. What follows, then, is the output record description:

```
01  OUTREC.
    02 FILLER                 PIC X(10).
    02 EMPLOYEE-NUM-OUT       PIC 9(7).
    02 FILLER                 PIC X(13).
    02 NAME-OUT               PIC X(20).
    02 FILLER                 PIC X(10).
    02 EXTENSION-OUT          PIC X(4).
    02 FILLER                 PIC X(6).
    02 DEPARTMENT-OUT         PIC X(10).
```

Notice the use of FILLER to "fill in" the areas where there are no field descriptions. Even if data were present it could be excluded from any processing by using a FILLER for that particular area in the record.

It now becomes necessary to move these fields from input to output; this is why the data-names are different in both record descriptions. These MOVE statements appear in the Procedure Division as follows:

```
MOVE SPACES TO OUTREC.
MOVE NAME-IN TO NAME-OUT.
MOVE EXTENSION-IN TO EXTENSION-OUT.
MOVE EMPLOYEE-NUM-IN TO EMPLOYEE-NUM-OUT.
MOVE DEPARTMENT-IN TO DEPARTMENT-OUT.
```

The MOVE SPACES TO OUTREC statement is necessary because you must put spaces in between the output fields. It is not necessary for the input records because the spaces are already present. The MOVE statements, along with the READ and WRITE statements, will be added to the Procedure Division. All these additional statements will be added to a paragraph called MIDDLE-LOOP-PARAGRAPH that will be "performed" until there are no more records. This is done by adding a switch (ENDOFFILE). The switch is activated when there are no records remaining. This is why there are two READ statements: the first, in the first paragraph, reads the first record; if there aren't any records, the program will stop there. Remaining records will be read with the READ statement in the "loop" paragraph, continuing to process (as the loop continues) until there are no more records (ENDOFFILE = "YES"). The statement that controls this loop function is in the main module paragraph along with the other PERFORM statements as follows:

```
PERFORM MAIN-LOOP-PARAGRAPH UNTIL ENDOFFILE = "YES".
```

All the additional statements have been added in lower case for clarification:

```
IDENTIFICATION DIVISION.
PROGRAM-ID. FIRSTX.
AUTHOR. SAMUELS.
ENVIRONMENT DIVISION.
INPUT-OUTPUT SECTION.
FILE-CONTROL.
      SELECT INFILE ASSIGN TO EMPLOYEE.
      SELECT OUTFILE ASSIGN TO EMPREPT.
DATA DIVISION.
FILE SECTION.
FD   INFILE
      DATA RECORD IS INREC.
01   INREC.
      02 name-in               pic x(20).
      02 em ployee-num-in      pic 9(7).
      02 filler                pic x(3).
      02 extension-in          pic x(4).
      02 deparment-in          pic x(10).
FD OUTFILE
      DATA RECORD IS OUTREC.
```

```
01  OUTREC.
        02 filerr               pic x(10).
        02 employee-num-out     pic 9(7).
        02 filler               pic x(13).
        02 name-out             pic x(20).
        02 filler               pic x(10).
        02 extension-out        pic x(4).
        02 filler               pic x(6).
        02 department-out       pic x(10).
WORKING-STORAGE SECTION.
PROCEDURE DIVISION.
HERE-WE-GO.
    PERFORM FIRST-PARAGRAPH.
    perform middle-loop-paragraph until endoffile = "yes".
    PERFORM LAST-PARAGRAPH.
FIRST-PARAGRAPH.
    OPEN INPUT INFILE OUTPUT OUTFILE.
    read infile at end move "yes" to endoffile.
middle-loop-paragraph.
    move spaces to outrec.
    move name-in to name-out.
    move extension-in to extension-out.
    move employee-num-in to employee-num-out.
    move department-in to deparment-out.
    write outrec.
    read infile at end move "yes" to endoffile.
LAST-PARAGRAPH.
    CLOSE INFILE OUTFILE.
    STOP RUN.
```

When we compile using $COB MOVER we get the following compiler errors:

```
$COB MOVER
    15                      02 em ployee-num-in pic 9(7).
                              1    2
%COBOL-E-ERROR      81, (1) PICTURE clause required
%COBOL-E-ERROR      65, (2) Missing period is assumed
%COBOL-E-ERROR      66, (2) Missing level-number—assumed same as
                    previous
    33                       perform middle-loop-paragraph until endoffile =
                         "yes".
                                          1              2
%COBOL-F-ERROR      349, (1) Undefined name
```

%COBOL-W-ERROR   297, (2) Processing of source program resumes at
                  this point
      37   read infile at end move "yes" to endoffile.
                                                                   1
%COBOL-F-ERROR   349, (1) Undefined name
      42   move employee-num-in to employee-num-out.
                                1
%COBOL-F-ERROR   349, (1) Undefined name
      43   move department-in to deparment-out.
                           1   2   3
%COBOL-W-ERROR   297, (1) Processing of source program resumes at
                  this point
%COBOL-F-ERROR   349, (2) Undefined name
%COBOL-F-ERROR   349, (3) Undefined name
      44   write outrec.
%COBOL-W-ERROR   297, (1) Processing of source program resumes at
                  this point
      45   read infile at end move "yes" to endoffile.
                                                                   1

%COBOL-F-ERROR   349, (1) Undefined name
%COBOL-F-ENDNOOBJ,   UD2:[SAMUELS]MOVER.COB;4   completed
with 12 diagnostics
—object deleted

Before attempting to edit this program it is appropriate, at this time, to create
a "listing" file of the above COBOL program. The errors listed above will be
more easily identified.

4.3   CREATING THE LISTING FILE

To obtain a "listing" file do the following:

$COB/LIS MOVER

The same compiler errors are shown but a new file has been added to the
directory:

MOVER.LIS

This is a "listing" of the COBOL program with the appropriate compiler
errors listed right after the error. There is also other information such as
STATISTICS, COMMAND QUALIFIERS, and the like that will be explained later. From now on "listing" versions of COBOL programs will be
used because:

1. Line numbers are automatically given.

2. Compiler errors are easier to find and fix.

3. Other statistical and informational data is present.

The statistics and other informational data will be shown this time only and in the last few chapters; however, the rest of the .LIS version will always be shown rather than the .COB version.

When $TYPE MOVER.LIS is entered, the following appears:

```
FIRSTX                                                      19-Oct-1983 13:3
4:55    VAX-11 COBOL V2.2-40                  Page   1
Source Listing                                             19-Oct-1983 13:1
3:22    UD2:[SAMUELS.BOOK]MOVER.COB;1  (1)

     1            IDENTIFICATION DIVISION.
     2            PROGRAM-ID. FIRSTX.
     3            AUTHOR. SAMUELS.
     4            ENVIRONMENT DIVISION.
     5            INPUT-OUTPUT SECTION.
     6            FILE-CONTROL.
     7                SELECT INFILE ASSIGN TO EMPLOYEE.
     8                SELECT OUTFILE ASSIGN TO EMPREPT.
     9            DATA DIVISION.
    10            FILE SECTION.
    11            FD  INFILE
    12                DATA RECORD IS INREC.
    13            01  INREC.
    14                02 name-in          pic x(20).
    15                02 employee-num-in  pic 9(7).
                     1  2
%COBOL-E-ERROR   81, (1) PICTURE clause required
%COBOL-E-ERROR   65, (2) Missing period is assumed
%COBOL-E-ERROR   66, (2) Missing level-number - assumed same as previous
    16                02 filler           pic x(3).
    17                02 extension-in      pic x(4).
    18                02 deparment-in      pic  x(10).
    19            FD  OUTFILE
    20                DATA RECORD IS OUTREC.
    21            01  OUTREC.
    22                02 filerr            pic x(10).
    23                02 employee-num-out  pic 9(7).
    24                02 filler            pic x(13).
    25                02 name-out          pic x(20).
    26                02 filler            pic x(10).
    27                02 extension-out     pic x(4).
    28                02 filler            pic x(6).
    29                02 department-out    pic x(10).
    30            WORKING-STORAGE SECTION.
    31            PROCEDURE DIVISION.
    32            HERE-WE-GO.
    33                PERFORM FIRST-PARAGRAPH.
    34                perform middle-loop-paragraph until endoffile = "yes".
                                                            1                2
%COBOL-F-ERROR   349, (1) Undefined name
%COBOL-W-ERROR   297, (2) Processing of source program resumes at this point
    35                PERFORM LAST-PARAGRAPH.
    36            FIRST-PARAGRAPH.
```

```
37              OPEN INPUT INFILE OUTPUT OUTFILE.
38              read infile at end move "yes" to endoffile.
                                                         1
%COBOL-F-ERROR  349, (1) Undefined name
39          middle-loop-paragraph.
40              move spaces to outrec.
41              move name-in to name-out.
42              move extension-in to extension-out.
43              move employee-num-in to employee-num-out.
                 1
%COBOL-F-ERROR  349, (1) Undefined name
44              move department-in to deparment-out.
                 1       2             3
%COBOL-W-ERROR  297, (1) Processing of source program resumes at this point
%COBOL-F-ERROR  349, (2) Undefined name
%COBOL-F-ERROR  349, (3) Undefined name
45              write outrec.
```

```
FIRSTX                                              19-Oct-1983 13:3
4:55   VAX-11 COBOL V2.2-40            Page   2
Source Listing                                      19-Oct-1983 13:1
3:22   UD2:[SAMUELS.BOOK]MOVER.COB;1 (1)


                 1
%COBOL-W-ERROR  297, (1) Processing of source program resumes at this point
46              read infile at end move "yes" to endoffile.
                                                         1
%COBOL-F-ERROR  349, (1) Undefined name
47          LAST-PARAGRAPH.
48              CLOSE  INFILE  OUTFILE.
49              STOP RUN.
```

```
FIRSTX                                              19-Oct-1983 13:3
4:55   VAX-11 COBOL V2.2-40            Page   3
Compilation Summary                                 19-Oct-1983 13:1
3:22   UD2:[SAMUELS.BOOK]MOVER.COB;1 (1)
```

PROGRAM SECTIONS

```
    Name                         Bytes    Attributes

  1 $LOCAL                        888     PIC   CON   REL   LCL NOSHR NO
EXE   RD   WRT Align(2)
```

DIAGNOSTICS

```
    Warning:        3
    Error:          3
    Severe Error:   6
```

COMMAND QUALIFIERS

```
    COBOL IS MOVER

    /NOCOPY_LIST  /NOMACHINE_CODE  /NOCROSS_REFERENCE
    /NOANSI_FORMAT  /NOSEQUENCE_CHECK  /NOMAP
    /NOTRUNCATE  /NOAUDIT  /NOCONDITIONALS
    /CHECK=(NOPERFORM,NOBOUNDS)  /DEBUG=(NOSYMBOLS,TRACEBACK)
    /WARNINGS=(NOSTANDARD,OTHER,NOINFORMATION)
   /NOFIPS
```

```
STATISTICS
        Run Time:           2.02 seconds
        Elapsed Time:       20.18 seconds
        Page Faults:        348
        Dynamic Memory:     381 pages
```

The following errors have to be fixed:

DATA DIVISION

a. Change em ployee-num-in to employee-num-in
b. Change deparment-in to department-in
c. Add a description for endoffile in WORKING-STORAGE.

PROCEDURE DIVISION

d. change deparment-out to department-out

Notice that in line 21, FILLER was misspelled. It makes no difference since FILERR acts as a data-name that is NOT used in the Procedure Division.

What follows is the input file (EMPLOYEE.DAT), the corrected program listing, and another of those "stack dump" messages produced when the .EXE module is executed. You realize that a successful compile produces the object module (MOVER.OBJ) in this case, and a successful link produces the executable module (MOVER.EXE). SUCCESSFUL COMPILATION DOES NOT MEAN SUCCESSFUL EXECUTION!!

The following commands will be used:

$COB/LIS MOVER (produces MOVER.LIS regardless of whether or not
                compile was successful)
$LINK MOVER

Input Data ———————————————————————————————

```
JACKSON SARAH      1241231   3443PERSONNEL
JONES PETE         1453221   3445PAYROLL
KILPATRICK JANE    5212342   3442SHIPPING
PRESTON SUSAN      2223124   3448ADVERTISING
FLORES SHARON      2593823   3440CORPORATE
```

Program Listing ———————————————————————————

```
1     IDENTIFICATION DIVISION.
2     PROGRAM-ID. FIRSTX.
3     AUTHOR. SAMUELS.
4     ENVIRONMENT DIVISION.
```

```
  5      INPUT-OUTPUT SECTION.
  6      FILE-CONTROL.
  7          SELECT INFILE ASSIGN TO EMPLOYEE.
  8          SELECT OUTFILE ASSIGN TO EMPREPT.
  9      DATA DIVISION.
 10      FILE SECTION.
 11      FD  INFILE
 12          DATA RECORD IS INREC.
 13      01  INREC.
 14          02 name-in            pic x(20).
 15          02 employee-num-in    pic 9(7).
 16          02 filler             pic x(3).
 17          02 extension-in       pic x(4).
 18          02 department-in      pic  x(10).
 19      FD  OUTFILE
 20          DATA RECORD IS OUTREC.
 21      01  OUTREC.
 22          02 filerr             pic x(10).
 23          02 employee-num-out   pic 9(7).
 24          02 filler             pic x(13).
 25          02 name-out           pic x(20).
 26          02 filler             pic x(10).
 27          02 extension-out      pic x(4).
 28          02 filler             pic x(6).
 29          02 department-out     pic x(10).
 30      WORKING-STORAGE SECTION.
 31      01  endoffile             pic xxx value spaces.
 32      PROCEDURE DIVISION.
 33      HERE-WE-GO.
 34          PERFORM FIRST-PARAGRAPH.
 35          perform middle-loop-paragraph until endoffile = "yes".
 36          PERFORM LAST-PARAGRAPH.
 37      FIRST-PARAGRAPH.
 38          OPEN INPUT INFILE OUTPUT OUTFILE.
 39          read infile at end move "yes" to endoffile.
 40      middle-loop-paragraph.
 41          move spaces to outrec.
 42          move name-in to name-out.
 43          move extension-in to extension-out.
 44          move employee-num-in to employee-num-out.
 45          move department-in to department-out.
 46          write outrec.
 47          read infile at end move "yes" to endoffile.
 48      LAST-PARAGRAPH.
 49          CLOSE  INFILE  OUTFILE.
 50          STOP RUN.


$RUN MOVER
%COB-F-ERRON_FIL, error on file UD2:[SAMUELS]EMPLOYEE.DAT;1
-RMS-W-RTB, 45 byte record too large for user's buffer
%TRACE-F-TRACEBACK, symbolic stack dump follows
module name       routine name       line    rel PC      abs PC

                                              0000DF66    0000DF66
FIRSTX           FIRSTX              47       00000154    00000B54
```

That certainly doesn't look like acceptable output data. What happened? If
you examine the input records you will see that the fourth record is too big

for the input record description. The above is an example of an error in execution, not compilation. If we take the "G" off ADVERTISING we will get a 44-byte record that will fit. Since the correct object module is present (MOVER.OBJ;5) in the directory, all that is necessary is:

$LINK MOVER (creates an EXE module from the OBJ + "fixed" input data)
$RUN MOVER

What follows are the output data:

1241231	JACKSON SARAH	3443 P E RSONNEL@
1453221	JONES PETE	3445 P AYROL L EL@
5212342	KILPATRICK JANE	3442 SH I P P I NGL@
2223124	PRESTON SUSAN	3448 ADVERT I S IN
2593823	FLORES SHARON	3440 CORPOR A TEN

It's looking better, but it's not perfect. There is some kind of file marker present at the end of the first three records. The last record should be CORPORATE, not CORPORATEN. Apparently, the "N" in ADVERTISING was included in CORPORATE. It must be concluded that variable length records were read. That is, the second record is 41 characters long. The first record is 43 characters long. This allows "EL" from PERSONNEL (9 bytes) to be included after PAYROLL (7-bytes). The same situation occurs for records four and five. One can avoid these problems by using "fixed" length data records. After PERSONNEL is entered, add one more blank (to make a 44-byte record), and then use the ⟨ret⟩ character. After PAYROLL (second record), add 3 blanks (spaces) before ⟨ret⟩. There is no need to do this for ADVERTISIN (fourth record) because it is already 44 bytes long. The blank is a character too!

It is perfectly acceptable to "manipulate" input test data because this whole process is a learning experience. In the "real world" data that may be perfect or imperfect, fixed or variable, etc. already exists. In time you will be able to write programs that can handle all kinds of input data. What follows are correct output data:

1241231	JACKSON SARAH	3443 PERSONNEL
1453221	JONES PETE	3445 PAYROLL
5212342	KILPATRICK JANE	3442 SHIPPING
2223124	PRESTON SUSAN	3448 ADVERTISIN
2593823	FLORES SHARON	3440 CORPORATE

It took a long time but it was worth the effort. You are urged to do all the programming exercises at the end of this chapter. The same modular design used for the above problem can be used; however, the input and output file descriptions will differ. You should also provide your own test data; that is, create your own files to be used as input to the programs. Input and output data will be shown for programming problem 1 only.

By "walking through" the above problem it becomes much easier to discuss and learn specific information about data types, movement of fields, and field descriptions.

4.4 DATA TYPES

Any field can be defined as:

1. Group
2. Alphabetic
3. Alphanumeric
4. Numeric
5. Numeric Edited

depending upon the type of picture clause (PIC) used with the field in question. The Group item CANNOT have a picture clause and all elementary items MUST have one. Numeric edited fields will be discussed in chapter 7. This author does not use alphabetic field descriptions, although they will be discussed.

What follows are some examples:

DATA TYPE ENTRY		DEFINITION AND EXAMPLES
04 CITY	PIC A(10)	10 alphabetic characters including blanks CHICAGO NEW LENNOX
02 QUANTITY	PIC 9(4) (or PIC 9999)	4 numeric characters only: 0432 9466
03 TAX-IDENTIFIER	PIC XXXXXXX (or PIC X(7))	7 characters allowed: 4226314 A–463–7 00–43–7
02 SALARY-IN	PIC 999V99 or PIC 9(3)V99	Five numbers only. The compiler assumes first three numbers are integers and the last two are decimal. 10000 04050

03 AMOUNT	PIC S9(4)V9(3) (or PIC S9999V999)	Seven numeric digits. First four represent integers followed by three numbers representing decimal portion. The amount can be negative because of the "S". If the "S" is absent, AMOUNT is always considered positive. The "S" represents SIGN and enables the field to be either + or –.
		9300400
		6742178
		2340000
01 REC-OUT.		Group item. No picture clause. It is as large as all subordinate fields put together. Always considered alphanumeric.

4.5   INPUT AND/OR OUTPUT RECORD FORMATS

Example 1:

Field	Columns
NAME	1–20
SALARY	21–25 (assumed decimal)
ADDRESS	31–50
CITY	51–60
ZIP	61–65

Data for example 1:

SAMUELS STEPHEN   60000   34 S. WABASH   CHICAGO 60604

Record description for 1:

```
01   EMPLOYEE-REC.
     02 NAME          PIC X(20).
     02 SALARY        PIC 999V99.
```

02 FILLER	PIC X(5).
02 ADDRESS	PIC X(20).
02 CITY	PIC X(10).
02 ZIP	PIC X(5).

Example 2:

Field	Columns
BRANCH NUMBER	1–2
REGION NUMBER	3–4
SALESMAN	5–24
COMMISSION RATE	25–26 (ASSUMED DECIMAL)
QUANTITY SOLD	27–30
UNIT PRICE	31–36 (ASSUMED DECIMAL)

Data for example 2:

0412JONES PETER   081500095000

Record description for 2:

01	SALES-REC.	
	02 IN-BRANCH	PIC XX.
	02 IN-REGION	PIC XX.
	02 IN-SALESMAN	PIC X(20).
	02 IN-COMM-RATE	PIC V99.
	02 IN-QUAN-SOLD	PIC 9999.
	02 IN-UNIT-PRICE	PIC 9(4)V99.

[The second example is obviously for some sort of input record.]

4.6 MOVEMENT OF DATA

The MOVE statement accomplishes the transfer of data from one storage location to another. The general form of the MOVE statement can be found in appendix D. The results of the MOVE statement depend on the picture of the receiving field. If the picture clause of the receiving field is different from that of the sending field, either an internal data conversion takes place or the move is invalid. Valid MOVE statements clear out what was previously in the receiving field's location. The following table gives the rules of the MOVE statement:

	Receiving Field			
Sending Field	Alphabetic	Alphanumeric	Numeric	Group
Alphabetic	ok	ok	INVALID	ok
Alphanumeric	ok	ok	ok	ok
Numeric	INVALID	ok*	ok	ok
Group	ok	ok	ok	ok

* [No assumed decimal picture, e.g., 99V99 > X(4) not allowed.]

Example of a MOVE statement:

MOVE FIELDA TO FIELDB.

The following table illustrates the results of MOVE statements using FIELDA with various picture clauses and FIELDB with the same or differing picture clauses:

Sending Field (fielda)		Received Field (fieldb)		Authors Comment
PIC	Contents	PIC	Contents	
9(4)	1234	9(4)	1234	
X(11)	326–55–3043	X(10)	326–55–304	right truncation
A(3)	HOP	A(5)	HOP	pad on right with blanks
9(5)	40293	9(3)	293	left truncation
99	23	999	023	pad on left with zeros
9(3)V99	42316	9999V9	04231	strange move! Not a smart idea. Pad on left with zeros because of increased integer size [9(3) > 9(4)]. Right truncation of decimal portion.
9(5)V99	1040703	9(5)V99	1040703	Much better!!
A(5)	DEATH	9(5)		INVALID
9(5)	00321	A(5)		INVALID
A(7)	SAMUELS	X(7)	SAMUELS	

One can also use the MOVE statement to move literals into receiving fields, such as:

MOVE 37 TO FIELDX.   (Where FIELDX has a picture of 99)

MOVE "FIRED" TO EMP-STATUS.   (Where EMP-STATUS has a picture of X(5) or A(5))

MOVE .05 TO RATE-OUT. (Where RATE-OUT has a picture of V99)

The compiler does not reserve storage areas for literals as it does for data-names. Non-numeric literals require quotation marks. A given quantity can also be moved to several data-names in one statement. For example:

MOVE ZEROS TO FIELDA FIELDB FIELDC.

puts all zeros into all three fields.

SUMMARY

This chapter provides the framework by which you should have learned to:

1. understand, detect, and fix compilation errors.
2. understand how to modularize your code—i.e., add code in relatively small amounts to easily detect and correct errors in compilation AND execution.
3. use correct input file descriptions for incoming data.
4. manage movement of data with appropriate data-names and data-types.
5. construct a listing file.

QUESTIONS

1. Write the input file description for the following:

Field	Columns
ADDRESS	1–20
ZIP	21–25
CITY	31–40
NAME	41–60
SALARY	61–65
YTD-SALARY	67–72

2. Give the contents for the receiving field after the move is successful. If not, write INVALID.

Sending Field PIC	Contents	Receiving Field PIC	Contents
9(6)	300040	9(6)	
9(5)V99	0235123	9(4)V999	
A(11)	INFORMATION	X(9)	
9(3)	200	9(5)	
99V99	2040	999V999	
V99	30	99	
A(7)	SAMUELS	9(7)	
X(5)	WORLD	A(9)	

3. Given the following:

```
01  REC-LINE.
    02  NAME.
        03  LASTER         PIC X(10).
        03  FIRSTER        PIC X(8).
        03  FILLER         PIC X.
        03  MIDDLER        PIC X.
    02  SOC-NUM            PIC 9(9).
    02  ADDRESS.
        03  NUM-STREET     PIC X(20).
        03  CITY           PIC X(10).
        03  ZIP            PIC X(5).
    02  PHONE.
        03  EXTENSION      PIC XXX.
        03  P-NUM          PIC 9(7).
```

a. How many bytes does REC-LINE contain?
b. List all elementary data-names.
c. List all group data-names.
d. What column does SOC-NUM start in?
e. What column does EXTENSION end in?

PROGRAMMING PROBLEMS

1. Write a program that will read records from an input file (SALES.DAT), move appropriate data fields, and create an output file (SALREPT.DAT). Given the following input record information:

Field	Columns
Salesman #	1–4
Salesman Name	7–26
Amount Sold	31–37
Commission Rate	38–39 (assumed decimal)

The output records should be as follows:

Field	Columns
Amount Sold	4–10
Salesman Name	21–40
Commission Rate	51–52 (assumed decimal)
Salesman #	71–74

Provide your own test data. You will learn more by doing so!

2. Try the same thing again this time using the following (choice of file names is yours):

a. Input

Field	Columns	
Name	1–20	
SS#	21–31	
Salary	32–37	(assumed decimal)
Tax	38–43	(assumed decimal)

b. Output

Field	Columns	
Name	31–50	
SS#	71–81	
Salary	101–106	(assumed decimal)
Tax	121–126	(assumed decimal)

If your terminal can only display 80 columns on one line, do you notice something interesting when you $TYPE your output file created in this second problem? It is called WRAPAROUND!

## 5

Arithmetic Operations

As with other programming languages, COBOL has a complete set of statements that can perform arithmetic operations. There are basically two types of arithmetic statements. One type uses the verbs ADD, SUBTRACT, MULTIPLY, and DIVIDE, permitting one calculation at a time. The other type uses the verb COMPUTE, which not only allows one to use the symbols + (add), − (subract), * (multiply), / (divide), and ** (exponentiation), but also allows for multiple operations in a single statement. For the above capability and its similarity with other languages, this author prefers COMPUTE over all other arithmetic statements.

5.1 A PARTIAL SOLUTION TO A PROGRAMMING PROBLEM

Both types of arithmetic statements can be demonstrated by writing a program to solve the following problem:

A department in a midwestern university wants a report of all graduating seniors. The input records of each student have the following format:

Field	Columns
Last Name	1–10
First Name	11–17
Middle I	19
Credits (freshman)	21–22
Grade Point Ave [F]	23–25
Credits (sophomore)	26–27
Grade Point Ave [S]	28–30
Credits (junior)	31–32
Grade Point Ave [J]	33–35
Credits (senior)	36–37
Grade Point Ave [Se]	38–40
Outside Credits	41–43

The report has the following format:

Field	Columns
First Name	2–8
Middle I	10
Last Name	12–21
Total Credits	31–34
4-yr Average Grade Pt	41–43
Resident Tot Credits	51–53
% Resident Credits	61–62

Processing entails the following:

Total Credits = Credits (freshman) + Credits (sophomore) + Credits (junior) + Credits (senior)

4-yr Average Grade Pt = [Grade Point Ave (freshman) + Grade Point Ave (sophomore) + Grade Point Ave (junior) + Grade Point Ave (senior)] / 4.

Resident Tot Credits = Total Credits − Outside Credits

% Resident Credits = Resident Tot Credits/Total Credits × (100)

It is strongly suggested that before any calculations are attempted, one should have a program that can move necessary data fields from input to output. This satisfies the basic modular design that was developed in the previous chapter and assures that all the data records have been accounted for. This kind of pattern will be shown throughout the text. Even though only three fields are being moved (last, first, and middle initial), basic compiler errors and unfortunate stack dumps can be solved before additional code,

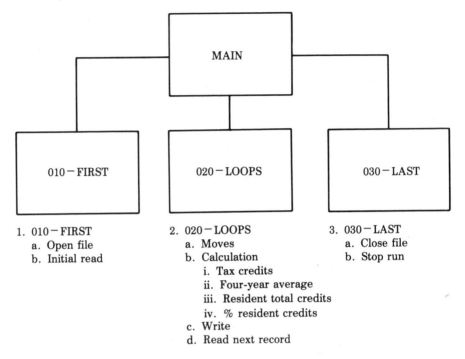

1. 010 – FIRST
   a. Open file
   b. Initial read

2. 020 – LOOPS
   a. Moves
   b. Calculation
      i. Tax credits
      ii. Four-year average
      iii. Resident total credits
      iv. % resident credits
   c. Write
   d. Read next record

3. 030 – LAST
   a. Close file
   b. Stop run

Figure 5-1

which would complicate the issue, is added. Essentially, we are programming in little steps.

The design and pseudocode are in Figure 5-1. Then examine the following program:

```
    1            IDENTIFICATION DIVISION.
    2            PROGRAM-ID. ARITHMETIC.
    3            AUTHOR. SAMUELS.
    4            ENVIRONMENT DIVISION.
    5            INPUT-OUPUT SECTION.
                 1
%COBOL-F-ERROR  117, (1) Invalid syntax
    6            FILE-CONTROL.
                 1
%COBOL-W-ERROR  297, (1) Processing of source program resumes at this point
%COBOL-E-ERROR  453, (1) Missing INPUT-OUTPUT SECTION header assumed
    7                SELECT FILE-IN ASSIGN TO STUDENTS.
    8                SELECT FILE-OUT ASSIGN TO UNIVREPT.
    9            DATA DIVISION.
   10            FILE SECTION.
   11            FD  FILE-IN
   12                DATA RECORD IS STU-REC.
   13            01  STU-REC.
   14                02 NAME.
   15                    03 LAST-IN         PIC X(10).
```

```
16                    03 FIRST-IN        PIC X(7).
17                    03 FILLER          PIC X.
18                    03 MIDDLE-IN       PIC X.
19                02 FILLER              PIC X.
20                02 FROSH-CREDITS       PIC 99.
21                02 FROSH-GR-AVE        PIC 9V99.
22                02 SOPH-CREDITS        PIC 99.
23                02 SOPH-GR-AVE         PIC 9V99.
24                02 JUN-CREDITS         PIC 99.
25                02 JUN-GR-AVE          PIC 9V99.
26                02 SEN-CREDITS         PIC 99.
27                02 SEN-GR-AVE          PIC 9V99.
28                02 OUTSIDE-CR-IN       PIC 999.
29          FD  FILE-OUT
30              DATA RECORD IS UNIVREPT-REC.
31          01  UNIVREPT-REC.
32                02  FILLER             PIC X.
33                02  FIRST-OUT          PIC X(7).
34                02  FILLER             PIC X.
35                02  MIDDLE-OUT         PIC X.
36                02  LAST-OUT           PIC X(10).
37                02  FILLER             PIC X(9).
38                02  TOT-CREDITS        PIC 999.
39                02  FILLER             PIC X(6).
40                02  4-YR-GR-AVE        PIC 9V99.
41                02  FILLER             PIC X(7).
42                02  RES-TOT-CREDITS    PIC 999.
43                02  FILLER             PIC X(7).
44                02  PERC-RES-CREDITS   PIC 99.
45          WORKING-STORAGE SECCTION.
                              1
%COBOL-F-ERROR  222, (1) "SECTION" required at this point
46          01  FINISHED       PIC XXX VALUE SPACES.
                  1
%COBOL-W-ERROR  297, (1) Processing of source program resumes at this point
47          PROCEDURE DIVISION.
48          BEGINNER.
49              PERFORM 010-FIRST.
50              PERFORM 020-LOOPS UNTIL FINISHED = "YES".
51              PERFORM 030-LAST.
52          010-FIRST.
53              OPEN INPUT FILE-IN OUTPUT FILE-OUT.
54              READ FILE-IN AT END MOVE "YES" TO FINISHED.
55          020-LOOPS.
56              MOVE SPACES TO UNIVREPT.
                              1
%COBOL-F-ERROR  349, (1) Undefined name
57              MOVE LAST-IN TO LAST-OUT.
58              MOVE FIRST-IN TO FIRST-OUT.
59              MOVE MIDDLE-IN TO MIDDLE-OUT.
60              WRITE UNIVREPT.
                      1
%COBOL-F-ERROR  349, (1) Undefined name
61              READ FILE-IN AT END MOVE "YES" TO FINISHED.
                      1
%COBOL-W-ERROR  297, (1) Processing of source program resumes at this point
62          030-LAST.
63              CLOSE FILE-IN FILE-OUT.
64              STOP RUN.
```

Once again we have some errors in compilation that must be fixed before an object module can be produced. A further explanation of the above errors is as follows:

Line 5	Misspelled INPUT-OUTPUT SECTION.
Line 6	Ok. We are shown where processing continues.
Line 45	Interesting way of spelling SECTION.
Line 46	Same as line 6.
Lines 56 and 60	Should be UNIVREPT-REC.
Line 61	Same as line 6.

Hence, we must use the Editor:

$EDT STUPROG.COB (the external file name of the program)

and do the following:

get to line 5 and use:

S/OUPUT/OUTPUT

get to line 45 and use:

S/SECC/SEC

get to lines 56 and 60 to use:

S/REPT/REPT-REC

What follows is a list of input records to this program, the program listing without compiler errors, and the output records produced by the program.

Input Records

ARTIBEY	KIM	A	202753327510275343000 3 8
BERNOT	JANE	M	323503327532200343000 0 0
DELSIT	PETER	L	242002617534300303250 1 6
GRANGER	JOSEPH		323503030036375283000 1 0
HARRISON	SHERRY	A	123001230034375343750 4 0
WILKERSON	AMY	D	322003217533275332750 O 0
ZAWORSKI	BARRY	I	324003340024325333750 0 8

Program Listing

```
1     IDENTIFICATION DIVISION.
2     PROGRAM-ID. ARITHMETIC.
3     AUTHOR. SAMUELS.
4     ENVIRONMENT DIVISION.
5     INPUT-OUTPUT SECTION.
6     FILE-CONTROL.
7          SELECT FILE-IN ASSIGN TO STUDENTS.
8          SELECT FILE-OUT ASSIGN TO UNIVREPT.
9     DATA DIVISION.
10    FILE SECTION.
11    FD  FILE-IN
12        DATA RECORD IS STU-REC.
13    01  STU-REC.
14        02 NAME.
15            03 LAST-IN          PIC X(10).
16            03 FIRST-IN         PIC X(7).
17            03 FILLER           PIC X.
18            03 MIDDLE-IN         PIC X.
19        02 FILLER               PIC X.
20        02 FROSH-CREDITS         PIC 99.
21        02 FROSH-GR-AVE          PIC 9V99.
22        02 SOPH-CREDITS          PIC 99.
23        02 SOPH-GR-AVE           PIC 9V99.
24        02 JUN-CREDITS           PIC 99.
25        02 JUN-GR-AVE            PIC 9V99.
26        02 SEN-CREDITS           PIC 99.
27        02 SEN-GR-AVE            PIC 9V99.
28        02 OUTSIDE-CR-IN         PIC 999.
29    FD  FILE-OUT
30        DATA RECORD IS UNIVREPT-REC.
31    01  UNIVREPT-REC.
32        02  FILLER              PIC X.
33        02  FIRST-OUT           PIC X(7).
34        02  FILLER              PIC X.
35        02  MIDDLE-OUT          PIC X.
36        02  LAST-OUT            PIC X(10).
37        02  FILLER              PIC X(9).
38        02  TOT-CREDITS         PIC 999.
39        02  FILLER              PIC X(6).
40        02  4-YR-GR-AVE         PIC 9V99.
41        02  FILLER              PIC X(7).
42        02  RES-TOT-CREDITS     PIC 999.
43        02  FILLER              PIC X(7).
44        02  PERC-RES-CREDITS    PIC 99.
45    WORKING-STORAGE SECTION.
46    01  FINISHED                PIC XXX VALUE SPACES.
47    PROCEDURE DIVISION.
48    BEGINNER.
49        PERFORM 010-FIRST.
50        PERFORM 020-LOOPS UNTIL FINISHED = "YES".
51        PERFORM 030-LAST.
52    010-FIRST.
53        OPEN INPUT FILE-IN OUTPUT FILE-OUT.
54        READ FILE-IN AT END MOVE "YES" TO FINISHED.
55    020-LOOPS.
56        MOVE SPACES TO UNIVREPT-REC.
57        MOVE LAST-IN TO LAST-OUT.
58        MOVE FIRST-IN TO FIRST-OUT.
```

```
59          MOVE MIDDLE-IN TO MIDDLE-OUT.
60          WRITE UNIVREPT-REC.
61          READ FILE-IN AT END MOVE "YES" TO FINISHED.
62      030-LAST.
63          CLOSE FILE-IN FILE-OUT.
64          STOP RUN.
```

Output Records ——————————————————————————————————————

KIM   AARTIBEY
JANE   MBERNOT
PETER   LDELSIT
JOSEPH   GRANGER
SHERRY   AHARRISON
AMY   DWILKERSON
BARRY   IZAWORSKI

Note that there is no space between the middle initial and last name of all the output records. This can be easily remedied by adding:

02   FILLER   PIC X.

between lines 35 and 36.

5.2   ADDITION OF ARITHMETIC STATEMENTS

Assume that the above change is made. It is not necessary to show the input, listing, and output again. The emphasis must be placed on the arithmetic operations that must be added to the program to complete its solution.

To get TOT-CREDITS we have to do the following:

ADD FROSH-CREDITS SOPH-CREDITS GIVING TOT-CREDITS.
ADD JUN-CREDITS TO TOT-CREDITS.
ADD SEN-CREDITS TO TOT-CREDITS.
ADD OUTSIDE-CR-IN TO TOT-CREDITS.

We need the Giving option to let the system add FROSH-CREDITS and SOPH-CREDITS, producing an answer that will be "moved" to TOT-CREDITS. If we do the following:

ADD FROSH-CREDITS TO TOT-CREDITS.
ADD SOPH-CREDITS TO TOT-CREDITS.
ADD JUN-CREDITS TO TOT-CREDITS.
ADD SEN-CREDITS TO TOT-CREDITS.
ADD OUTSIDE-CR-IN TO TOT-CREDITS.

a stack dump will result because the contents of TOT-CREDITS is unknown when the first ADD statement is executed. The compiler has set up a storage area for TOT-CREDITS but, after compilation, it has no way of knowing what is initially in TOT-CREDITS. The Giving option in the ADD statement provides the move that "puts" the answer in TOT-CREDITS. Once a number is in TOT-CREDITS the other form of the ADD statement can be used. (See section 5–3 for examples of all arithmetic statements. Also consult appendix D for the general forms of all arithmetic statements.)

There are two better and shorter methods for getting the correct answer in TOT-CREDITS:

a. ADD FROSH-CREDITS SOPH-CREDITS JUN-CREDITS SEN-CREDITS
    OUTSIDE-CR-IN GIVING TOT-CREDITS.

b. COMPUTE TOT-CREDITS = FROSH-CREDITS + SOPH-CREDITS
    + JUN-CREDITS + SEN-CREDITS + OUTSIDE-CR-IN.

The ADD and SUBTRACT statements allow for more than two operands to be used for addition and subtraction. This is not the case with MULTIPLY or DIVIDE. Method "b" is preferred anyway. Since the compiler "views" many blanks as one blank, the above statements can be split up into two or more lines of code; however, one should not "split up" a word (reserved or data-name)! Since method "b" is preferred, it will be used in the program that will follow.

To get RES-TOT-CREDITS we can use:

SUBTRACT OUTSIDE-CR-IN FROM TOT-CREDITS
GIVING RES-TOT-CREDITS.

or:

COMPUTE RES-TOT-CREDITS = TOT-CREDITS − OUTSIDE-CR-IN.

One could make a case about the above arithmetic logic since the credits for all four years could be added up to give RES-TOT-CREDITS (resident credits). Then RES-TOT-CREDITS could be added to OUTSIDE-CR-IN (credits earned outside the university) to give TOT-CREDITS. This approach was not taken so that the SUBTRACT statement could be shown.

There is a problem, however, in getting 4-YR-GR-AVE. If we used appropriate ADD statements we would get a total of all grade point averages. But we want an average for all four years; that is, we need a statement to add up all four-year grade point averages and divide by 4 to get 4-YR-GR-AVE. There has been no provision made for an area that contains the sum of all grade point averages in the DATA DIVISION. If another area were set up then one could use an ADD statement and a DIVIDE statement to obtain the result. In this case the only way is to do the following:

COMPUTE 4-YR-GR-AVE = (FROSH-GR-AVE + SOPH-GR-AVE +
JUN-GR-AVE + SEN-GR-AVE) / 4.

Notice that parentheses were used to change the order of operations. In all
COMPUTE statements at least one blank must appear between arithmetic
operators and the assignment operator (=). No blank is needed or should be
used between the left or right parenthesis and a data-name. See section 5-4
for a table showing the hierarchy of arithmetic operations and some examples of COMPUTE statements with and without parentheses.

   To get PERC-RES-CREDITS a COMPUTE statement is best:

COMPUTE PERC-RES-CREDITS = RES-TOT-CREDITS / TOT-CREDITS
* 100.

Parentheses are not required although they can be used for clarification:

COMPUTE PREC-RES-CREDITS = (RES-TOT-CREDITS /
TOT-CREDITS) * 100.

Since the author only uses ADD and SUBTRACT statements to increment or
decrement totals, COMPUTE statements will be added to perform the necessary arithmetic operations.

   The following is the modified program with output records shown after
the listing:

```
 1      IDENTIFICATION DIVISION.
 2      PROGRAM-ID. ARITHMETIC.
 3      AUTHOR. SAMUELS.
 4      ENVIRONMENT DIVISION.
 5      INPUT-OUTPUT SECTION.
 6      FILE-CONTROL.
 7          SELECT FILE-IN ASSIGN TO STUDENTS.
 8          SELECT FILE-OUT ASSIGN TO UNIVREPT.
 9      DATA DIVISION.
10      FILE SECTION.
11      FD  FILE-IN
12          DATA RECORD IS STU-REC.
13      01  STU-REC.
14          02 NAME.
15              03 LAST-IN         PIC X(10).
16              03 FIRST-IN        PIC X(7).
17              03 FILLER          PIC X.
18              03 MIDDLE-IN       PIC X.
19          02 FILLER              PIC X.
20          02 FROSH-CREDITS       PIC 99.
21          02 FROSH-GR-AVE        PIC 9V99.
22          02 SOPH-CREDITS        PIC 99.
23          02 SOPH-GR-AVE         PIC 9V99.
24          02 JUN-CREDITS         PIC 99.
```

```
25          02 JUN-GR-AVE          PIC 9V99.
26          02 SEN-CREDITS         PIC 99.
27          02 SEN-GR-AVE          PIC 9V99.
28          02 OUTSIDE-CR-IN       PIC 999.
29      FD  FILE-OUT
30          DATA RECORD IS UNIVREPT-REC.
31      01  UNIVREPT-REC.
32          02  FILLER             PIC X.
33          02  FIRST-OUT          PIC X(7).
34          02  FILLER             PIC X.
35          02  MIDDLE-OUT         PIC X.
36          02  filler             pic x.
37          02  LAST-OUT           PIC X(10).
38          02  FILLER             PIC X(9).
39          02  TOT-CREDITS        PIC 999.
40          02  FILLER             PIC X(6).
41          02  4-YR-GR-AVE        PIC 9V99.
42          02  FILLER             PIC X(7).
43          02  RES-TOT-CREDITS    PIC 999.
44          02  FILLER             PIC X(7).
45          02  PERC-RES-CREDITS   PIC 99.
46      WORKING-STORAGE SECTION.
47      01  FINISHED               PIC XXX VALUE SPACES.
48      PROCEDURE DIVISION.
49      BEGINNER.
50          PERFORM 010-FIRST.
51          PERFORM 020-LOOPS UNTIL FINISHED = "YES".
52          PERFORM 030-LAST.
53      010-FIRST.
54          OPEN INPUT FILE-IN OUTPUT FILE-OUT.
55          READ FILE-IN AT END MOVE "YES" TO FINISHED.
56      020-LOOPS.
57          MOVE SPACES TO UNIVREPT-REC.
58          MOVE LAST-IN TO LAST-OUT.
59          MOVE FIRST-IN TO FIRST-OUT.
60          MOVE MIDDLE-IN TO MIDDLE-OUT.
61          compute tot-credits = frosh-credits + soph-credits
62              + jun-credits + sen-credits + outside-cr-in.
63          compute res-tot-credits = tot-credits - outside-cr-in.
64          compute 4-yr-gr-ave = (frosh-gr-ave + soph-gr-ave +
65              jun-gr-ave + sen-gr-ave) / 4.
66          compute perc-res-credits = (res-tot-credits / tot-credits)
67              * 100.
68          WRITE UNIVREPT-REC.
69          READ FILE-IN AT END MOVE "YES" TO FINISHED.
70      030-LAST.
71          CLOSE FILE-IN FILE-OUT.
72          STOP RUN.
```

Output Records ───────────────────────────────────────

KIM	A	ARTIBEY	135	281	097	71
JANE	M	BERNOT	131	281	131	00
PETER	L	DELSIT	130	250	114	87
JOSEPH		GRANGER	136	331	126	92
SHERRY	A	HARRISON	132	337	092	69

When the program was run we not only got the above records in UNIVREPT.DAT but also the following message on the "tube."

%COB-F-INVDECDAT, invalid decimal data
%TRACE-F-TRACEBACK, symbolic stack dump follows

module name	routine name	line	rel PC	abs PC
ARITHMETIC	ARITHMETIC	61	00000172	00000B72

There are two things wrong. Jane Bernot, the second output record, shows 00 for a percentage instead of 100. Obviously, the output field for PERC-RES-CREDITS was too small, causing truncation on the left. Amy Wilkerson's record cannot be processed since there is an "O" instead of an "0" in the OUTSIDE-CR-IN field. If we expand the PERC-RES-CREDITS field and "fix" the incoming data, we get the following:

KIM	A	ARTIBEY	135	281	097	071
JANE	M	BERNOT	131	281	131	100
PETER	L	DELSIT	130	250	114	087
JOSEPH		GRANGER	136	331	126	092
SHERRY	A	HARRISON	132	337	092	069
AMY	D	WILKERSON	130	231	130	100
BARRY	I	ZAWORSKI	130	375	122	093

One must always examine the output. Those stack dump errors are sometimes quite difficult to fix. It is no easy task when examining test data to find a "O" instead of a "0." The computer cannot handle a "O" arithmetically. The compiler did its job; that is, it found no syntax errors, and created the object module with appropriate storage areas. A stack dump like you have just seen is an error in execution, not compilation. The compiler has no way of knowing what will wind up in the created storage areas in main memory.

Suppose someone asked you to go to the twentieth floor of a high-rise building and jump out a window. You understand the instructions (compilation) but would you execute them (run)?

Or how about this statement:

COMPUTE Q-FIELD = Y-FIELD / Z-FIELD.

This makes sense to the compiler but will cause a stack dump after an attempted RUN if Z-FIELD = 0.

In future chapters, test data that include invalid data will be used as input to programs. Our programs will have to handle invalid input as well as test for all possible "legal" situations. It is most important to understand that it is better to write programs in "little pieces" using test data at various points rather than to write the complete program and spend inordinate amounts of time "debugging" it.

5.3   EXAMPLES OF ARITHMETIC STATEMENTS

The ADD Statement

a. ADD Q-FIELD R-FIELD GIVING Z-FIELD.

$$\text{where Q-FIELD (PIC 999)} = |4|2|3|$$
$$\text{R-FIELD (PIC 99)} = |6|7|$$
$$\text{then} \quad \text{Z-FIELD (PIC 9999)} = |0|4|9|0|$$

b. ADD 1 TO COUNTX

where   COUNTX (PIC 999) = $|A|B|C|$ results in a stack dump (cannot add to non-numeric quantity)

but when COUNTX (PIC 999) = $|0|0|0|$ then, after execution

$$\text{COUNTX (PIC 999)} = |0|0|1|$$

c. ADD M-FIELD 7.2 N-FIELD GIVING O-FIELD

where M-FIELD (PIC 99V9) = $|2|3|7|$

N-FIELD (PIC 9V9)   = $|7|4|$

then   O-FIELD (PIC 99V9) = $|3|8|3|$ (we didn't forget to also add 7.2)

General rules:

1. Make sure receiving fields are large enough to accommodate the result; otherwise, left truncation will occur on the integer side and right truncation will occur on the decimal side. If receiving field is too large, then padding with zeros occurs on the left of the integer field and on the right of the decimal field. [ON SIZE ERROR discussed later]

2. Initialize (MOVE 0 or VALUE 0) all data-names that act as accumulators.

The SUBTRACT Statement

a. SUBTRACT R-FIELD FROM Q-FIELD GIVING Z-FIELD.

$$\text{where Q-FIELD (PIC 999)} = |6|2|8|$$

R- FIELD (PIC 999) $= |0|3|7|$

then   Z- FIELD (PIC 999) $= |5|9|1|$

b. SUBTRACT 1 FROM COUNTX

where before COUNTX (PIC 99V9) $= |2|3|0|$

now COUNTX becomes $\qquad = |2|2|0|$

c. SUBTRACT Q-FIELD R-FIELD S-FIELD FROM Z-FIELD.

where $\qquad$ Q-FIELD (PIC 99V99) $= |3|2|4|8|$

R-FIELD (PIC 99V99) $= |2|2|8|3|$

S-FIELD (PIC 99V99) $= |4|4|8|0|$

and before Z-FIELD (PIC 999V99) $= |2|0|0|0|0|$

now $\qquad$ Z-FIELD becomes $\qquad = |0|9|9|8|9|$

General rules:

1. Make sure you use a signed field if the result is going to be negative (or has that possibility). This will be discussed in a later chapter.

2. If you are decrementing a data-name (as in "b"), make sure this field has been initialized.

The MULTIPLY Statement

a. MULTIPLY PAY BY 0.065 GIVING FICA

where PAY (PIC 9999V99) $\qquad = |0|5|2|3|4|6|$

now FICA (PIC 9999V99) becomes $= |0|0|3|4|0|2|$

b. MULTIPLY C-FIELD BY D-FIELD

where C-FIELD (PIC 99V99) $\qquad = |1|2|3|4|$

and before D-FIELD (PIC 9999V99) $= |0|0|1|0|0|0|$

now D-FIELD becomes $\qquad = |0|1|2|3|4|0|$

General rules:

1. As before, make sure receiving field is large enough.

2. Example "b," although valid, is not a recommended method of doing multiplication.

The DIVIDE Statement

Using format 1 (see appendix)

a. DIVIDE X-FIELD INTO Y-FIELD GIVING Z-FIELD.

where X-FIELD (PIC 99) $= |2|5|$

Y-FIELD (PIC 999) $= |2|0|0|$

and Z-FIELD (PIC 999) becomes $= |0|0|8|$

b. DIVIDE X-FIELD INTO Y-FIELD

where X-FIELD (PIC 9V99) $= |1|2|0|$

and before Y-FIELD (PIC 99V9) $= |2|7|6|$

now Y-FIELD becomes $= |2|3|0|$

Using format 2 (see appendix)

a. DIVIDE Q-FIELD BY 5 GIVING M-FIELD

where Q-FIELD (PIC 999) $= |3|0|0|$

and M-FIELD (PIC 999) becomes $= |0|6|0|$

b. DIVIDE A-FIELD BY B-FIELD

where A-FIELD (PIC 99V9) $= |2|7|6|$

and before B-FIELD (PIC 99V9) $= |0|9|2|$

now B-FIELD becomes $= |0|0|3|$

c. DIVIDE 8.2 BY Z-FIELD GIVING Q-FIELD REMAINDER D-FIELD

where Z-FIELD (PIC 9V99) $= |2|0|6|$

and Q-FIELD (PIC 99V99) becomes $= |0|3|9|8|$

and D-FIELD (PIC 9V99) becomes $= |0|1|2|$

General rules:

1. Make sure you have proper picture clauses for divisor and dividend; otherwise, you may lose integers and/or decimal portions.

2. The "b" examples require initialization of some kind.

The COMPUTE Statement (author's favorite)

a. COMPUTE Q-FIELD = Z-FIELD

where Z-FIELD (PIC 99) $= |0|8|$

and Q-FIELD (PIC 999) becomes $= |0|0|8|$

b. COMPUTE A-FIELD = B-FIELD + 36 / D-FIELD

where B-FIELD (PIC 999) $= |3|0|0|$

D-FIELD (PIC 9) $= |3|$

and A-FIELD (PIC 9999) becomes $= |0|3|1|2|$

c. COMPUTE X-FIELD = B-FIELD ** 2 + (M-FIELD − D-FIELD) * 4.

where B-FIELD (PIC 9) $= |8|$

M-FIELD (PIC 99V9) $= |2|3|6|$

D-FIELD (PIC 99V9) $= |2|1|5|$

and X-FIELD (PIC 999V9) becomes $= |0|7|2|4|$

[the above order of operations is as follows:

−	first
**	second
*	third
+	fourth]

General rules:

1. Make sure you know what you want in terms of order of operations.

2. Avoid the use of unnecessary parentheses.

5.4 HIERARCHY OF ARITHMETIC OPERATIONS

**	Exponentiation	Highest
* /	Multiplication and Division	
	(whichever is seen first after =)	
+ −	Addition and Subtraction	Lowest
	(whichever is seen first after =)	

Specific examples using COMPUTE statements follow (the number underneath the operation shows the order):

COMPUTE XYZ = QRS + PMB * FDK.
                        2   1

COMPUTE SAL = REGULAR + (HOURS − 40) * RATE * 1.5.
                       4   1   2   3

COMPUTE M   = ((M − R) * P) / Z ** (F + 4).
                 1   2   5   4   3

Note: Operations within parentheses are performed first.

SUMMARY

As in the previous chapter, you should now understand how to write COBOL statements in "small steps." Correcting errors in compilation should NOT be such a horrendous task. Also, errors in execution can be more easily identified and the program changed accordingly so that the right output is produced.

    The following additional syntax should have been learned:

1. ADD
2. SUBTRACT
3. MULTIPLY
4. DIVIDE
5. COMPUTE

    Finally, you should thoroughly understand the hierarchy of arithmetic operations if more than one operator is used in a COMPUTE statement—with or without parentheses.

QUESTIONS

1. Arrange in order the following statements so that the computer can execute each one properly.

    a. COMPUTE Z = X + Y * 5.
    b. MULTIPLY P BY 3 GIVING B.
    c. DIVIDE Q BY 6 GIVING M.
    d. MOVE B TO A Y X.
    e. MOVE 12 TO X Y.
    f. COMPUTE U = (A + B) ** 2 / (B + L).
    g. SUBTRACT Y FROM M GIVING L.
    h. ADD U M B A GIVING P.

i. ADD Z X X GIVING Q.
j. MOVE L TO P Y.

2. What values are in the above data-names after the last instruction is executed? (Assume large enough numeric picture clauses are associated with the data-names.)

3. Write COBOL statements for the following (use ADD, SUBTRACT, MULTIPLY, DIVIDE, or preferably, COMPUTE):

   a. C = A + B
   b. Net pay is equal to gross pay minus deductions.
   c. V = 4/3 πr^3
   d. F = F − 1
   e. A = P(1 − r)^n
   f. Commission is equal to quantity sold times the unit price times the commission rate

4. Suppose X=5, Y=3, Z=7.1, and P=16. What is the value of Q after each statement of a set of statements is executed (assume Q has a PIC 999V9)?

   a. COMPUTE Q = (X + Z) * P − Z   Q = ?
   b. ADD X P GIVING Q.
      SUBTRACT Y FROM Q.
      MULTIPLY Q BY Z GIVING Q.   Q = ?
   c. COMPUTE Q = X ** (Y − 1) / ((P − Z) * Y)   Q = ?

5. What is in X-FIELD, Y-FIELD, and Z-FIELD after the following is executed:

```
        PROCEDURE DIVISION.
        STARTER.
            PERFORM 010–FIRST.
            PERFORM 020–SECOND.
            PERFORM 030–THIRD UNTIL Y > 3.
            PERFORM 020–SECOND.
            STOP RUN.
        010–FIRST.
            MOVE 0 TO Z-FIELD.
            MOVE 3 TO X-FIELD.
            MOVE 5 TO Y-FIELD.
        020–SECOND.
            ADD Y-FIELD TO Z-FIELD.
            COMPUTE Y-FIELD = Y-FIELD + 2.
        030–THIRD.
            COMPUTE Z-FIELD = Z-FIELD + X-FIELD.
            ADD 1 TO Y-FIELD.
```

PROGRAMMING PROBLEMS

1. Write a program that reads in records with the following format:

Field	Columns
Name	1–20
Amount	21–26 (assumed decimal)
Interest Rate	27–28 (assumed decimal)

and produces the following:

Field	Columns
Name	11–30
Amount	31–36
Interest	41–46
New Balance	51–56

where:

$$\text{Interest} = (\text{Amount})(\text{Interest Rate})$$
$$\text{New Balance} = \text{Amount} + \text{Interest}$$

using the following data:

```
JOE SMITH              80000006
SARAH DINERO           75000007
SIDNEY GREENSTREET     08000005
FRED PALLADIN          30000008
```

one should get:

```
JOE SMITH              800000  048000  848000
SARAH DINERO           750000  052500  802500
SIDNEY GREENSTREET     080000  004000  084000
FRED PALLADIN          300000  024000  324000
```

2. A publishing company pays a certain COST to have a book printed and bound. The author receives a ROYALTY (fixed percentage) of the WHOLE-SALE price for each book and the unsold books have a certain SALVAGE value per book. Write a program that reads in records containing the following fields:

Number of books printed

Cost to print each book

Fixed royalty percentage

Wholesale price

Number of books sold

Salvage value for each book

[Provide your own input file description and test data.]
The output should have a line printed for each record that contains the above fields plus the PROFIT (if any)!

* 3. Write a program to read in records with the following format:

Field	Columns
Name	1–20
Mortgage Amount	21–27 (assumed decimal)
Interest Rate	31–33 (assumed decimal)
Number of years	35–36

The output consists of all the above fields plus the monthly mortgage payment. I'm afraid you must use the following formula:

$$M = \frac{P \times \dfrac{R}{12}}{1 - \left[\dfrac{1}{1 + \dfrac{R}{12}}\right]^{T \times 12}}$$

M = monthly payment
P = principal (mortgage amount)
R = interest
T = time (years)

[HINT: Consult your local bank or S/L for correct monthly payments for various mortgage amounts over certain time frames. Your answer may differ slightly due to internal differences among computers. So if you are "off" a few cents, no bank auditor will come to call!]

Condition (IF) Statements

Most COBOL programs are written to have the computer make decisions. In many cases one action or the other is taken based on a condition. Examine the general form of IF statements in the Appendix. Also examine Figure 6–1 for various flowcharts and the related "translations" into COBOL condition statements.

6.1 BASIC CONDITION STATEMENTS

In the previous chapter, we wrote a program for that midwestern university, producing a report containing certain information for every input record. But suppose we wanted the computer to only produce output records of students who had taken no courses outside this university (OUTSIDE-CR-IN = 000). Examine the flowchart in Figure 6–2 for this situation. The condition must be TRUE for any output record to be written.

What follows is the program developed from the previous chapter with the proper IF statement included in lower case. The output follows the program.

```
1    IDENTIFICATION DIVISION.
2    PROGRAM-ID. CONDTION.
3    AUTHOR. SAMUELS.
4    ENVIRONMENT DIVISION.
5    INPUT-OUTPUT SECTION.
```

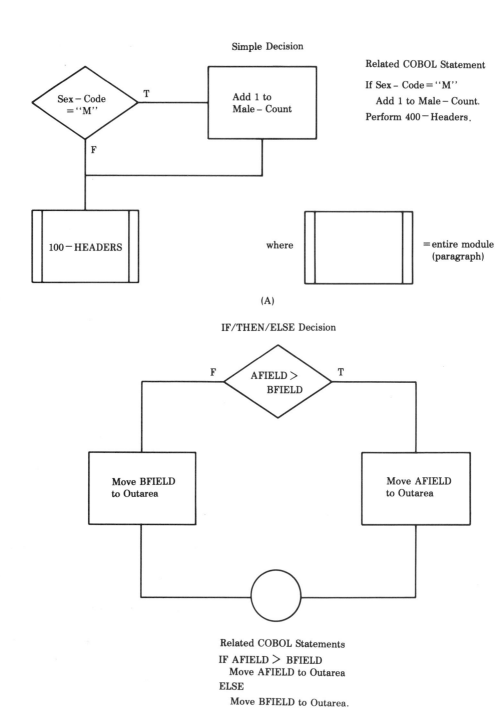

Simple Decision

Related COBOL Statement

If Sex – Code = ''M''
    Add 1 to Male – Count.
Perform 400 – Headers.

(A)

IF/THEN/ELSE Decision

Related COBOL Statements

IF AFIELD > BFIELD
    Move AFIELD to Outarea
ELSE
    Move BFIELD to Outarea.

(B)

Figure 6–1

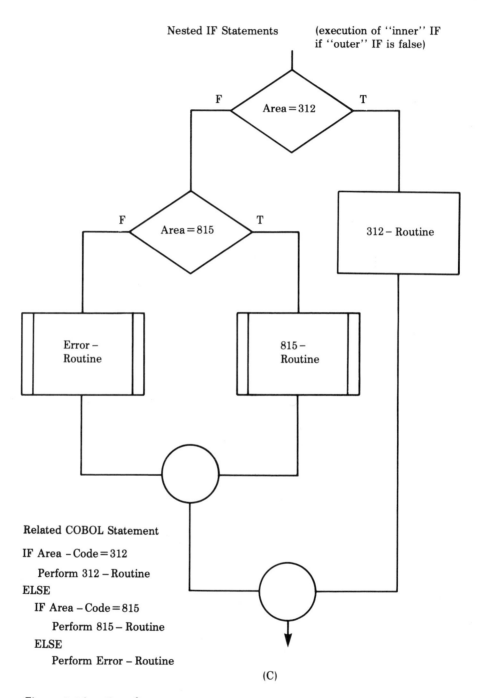

Nested IF Statements (execution of ''inner'' IF if ''outer'' IF is false)

Related COBOL Statement

IF Area – Code = 312

    Perform 312 – Routine
ELSE
  IF Area – Code = 815
     Perform 815 – Routine
  ELSE
     Perform Error – Routine

(C)

Figure 6-1 (continued)

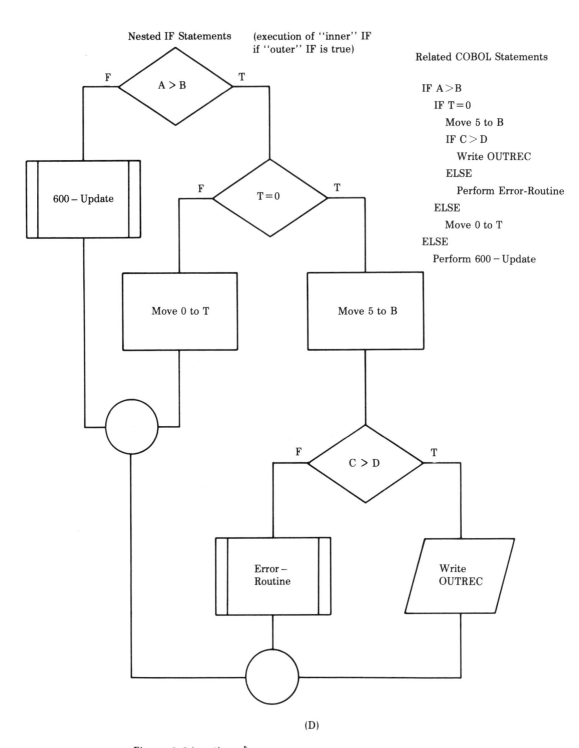

Nested IF Statements   (execution of "inner" IF
                        if "outer" IF is true)

Related COBOL Statements

```
IF A>B
    IF T=0
        Move 5 to B
        IF C>D
            Write OUTREC
        ELSE
            Perform Error-Routine
    ELSE
        Move 0 to T
ELSE
    Perform 600 – Update
```

(D)

Figure 6-1 (continued)

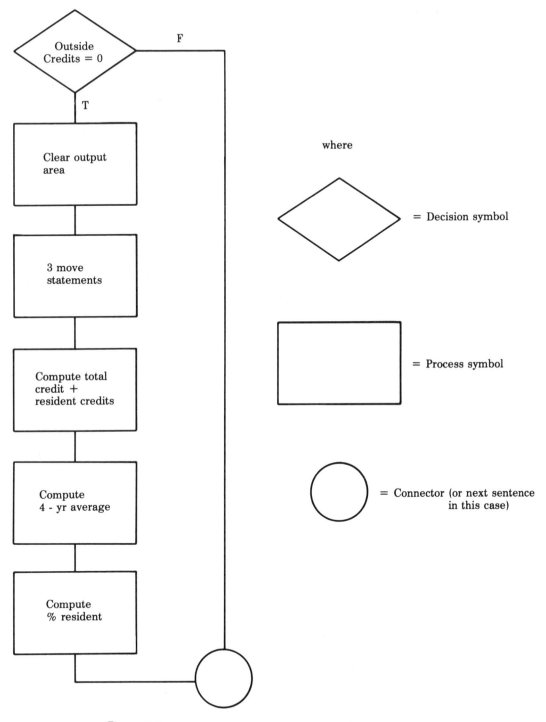

Figure 6-2

where

= Decision symbol

= Process symbol

= Connector (or next sentence
in this case)

```
 6    FILE-CONTROL.
 7        SELECT FILE-IN ASSIGN TO STUDENTS.
 8        SELECT FILE-OUT ASSIGN TO UNIVREPT.
 9    DATA DIVISION.
10    FILE SECTION.
11    FD  FILE-IN
12        DATA RECORD IS STU-REC.
13    01  STU-REC.
14        02 NAME.
15            03 LAST-IN        PIC X(10).
16            03 FIRST-IN       PIC X(7).
17            03 FILLER         PIC X.
18            03 MIDDLE-IN       PIC X.
19        02 FILLER            PIC X.
20        02 FROSH-CRED        PIC 99.
21        02 FROSH-GR-AVE      PIC 9V99.
22        02 SOPH-CREDITS      PIC 99.
23        02 SOPH-GR-AVE       PIC 9V99.
24        02 JUN-CREDITS       PIC 99.
25        02 JUN-GR-AVE        PIC 9V99.
26        02 SEN-CREDITS       PIC 99.
27        02 SEN-GR-AVE        PIC 9V99.
28        02 OUTSIDE-CR-IN     PIC 999.
29    FD  FILE-OUT
30        DATA RECORD IS UNIVREPT-REC.
31    01  UNIVREPT-REC.
32        02  FILLER           PIC X.
33        02  FIRST-OUT        PIC X(7).
34        02  FILLER           PIC X.
35        02  MIDDLE-OUT       PIC X.
36        02  FILLER           PIC X.
37        02  LAST-OUT         PIC X(10).
38        02  FILLER           PIC X(9).
39        02  TOT-CREDITS      PIC 999.
40        02  FILLER           PIC X(6).
41        02  4-YR-GR-AVE      PIC 9V99.
42        02  FILLER           PIC X(7).
43        02  RES-TOT-CREDITS  PIC 999.
44        02  FILLER           PIC X(7).
45        02  PERC-RES-CREDITS PIC 999.
46    WORKING-STORAGE SECTION.
47    01  FINISHED             PIC XXX VALUE SPACES.
48    PROCEDURE DIVISION.
49    BEGIN.
50        PERFORM 010-FIRST.
51        PERFORM 020-LOOPS UNTIL FINISHED = "YES".
52        PERFORM 030-LAST.
53    010-FIRST.
54        OPEN INPUT FILE-IN OUTPUT FILE-OUT.
55        READ FILE-IN AT END MOVE "YES" TO FINISHED.
56    020-LOOPS.
57        if outside-cr-in = 0
58          MOVE SPACES TO UNIVREPT-REC
59          MOVE LAST-IN TO LAST-OUT
60          MOVE FIRST-IN TO FIRST-OUT
61          MOVE MIDDLE-IN TO MIDDLE-OUT
62          COMPUTE TOT-CREDITS = FROSH-CREDITS + SOPH-CREDITS
63              + JUN-CREDITS + SEN-CREDITS + OUTSIDE-CR-IN
64          COMPUTE RES-TOT-CREDITS = TOT-CREDITS - OUTSIDE-CR-IN
65          COMPUTE 4-YR-GR-AVE = (FROSH-GR-AVE + SOPH-GR-AVE +
66              JUN-GR-AVE + SEN-GR-AVE) / 4
67          COMPUTE PERC-RES-CREDITS = (RES-TOT-CREDITS / TOT-CREDITS)
```

```
68                    * 100
69              WRITE UNIVREPT-REC.
70              READ FILE-IN AT END MOVE "YES" TO FINISHED.
71          030-LAST.
72              CLOSE FILE-IN FILE-OUT.
73              STOP RUN.
```

Output Records

JANE M BERNOT	131	281	131	100
AMY D WILKERSON	130	231	130	100

The following changes were made:

a. The program-id was changed.

b. Periods were removed from statements 58–68 so that lines 58–69 could be executed if OUTSIDE-CR-IN = 0.

You are encouraged to put the above program into your directory with the related input file. Experiment by putting a period after statement 66 and see what happens.

Reverse logic could have been employed by using the following:

```
        IF OUTSIDE-CR-IN NOT = 0
                    NEXT SENTENCE
    ELSE
            statement 58
            statement 59

                    .
                    .
                    .
        WRITE  UNIVREPT-REC.
```

This would have produced the same result. The YES and NO in the flowchart have just been reversed. YOU SHOULD TRY IT!!

The clause NEXT SENTENCE means to execute the following statement.

What would happen if we used this conditional statement?

```
    IF FROSH-GR-AVE > 3 AND OUTSIDE-CR-IN NOT = 0
            statement 58
            statement 59

                .
                .
                .
        WRITE UNIVREPT-REC.
????????
```

6.2 PARTIAL SOLUTION TO A PAYROLL PROBLEM

Suppose you want to produce a payroll register for hourly workers. The input file contains records having the following format:

Field	Columns
NAME	1–20
RATE	21–24 (NUMERIC – ASSUMED DECIMAL)
HOURS	25–26

Output records have the following format:

Field	Columns
NAME	11–30
RATE	41–44 (ASSUMED DECIMAL)
HOURS	55–56
GROSS SALARY	67–72 (ASSUMED DECIMAL)
FEDERAL TAX	83–88 (ASSUMED DECIMAL)
NET PAY	99–104 (ASSUMED DECIMAL)

Before calculating pay, overtime, taxes, etc., one should start by coding a simple program that just moves the data. That way, a standard type of operating procedure for coding can be developed and input data can be checked against the COBOL file descriptions.

Input Data

JOHN WORKHOUSE   125040

JUNE BRICNBRAC   060030

SAM DINERO   095050

SUSAN MASON   112038

ANN WORTHMORE   080053

Figure 6-3 depicts a diagram illustrating, again, our basic modular design with appropriate pseudocode and the COBOL program that just moves data from input (WORKERS.DAT) to output (CHECKS.DAT).
And now the COBOL program:

```
1    IDENTIFICATION DIVISION.
2    PROGRAM-ID.  SECOND.
3    AUTHOR.  SAMUELS.
```

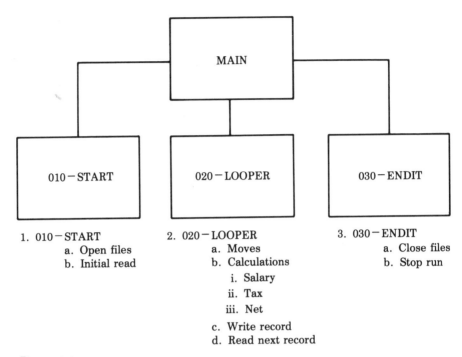

1. 010 – START
   a. Open files
   b. Initial read

2. 020 – LOOPER
   a. Moves
   b. Calculations
      i. Salary
      ii. Tax
      iii. Net
   c. Write record
   d. Read next record

3. 030 – ENDIT
   a. Close files
   b. Stop run

Figure 6–3

```
 4      ENVIRONMENT DIVISION.
 5      INPUT-OUTPUT SECTION.
 6      FILE-CONTROL.
 7      SELECT RAW-FILE ASSIGN TO WORKERS.
 8      SELECT MONEY-FILE ASSIGN TO CHECKS.
 9      DATA DIVISION.
10      FD   RAW-FILE
        1
%COBOL-E-ERROR   453, (1) Missing FILE SECTION header assumed
11      DATA RECORD IS IN-REC.
12      01   IN-REC.
13           02   IN-NAME        PIC X(20).
14           02   IN-RATE        PIC 99V99.
15           02   IN-HOURS       PIC 99.
16      FD   MONEY-FILE
17           DATA RECORD IS OUT-REC.
18      01   OUT-REC.
19           02   FILLER         PIC X(10).
20           02   OUT-NAME       PIC X(20).
21           02   FILLER         PIC X(10).
22           02   OUT-RATE       PIC 99V99.
23           02   FILLER         PIC X(10).
24           02 OUT-HOURS        PIC 99.
25      WORKING-STORAGE SECTION.
26      01   BEDTIME            PIC XX VALUE SPACES.
27      PROCEDURE DIVISION.
28      BEGIN.
```

```
29          PERFORM 010-START.
30          PERFORM 020-LOOPER.
31          PERFORM 030-ENDIT.
32      010-START.
33          OPEN INPUT RAW-FILE OUTPUT MONEY-FILE.
34          READ RAW-FILE AT END MOVE "NO" TO BEDTIME.
35      020-LOOPER.
36          MOVE SPACES TO OUT-REC.
37          MOVE IN-NAME TO OUT-NAME.
38          MOVE IN-RATE TO OU-RATE.
                                    1
%COBOL-F-ERROR  349, (1) Undefined name
39          MOVE IN-HOURS TO OUT-HOURS.
40          WRITE OUT-REC.
41          READ RAW-FILE AT END MOVE "NO" TO BEDTIME.
42      030-ENDIT.
43          CLOSE RAW-FILE MONEY-FILE.
44          STOP RUN.
```

As you can see, there are two compiler errors that must be fixed. First, the editor must be used as follows:

$EDT PAYROLL.COB (name of external COBOL file)

Locate line 11 and do the following;

*I

FILE SECTION.

^

Z

*38

MOVE IN-RATE TO OU-RATE.

*S/OU/OUT

MOVE IN-RATE TO OUT-RATE.

*EX

Then, in the command mode do:

$COB/LIS PAYROLL
$LINK PAYROLL
$RUN PAYROLL

What follows is the listing version (PAYROLL.LIS) and the output from CHECKS.DAT.

```
1   IDENTIFICATION DIVISION.
2   PROGRAM-ID.  SECOND.
3   AUTHOR.  THE GREAT ONE.
4   ENVIRONMENT DIVISION.
5   INPUT-OUTPUT SECTION.
6   FILE-CONTROL.
```

```
 7          SELECT RAW-FILE ASSIGN TO WORKERS.
 8          SELECT MONEY-FILE ASSIGN TO CHECKS.
 9      DATA DIVISION.
10      FILE SECTION.
11      FD  RAW-FILE
12          DATA RECORD IS IN-REC.
13      01  IN-REC.
14          02  IN-NAME        PIC X(20).
15          02  IN-RATE        PIC 99V99.
16          02  IN-HOURS       PIC 99.
17      FD  MONEY-FILE
18          DATA RECORD IS OUT-REC.
19      01  OUT-REC.
20          02  FILLER         PIC X(10).
21          02  OUT-NAME       PIC X(20).
22          02  FILLER         PIC X(10).
23          02  OUT-RATE       PIC 99V99.
24          02  FILLER         PIC X(10).
25          02 OUT-HOURS       PIC 99.
26      WORKING-STORAGE SECTION.
27      01  BEDTIME            PIC XX VALUE SPACES.
28      PROCEDURE DIVISION.
29      BEGIN.
30          PERFORM 010-START.
31          PERFORM 020-LOOPER.
32          PERFORM 030-ENDIT.
33      010-START.
34          OPEN INPUT RAW-FILE OUTPUT MONEY-FILE.
35          READ RAW-FILE AT END MOVE "NO" TO BEDTIME.
36      020-LOOPER.
37          MOVE SPACES TO OUT-REC.
38          MOVE IN-NAME TO OUT-NAME.
39          MOVE IN-RATE TO OUT-RATE.
40          MOVE IN-HOURS TO OUT-HOURS.
41          WRITE OUT-REC.
42          READ RAW-FILE AT END MOVE "NO" TO BEDTIME.
43      030-ENDIT.
44          CLOSE RAW-FILE MONEY-FILE.
45          STOP RUN.
```

JOHN WORKHORSE   1250   40

HUH??? We were supposed to get five records in CHECKS.DAT because we read in five input records from WORKERS.DAT.

What happened? Examine line 31. That should be:

PERFORM 020-LOOPER UNTIL BEDTIME = "NO".

If that change is made CHECKS.DAT contains:

JOHN WORKHORSE	1250	40
JUNE BRICNBRAC	0600	30
SAM DINERO	0950	50
SUSAN MASON	1120	38
ANN WORTHMORE	0800	53

6.3   PAYROLL PROBLEM INCLUDING CONDITION STATEMENTS

It is time to add the gross salary calculation to our program. In order to do that the following conditions are imposed:

An hourly worker gets double-time for hours worked in excess of 48.

An hourly worker gets time-and-one-half for hours worked over 40.

An hourly worker gets regular pay (hours * rate) for 40 hours or less.

This calculation is added to our 020–LOOPER module. But what logic should we use? Examine the two flowcharts in Figure 6–4. Diagram "b" is correct. If one uses the logic developed in diagram "a" an hourly worker who works over 48 hours does not receive any double-time.

The coding for the gross salary routine, in lower case, is added to the following program:

```
 1      IDENTIFICATION DIVISION.
 2      PROGRAM-ID.   SECOND.
 3      AUTHOR.   THE GREAT ONE.
 4      ENVIRONMENT DIVISION.
 5      INPUT-OUTPUT SECTION.
 6      FILE-CONTROL.
 7          SELECT RAW-FILE ASSIGN TO WORKERS.
 8          SELECT MONEY-FILE ASSIGN TO CHECKS.
 9      DATA DIVISION.
10      FILE SECTION.
11      FD  RAW-FILE
12          DATA RECORD IS IN-REC.
13      01  IN-REC.
14          02  IN-NAME          PIC X(20).
15          02  IN-RATE          PIC 99V99.
16          02  IN-HOURS         PIC 99.
17      FD  MONEY-FILE
18          DATA RECORD IS OUT-REC.
19      01  OUT-REC.
20          02  FILLER           PIC X(10).
21          02  OUT-NAME         PIC X(20).
22          02  FILLER           PIC X(10).
23          02  OUT-RATE         PIC 99V99.
24          02  FILLER           PIC X(10).
25          02 OUT-HOURS         PIC 99.
26          02  filler           pic x(10).
27          02  out-salary       pic 9999v99.
28      WORKING-STORAGE SECTION.
29      01  BEDTIME              PIC XX VALUE SPACES.
30      PROCEDURE DIVISION.
31      BEGIN.
32          PERFORM 010-START.
33          PERFORM 020-LOOPER UNTIL BEDTIME = "NO".
34          PERFORM 030-ENDIT.
35      010-START.
36          OPEN INPUT RAW-FILE OUTPUT MONEY-FILE.
37          READ RAW-FILE AT END MOVE "NO" TO BEDTIME.
```

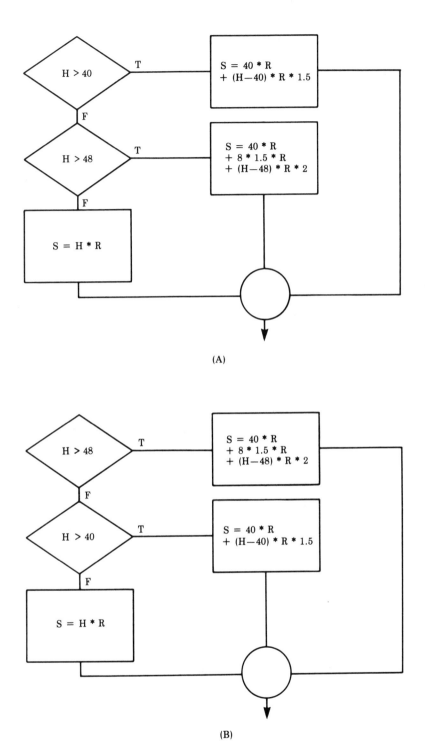

(A)

(B)

Figure 6-4

```
38      020-LOOPER.
39          MOVE SPACES TO OUT-REC.
40          MOVE IN-NAME TO OUT-NAME.
41          MOVE IN-RATE TO OUT-RATE.
42          MOVE IN-HOURS TO OUT-HOURS.
43          if in-hours > 48
44              compute out-salary = 40 * in-rate + 1.5 * 8 * in-rate
45                  + (in-hours - 48) * 2 * in-rate
46          else if in-hours > 40
47                  compute out-salary = 40 * in-rate + (in-hours -40)
                                                                      1
%COBOL-F-ERROR   328, (1) Invalid expression
48                                           * 1.5 * in-rate
49              else
50                  compute out-salary = in-hours * in-rate.
                      1
%COBOL-W-ERROR   297, (1) Processing of source program resumes at this point
51          WRITE OUT-REC.
52          READ RAW-FILE AT END MOVE "NO" TO BEDTIME.
53      030-ENDIT.
54          CLOSE RAW-FILE MONEY-FILE.
55          STOP RUN.
```

Can you see the error? If a space is put after the minus sign and we recompile, link, and run, the following output is produced:

JOHN WORKHORSE	1250	40	050000
JUNE BRICNBRAC	0600	30	018000
SAM DINERO	0950	50	053200
SUSAN MASON	1120	38	042560
ANN WORTHMORE	0800	53	049600

6.4   ENHANCEMENT OF PAYROLL PROGRAM WITH FEDERAL TAX CODE

The output records look good. One should perform hand calculations before adding a federal tax routine to this program.

The following conditions are used for calculating federal tax. Once the federal tax is found, the net pay can be found by simple subtraction. (State tax, voluntary deductions, etc. are not included at this time. Let's give 'em a few extra bucks to spend!!)

Anyone making over $400 is in the 30% tax bracket.

Anyone making over $300 is in the 20% tax bracket.

Anyone making over $200 is in the 10% tax bracket.

No tax for $200 or less (too poor for Uncle Sam).

Examine the flowchart in Figure 6–5 to solve the above conditions:

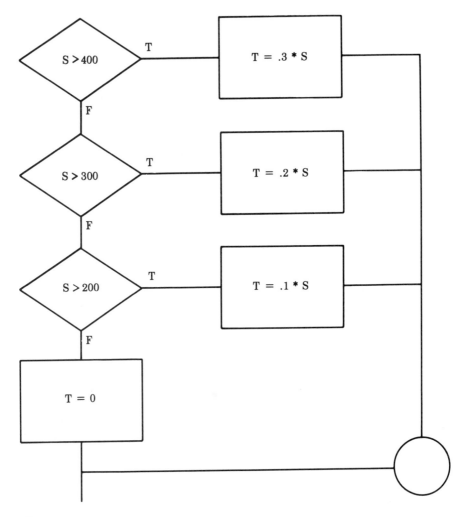

Figure 6-5

And now the program with code for calculating the federal tax and net pay.
Also notice the necessary additions to the Data Division as well:

```
1      IDENTIFICATION DIVISION.
2      PROGRAM-ID.   SECOND.
3      AUTHOR.   THE GREAT ONE.
4      ENVIRONMENT DIVISION.
5      INPUT-OUTPUT SECTION.
6      FILE-CONTROL.
7           SELECT RAW-FILE ASSIGN TO WORKERS.
8           SELECT MONEY-FILE ASSIGN TO CHECKS.
9      DATA DIVISION.
10     FILE SECTION.
11     FD   RAW-FILE
```

```
12              DATA RECORD IS IN-REC.
13      01   IN-REC.
14          02   IN-NAME        PIC X(20).
15          02   IN-RATE        PIC 99V99.
16          02   IN-HOURS       PIC 99.
17      FD  MONEY-FILE
18          DATA RECORD IS OUT-REC.
19      01   OUT-REC.
20          02   FILLER         PIC X(10).
21          02   OUT-NAME       PIC X(20).
22          02   FILLER         PIC X(10).
23          02   OUT-RATE       PIC 99V99.
24          02   FILLER         PIC X(10).
25          02  OUT-HOURS       PIC 99.
26          02   FILLER         PIC X(10).
27          02   OUT-SALARY     PIC 9999V99.
28          02   filler         pic x(10).
29          02   fed-tax        pic 9999v99.
30          02   filler         pic x(10).
31          02   net-pay        pic 9999v99.
32      WORKING-STORAGE SECTION.
33      01   BEDTIME            PIC XX VALUE SPACES.
34      PROCEDURE DIVISION.
35      BEGIN.
36          PERFORM 010-START.
37          PERFORM 020-LOOPER UNTIL BEDTIME = "NO".
38          PERFORM 030-ENDIT.
39      010-START.
40          OPEN INPUT RAW-FILE OUTPUT MONEY-FILE.
41          READ RAW-FILE AT END MOVE "NO" TO BEDTIME.
42      020-LOOPER.
43          MOVE SPACES TO OUT-REC.
44          MOVE IN-NAME TO OUT-NAME.
45          MOVE IN-RATE TO OUT-RATE.
46          MOVE IN-HOURS TO OUT-HOURS.
47          IF IN-HOURS > 48
48              COMPUTE OUT-SALARY = 40 * IN-RATE + 1.5 * 8 * IN-RATE
49                                  + (IN-HOURS - 40 ) * 2 * IN-RATE
50          ELSE IF IN-HOURS > 40
51              COMPUTE OUT-SALARY = 40 * IN-RATE + (IN-HOURS - 40)
52                                  * 1.5 * IN-RATE
53              ELSE
54                  COMPUTE OUT-SALARY = IN-HOURS * IN-RATE.
55          if out-salary > 400 compute fed-tax = 0.3 * out-salary
56          else if out-salary > 300 compute fed-tax = 0.2 * out-salary
57              else if out-salary > 200 compute fed-tax = 0.1 * out-salary
58                  else move 0 to fed-tax.
59          compute net-pay = out-salary - fed-tax.
60          WRITE OUT-REC.
61          READ RAW-FILE AT END MOVE "NO" TO BEDTIME.
62      030-ENDIT.
63          CLOSE RAW-FILE MONEY-FILE.
64          STOP RUN.
```

Let us hand check to see if the following output is correct.

JOHN WORKHORSE	1250	40	050000
015000 035000			
JUNE BRICNBRAC	0600	30	018000

000000		018000			
	SAM DINERO		0950	50	053200
15960		037240			
	SUSAN MASON		1120	38	042560
012768		029792			
	ANN WORTHMORE		0800	53	049600
014880		034720			

Is it correct??

There is "wraparound" because the output records are greater than 80 bytes (characters). Can you correct this??

SUMMARY

The step by step programming process has been demonstrated in this chapter as well as the previous ones. As you progress through this text, it is hoped that you encounter fewer and fewer compiler errors with each compilation. You should also be testing additonal code by doing hand calculations to see if the output is correct.

You should have a good understanding of the following syntax:

1. IF

2. IF.... ELSE

QUESTIONS

1. Write COBOL statements for the diagrams in Figure 6–6.

2. Write flowcharts for the following:
   a.
   ```
              IF X = 5
                   MOVE 10 TO Q
          ELSE
                   IF Y = 5
                        MOVE 10 TO R
                   ELSE
                        IF Z = 5
                             MOVE 10 TO S
                        ELSE
                             NEXT SENTENCE.
   ```

   b.
   ```
              IF NAME = "SOLD"
   ```

        PERFORM 300-ESTATE-ROUTINE
        PERFORM 400-LISTING-ROUTINE
        MOVE 0 TO TOT
    ELSE

        PERFORM 200-REG-ROUTINE.

  c.

    IF X > Y
      MOVE 0 TO X
      IF Y > Z
        WRITE OUTREC
      ELSE
        PERFORM 600-GAR-ROUTINE
        PERFORM 200-READ-ROUTINE
    ELSE

      NEXT SENTENCE.

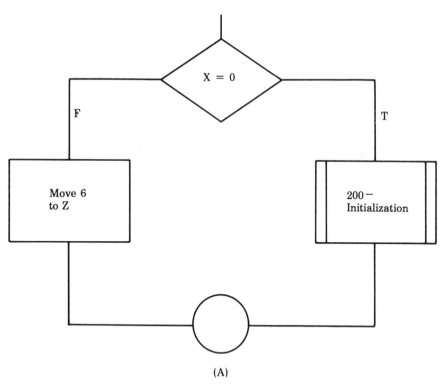

(A)

Figure 6-6

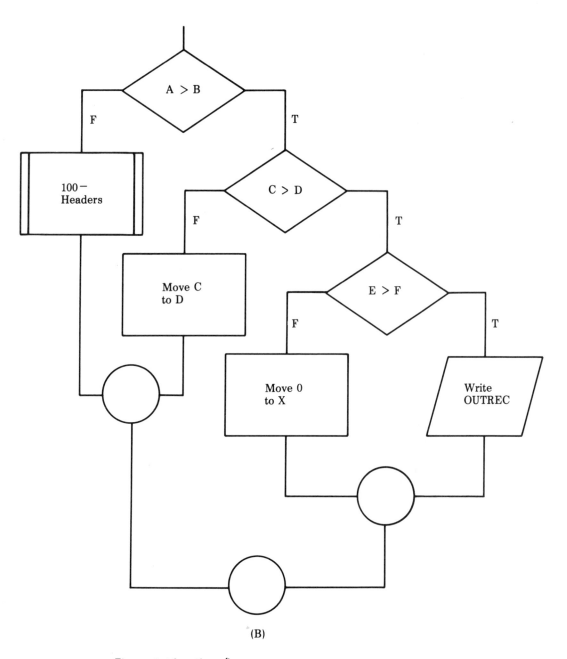

(B)

Figure 6-6 (continued)

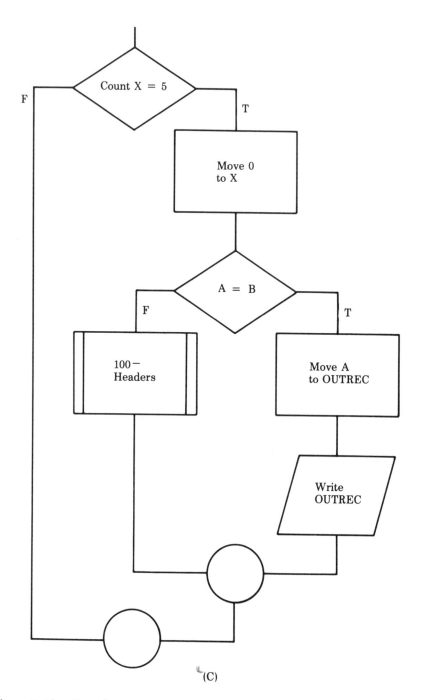

Figure 6-6 (continued)

3. What is in X,Y, and Z after the following is executed:

```
PROCEDURE DIVISION.
STARTER.
        PERFORM 010-INITIAL.
        PERFORM 020-PROCESS.
        PERFORM 030-ENDER.
010-INITIAL.
        MOVE 3 TO X.
        MOVE 5 TO Y Z.
020-PROCESS.
        IF X < Y
                ADD Y TO Z
                SUBTRACT 1 FROM Y
        ELSE
                MOVE 5 TO X.
030-ENDER.
        IF Z < Y
            IF X < Y
                COMPUTE Z = 5
                COMPUTE Y = Y + X
            ELSE
                COMPUTE X = X - 1
        ELSE
            ADD 4 TO Y.
```

4. Write an IF statement and flowchart that solves the following:

minimum payment = balance, if balance is less than or equal to $60:

$20 + 8% of (balance − $60), if $60 < balance < $200:

$40 + 15% of (balance − $200), if balance is equal or greater than $200.

PROGRAMMING PROBLEMS

1. It is October, 1983, and JOHN PULLTOOTH, a renowned dentist, needs accurate records of dental insurance payments on his patients. Some insurance companies have been delinquent in payments so he wants a report listing all those patients from whom he has NOT received a payment since August of this year and whose balance exceeds $100.00. The input records have the following format:

Field	Columns
Patient Name	1–20
Insurance Co.	21–30
Ins. Co. Address	31–50
Zip	51–55
Date of last payment	61–66
Balance	71–76

The output records have the following format:

Field	Columns
Patient Name	1–20
Insurance Co.	31–40
Ins. Co. Address	51–70
Zip	71–75
Date of last payment	81–86
Balance	91–96

Use the following data:

JACK SHEA	XYZ-CROSS	801 W. MADISON	60633 090383 015000
NATE COLDIRON	BLUEFIRE	600 N. DEARBORN	60603 050683 012300
SARAH CAVITY	HMO-INS	1212 W. ADDISON	60644 070583 004000
FREDDIE FLUORIDE	XYZ-CROSS	801 W. MADISON	60633 101282 020000
JANE LAUGHGAS	HMO-INS	1212 W. ADDISON	60644 081983 125000

2. Salesmen for Psycho Products get paid solely on commission basis. Their salary is determined by the type of product they sell and the quantity of the sale.

Psycho Products consists of three regions. Each region has a certain number of branches; each branch has a certain number of salesmen.

A record consists of one sale. Examine the following input format for a particular sale (all the records are sorted by salesman number WITHIN branch number WITHIN region number).

INPUT RECORD SPECIFICATIONS

Field	Columns
Region number	1–2
Branch number	3–4
Salesman number	5–6
Product number	8–13
Quantity	14–17
Type	18
Price (assumed dec.)	20–24
Salesman name	25–44

Each output record should have the following format:

OUTPUT RECORD (REPORT LINE) SPECIFICATIONS

Field	Columns
Region number	1–2
Branch number	5–6
Salesman number	9–10
Product number	13–18
Quantity	21–24
Price	27–31
Commission rate	34–35 (assumed decimal)
Amount sold	38–47 (assumed decimal)
Commission	50–57 (assumed decimal)
Salesman name	60–79

You need to include the commission rate, amount sold, and commission. The following processing must occur:

Type   = A then Commission Rate = .05
Type   = B then Commission Rate = .07
Type   = C then Commission Rate = .10
Amount sold = Quantity * Price
Commission = Amount Sold * Commission Rate

A correctly designed and coded program should yield the following output (for each sales record):

01   04   13   328204   0300   02000   05   00600000   00030000   SMYTH J.

... given the following input

```
010413 3282040300A 02000SMYTH J.
010413 5918230010B 15000SMYTH J.
010423 2918231000A 00500COLBY S.
010423 3910280400C 01000COLBY S.
010423 3917810003A 15000COLBY S.
010425 3948830020B 05000HOE A.
011114 9283230040B 06000JACKSON J.
011114 3728190100C 10000JACKSON J.
011114 9584920300B 02200JACKSON J.
140517 7653810015A 00341SAMUELS S.
140517 1284550100B 20381SAMUELS S.
140517 2222225666A 00022SAMUELS S.
140517 1212120003C 29317SAMUELS S.
140525 4477150581B 00450BABBAGE C.
140525 6189030021C 14683BABBAGE C.
140545 4442280956A 00351NORAD D.
140545 1186451111B 29190NORAD D.
140545 6371006716C 00123NORAD D.
140561 9501430004C 00011DEMKINS S.
140561 0000130381B 00234DEMKINS S.
140577 0371850031A 00032LEMONHEAD D.
145501 6529610378B 08312BIRDIE B.
145501 4085000371C 00173BIRDIE B.
145501 3017402874A 10892BIRDIE B.
145537 5555550028B 02398TAMERLIN T.
145537 4329019999A 99999TAMERLIN T.
145545 2139750012C 00827TUT K.
145545 3901270871B 00013TUT K.
145545 8839170005C 03821TUT K.
148715 6730170987B 11173DEETLE D.
148715 3333360771A 00153DEETLE D.
148715 2283611738B 00024DEETLE D.
148731 3927440831A 02871TANNY V.
148731 3975811183B 00037TANNY V.
148731 7771110031A 00002TANNY V.
148759 6620980002C 88754WILKE T.
148759 2215930038C 74861WILKE T.
148763 0028420204A 00023DURAN D.
148763 8937620014B 03851DURAN D.
148763 3829485612A 00183DURAN D.
662018 8290000381B 00012DUWOP D.
662018 3829001821C 02845DUWOP D.
662027 5647630284B 00284CARNIGIE D.
662027 7690239999A 99934CARNIGIE D.
662027 5629409999B 99274CARNIGIE D.
662027 8267319999C 99927CARNIGIE D.
663705 7372890012A 00012PEABRAIN D.
663705 7294870000C 00002PEABRAIN D.
663718 5438230283A 03872DAPPER V.
663718 7802630028B 00012DAPPER V.
663718 8888880274C 93721DAPPER V.
663718 3645310026A 07382DAPPER V.
663729 9274830123B 00028GRAUER R.
663729 8282190057C 02847GRAUER R.
663751 7382150382B 93721LULU P.
669737 8927370012A 08274TRIPP U.
669737 3673018392C 00012TRIPP U.
669737 2287013284B 01274TRIPP U.
669743 2946520035B 00274WHIZ G.
669743 0037210003C 23472WHIZ G.
669775 0002340028A 00264BUMBLE B.
669775 9375830372C 00027BUMBLE B.
669775 3756410038A 75643BUMBLE B.
669775 8787679372C 98676BUMBLE B.
669781 6453649898A 00274LATER C. U.
669781 3746320387B 07823LATER C. U.
```

Figure 6-7

010413   3282040300A   02000SMYTH J.

You are urged to complete the above program because you will be asked to embellish it in future chapters. Use the data presented in Figure 6-7.

*3. Programming problem #3 of the previous chapter asked you to calculate a monthly mortgage payment given the mortgage amount, number of years, and interest rate. Once the monthly payment is determined, other vital information about the loan can be calculated:

interest   = interest rate/12 * mortgage balance
principal reduction = monthly payment — interest
mortgage balance   = mortgage balance — principal reduction

For each record print out the ENTIRE amortization for each mortgage. If a record has a mortgage of $20,000 for 25 years at 11%, output should show four columns of figures (monthly payment, interest, principal reduction, and remaining balance) for 300 payments!! Don't forget that the last payment will be less than the monthly payment itself—unless you want to give that bank or S/L a monetary GIFT!! [Let your bank or S/L give you some figures on typical mortgages over a period of time so that you can compare your results.]

Editing Data

7.1 HEADER LINES

If you examined the output data produced from the program in the previous chapter, you noticed that it looked rather barren. That is, there wasn't a header showing what the various output data meant, the data itself was not edited and there were no final totals. In other words, it certainly didn't resemble a report.

We can modify our previous program to make the output data look rather decent—something you could give another party and feel confident that the report made sense. To do this we will add the syntax necessary to:

a. Produce header lines.

b. Form edited output.

c. Prepare final figures.

The following program produces the output as before but now includes header lines.

```
1     IDENTIFICATION DIVISION.
2     PROGRAM-ID.   THIRD.
3     AUTHOR.   SAMUELS.
4     ENVIRONMENT DIVISION.
5     INPUT-OUTPUT SECTION.
```

```
 6    FILE-CONTROL.
 7        SELECT RAW-FILE ASSIGN TO WORKERS.
 8        SELECT MONEY-FILE ASSIGN TO CHECKS.
 9    DATA DIVISION.
10    FILE SECTION.
11    FD  RAW-FILE
12        DATA RECORD IS IN-REC.
13    01  IN-REC.
14        02  IN-NAME       PIC X(20).
15        02  IN-RATE       PIC 99V99.
16        02  IN-HOURS      PIC 99.
17    FD  MONEY-FILE
18        DATA RECORD IS OUT-REC.
19    01  OUT-REC       PIC X(80).
20    WORKING-STORAGE SECTION.
21    01  DETAIL-LINE.
22        02  OUT-NAME      PIC X(20).
23        02  OUT-RATE      PIC 99V99.
24        02  FILLER        PIC X(10)  value spaces.
25        02 OUT-HOURS      PIC 99.
26        02  FILLER        PIC X(8)  value spaces.
27        02  SALARY        PIC 9999V99.
28        02  FILLER        PIC X(8)  value spaces.
29        02  FED-TAX       PIC 9999V99.
30        02  FILLER        PIC X(8)  value spaces.
31        02  NET-PAY       PIC 9999V99.
32    01  BEDTIME           PIC XX VALUE SPACES.
33    01  header-one.
34        02  filler            pic x(80) value all "*".
35    01  header-two.
36        02  filler            pic x(4) value "NAME".
37        02  filler            pic x(10) value spaces.
38        02  filler            pic x(11) value "HOURLY RATE".
39        02  filler            pic x(3) value spaces.
40        02  filler            pic x(12) value "HOURS WORKED".
41        02  filler            pic x(5) value spaces.
42        02  filler            pic x(12) value "GROSS SALARY".
43        02  filler            pic x(5) value spaces.
44        02  filler            pic x(7) value "FED TAX".
45        02  filler            pic x(4) value spaces.
46        02  filler            pic x(7) value "NET PAY".
47    PROCEDURE DIVISION.
48    BEGIN.
49        PERFORM 010-START.
50        PERFORM 020-LOOPER UNTIL BEDTIME = "NO".
51        PERFORM 030-ENDIT.
52    010-START.
53        OPEN INPUT RAW-FILE OUTPUT MONEY-FILE.
54        write out-rec from header-one after 1.
55        write out-rec from header-two after 1.
56        write out-rec from header-one after 1.
57        READ RAW-FILE AT END MOVE "NO" TO BEDTIME.
58    020-LOOPER.
59        MOVE IN-NAME TO OUT-NAME.
60        MOVE IN-RATE TO OUT-RATE.
61        MOVE IN-HOURS TO OUT-HOURS.
62        IF IN-HOURS > 48
63            COMPUTE SALARY = (40 * IN-RATE) + (1.5 * 8 * IN-RATE)
64                             + ((IN-HOURS - 48) * 2 * IN-RATE)
65        ELSE IF IN-HOURS > 40
66                COMPUTE SALARY = (40 * IN-RATE) + ((IN-HOURS - 40)
```

```
67                                     * 1.5 * IN-RATE)
68              ELSE
69                      COMPUTE SALARY = IN-HOURS * IN-RATE.
70          IF SALARY > 400 COMPUTE FED-TAX = 0.3 * SALARY
71          ELSE IF SALARY > 300 COMPUTE FED-TAX = 0.2 * SALARY
72              ELSE IF SALARY > 200 COMPUTE FED-TAX = 0.1 * SALARY
73                  ELSE MOVE 0 TO FED-TAX.
74          COMPUTE NET-PAY = SALARY - FED-TAX.
75          write out-rec from detail-line after 1.
76          READ RAW-FILE AT END MOVE "NO" TO BEDTIME.
77      030-ENDIT.
78          CLOSE RAW-FILE MONEY-FILE.
79          STOP RUN.
```

Please notice several things about the above modifications to the previous program:

1. The program-id was changed.

2. The output line from the previous program was moved to Working-Storage—hence VALUE SPACES can be included.

3. Two header lines were included in Working-Storage. This is presented in lower case—except for literal entry.

4. All output lines were made 80 columns wide so that one would NOT get wraparound when the output file was typed.

5. The following additional Procedure Division options were used:

    a. WRITE FROM
    b. AFTER #

Before we elucidate further let us see what the output looks like:

```
***************************************************************************
```

NAME	HOURLY RATE	HOURS WORKED	GROSS SALARY	FED TAX	NET PAY

```
***************************************************************************
```

NAME	HOURLY RATE	HOURS WORKED	GROSS SALARY	FED TAX	NET PAY
JOHN WORKHORSE	1250	40	050000	015000	035000
JUNE BRICNBRAC	0600	30	018000	000000	018000
SAM DINERO	0950	50	053200	015960	037240
SUSAN MASON	1120	38	042560	012768	029792
ANN WORTHMORE	0800	53	049600	014880	034720

Notice that the alignment of the headers and data is off center. We can resolve this problem by changing the appropriate numbers in the various FILLER picture clauses in the Working-Storage area of the program, listed above the output data. Actually, it would be better to use printer spacing charts. A printer spacing chart (see Figure 7-1) allows the program to manually write what his/her report should look like. One can then count the proper number of spaces in between literals and output data so that the alignment is correct the first time.

150/10/6 PRINT CHART   PROG. ID _____   PAGE_____

(SPACING: 150 POSITION SPAN, AT 10 CHARACTERS PER INCH, 6 LINES PER VERTICAL INCH)   DATE _____

PROGRAM TITLE _____

PROGRAMMER OR DOCUMENTALIST: _____

CHART TITLE _____

Figure 7-1

112

Id back at dotted line.

Fold in at dotted line.

NOTE: Dimensions on this sheet vary with humidity. Exact measurements should be calculated or scaled with a ruler rather than with the lines on this chart.

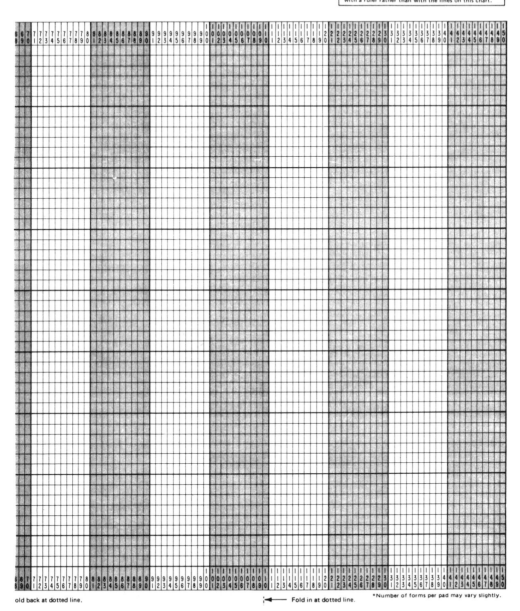

old back at dotted line.

Fold in at dotted line.

*Number of forms per pad may vary slightly.

Figure 7-1 (continued)

7.2 WORKING-STORAGE SECTION

This is a second part of the Data Division. In contrast to the File Section that describes incoming and outgoing data, one can set aside records and/or fields to work with in this section. It is best to format all detail lines, header lines, final lines, etc., in this section. All counters, switches, table entries, and even input record descriptions should be put here. Hence, although you may describe the size of an input or output area in the File Section, different lines, using this size, can be formatted in Working-Storage. The coding is more understandable. The MOVE SPACES statement can be eliminated because each line can have a VALUE SPACES entry after the PIC clauses. Schematically, this can be represented in Figure 7-2.

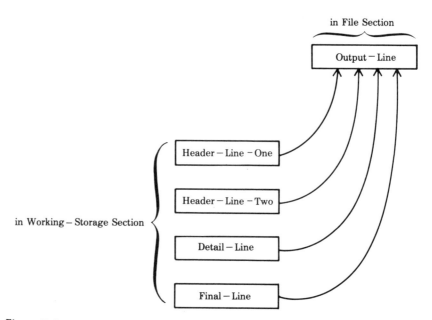

Figure 7-2

In the above example (THIRD) the detail line and header lines are formatted in this section along with a switch.

Another way to format the THIRD header line is as follows:

```
01  HEADER-TWO.
    02  FILLER          PIC X(14) VALUE "NAME".
    02  FILLER          PIC X(14) VALUE "HOURLY RATE".
    02  FILLER          PIC X(17) VALUE "HOURS WORKED".
    02  FILLER          PIC X(17) VALUE "GROSS SALARY".
    02  FILLER          PIC X(11) VALUE "FED TAX".
    02  FILLER          PIC X(7)  VALUE "NET PAY".
```

The literal entry is entered from left to right and "padded" by blanks on the right if there is extra room [Figure 7–3].

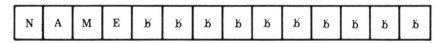

Figure 7–3

Although this method avoids the use of VALUE SPACES, the format included in the program appears to handle alignment changes easier. In either case, the entire line is formatted with literals and spaces so that the MOVE SPACES entry in the Procedure Division is not necessary. Notice that the detail line also has the VALUE SPACES clause. VALUE clauses are not allowed in the File Section except under certain circumstances that will be discussed in a later chapter. Incidentally, literals that are too large for the corresponding PIC clauses will cause an error in compilation.

7.3 ADDITIONAL PROCEDURE DIVISION ENTRIES

The WRITE FROM option combines the MOVE and WRITE statements shown in previous programs. Instead of the following:

MOVE DETAIL-LINE TO OUT-REC.
WRITE OUT-REC AFTER 1.

one can use:

WRITE OUT-REC FROM DETAIL-LINE AFTER 1.

The AFTER option is necessary for line spacing. "AFTER 2" causes the printer to skip one line (double spacing). "AFTER 3" causes triple spacing, and "AFTER PAGE" causes the printer to eject to the next page and write a line. For example:

WRITE OUT-REC FROM HEADER-LINE AFTER PAGE.

Logically, the BEFORE option causes the line to be printed first, after which the specified number of lines are skipped. You should use the AFTER or BEFORE option on all WRITE statements. It provides a consistent method of code. [Some compilers give error messages if a COBOL program contains some WRITE statements with and without the After option.]

If a report requires more than one page, as most do, we usually want to print header lines on top of each page. This will require a change in our basic design structure. Our purpose in this chapter is not to show changes in design strategy, but the syntax required for editing data, so we'll put that off for now. Chapter 8 concentrates on the additions to the basic design.

QUESTIONS

1. Format a line in working storage that will cause the following to be printed out with the appropriate WRITE statement:

NUMBER OF STUDENTS   PERCENTAGE OF FAILURES
^   ^

^   ^

(col. 14)   (col. 74)

2. Embellish your program from question #2 of the previous chapter to include header lines as follows:

```
*****************************************************************
INVENTORY   DESCRIPTION   PRICE   QUANTITY   INVENTORY
NUMBER                                       AMOUNT
*****************************************************************
```

3. Write the Procedure Division code necessary to print out the header lines formatted in #2.

7.4   EDITING OUTPUT DATA

COBOL is a business-oriented language and can produce reports with data containing dollar signs, commas, credit and debit symbols, decimal points, check protection (asterisk fill), and so on. The following program listing with accompanying output data shows how to edit data to produce a decent looking report—that is, by ridding oneself of those ridiculous leading zeros and by including of the dollar sign (floating, in this case). This is discussed in the next section.

```
1     IDENTIFICATION DIVISION.
2     PROGRAM-ID.  THIRD.
3     AUTHOR.   SAMUELS.
4     ENVIRONMENT DIVISION.
5     INPUT-OUTPUT SECTION.
6     FILE-CONTROL.
7         SELECT RAW-FILE ASSIGN TO WORKERS.
8         SELECT MONEY-FILE ASSIGN TO CHECKS.
9     DATA DIVISION.
10    FILE SECTION.
```

```
11   FD   RAW-FILE
12        DATA RECORD IS IN-REC.
13   01   IN-REC.
14        02   IN-NAME        PIC X(20).
15        02   IN-RATE        PIC 99V99.
16        02   IN-HOURS       PIC 99.
17   FD   MONEY-FILE
18        DATA RECORD IS OUT-REC.
19   01   OUT-REC        PIC X(80).
20   WORKING-STORAGE SECTION.
21   01   DETAIL-LINE.
22        02   OUT-NAME       PIC X(20).
23        02   OUT-RATE       PIC $$$.99.
24        02   FILLER         PIC X(8)   VALUE SPACES.
25        02   OUT-HOURS      PIC z9.
26        02   FILLER         PIC X(8)   VALUE SPACES.
27        02   SALARY         PIC $$,$$$.99.
28        02   FILLER         PIC X(5)   VALUE SPACES.
29        02   FED-TAX        PIC $$,$$$.99.
30        02   FILLER         PIC X(4)   VALUE SPACES.
31        02   NET-PAY        PIC $$,$$$.99.
32   01   BEDTIME            PIC XX VALUE SPACES.
33   01   HEADER-ONE.
34        02   FILLER          PIC X(80) VALUE ALL "*".
35   01   HEADER-TWO.
36        02   FILLER          PIC X(4) VALUE "NAME".
37        02   FILLER          PIC X(10) VALUE SPACES.
38        02   FILLER          PIC X(11) VALUE "     RATE".
39        02   FILLER          PIC X(3) VALUE SPACES.
40        02   FILLER          PIC X(12) VALUE "HOURS WORKED".
41        02   FILLER          PIC X(4) VALUE SPACES.
42        02   FILLER          PIC X(12) VALUE "GROSS SALARY".
43        02   FILLER          PIC X(4) VALUE SPACES.
44        02   FILLER          PIC X(7) VALUE "FED TAX".
45        02   FILLER          PIC X(5) VALUE SPACES.
46        02   FILLER          PIC X(7) VALUE "NET PAY".
47   01   temp-areas.
48        02   temp-salary         pic 9999v99.
49        02   temp-fed-tax        pic 9999v99.
50   PROCEDURE DIVISION.
51   BEGIN.
52      PERFORM 010-START.
53      PERFORM 020-LOOPER UNTIL BEDTIME = "NO".
54      PERFORM 030-ENDIT.
55   010-START.
56      OPEN INPUT RAW-FILE OUTPUT MONEY-FILE.
57      WRITE OUT-REC FROM HEADER-ONE AFTER 1.
58      WRITE OUT-REC FROM HEADER-TWO AFTER 1.
59      WRITE OUT-REC FROM HEADER-ONE AFTER 1.
60      READ RAW-FILE AT END MOVE "NO" TO BEDTIME.
61   020-LOOPER.
62      MOVE IN-NAME TO OUT-NAME.
63      MOVE IN-RATE TO OUT-RATE.
64      MOVE IN-HOURS TO OUT-HOURS.
65      IF IN-HOURS > 48
66           COMPUTE temp-salary = (40 * IN-RATE) + (1.5 * 8 * IN-RATE)
67                             + ((IN-HOURS - 48) * 2 * IN-RATE)
68      ELSE IF IN-HOURS > 40
69           COMPUTE temp-salary = (40 * IN-RATE) + ((IN-HOURS - 40)
70                            * 1.5 * IN-RATE)
71           ELSE
72                COMPUTE temp-salary = IN-HOURS * IN-RATE.
73      IF temp-salary > 400 COMPUTE temp-fed-tax = 0.3 * temp-salary
```

```
74          ELSE IF temp-salary > 300 COMPUTE temp-fed-tax = 0.2 * temp-salary
75             ELSE IF temp-salary > 200 COMPUTE temp-fed-tax = 0.1 *
                  temp-salary
76                ELSE MOVE 0 TO temp-fed-tax.
77          COMPUTE NET-PAY = temp-salary - temp-fed-tax.
78          move temp-salary to salary.
79          move temp-fed-tax to fed-tax.
80          WRITE OUT-REC FROM DETAIL-LINE after 1.
81          READ RAW-FILE AT END MOVE "NO" TO BEDTIME.
82      030-ENDIT.
83          CLOSE RAW-FILE MONEY-FILE.
84          STOP RUN.
```

and the output—which doesn't look so bad!!

```
*****************************************************************************
```

NAME	RATE	HOURS WORKED	GROSS SALARY	FED TAX	NET PAY
JOHN WORKHORSE	$12.50	40	$500.00	$150.00	$350.00
JUNE BRICNBRAC	$6.00	30	$180.00	$.00	$180.00
SAM DINERO	$9.50	50	$532.00	$159.60	$372.40
SUSAN MASON	$11.20	38	$425.60	$127.68	$297.92
ANN WORTHMORE	$8.00	53	$496.00	$148.80	$347.20

The above program contained the following modification:

1. Edited output lines.

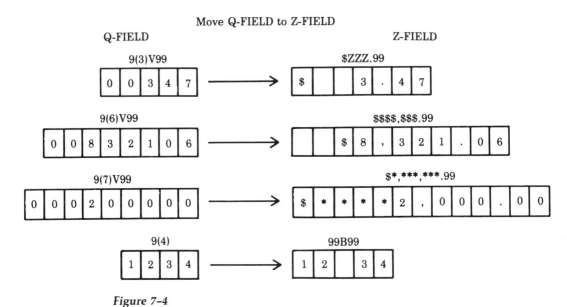

Figure 7-4

2. Temporary storage areas because one cannot use edited fields in arithmetic calculations (lines 47–49 plus lower-case entries in Procedure Division).

3. Refinement of header-line (lines 35–46).

7.5   EDITING DATA

The following table illustrates editing data with:

a. Decimal points

b. Leading zero suppression

c. Floating dollar sign

d. Fixed dollar sign—zero suppression

e. Check protection (asterisk fill)

f. Blank insertion

Source Field		Receiving Field	
Picture	*Contents*	*Picture*	*Contents*
9(3)V99	04564	999.99	045.64
9(5)	00042	Z(5)	42
9(4)	0000	Z(4)	
9(3)V99	00000	ZZZ.99	.00
9(6)	000000	Z(5)9	0
9(5)	010306	Z(4)9	10306
9(4)V99	133231	$$$$$9.99	$1332.31
9(3)V99	000463	$$$$.99	$4.63
9(5)V99	0443634	$$$,$$$.99	$4,436.34
9(4)V99	0005423	$Z,ZZZ.99	$ 54.23
9(5)V99	0034212	$**,***.99	$**342.12
9(6)	102283	99B99B99	10 22 83

It is very important to know the maximum size of your output fields. For example, the field PIC $$$,$$$.99 contains 10 print positions, whether they are all used or not. The dollar sign edit pictures require the "extra" dollar sign. PIC $$$,$$$.99 can only accommodate 9(5)V99!!

See Figure 7–4 for some diagrams illustrating in greater detail the moves from unedited input to edited output fields.

COBOL cannot handle arithmetic statements using edited fields. You will always get compilation errors pointing to those PROCEDURE DIVISION statements that attempt to do any arithmetic using source fields having pictures other than unedited integer [9(3) or 9999 for example] or unedited assumed decimal [9(4)V99]. Any other picture descriptions of source fields (X, $, B, etc.) will cause an error message. If TEMP-FED-TAX was left out of the Data Division and FED-TAX was computed in the Procedure Division, one would get the following, upon compilation:

```
$COB PROG3
    77 COMPUTE NET-PAY = temp-salary − FED-TAX.
%COBOL-F-ERROR 276, (1) Operand must be a numeric data-
name or a numeric literal
%COBOL-F-ENDNOOBJ, UD2:[SAMUELS.BOOK]PROG3.COB;5
    completed with 1 diagnostic—object deleted
```

7.6   TEMPORARY STORAGE AREAS

Now suppose you had a glass of coffee and a cup of orange juice in front of you. No matter how hungry or thirsty you might be you KNOW it is IM-PROPER to drink these liquids in their existing containers. So what do you do? Of course, you have to get a THIRD container. You can pour the orange juice into this THIRD container, and now the coffee can be poured into the cup. The orange juice can be poured into the glass so—VOILA—you have solved that problem.

Temporary storage areas work the same way. Since you cannot do arithmetic with edited fields you create these temporary areas so that you can do these calculations. After the calculations are completed you can, of course, move them to edited fields. The program above illustrates this quite clearly. Notice the addition of more Data Division entries (lower case, of course) and additional PROCEDURE DIVISION statements for the corresponding calculations and moves that are required.

These temporary storage areas are neither input nor output fields; rather, they are created by the programmer to satisfy the requirements for arithmetic calculations. The CPU does not know how to multiply commas or divide by dollar signs, etc.

QUESTIONS

1. Further enhance your inventory problem (#2 of previous chapter) to include edited data.

2. Show the value of the edited result for each of the following entries:

Sending Field		Receiving Field	
Picture	*Contents*	*Picture*	*Contents*
(A) 9(7)	0843928	Z,ZZZ,ZZZ	
(B) 9(4)	1254	99B99	
(C) 9(4)V99	005394	$$,$$$.99	
(D) 9(6)V99	02123423	$$$$,$$9.99	
(E) 9(3)V99	00004	$ZZZ.99	
(F) 99V99	0534	99.99	
(G) 9(5)V99	0100000	$**,***.99	

7.7   TOTAL LINES

Most reports are not complete without the addition of accumulated totals. The program below contains additional code to provide for a final total. Notice that the two temporary storage areas provided for number of employees and total payroll are both initialized to zero.

   If accumulators are not initialized, you will probably wind up with a stack dump. It will be similar to previous "stack dumps" shown in earlier chapters. First, the program is shown followed by the output data, and finally, by another example of a "stack dump."

```
 1     IDENTIFICATION DIVISION.
 2     PROGRAM-ID.  THIRD.
 3     AUTHOR.  SAMUELS.
 4     ENVIRONMENT DIVISION.
 5     INPUT-OUTPUT SECTION.
 6     FILE-CONTROL.
 7          SELECT RAW-FILE ASSIGN TO WORKERS.
 8          SELECT MONEY-FILE ASSIGN TO CHECKS.
 9     DATA DIVISION.
10     FILE SECTION.
11     FD  RAW-FILE
12         DATA RECORD IS IN-REC.
13     01  IN-REC.
14         02  IN-NAME        PIC X(20).
15         02  IN-RATE        PIC 99V99.
16         02  IN-HOURS       PIC 99.
17     FD  MONEY-FILE
18         DATA RECORD IS OUT-REC.
19     01  OUT-REC        PIC X(80).
20     WORKING-STORAGE SECTION.
21     01  DETAIL-LINE.
22         02  OUT-NAME       PIC X(20).
23         02  OUT-RATE       PIC $$$.99.
24         02  FILLER         PIC X(8)  VALUE SPACES.
25         02  OUT-HOURS       PIC Z9.
26         02  FILLER         PIC X(8)  VALUE SPACES.
27         02  SALARY         PIC $$,$$$.99.
28         02  FILLER         PIC X(5)  VALUE SPACES.
29         02  FED-TAX        PIC $$,$$$.99.
30         02  FILLER         PIC X(4)  VALUE SPACES.
31         02  NET-PAY        PIC $$,$$$.99.
```

```
32   01  BEDTIME              PIC XX VALUE SPACES.
33   01  HEADER-ONE.
34       02  FILLER          PIC X(80) VALUE ALL "*".
35   01  HEADER-TWO.
36       02  FILLER          PIC X(4) VALUE "NAME".
37       02  FILLER          PIC X(10) VALUE SPACES.
38       02  FILLER          PIC X(11) VALUE "       RATE".
39       02  FILLER          PIC X(3) VALUE SPACES.
40       02  FILLER          PIC X(12) VALUE "HOURS WORKED".
41       02  FILLER          PIC X(4) VALUE SPACES.
42       02  FILLER          PIC X(12) VALUE "GROSS SALARY".
43       02  FILLER          PIC X(4) VALUE SPACES.
44       02  FILLER          PIC X(7) VALUE "FED TAX".
45       02  FILLER          PIC X(5) VALUE SPACES.
46       02  FILLER          PIC X(7) VALUE "NET PAY".
47   01  temp-areas.
48       02  TEMP-SALARY          pic 9999v99.
49       02  TEMP-FED-TAX         pic 9999v99.
50       02  temp-total-payroll   pic 99999v99 value 0.
51       02  temp-num-employees   pic 999 value 0.
52   01  final-line.
53       02  filler          pic x(5) value spaces.
54       02  filler          pic x(30) value
55           "TOTAL NUMBER OF EMPLOYEES = ".
56       02  num-employees-out  pic zz9.
57       02  filler          pic x(5) value spaces.
58       02  filler          pic x(20) value
59           "TOTAL PAYROLL = ".
60       02  total-payroll-out   pic $$$,$$$.99.
61   PROCEDURE DIVISION.
62   BEGIN.
63       PERFORM 010-START.
64       PERFORM 020-LOOPER UNTIL BEDTIME = "NO".
65       PERFORM 030-ENDIT.
66   010-START.
67       OPEN INPUT RAW-FILE OUTPUT MONEY-FILE.
68       WRITE OUT-REC FROM HEADER-ONE AFTER 1.
69       WRITE OUT-REC FROM HEADER-TWO AFTER 1.
70       WRITE OUT-REC FROM HEADER-ONE AFTER 1.
71       READ RAW-FILE AT END MOVE "NO" TO BEDTIME.
72   020-LOOPER.
73       add 1 to temp-num-employees.
74       MOVE IN-NAME TO OUT-NAME.
75       MOVE IN-RATE TO OUT-RATE.
76       MOVE IN-HOURS TO OUT-HOURS.
77       IF IN-HOURS > 48
78           COMPUTE TEMP-SALARY = (40 * IN-RATE) + (1.5 * 8 * IN-RATE)
79                               + ((IN-HOURS - 48) * 2 * IN-RATE)
80       ELSE IF IN-HOURS > 40
81               COMPUTE TEMP-SALARY = (40 * IN-RATE) + ((IN-HOURS - 40)
82                               * 1.5 * IN-RATE)
83           ELSE
84               COMPUTE TEMP-SALARY = IN-HOURS * IN-RATE.
85       IF TEMP-SALARY > 400 COMPUTE TEMP-FED-TAX = 0.3 * TEMP-SALARY
86       ELSE IF TEMP-SALARY > 300 COMPUTE TEMP-FED-TAX = 0.2 * TEMP-SALARY
87           ELSE IF TEMP-SALARY > 200 COMPUTE TEMP-FED-TAX = 0.1 *
88                   TEMP-SALARY
                     ELSE MOVE 0 TO TEMP-FED-TAX.
89       add temp-salary to temp-total-payroll.
90       COMPUTE NET-PAY = TEMP-SALARY - TEMP-FED-TAX.
```

```
 91          MOVE TEMP-SALARY TO SALARY.
 92          MOVE TEMP-FED-TAX TO FED-TAX.
 93          WRITE OUT-REC FROM DETAIL-LINE after 1.
 94          READ RAW-FILE AT END MOVE "NO" TO BEDTIME.
 95     030-ENDIT.
 96          move temp-num-employees to num-employees-out.
 97          move temp-total-payroll to total-payroll-out.
 98          write out-rec from final-line after 5.
 99          CLOSE RAW-FILE MONEY-FILE.
100          STOP RUN.
```

****

NAME	RATE	HOURS WORKED	GROSS SALARY	FED TAX	NET PAY
JOHN WORKHORSE	$12.50	40	$500.00	$150.00	$350.00
JUNE BRICNBRAC	$6.00	30	$180.00	$.00	$180.00
SAM DINERO	$9.50	50	$532.00	$159.60	$372.40
SUSAN MASON	$11.20	38	$425.60	$127.68	$297.92
ANN WORTHMORE	$8.00	53	$496.00	$148.80	$347.20

TOTAL NUMBER OF EMPLOYEES = 5   TOTAL PAYROLL = $2,133.60

As one can see, an additional line was formatted in the Working-Storage section. Additional MOVE and WRITE statements appear in the Procedure Division, particularly in the final paragraph.

What follows is another stack dump that occurred when the value 0 clause was left off one of the accumulators. The line number gives the statement that caused the "dump" so it is easy to find the culprit.

$RUN PROG3
%COB-F-INVDECDAT, invalid decimal data
%TRACE-F-TRACEBACK, symbolic stack dump follows

module name	routine name	line	rel PC	abs PC
THIRD	THIRD	73	000001E4	000011E4

Examining line 73 we find the following statement:

add 1 to temp-num-employees.

If this data name were not initialized, we would be attempting to add 1 to a storage area with unknown contents. If the contents of this storage area are not numeric, a stack dump occurs.

Our basic design structure has remained the same. There are still three modules emanating from the MAIN module. Additional pseudocode has been provided under each except the MAIN module [Figure 7-5].

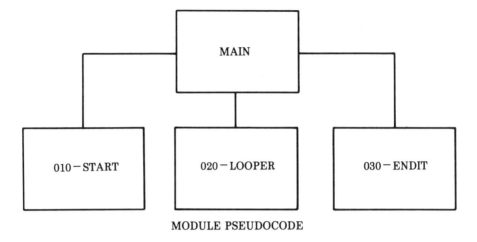

MODULE PSEUDOCODE

1. 010 – START
   a. Open files
   * b. Write headers
   c. Initial read

2. 020 – LOOPER
   a. Calculations
   b. Moves
   c. Write output (detail)
   d. "Looped" read

3. 030 – ENDIT
   * a. Write final totals
   b. Close files
   c. Stop

* = additions to
  pseudocode
  from previous
  diagrammed
  design

Figure 7-5

QUESTION

Provide the additional code necessary for you to create the final lines of the
report of your inventory program to look like this:

TOTAL ITEMS = (some #) TOTAL QUANTITY SOLD = (some #)

two spaces

TOTAL INVENTORY = (some $ amount)

SUMMARY

In order to produce reports with acceptable output format, the following additional syntax was learned:

1. WORKING-STORAGE SECTION
   a. VALUE clauses
   b. Formatted header lines
   c. Formatted detail lines consisting of edited output:
      i. zero suppression
      ii. floating dollar sign
   d. creating temporary storage areas

2. PROCEDURE DIVISION
   a. WRITE FROM
   b. AFTER #

PROGRAMMING PROBLEMS

1. From the following student input data with the following format:

Field	Columns
Name	1–20
Grade	21
Grade	23
Grade	25
Grade	27
Grade	29
Grade	31

Calculate and print out the following:

Field	Columns
Name	21–40
Grade Point Average	71–74

where an "A" = 4, "B" = 3, "C" = 2, "D" = 1, and "F" = 0

For example—an input record containing the following:

| JOE SMITH | A C D C D B |
| SARAH HAMMER | B   B A A D |

produces the following:

| JOE SMITH | 2.16 |
| SARAH HAMMER | 3.00 |

[Blanks in the grade fields are not included in the grade-point tally!!!]

Provide for header lines, edited detail lines for each student, and a total line showing the average grade-point average for all students.

*2. It is necessary to find out how much DADDY WARBUCKS (a stock broker) made on commissions last week on all his transactions. Each transaction is a record consisting of:

Field	Columns
Transaction #	1–5
Name of stock	6–35
Date of transaction	36–41
Transaction type	42
Amount bought/sold	43–47
Stock price	48–52 (assumed decimal)

where transaction type

$$A=2\%$$
$$B=3\%$$
$$C=4\%$$

Any amount bought/sold exceeding 100 shares reduces the commission rate .5%. Any amount bought/sold exceeding 1000 shares reduces the commission rate 1%.

For example, input records like this:

```
00235   PACIFIC GAS AND ELECTRIC              092683B0020015000
00044   DIGITAL EQUIPMENT CORPORATION         092883A0150006000
10443   TELEX                                 092983C0004002550
```

Produces:

```
  234 PACIFIC GAS AND ELECTRIC              9/26/83   2.5% $750.00
   44 DIGITAL EQUIPMENT CORPORATION         9/28/83   1.0% $900.00
10443 TELEX                                 9/29/83   4.0%  $40.80
```

Provide total lines as follows:

```
NUMBER OF TRANSACTIONS = #
TOTAL AMOUNT OF STOCK SOLD + #
TOTAL COMMISSION = $ amount
HIGHEST ONE-TRANSACTION COMMISSION TOTAL = $ amount
LOWEST ONE-TRANSACTION COMMISSION TOTAL = $ amount
```

Provide good, "clean" test data to cover all conditions. Include appropriate header lines.

For the above problems, develop a modular design plus pseudocode for just moving data from input to output. Then make the necessary additions to enhance your design, program, and produce your report.

Expansion of the Basic Modular Design

8.1 ADDITION OF ANOTHER PARAGRAPH (MODULE)

In order to incorporate a routine in our previous program that will handle invalid input data, we must focus our attention on expansion of our basic modular design structure. As programming problems become more complex, COBOL programs themselves become more complex with the inclusion of additional paragraphs.

It was mentioned in the previous chapter that no provision was made for reports exceeding one page in length, when in reality this happens all the time. Line counters should be set up and header lines should be printed on top of each page of the report. This requires us to modify our design so that a separate header module is added.

Examine the design in Figure 8–1.

The following program shows the addition of a paragraph that can be performed by two other paragraphs. Added code is in lower case.

```
1    IDENTIFICATION DIVISION.
2    PROGRAM-ID. FOURTH.
3    AUTHOR. SAMUELS.
4    ENVIRONMENT DIVISION.
5    INPUT-OUTPUT SECTION.
6    FILE-CONTROL.
```

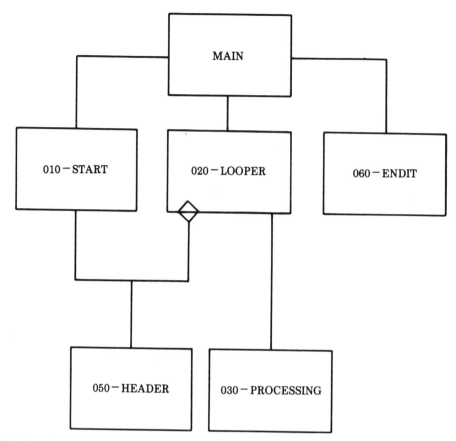

Modified Payroll Design Plan

Module Pseudocode:

1. 010 – START
   a. Open files
   * b. Transfer control to header routine
   c. Initial read

2. 020 – LOOPER
   * a. Transfer control to header routine upon line counter condition
   * b. Transfer control to processing
   c. "Looped" read

* 3. 030 – PROCESSING
   a. Calculations
   b. Moves
   c. Write output (detail)
   * d. Increment line counter

* 4. 050 – HEADER
   a. Write header lines

5. 060 – ENDIT
   a. Write final totals
   b. Close files
   c. Stop

* = additions to pseudocode from previous diagrammed design

Figure 8-1

```
 7          SELECT RAW-FILE ASSIGN TO WORKERS.
 8          SELECT MONEY-FILE ASSIGN TO CHECKS.
 9     DATA DIVISION.
10     FILE SECTION.
11     FD  RAW-FILE
12         DATA RECORD IS IN-REC.
13     01  IN-REC.
14         02  IN-NAME        PIC X(20).
15         02  IN-RATE        PIC 99V99.
16         02  IN-HOURS       PIC 99.
17     FD  MONEY-FILE
18         DATA RECORD IS OUT-REC.
19     01  OUT-REC           PIC X(80).
20     WORKING-STORAGE SECTION.
21     01  DETAIL-LINE.
22         02  OUT-NAME        PIC X(20).
23         02  OUT-RATE        PIC $$$.99.
24         02  FILLER          PIC X(8) VALUE SPACES.
25         02  OUT-HOURS       PIC Z9.
26         02  FILLER          PIC X(8) VALUE SPACES.
27         02  OUT-SALARY      PIC $$,$$$.99.
28         02  FILLER          PIC X(5) VALUE SPACES.
29         02  FED-TAX         PIC $$,$$$.99.
30         02  FILLER          PIC X(4) VALUE SPACES.
31         02  NET-PAY         PIC $$,$$$.99.
32     01  HEADER-ONE.
33         02  FILLER          PIC X(80) VALUE ALL "*".
34     01  HEADER-TWO.
35         02  FILLER          PIC X(4) VALUE "NAME".
36         02  FILLER          PIC X(10) VALUE SPACES.
37         02  FILLER          PIC X(11) VALUE "     RATE".
38         02  FILLER          PIC X(3) VALUE SPACES.
39         02  FILLER          PIC X(12) VALUE "HOURS WORKED".
40         02  FILLER          PIC X(4) VALUE SPACES.
41         02  FILLER          PIC X(12) VALUE "GROSS SALARY".
42         02  FILLER          PIC X(4) VALUE SPACES.
43         02  FILLER          PIC X(7) VALUE "FED TAX".
44         02  FILLER          PIC X(6) VALUE SPACES.
45         02  FILLER          PIC X(7) VALUE "NET PAY".
46     01  FINAL-LINE.
47         02 FILLER      PIC X(5) VALUE SPACES.
48         02 FILLER      PIC X(30) VALUE
49            "TOTAL NUMBER OF EMPLOYEES = ".
50         02  NUM-EMPLOYEES-OUT          PIC ZZ9.
51         02 FILLER      PIC X(5) VALUE SPACES.
52         02 FILLER      PIC X(20) VALUE
53            "TOTAL PAYROLL = ".
54         02 TOTAL-PAYROLL-OUT          PIC $$$,$$$.99.
55     01  BEDTIME        PIC XXX    VALUE SPACES.
56         88 there-are-no-more-records       value "yes".
57     01  LINE-COUNT     PIC 99 VALUE 0.
58     01  TEMP-AREAS.
59         02  TEMP-SALARY        PIC 9999V99.
60         02  TEMP-FED-TAX       PIC 9999V99.
61         02  TEMP-TOTAL-PAYROLL PIC 9999V99 VALUE 0.
62         02  TEMP-NUM-EMPLOYEES PIC 999 VALUE 0.
63     PROCEDURE DIVISION.
64     BEGIN.
65         PERFORM 010-START.
66         PERFORM 020-LOOPER UNTIL there-are-no-more-records.
67         PERFORM 060-ENDIT.
```

```
68      010-START.
69          OPEN INPUT RAW-FILE
70              OUTPUT MONEY-FILE.
71          perform 050-header-routine.
72
73          READ RAW-FILE AT END MOVE "YES" TO BEDTIME.
74      020-LOOPER.
75          if line-count > 64
76              perform 050-header-routine.
77              perform 030-normal-processing.
78          READ RAW-FILE AT END MOVE "YES" TO BEDTIME.
79      030-normal-processing.
80          ADD 1 TO TEMP-NUM-EMPLOYEES.
81          MOVE IN-NAME TO OUT-NAME.
82          MOVE IN-RATE TO OUT-RATE.
83          MOVE IN-HOURS TO OUT-HOURS.
84          IF IN-HOURS > 48
85              COMPUTE TEMP-SALARY = (40 * IN-RATE) + (1.5 * 8 *
86                          IN-RATE) + ((IN-HOURS - 48) * 2 * IN-RATE)
87          ELSE IF IN-HOURS > 40
88              COMPUTE TEMP-SALARY = (40 * IN-RATE) + ((IN-HOURS - 40)
89                          * 1.5 * IN-RATE)
90              ELSE
91                      COMPUTE TEMP-SALARY = IN-HOURS * IN-RATE.
92              IF TEMP-SALARY > 400
93                      COMPUTE TEMP-FED-TAX = 0.3 * TEMP-SALARY
94              ELSE IF TEMP-SALARY > 300
95                      COMPUTE TEMP-FED-TAX = 0.2 * TEMP-SALARY
96                  ELSE IF TEMP-SALARY > 200
97                          COMPUTE TEMP-FED-TAX = 0.1 * TEMP-SALARY
98                      ELSE MOVE 0 TO TEMP-FED-TAX.
99          ADD TEMP-SALARY TO TEMP-TOTAL-PAYROLL.
100         COMPUTE NET-PAY = TEMP-SALARY - TEMP-FED-TAX.
101         MOVE TEMP-SALARY TO OUT-SALARY.
102         MOVE TEMP-FED-TAX TO FED-TAX.
103         WRITE OUT-REC FROM DETAIL-LINE AFTER 1.
104         add 1 to line-count.
105     050-header-routine.
106         WRITE OUT-REC FROM HEADER-ONE AFTER PAGE.
107         WRITE OUT-REC FROM HEADER-TWO AFTER 1.
108         WRITE OUT-REC FROM HEADER-ONE AFTER 1.
109         move 3 to line-count.
110     060-ENDIT.
111         MOVE TEMP-NUM-EMPLOYEES TO NUM-EMPLOYEES-OUT.
112         MOVE TEMP-TOTAL-PAYROLL TO TOTAL-PAYROLL-OUT.
113         WRITE OUT-REC FROM FINAL-LINE AFTER 5.
114         CLOSE RAW-FILE MONEY-FILE.
115         STOP RUN.
```

The above program (FOUR) is quite similar to the one in the previous chapter except for the following:

a. The program-id was changed again.

b. A separate paragraph was entered for the header lines. It is performed by two other paragraphs (010-START and 020-LOOPER). If you attempt to include WRITE statements for header lines in 010-START, as in the previous chapter, and attempt to perform this routine more than once, you will cause an error by attempting to OPEN files after they are already opened. The header paragraph is executed when LINE-COUNTER > 64.

c. 030–PROCESSING is a separate paragraph. Later, you will see the inclusion of an error-routine that is another module entirely separate from processing.

d. The addition of a new level entry—88.

e. The concept of nested performs—enhancement of top-down structure.

8.2 LEVEL 88 [CONDITIONAL DATA-NAMES]

Condition names (88-level entries) provide superior documentation. As the name implies, the condition is built into the data-name. These entries have only VALUE clauses since they are subordinate to a level number with a PIC clause. Instead of using:

PERFORM 020–LOOPER UNTIL BEDTIME = "YES".

the following is better understood [especially if one has many switches of this type in a program]:

PERFORM 020–LOOPER UNTIL THERE-ARE-NO-MORE-RECORDS.

Notice that THERE-ARE-NO-MORE-RECORDS is the same as SWITCH = "YES".
Examine this Data Division entry:

```
02 EMPLOYEE-STATUS              PIC 9.
   88 SALARIED                  VALUES ARE 1, 2.
   88 HOURLY                    VALUE 3.
   88 MANAGERIAL                VALUES ARE 4 THRU 7.
   88 EXECUTIVE                 VALUE 8.
   88 PART-TIME                 VALUE 9.
```

In this case, for example, PART-TIME is the same as EMPLOYEE-STATUS = 9. The advantages for using condition names are as follows:

a. Documentation is clearer. It makes more sense to say:

IF EXECUTIVE OR MANAGERIAL PERFORM HIGH-SAL-ROUTINE.

rather than:

IF EMPLOYEE-STATUS > 3 AND EMPLOYEE-STATUS < 9
PERFORM HIGH-SAL-ROUTINE.

Cumbersome compound conditional statements are avoided.

b. Program maintenance is facilitated. Suppose codes of HOURLY and PART-TIME have to be changed. Only two changes are required in the 88-level entries (switch codes). If 88-level entries are not used, then one must find all the occurrences of EMPLOYEE-STATUS = 3 and EMPLOYEE-STATUS = 9 in the Procedure Division. The latter would increase the chance for errors.

c. 88-level entries are the only level numbers that enable the programmer to use VALUE clauses in the File Section.

d. Finally, the VALUES ARE clause groups all codes together, making it easy to test for error conditions.

8.3 NESTED PERFORM STATEMENTS

The additional modules attached below our previous design structure necessitate complementary code in the Procedure Division. Statements 71 and 76 of the program listed above represent nested PERFORM statements because both are in paragraphs that are being performed.

Statement 71 transfers control to statement 105 (050–HEADER-ROUTINE). After all statements in that paragraph are executed (106–109), transfer of control passes back to statement 72. After statement 73 is executed, transfer of control passes back to statement 66 that is at the highest level (MAIN—in the design). It appears that statement 71 (PERFORM 050–HEADER-ROUTINE) is "caught in the middle." It can only be executed if performed by a higher module and can perform a routine or module beneath it. Statement 71 is "nested." The same thing can be said about statement 76.

Nesting of PERFORM statements is important if one remembers two general rules:

a. Always attempt to "perform down." That is, one PERFORM statement should transfer control to a paragraph beneath it. Performing paragraphs above and below are contrary to top-down code methodolgy and can lead to serious errors.

b. Don't get carried away with nested PERFORM statements. Generally, one should never "nest" more than three times. After that, coding becomes so complex that it is hard to maintain and/or change.

QUESTIONS

1. Students at a university have 6 possible registration categories.

Category	Codes
FULL-TIME-UNDERGRADUATE	3, 24–26
PART-TIME-UNDERGRADUATE	6, 8
FULL-TIME-GRADUATE	1, 2, 14–16
PART-TIME-GRADUATE	7, 11, 12
SPECIAL-DAY	4
SPECIAL-EVENING	17

a. Establish condition-name entries so that a category can be determined for a given value of STUDENT-STATUS.

b. It is possible to have an invalid STUDENT-STATUS code. Provide for that by including an 88-level entry for INVALID-CODES. Include a PROCEDURE DIVISION statement that would verify whether or not a STUDENT-STATUS code was valid. If the code is invalid transfer control to 080–INVALID-ROUTINE. Any code not shown above is invalid.

2. Enhance your inventory program from the previous chapter to include a separate paragraph for a header routine and also use an 88-level entry. Include a modified design structure and appropriate pseudocode.

3. Given the following Procedure Division code:

```
PROCEDURE DIVISION.
BEGIN.
        PERFORM PAR-A.
        PERFORM PAR-B UNTIL Y > 30.
        PERFORM PAR-C.
        PERFORM PAR-D.
        STOP RUN.
    PAR-A.
        MOVE 10 TO Q.
        MOVE 25 TO Y.
        MOVE 13 TO Z.
    PAR-B.
        ADD 2 TO Q.
        PERFORM PAR-C.
        ADD 2 TO Z.
    PAR-C.
        ADD 1 TO Y.
        PERFORM PAR-E.
```

PAR-D.
    MOVE Z TO Q.
    ADD 10 TO Y.
PAR-E.
    SUBTRACT 1 FROM Z.

What is in Q,Y,Z after the above is executed?

8.4 DATA VALIDATION

The importance of validating incoming data cannot be stressed enough. Even after data are checked and cleared of invalid entries, there is always the possibility that an invalid code, number sequence, or other "weird" field or record contents will cause a programmer many sleepless nights. "This program is absolutely perfect. No invalid data can sneak through." You've got to be kidding!!

In any case, we can further modify our design to incorporate a basic error routine [see Figure 8–2]. Examine the following program:

```
1        IDENTIFICATION DIVISION.
2        PROGRAM-ID. FOURTH.
3        AUTHOR. SAMUELS.
4        ENVIRONMENT DIVISION.
5        INPUT-OUTPUT SECTION.
6        FILE-CONTROL.
7            SELECT RAW-FILE ASSIGN TO WORKERS.
8            SELECT MONEY-FILE ASSIGN TO CHECKS.
9            select error-file assign to ERRORS.
10       DATA DIVISION.
11       FILE SECTION.
12       FD  RAW-FILE
13           DATA RECORD IS IN-REC.
14       01  IN-REC.
15           02  IN-NAME      PIC X(20).
16           02  IN-RATE      PIC 99V99.
17           02  IN-HOURS     PIC 99.
18       fd  error-file
19           data record is error-rec.
20       01  error-rec        pic x(80).
21       FD  MONEY-FILE
22           DATA RECORD IS OUT-REC.
23       01  OUT-REC          PIC X(80).
24       WORKING-STORAGE SECTION.
25       01  DETAIL-LINE.
26           02  OUT-NAME         PIC X(20).
27           02  OUT-RATE         PIC $$$.99.
28           02  FILLER           PIC X(8) VALUE SPACES.
29           02  OUT-HOURS        PIC Z9.
30           02  FILLER           PIC X(8) VALUE SPACES.
31           02  OUT-SALARY       PIC $$,$$$.99.
32           02  FILLER           PIC X(5) VALUE SPACES.
33           02  FED-TAX          PIC $$,$$$.99.
34           02  FILLER           PIC X(4) VALUE SPACES.
```

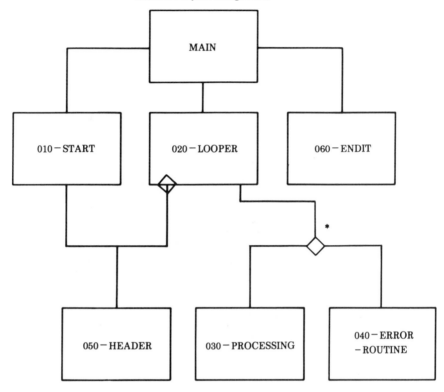

Modified Payroll Design Plan

*=decision to go to either 030 – PROCESSING or 040 – ERROR – ROUTINE
(other ◇ in 020 – LOOPER signifies that either control is passed
to 050 – HEADER or continue in 020 – LOOPER)

Additional Pseudocode:

1. 010 – START
   a. Open files
   b. Transfer control to header routine
   c. Initial read
2. 020 – LOOPER
   a. Transfer control to header routine
      upon line counter condition
   b. Transfer control to processing
   c. "Looped" read
3. 030 – PROCESSING
   a. Calculations
   b. Moves
   c. Write output (detail)
   d. Increment line counter

4. 050 – HEADER
   a. Write header line
5. 060 – ENDIT
   a. Write final totals
   b. Close files
   c. Stop
6. 040 – ERROR – ROUTINE
   a. Moves
   b. Write output to error report

Figure 8–2

```
35          02  NET-PAY          PIC $$,$$$.99.
36    01  HEADER-ONE.
37          02  FILLER        PIC X(80) VALUE ALL "*".
38    01  HEADER-TWO.
39          02  FILLER        PIC X(4) VALUE "NAME".
40          02  FILLER        PIC X(10) VALUE SPACES.
41          02  FILLER        PIC X(11) VALUE "     RATE".
42          02  FILLER        PIC X(3) VALUE SPACES.
43          02  FILLER        PIC X(12) VALUE "HOURS WORKED".
44          02  FILLER        PIC X(4) VALUE SPACES.
45          02  FILLER        PIC X(12) VALUE "GROSS SALARY".
46          02  FILLER        PIC X(4) VALUE SPACES.
47          02  FILLER        PIC X(7) VALUE "FED TAX".
48          02  FILLER        PIC X(6) VALUE SPACES.
49          02  FILLER        PIC X(7) VALUE "NET PAY".
50    01  FINAL-LINE.
51          02 FILLER       PIC X(5) VALUE SPACES.
52          02 FILLER       PIC X(30) VALUE
53              "TOTAL NUMBER OF EMPLOYEES = ".
54          02   NUM-EMPLOYEES-OUT          PIC ZZ9.
55          02 FILLER       PIC X(5) VALUE SPACES.
56          02 FILLER       PIC X(20) VALUE
57              "TOTAL PAYROLL = ".
58          02 TOTAL-PAYROLL-OUT          PIC $$$,$$$.99.
59    01  BEDTIME        PIC XXX    VALUE SPACES.
60          88 THERE-ARE-NO-MORE-RECORDS      VALUE "YES".
61    01  LINE-COUNT     PIC 99 VALUE 0.
62    01  TEMP-AREAS.
63          02  TEMP-SALARY      PIC 9999V99.
64          02  TEMP-FED-TAX     PIC 9999V99.
65          02  TEMP-TOTAL-PAYROLL PIC 9999V99 VALUE 0.
66          02  TEMP-NUM-EMPLOYEES PIC 999 VALUE 0.
67    PROCEDURE DIVISION.
68    BEGIN.
69          PERFORM 010-START.
70          PERFORM 020-LOOPER UNTIL THERE-ARE-NO-MORE-RECORDS.
71          PERFORM 060-ENDIT.
72    010-START.
73          OPEN INPUT RAW-FILE
74                OUTPUT MONEY-FILE
75                     error-file.
76          PERFORM 050-HEADER-ROUTINE.
77
78          READ RAW-FILE AT END MOVE "YES" TO BEDTIME.
79    020-LOOPER.
80          IF LINE-COUNT > 64
81              PERFORM 050-HEADER-ROUTINE.
82          If in-hours not numeric or in-rate not numeric
83              perform 040-error-routine
84          else
85              perform 030-normal-processing.
86          READ RAW-FILE AT END MOVE "YES" TO BEDTIME.
87    ********************************************************
88    *       PROCESSING OF GOOD RECORDS                    *
89    ********************************************************
90    030-NORMAL-PROCESSING.
91          ADD 1 TO TEMP-NUM-EMPLOYEES.
92          MOVE IN-NAME TO OUT-NAME.
93          MOVE IN-RATE TO OUT-RATE.
94          MOVE IN-HOURS TO OUT-HOURS.
```

```
95          IF IN-HOURS > 48
96              COMPUTE TEMP-SALARY = (40 * IN-RATE) + (1.5 * 8 *
97                      IN-RATE) + ((IN-HOURS - 48) * 2 * IN-RATE)
98          ELSE IF IN-HOURS > 40
99              COMPUTE TEMP-SALARY = (40 * IN-RATE) + ((IN-HOURS - 40)
100                     * 1.5 * IN-RATE)
101             ELSE
102                     COMPUTE TEMP-SALARY = IN-HOURS * IN-RATE.
103         IF TEMP-SALARY > 400
104                 COMPUTE TEMP-FED-TAX = 0.3 * TEMP-SALARY
105         ELSE IF TEMP-SALARY > 300
106                 COMPUTE TEMP-FED-TAX = 0.2 * TEMP-SALARY
107             ELSE IF TEMP-SALARY > 200
108                     COMPUTE TEMP-FED-TAX = 0.1 * TEMP-SALARY
109                 ELSE MOVE 0 TO TEMP-FED-TAX.
110         ADD TEMP-SALARY TO TEMP-TOTAL-PAYROLL.
111         COMPUTE NET-PAY = TEMP-SALARY - TEMP-FED-TAX.
112         MOVE TEMP-SALARY TO OUT-SALARY.
113         MOVE TEMP-FED-TAX TO FED-TAX.
114         WRITE OUT-REC FROM DETAIL-LINE AFTER 1.
115         ADD 1 TO LINE-COUNT.
116     ********************************************************
117     *       INVALID RECORD PROCESSING                     *
118     ********************************************************
119     040-error-routine.
120          display "THIS MODULE DOES NOT FUNCTION YET".
121     050-HEADER-ROUTINE.
122         WRITE OUT-REC FROM HEADER-ONE AFTER PAGE.
123         WRITE OUT-REC FROM HEADER-TWO AFTER 1.
124         WRITE OUT-REC FROM HEADER-ONE AFTER 1.
125         MOVE 3 TO LINE-COUNT.
126     060-ENDIT.
127         MOVE TEMP-NUM-EMPLOYEES TO NUM-EMPLOYEES-OUT.
128         MOVE TEMP-TOTAL-PAYROLL TO TOTAL-PAYROLL-OUT.
129         WRITE OUT-REC FROM FINAL-LINE AFTER 5.
130         CLOSE RAW-FILE MONEY-FILE error-file.
131         STOP RUN.
```

Notice the following changes to our program:

a. This program contains comments which are a form of documentation to help clarify certain sections of code. Any comment line starts with an "*" in the first column, or A margin. This makes the entire line non-executable. Comments are needed to further clarify various parts of a program. You are urged to use them. Actually, one should add comments when new modules (paragraphs) are added. One should NOT add them AFTER the entire program is written!!

b. A new file has been set up. All invalid records will eventually be written to this file (external file name = ERRORS.DAT). At the moment a "stub" has been created. A "stub" is a paragraph that will be further enhanced at a later date. It is put there to test out main logic sequences. You should examine the additional code in the Procedure Division before proceeding any further. Notice that a new nested PERFORM statement has been added (line 83).

8.5   THE DISPLAY STATEMENT

A new verb (DISPLAY) has been added to our Procedure Division. A literal or the contents of a storage area (data-name) can be "displayed" on the CRT. This storage area must be defined in the working-storage section. For example:

DISPLAY "THE NAME OF THE GAME."

causes THE NAME OF THE GAME to be "put on the screen."

DISPLAY THE-GAME.

causes whatever is in THE-GAME to be "put on the screen." If THE-GAME has a PIC X(10) and contains MONOPOLY then:

DISPLAY "THE NAME OF THE GAME IS" THE-GAME.

will show on the CRT:

THE NAME OF THE GAME IS MONOPOLY

DISPLAY statements are quite useful as a debugging tool. That is, a programmer can follow the logical execution of his/her program if DISPLAY statements are added to most or all of the paragraphs. You should try adding DISPLAY statements to each paragraph of your inventory program and see what happens during execution. Use statements like this:

DISPLAY "HI—I AM IN THE START MODULE".
DISPLAY "HI—I AM IN THE LOOP MODULE".
DISPLAY "HI—I AM IN THE FINAL MODULE".

Of course, you have to put them in the appropriate paragraphs. The following data:

JOHN WORKHORSE	1 2 504 0
JUNE BRICNBRAC	0 6 003 0
BAD MOVER	0 4 G34 2
SAM DINERO	0 9 505 0
MR. ERROR	0 9 003M
SUSAN MASON	1 1 203 8
ANN WORTHMORE	0 8 005 3
TOOBAD JONES	C D L *K %
BENNY HILLER	1 0 004 3

produced the following report:

```
*******************************************************************************
NAME                 RATE    HOURS WORKED    GROSS SALARY    FED TAX    NET PAY
*******************************************************************************
```

NAME	RATE	HOURS WORKED	GROSS SALARY	FED TAX	NET PAY
JOHN WORKHORSE	$12.50	40	$500.00	$150.00	$350.00
JUNE BRICNBRAC	$6.00	30	$180.00	$.00	$180.00
SAM DINERO	$9.50	50	$532.00	$159.60	$372.40
SUSAN MASON	$11.20	38	$425.60	$127.68	$297.92
ANN WORTHMORE	$8.00	53	$496.00	$148.80	$347.20
BENNY HILLER	$10.00	43	$445.00	$133.50	$311.50

TOTAL NUMBER OF EMPLOYEES = 6   TOTAL PAYROLL = $2,578.60

and the following to be "put on the screen":

THIS MODULE DOES NOT FUNCTION YET
THIS MODULE DOES NOT FUNCTION YET
THIS MODULE DOES NOT FUNCTION YET

Do you know why??

One more valid record has been included to test for someone working over 40 hours but fewer than 49 hours (see above).

The input data (WORKERS.DAT) contain non-numeric information in numeric fields as tested by the NON-NUMERIC option. The following table shows the valid forms of class test:

Data Type	PIC	Valid Tests
Numeric	9	NUMERIC, NOT NUMERIC
Alphanumeric	X	NUMERIC, NOT NUMERIC, ALPHABETIC NOT ALPHABETIC
Alphabetic	A	ALPHABETIC, NOT ALPHABETIC

You cannot use, for example:

IF FIELD-M IS NUMERIC. . . . . . . (if FIELD-M has a PIC = A)

or

IF FIELD-Q IS NOT ALPHABETIC. . . . . . (if FIELD-Q has
a PIC = 9)

8.6 ADDITION OF AN ERROR FILE

Finally, with the "real-world" input data listed above we enhance our program to produce two external files:

CHECKS.DAT that contains output for valid records
ERRORS.DAT that contains output for invalid records

The following program now includes the production of an error report with appropriate headers. A line counter for this report has been left out for the sake of brevity.

First the program and then the error report (the previous output report has already been given).

```
 1     IDENTIFICATION DIVISION.
 2     PROGRAM-ID. FOURTH.
 3     AUTHOR. SAMUELS.
 4     ENVIRONMENT DIVISION.
 5     INPUT-OUTPUT SECTION.
 6     FILE-CONTROL.
 7         SELECT RAW-FILE ASSIGN TO WORKERS.
 8         SELECT MONEY-FILE ASSIGN TO CHECKS.
 9         SELECT ERROR-FILE ASSIGN TO ERRORS.
10     DATA DIVISION.
11     FILE SECTION.
12     FD  RAW-FILE
13         DATA RECORD IS IN-REC.
14     01  IN-REC.
15         02  IN-NAME       PIC X(20).
16         02  IN-RATE       PIC 99V99.
17         02  IN-HOURS      PIC 99.
18     FD  ERROR-FILE
19         DATA RECORD IS ERROR-REC.
20     01  ERROR-REC     PIC X(80).
21     FD  MONEY-FILE
22         DATA RECORD IS OUT-REC.
23     01  OUT-REC       PIC X(80).
24     WORKING-STORAGE SECTION.
25     01  DETAIL-LINE.
26         02  OUT-NAME    PIC X(20).
27         02  OUT-RATE    PIC $$$.99.
28         02  FILLER      PIC X(8) VALUE SPACES.
29         02  OUT-HOURS   PIC Z9.
30         02  FILLER      PIC X(8) VALUE SPACES.
31         02  OUT-SALARY  PIC $$,$$$.99.
32         02  FILLER      PIC X(5) VALUE SPACES.
33         02  FED-TAX     PIC $$,$$$.99.
34         02  FILLER      PIC X(4) VALUE SPACES.
35         02  NET-PAY     PIC $$,$$$.99.
36     01  error-line.
37         02  error-name        pic x(20).
38         02  filler            pic x(15) value spaces.
39         02  error-message     pic x(45).
40     01  HEADER-ONE.
41         02  FILLER            PIC X(80) VALUE ALL "*".
42     01  HEADER-TWO.
43         02  FILLER            PIC X(4) VALUE "NAME".
44         02  FILLER            PIC X(10) VALUE SPACES.
45         02  FILLER            PIC X(11) VALUE "    RATE".
46         02  FILLER            PIC X(3) VALUE SPACES.
47         02  FILLER            PIC X(12) VALUE "HOURS WORKED".
48         02  FILLER            PIC X(4) VALUE SPACES.
49         02  FILLER            PIC X(12) VALUE "GROSS SALARY".
50         02  FILLER            PIC X(4) VALUE SPACES.
51         02  FILLER            PIC X(7) VALUE "FED TAX".
52         02  FILLER            PIC X(6) VALUE SPACES.
53         02  FILLER            PIC X(7) VALUE "NET PAY".
```

```
54    01  error-header.
55        02  filler        pic x(50) value "      NAME".
56        02  filler        pic x(30) value
57            "ERROR MESSAGE".
58    01  FINAL-LINE.
59        02 FILLER      PIC X(5) VALUE SPACES.
60        02 FILLER      PIC X(30) VALUE
61            "TOTAL NUMBER OF EMPLOYEES = ".
62        02  NUM-EMPLOYEES-OUT     PIC ZZ9.
63        02 FILLER      PIC X(5) VALUE SPACES.
64        02 FILLER      PIC X(20) VALUE
65            "TOTAL PAYROLL = ".
66        02 TOTAL-PAYROLL-OUT      PIC $$$,$$$.99.
67    01  BEDTIME    PIC XXX    VALUE SPACES.
68        88 THERE-ARE-NO-MORE-RECORDS      VALUE "YES".
69    01  LINE-COUNT      PIC 99 VALUE 0.
70    01  TEMP-AREAS.
71        02  TEMP-SALARY      PIC 9999V99.
72        02  TEMP-FED-TAX     PIC 9999V99.
73        02  TEMP-TOTAL-PAYROLL PIC 9999V99 VALUE 0.
74        02  TEMP-NUM-EMPLOYEES PIC 999 VALUE 0.
75    PROCEDURE DIVISION.
76    BEGIN.
77        PERFORM 010-START.
78        PERFORM 020-LOOPER UNTIL THERE-ARE-NO-MORE-RECORDS.
79        PERFORM 060-ENDIT.
80    010-START.
81        OPEN INPUT RAW-FILE
82          OUTPUT MONEY-FILE
83            ERROR-FILE.
84        PERFORM 050-HEADER-ROUTINE.
85
86        READ RAW-FILE AT END MOVE "YES" TO BEDTIME.
87    020-LOOPER.
88        IF LINE-COUNT > 64
89            PERFORM 050-HEADER-ROUTINE.
90        IF IN-HOURS NOT NUMERIC OR IN-RATE NOT NUMERIC
91            PERFORM 040-ERROR-ROUTINE
92        ELSE
93            PERFORM 030-NORMAL-PROCESSING.
94        READ RAW-FILE AT END MOVE "YES" TO BEDTIME.
95    ******************************************************
96    *            PROCESSING OF GOOD RECORDS            *
97    ******************************************************
98    030-NORMAL-PROCESSING.
99        ADD 1 TO TEMP-NUM-EMPLOYEES.
100       MOVE IN-NAME TO OUT-NAME.
101       MOVE IN-RATE TO OUT-RATE.
102       MOVE IN-HOURS TO OUT-HOURS.
103       IF IN-HOURS > 48
104           COMPUTE TEMP-SALARY = (40 * IN-RATE) + (1.5 * 8 *
105                     IN-RATE) + ((IN-HOURS - 48) * 2 * IN-RATE)
106       ELSE IF IN-HOURS > 40
107           COMPUTE TEMP-SALARY = (40 * IN-RATE) + ((IN-HOURS - 40)
108                     * 1.5 * IN-RATE)
109            ELSE
110              COMPUTE TEMP-SALARY = IN-HOURS * IN-RATE.
111       IF TEMP-SALARY > 400
112               COMPUTE TEMP-FED-TAX = 0.3 * TEMP-SALARY
113       ELSE IF TEMP-SALARY > 300
114               COMPUTE TEMP-FED-TAX = 0.2 * TEMP-SALARY
```

```
115              ELSE IF TEMP-SALARY > 200
116                 COMPUTE TEMP-FED-TAX = 0.1 * TEMP-SALARY
117              ELSE MOVE 0 TO TEMP-FED-TAX.
118          ADD TEMP-SALARY TO TEMP-TOTAL-PAYROLL.
119          COMPUTE NET-PAY = TEMP-SALARY - TEMP-FED-TAX.
120          MOVE TEMP-SALARY TO OUT-SALARY.
121          MOVE TEMP-FED-TAX TO FED-TAX.
122          WRITE OUT-REC FROM DETAIL-LINE AFTER 1.
123          ADD 1 TO LINE-COUNT.
124          ****************************************************
125          *          INVALID RECORD PROCESSING              *
126          ****************************************************
127      040-ERROR-ROUTINE.
128          move in-name to error-name.
129          move "invalid contents in rate and/or hours data" to
130          error-message.
131          write error-rec from error-line after 2.
132      050-HEADER-ROUTINE.
133          WRITE OUT-REC FROM HEADER-ONE AFTER PAGE.
134          WRITE OUT-REC FROM HEADER-TWO AFTER 1.
135          WRITE OUT-REC FROM HEADER-ONE AFTER 1.
136          write error-rec from header-one after 1.
137          write error-rec from error-header after 1.
138          write error-rec from header-one after 1.
139          MOVE 3 TO LINE-COUNT.
140      060-ENDIT.
141          MOVE TEMP-NUM-EMPLOYEES TO NUM-EMPLOYEES-OUT.
142          MOVE TEMP-TOTAL-PAYROLL TO TOTAL-PAYROLL-OUT.
143          WRITE OUT-REC FROM FINAL-LINE AFTER 5.
144          CLOSE RAW-FILE MONEY-FILE ERROR-FILE.
145          STOP RUN.
```

```
*********************************************************************
          NAME                          ERROR MESSAGE
*********************************************************************
```

NAME	ERROR MESSAGE
BAD MOVER	invalid contents in rate and/or hours data
MR. ERROR	invalid contents in rate and/or hours data
TOOBAD JONES	invalid contents in rate and/or hours data

One could embellish this error report by adding more types of error messages. Instead of line 129 that just moves one literal to one message area, one could have many messages sent to many areas on the line depending upon the type of specific error. The messages could read:

> INVALID RATE
> INVALID HOURS
> INVALID RATE AND INVALID HOURS

etc.

QUESTION

Provide the additional code necessary for you to create an appropriate error report for your inventory program from chapter 7.

SUMMARY

By now you should be able to add modules (and, therefore, coded paragraphs) to programs you have already developed, WITHOUT removing existing code. Additionally you should have learned the following syntax:

1. Conditional data-names (level 88)

2. DISPLAY

3. comments (*)

You should have also learned how to use nested PERFORM statements and class tests to properly handle the additional modules employing data validation techniques.

PROGRAMMING PROBLEMS

1. The FHA insures home mortgages up to $90,000. The down payment schedule is as follows:

3% of the first $40,000,
8% of the next $15,000,
9% of the remainder.

The first monthly payment is computed as follows:

0.9% per month on any amount over $50,000
+
1.0% per month on any amount $50,000 or less.

Write a program to accept input records containing an applicant's name and the amount of loan requested. Output should consist of all input fields, the amount of the down payment required, and the monthly payment. This report should include totals for number of requests, total of all down payments, average down payment, total monthly payments, and average monthly payment. An error report should also be produced that will show records containing invalid loan requests (non-numeric data plus loan requests above $90,000). Design your own input format and provide appropriate test data.

*2. Ace Conglomerate has been having trouble with data entry. There have been rumors that the ax will fall on this department because the data files have records with so many errors in them. A particular file to be audited is the personnel file. It contains records with the following format:

Field	Columns	Type	Range (if any)
Name	1–20		
SS#	21–29	Numeric	
Sex	30	Alphanumeric	S or F
Med Plan	31	Numeric	1 2 or 3
Birthdate	32–37	Numeric	
Department	39–54	Alpha	
Marital Status	55	Numeric	1 or 2
Deductions	56–57	Numeric	>0 and <8

Given the following data:

SAMUELS JOE	312093827Q2114B54	ACCOUNTING	2V3
FEZZO FRED	432123412M4092228	SHIPP34G	204
PETERSON JANE	519201923 F 1030344	ADVERTISING	101

The following report should be produced:

NAME	SS#	SEX	MED-PLAN	BIRTH	DEPT.	MAR-ST	DED
SAMUELS JOE	*	R	*	I	*	*	I
FEZZO FRED	*	*	R	*	I	*	*
PETERSON JANE	*	*	*	*	*	*	*

TOTAL RECORDS =
TOTAL NUMBER OF INVALID ENTRIES =
TOTAL NUMBER OF RANGE ERRORS =
TOTAL NUMBER OF VALID RECORDS =
PERCENTAGE OF VALID RECORDS =

(where * denotes field is ok, I = invalid, and R = range error)

Use the DISPLAY option for the final totals and percentage.

Provide appropriate test data!

For the above problems, develop a modular design + pseudocode. Do these programs in small discrete steps.

## 9

Control Breaks

If you have done most or all of the questions in the previous chapters and have successfully executed programs for the related programming problems at the end of each chapter, you have learned over 70% of the COBOL syntax.

It is important, at this time, to further develop the ability to modify (add to) existing designs and, therefore, programs. In doing so the following rules should be followed:

a. Always proceed in small, incremental steps. Add to the design, then add additional code to your program.

b. Use appropriate test data to check all conditions, overflow possibilities, errors, etc.

c. Attempt to make your program conform to top-down structure. Always try to "perform down." Avoid GO TO statements, except under rare circumstances that will be explained in the chapter on sorting. [*** **The GO TO statement has been purposely left out because its use leads to unstructured programming ***.**]

d. Do not put in overly complex code that only YOU will understand. Avoid massive nesting of IF statements and PERFORM statements (up to three nests is enough). In other words, make it as simple as possible.

The purpose of this chapter is to enhance your programming style by using input data to create reports that have one or more subtotals for various subsets of the data. You will also learn additional COBOL syntax along the way.

9.1   A PROBLEM

Examine the following problem:

Salesmen for Psycho Products get paid solely on a commission basis. Their salary is determined by the type of product they sell and the quantity of the sale.

Psycho Products consists of three regions. Each region has a certain number of branches; each branch has a certain number of salespersons.

A record consists of one sale. Examine the following input format for a particular sale (all the records are sorted by salesman number WITHIN branch number WITHIN region number):

Field	Columns
Region number	1–2
Branch number	3–4
Salesman number	5–6
Product number	8–13
Quantity	14–17
Type	18
Price (assumed dec.)	20–24
Salesman name	25–44

The company has decided to run a sales contest. Three prizes will be awarded: 1) a one-week, all-expense paid trip for two to Acapulco to the SALESPERSON with the highest sales commissions, 2) a pair of tickets to a Broadway play to each salesperson within the BRANCH achieving the highest sales commissions, and 3) a five dollar gift certificate to Duffy's Drive-In to each salesperson within the REGION achieving the highest sales commissions.

Each salesperson employed at Psycho Products has three chances to win a prize. He/She may be the salesperson achieving the highest sales commissions for an INDIVIDUAL, he/she may be a member of the BRANCH achieving the highest total sales commissions for a branch, and/or he/she may be a member of the REGION achieving the highest sales commissions for a region.

In order to determine the winner(s) in each of the above categories the company must have a report that 1) calculates and prints the total sales commissions for each individual salesperson, 2) calculates and prints the total sales commissions for each branch within Psycho Products, and 3) calculates and prints the total sales commissions for each region within Psycho Products. The company would still like to see a printed sales total for the entire company and a printed sales commission total for the entire company.

Each output record should have the following format:

Field	
Region number	(zero suppressed)
Branch number	(zero suppressed)
Salesman number	(zero suppressed)
Product number	
Quantity	(zero suppressed)
Price	(dollar sign, decimal point, zero suppressed dollar portion)
Commission rate	(percent sign)
Amount sold	(dollar sign, decimal point, zero suppressed dollar portion)
Commission	(dollar sign, decimal point, zero suppressed dollar portion)
Salesman name	

Interesting!! No mention is made of the exact nature of this report. What is known is that a detail line MUST be printed for each record. In addition, subtotals should be printed every time there is a change in salesman number, branch number, and region number. Final totals should also be printed.

Three things are assumed:

1. Processing calculations involves the following:

$$\text{Amount Sold} = (\text{Quantity})(\text{Price})$$
$$\text{Commission Rate} = (\text{Amount Sold})(\text{Commission Rate})$$

2. The initial test data is all valid.

3. You are sufficiently knowledgeable in the basics modular design code to design, code, and execute a program that would give a report showing header lines, detail lines, and a final line in well-defined, incremental steps as in previous chapters.

9.2 A PARTIAL SOLUTION

Examine this modular design with pseudocode (Figure 9–1) plus the printer spacing chart (Figure 9–2) that will help us format header lines, detail lines, and the final line.

Notice that the modular design provides for five performed paragraphs.

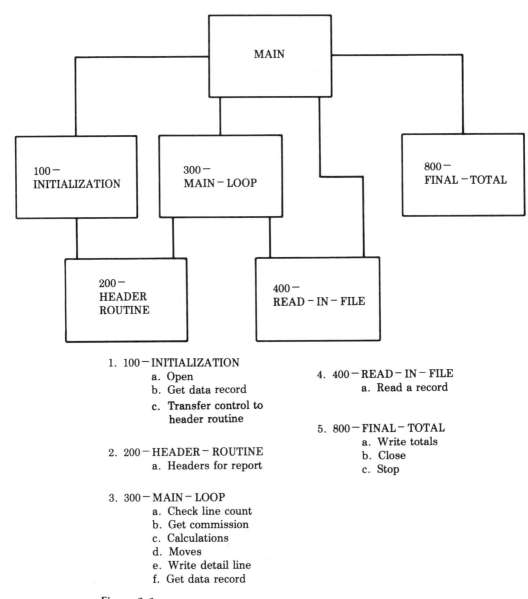

1. 100 – INITIALIZATION
   a. Open
   b. Get data record
   c. Transfer control to
      header routine

2. 200 – HEADER – ROUTINE
   a. Headers for report

3. 300 – MAIN – LOOP
   a. Check line count
   b. Get commission
   c. Calculations
   d. Moves
   e. Write detail line
   f. Get data record

4. 400 – READ – IN – FILE
   a. Read a record

5. 800 – FINAL – TOTAL
   a. Write totals
   b. Close
   c. Stop

Figure 9–1

A module has been included that will only contain the READ statement. This method uses only one READ statement but more PERFORM statements. The output record is also 132 lines long, instead of 80 columns.

The program that follows satisfies the first report (with no subtotals). [Figure 9–3 shows the input data and Figure 9–4 shows the output data.]

```
 1      IDENTIFICATION DIVISION.
 2      PROGRAM-ID.              FIFTH.
 3      AUTHOR.                  STEVE SAMUELS.
 4      INSTALLATION.            DEPAUL UNIVERSITY.
 5      DATE-WRITTEN.            10/3/83.
 6
 7      **************************************************************
 8      *****     INPUT:  THE INPUT TO THIS PROGRAM IS A FILE CALLED
 9      *****             "FIVE.DAT".  EACH RECORD IN
10      *****             THIS FILE CONSISTS OF ONE SALE AND INCLUDES
11      *****             REGION NUMBER, BRANCH NUMBER, SALESMAN
12      *****             NUMBER, PRODUCT NUMBER, QUANTITY, TYPE,
13      *****             PRICE AND SALESMAN NAME.  ALL THE RECORDS
14      *****             ARE SORTED BY SALESMAN NUMBER WITHIN BRANCH
15      *****             NUMBER WITHIN REGION NUMBER.
16      **************************************************************
17
18      **************************************************************
19      *****     OUTPUT:  THE OUTPUT FROM THIS PROGRAM CONSISTS OF
20      *****             A PRINTED REPORT, WITH HEADING LINES, CON-
21      *****             TAINING EDITED FIELDS FOR REGION NUMBER,
22      *****             BRANCH NUMBER, SALESMAN NUMBER, PRODUCT
23      *****             NUMBER, QUANTITY, PRICE, COMMISSION RATE,
24      *****             AMOUNT SOLD, COMMISSION AND SALESMAN NAME
25      *****             FOR EACH RECORD PROCESSED AS WELL AS
26      *****             FINAL TOTALS FOR AMOUNT SOLD AND COMMISSIONS.
27      **************************************************************
28
29      **************************************************************
30      *****     PROCESSING:  THE PROCESSING REQUIRED TO PREPARE
31      *****             THE REPORT CONSISTS OF READING AN INPUT
32      *****             RECORD, FINDING THE CORRECT COMMISSION
33      *****             RATE, CALCULATING COMMISSION AND AMOUNT
34      *****             SOLD, MOVING EACH OF THE REQUIRED FIELDS
35      *****             FROM THE INPUT OR WORKING STORAGE AREA
36      *****             TO THE OUTPUT AREA, WRITING A REPORT LINE,
37      *****             AND ACCUMULATING FINAL TOTALS.
38      **************************************************************
39
40      ENVIRONMENT DIVISION.
41
42      CONFIGURATION SECTION.
43
44      SOURCE-COMPUTER.     VAX-11-750.
45      OBJECT-COMPUTER.     VAX-11-750.
46
47      INPUT-OUTPUT SECTION.
48
49      FILE-CONTROL.
50          SELECT IN-FILE ASSIGN TO FIVE.
51          SELECT OUT-FILE ASSIGN TO OUTLOOK.
52
53      DATA DIVISION.
54
55      FILE SECTION.
56
57      FD  IN-FILE
58          DATA RECORD IS IN-REC.
59      01  IN-REC.
60          05  REGION-IN            PIC XX.
61          05  BRANCH-IN            PIC XX.
62          05  SMAN-NUMBER-IN       PIC XX.
```

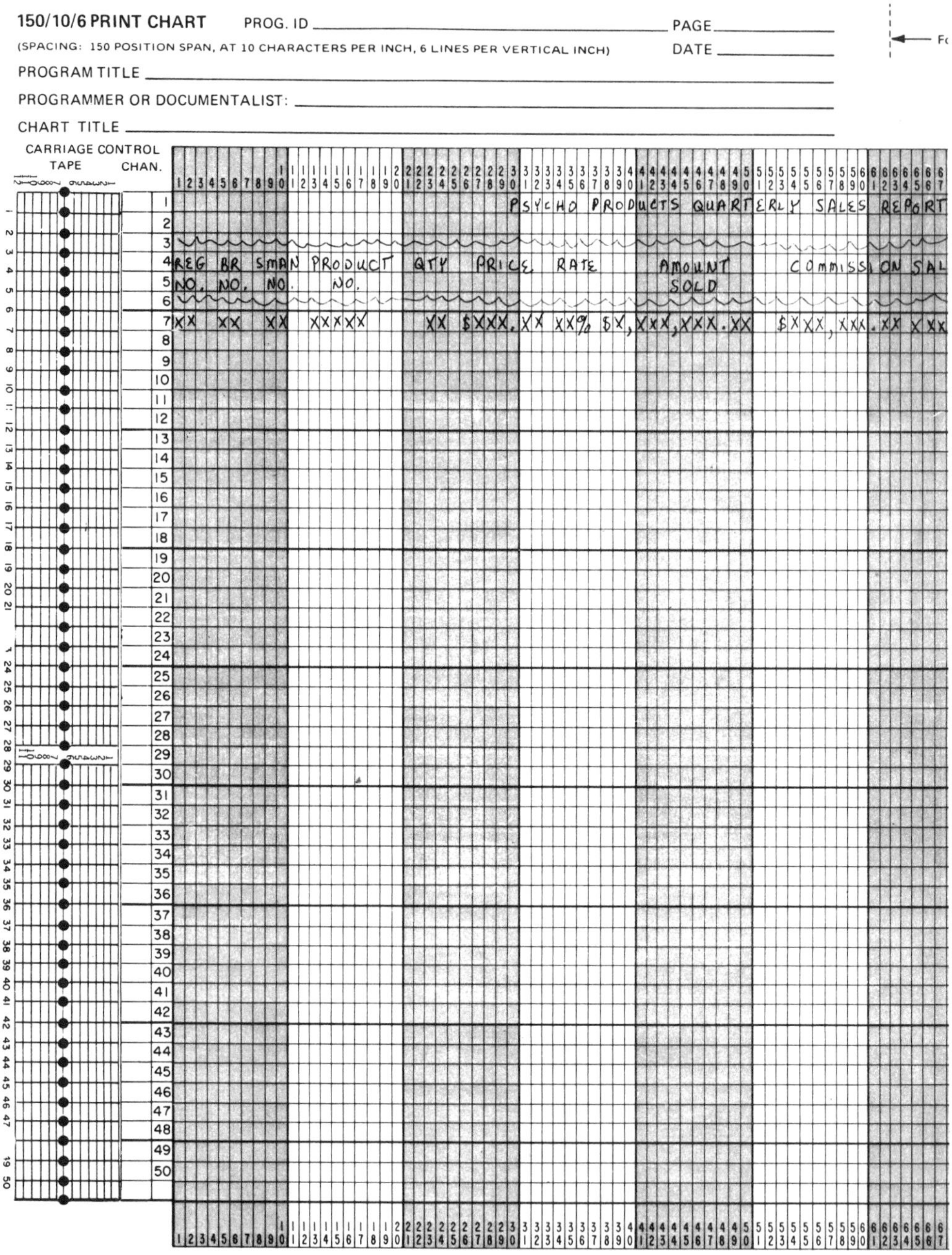

150/10/6 PRINT CHART PROG. ID ______ PAGE ______

(SPACING: 150 POSITION SPAN, AT 10 CHARACTERS PER INCH, 6 LINES PER VERTICAL INCH) DATE ______

PROGRAM TITLE ______

PROGRAMMER OR DOCUMENTALIST: ______

CHART TITLE ______

CARRIAGE CONTROL TAPE CHAN.

1 PSYCHO PRODUCTS QUARTERLY SALES REPORT

4 REG BR SMAN PRODUCT QTY PRICE RATE AMOUNT COMMISSION SAL

5 NO. NO. NO. NO. SOLD

7 XX XX XX XXXXX XX $XXX.XX XX% $X,XXX,XXX.XX $XXX,XXX.XX XXX

Figure 9-2

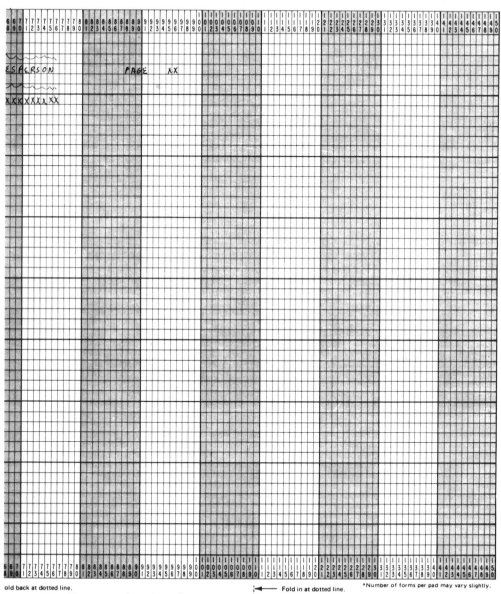

Figure 9-2 (continued)

```
63       05  FILLER                    PIC X.
64       05  PROD-NUMBER-IN            PIC X(6).
65       05  QUANTITY-IN               PIC 9(4).
66       05  COMMISSION-TYPE-IN        PIC X.
67           88 COMMISSION-RATE-CODE-A              VALUE "A".
68           88 COMMISSION-RATE-CODE-B              VALUE "B".
69           88 COMMISSION-RATE-CODE-C              VALUE "C".
70       05  FILLER                    PIC X.
71       05  PRICE-IN                  PIC 999V99.
72       05  SMAN-NAME-IN              PIC X(20).
73
74   FD  OUT-FILE
75       DATA RECORD IS OUT-REC.
76   01  OUT-REC                       PIC X(132).
77
78
79
80   WORKING-STORAGE SECTION.
81
82   01  FINISHED              PIC XXX VALUE SPACES.
83       88 THERE-ARE-NO-MORE-RECORDS    VALUE "YES".
84   01  COUNTERS.
85       05  WS-LINE-COUNT             PIC 99 VALUE 0.
86       05  WS-PAGE-NUMBER            PIC 99 VALUE 0.
87
88   01  WS-DATE-WORK-AREA.
89       05  TODAY-YEAR                PIC 99     VALUE ZEROS.
90       05  TODAY-MONTH               PIC 99     VALUE ZEROS.
91       05  TODAY-DAY                 PIC 99     VALUE ZEROS.
92
93   01  WS-CALCULATION-REGISTERS.
94       05  WS-AMT-SOLD               PIC 9(7)V99  VALUE ZEROS.
95       05  WS-COMMISS-RATE           PIC 99       VALUE ZEROS.
96       05  WS-COMMISSION             PIC 9(9)V99  VALUE ZEROS.
97       05  WS-TOTAL-COMMISSIONS      PIC 9(11)V99 VALUE ZEROS.
98       05  WS-TOTAL-SALES            PIC 9(11)V99 VALUE ZEROS.
99
100  01  WS-TITLE-LINE.
101      05  FILLER                    PIC X(29)    VALUE SPACES.
102      05  FILLER                    PIC X(38)    VALUE
                     "PSYCHO PRODUCTS QUARTERLY SALES REPORT".
103      05  FILLER                    PIC X(65)    VALUE SPACES.
104
105  01  WS-DATE-LINE.
106      05  FILLER                    PIC X(44)    VALUE SPACES.
107      05  DATE-OUT.
108          10 MONTH-OUT              PIC Z9       VALUE ZEROS.
109          10 FILLER                 PIC X        VALUE "/".
110          10 DAY-OUT                PIC Z9       VALUE ZEROS.
111          10 FILLER                 PIC X        VALUE "/".
112          10 YEAR-OUT               PIC 99       VALUE ZEROS.
113      05  FILLER                    PIC X(80)    VALUE SPACES.
114
115  01  WS-HEADING-LINE-FILLER.
116      05  FILLER                    PIC X(96)    VALUE ALL "&".
117      05  FILLER                    PIC X(36)    VALUE SPACES.
118
119  01  WS-HEADING-LINE-ONE.
120      05  FILLER                    PIC X(4)     VALUE "REG ".
121      05  FILLER                    PIC X(3)     VALUE "BR ".
122      05  FILLER                    PIC X(5)     VALUE "SMAN ".
```

```
123        05  FILLER                    PIC X(8)     VALUE "PRODUCT ".
124        05  FILLER                    PIC X(6)     VALUE " QTY  ".
125        05  FILLER                    PIC X(6)     VALUE "PRICE ".
126        05  FILLER                    PIC X(7)     VALUE " RATE   ".
127        05  FILLER                    PIC X(12)    VALUE "   AMOUNT      ".
128        05  FILLER                    PIC X(12)    VALUE "  COMMISSION".
129        05  FILLER                    PIC X(14)    VALUE " SALESPERSON  ".
130        05  FILLER                    PIC X(10)    VALUE SPACES.
131        05  FILLER                    PIC X(5)     VALUE "PAGE ".
132        05  PAGE-NUMBER-OUT           PIC ZZZ9     VALUE ZEROS.
133        05  FILLER                    PIC X(36)    VALUE SPACES.
134
135    01  WS-HEADING-LINE-TWO.
136        05  FILLER                    PIC X(4)     VALUE "NO. ".
137        05  FILLER                    PIC X(3)     VALUE "NO.".
138        05  FILLER                    PIC X(5)     VALUE " NO. ".
139        05  FILLER                    PIC X(8)     VALUE "  NO.    ".
140        05  FILLER                    PIC X(19)    VALUE SPACES.
141        05  FILLER                    PIC X(10)    VALUE "   SOLD  ".
142        05  FILLER                    PIC X(83)    VALUE SPACES.
143
144    01  WS-DATA-LINE.
145        05  REGION-OUT                PIC XX.
146        05  FILLER                    PIC XX  VALUE SPACES.
147        05  BRANCH-OUT                PIC XX.
148        05  FILLER                    PIC XX  VALUE SPACES.
149        05  SMAN-NUMBER-OUT           PIC XX.
150        05  FILLER                    PIC XX  VALUE SPACES.
151        05  PROD-NUMBER-OUT           PIC X(6).
152        05  FILLER                    PIC XX  VALUE SPACES.
153        05  QUANTITY-OUT              PIC ZZZ9.
154        05  FILLER                    PIC X  VALUE SPACES.
155        05  PRICE-OUT                 PIC $$$9.99.
156        05  FILLER                    PIC X  VALUE SPACES.
157        05  COMMISS-RATE-OUT          PIC Z9.
158        05  PERCENT-SIGN              PIC X  VALUE "%".
159        05  FILLER                    PIC X  VALUE SPACES.
160        05  AMT-SOLD-OUT              PIC $$,$$$,$$9.99.
161        05  FILLER                    PIC X  VALUE SPACES.
162        05  COMMISSION-OUT            PIC $$,$$$,$$9.99.
163        05  FILLER                    PIC X  VALUE SPACES.
164        05  SMAN-NAME-OUT             PIC X(20).
165        05  FILLER                    PIC X(20).
166
16     01  WS-TOTAL-LINE.
168        05  FILLER                    PIC X(16)   VALUE "FINAL TOTALS:   ".
169        05  TOTAL-SALES-OUT           PIC $$$$,$$$,$$$,$$9.99  VALUE ZEROS.
170        05  FILLER                    PIC X(10)   VALUE " SALES,  ".
171        05  TOTAL-COMMISSIONS-OUT     PIC $$$,$$$,$$$,$$9.99 VALUE ZEROS.
172        05  FILLER                    PIC X(13)   VALUE "  COMMISSIONS".
173        05  FILLER               PIC X(56)   VALUE " FOR PSYCHO PRODUCTS".
174
175    01  WS-UNDERLINE.
176        05  FILLER                    PIC X(132)  VALUE "*************".
177
178    PROCEDURE DIVISION.
179
180    000-MAINLINE.
181        PERFORM 100-INITIALIZATION THRU 100-EXIT.
182        PERFORM 200-HEADING-ROUTINE THRU 200-EXIT.
183        PERFORM 400-READ-IN-FILE THRU 400-EXIT.
```

```
184          PERFORM 300-MAIN-LOOP THRU 300-EXIT
185              UNTIL THERE-ARE-NO-MORE-RECORDS.
186          PERFORM 800-FINAL-TOTAL THRU 800-EXIT.
187
188      100-INITIALIZATION.
189          OPEN INPUT  IN-FILE
190              OUTPUT OUT-FILE.
191          ACCEPT WS-DATE-WORK-AREA FROM DATE.
192              MOVE TODAY-MONTH TO MONTH-OUT.
193              MOVE TODAY-DAY   TO   DAY-OUT.
194              MOVE TODAY-YEAR  TO  YEAR-OUT.
195      100-EXIT.
196          EXIT.
197
198      200-HEADING-ROUTINE.
199          ADD 1 TO WS-PAGE-NUMBER.
200          MOVE WS-PAGE-NUMBER TO PAGE-NUMBER-OUT.
201          WRITE OUT-REC FROM WS-TITLE-LINE AFTER PAGE.
202          WRITE OUT-REC FROM WS-DATE-LINE AFTER 1.
203          WRITE OUT-REC FROM WS-HEADING-LINE-FILLER AFTER 2.
204          WRITE OUT-REC FROM WS-HEADING-LINE-ONE AFTER 1.
205          WRITE OUT-REC FROM WS-HEADING-LINE-TWO AFTER 1.
206          WRITE OUT-REC FROM WS-HEADING-LINE-FILLER AFTER 1.
207          MOVE 6 TO WS-LINE-COUNT.
208      200-EXIT.
209          EXIT.
210
211      300-MAIN-LOOP.
212          IF WS-LINE-COUNT > 54
213              PERFORM 200-HEADING-ROUTINE THRU 200-EXIT.
214
215              IF COMMISSION-RATE-CODE-A
216                  MOVE 05 TO WS-COMMISS-RATE
217              ELSE IF COMMISSION-RATE-CODE-B
218                      MOVE 07 TO WS-COMMISS-RATE
219                  ELSE MOVE 10 TO WS-COMMISS-RATE.
220
221          COMPUTE WS-AMT-SOLD = QUANTITY-IN * PRICE-IN.
222          COMPUTE WS-COMMISSION ROUNDED =
                          WS-AMT-SOLD * WS-COMMISS-RATE / 100.
223          ADD WS-COMMISSION TO WS-TOTAL-COMMISSIONS
224            ON SIZE ERROR DISPLAY "COMMISSION TOTAL FIELD TOO SMALL".
225          ADD WS-AMT-SOLD TO WS-TOTAL-SALES
226            ON SIZE ERROR DISPLAY "TOTAL COMPANY SALES FIELD TOO SMALL".
227
228          MOVE REGION-IN TO REGION-OUT.
229          MOVE BRANCH-IN TO BRANCH-OUT.
230          MOVE SMAN-NUMBER-IN TO SMAN-NUMBER-OUT.
231          MOVE PROD-NUMBER-IN   TO PROD-NUMBER-OUT.
232          MOVE QUANTITY-IN      TO QUANTITY-OUT.
233          MOVE PRICE-IN         TO PRICE-OUT.
234          MOVE WS-COMMISS-RATE  TO COMMISS-RATE-OUT.
235          MOVE WS-AMT-SOLD      TO AMT-SOLD-OUT.
236          MOVE WS-COMMISSION    TO COMMISSION-OUT.
237          MOVE SMAN-NAME-IN TO SMAN-NAME-OUT.
238
239          WRITE OUT-REC FROM WS-DATA-LINE  AFTER 1.
240          ADD 1 TO WS-LINE-COUNT.
241          PERFORM 400-READ-IN-FILE THRU 400-EXIT.
```

```
242    300-EXIT.
243        EXIT.
244
245    400-READ-IN-FILE.
246        READ IN-FILE
247            AT END MOVE "YES" TO FINISHED.
248    400-EXIT.
249        EXIT.
250
251    800-FINAL-TOTAL.
252        MOVE WS-TOTAL-COMMISSIONS TO TOTAL-COMMISSIONS-OUT.
253        MOVE WS-TOTAL-SALES TO TOTAL-SALES-OUT.
254
255        WRITE OUT-REC FROM WS-TOTAL-LINE AFTER 5.
256        WRITE OUT-REC FROM WS-UNDERLINE.
257
258        CLOSE IN-FILE OUT-FILE.
259        STOP RUN.
260    800-EXIT.
261        EXIT.
262
```

Before we proceed with any enhancements to the above program notice the following:

a. Blank lines are permitted—they are used for clarification purposes.

b. Some documentation appears in the Identification Division.

c. 05 level numbers were used instead of 02.

The following, additional COBOL syntax was used:

a. INSTALLATION.

b. DATE-WRITTEN.

c. CONFIGURATION SECTION.

d. PERFORM . . . . THRU

e. ACCEPT

f. ON SIZE ERROR

g. ROUNDED

INSTALLATION and DATE-WRITTEN are optional paragraphs one can use in the Identification Division. CONFIGURATION SECTION is another section in the Environment Division and, if used, must precede the INPUT-OUTPUT SECTION. It details which processor is being used to compile the source program and which processor is being used to execute the object (machine language) program—usually the same one.

```
010413 3282040300A 02000SMYTH J.
010413 5918230010B 15000SMYTH J.
010423 2918231000A 00500COLBY S.
010423 3910280400C 01000COLBY S.
010423 3917810003A 15000COLBY S.
010425 3948830020B 05000HOE A.
011114 9283230040B 06000JACKSON J.
011114 3728190100C 10000JACKSON J.
011114 9584920300B 02200JACKSON J.
140517 7653810015A 00341SAMUELS S.
140517 1284550100B 20381SAMUELS S.
140517 2222225666A 00022SAMUELS S.
140517 1212120003C 29317SAMUELS S.
140525 4477150581B 00450BABBAGE C.
140525 6189030021C 14683BABBAGE C.
140545 4442280956A 00351NORAD D.
140545 1186451111B 29190NORAD D.
140545 6371006716C 00123NORAD D.
140561 9501430004C 00011DEMKINS S.
140561 0000130381B 00234DEMKINS S.
140577 0371850031A 00032LEMONHEAD D.
145501 6529610378B 08312BIRDIE B.
145501 4085000371C 00173BIRDIE B.
145501 3017402874A 10892BIRDIE B.
145537 5555550028B 02398TAMERLIN T.
145537 4329019999A 99999TAMERLIN T.
145545 2139750012C 00827TUT K.
145545 3901270871B 00013TUT K.
145545 8839170005C 03821TUT K.
148715 6730170987B 11173DEETLE D.
148715 3333360771A 00153DEETLE D.
148715 2283611738B 00024DEETLE D.
148731 3927440831A 02871TANNY V.
148731 3975811183B 00037TANNY V.
148731 7771110031A 00002TANNY V.
148759 6620980002C 88754WILKE T.
148759 2215930038C 74861WILKE T.
148763 0028420204A 00023DURAN D.
148763 8937620014B 03851DURAN D.
148763 3829485612A 00183DURAN D.
662018 8290000381B 00012DUWOP D.
662018 3829001821C 02845DUWOP D.
662027 5647630284B 00284CARNIGIE D.
662027 7690239999A 99934CARNIGIE D.
662027 5629409999B 99274CARNIGIE D.
662027 8267319999C 99927CARNIGIE D.
663705 7372890012A 00012PEABRAIN D.
663705 7294870000C 00002PEABRAIN D.
663718 5438230283A 03872DAPPER V.
663718 7802630028B 00012DAPPER V.
663718 8888880274C 93721DAPPER V.
663718 3645310026A 07382DAPPER V.
663729 9274830123B 00028GRAUER R.
663729 8282190057C 02847GRAUER R.
663751 7382150382B 93721LULU P.
669737 8927370012A 08274TRIPP U.
669737 3673018392C 00012TRIPP U.
669737 2287013284B 01274TRIPP U.
669743 2946520035B 00274WHIZ G.
669743 0037210003C 23472WHIZ G.
669775 0002340028A 00264BUMBLE B.
669775 9375830372C 00027BUMBLE B.
669775 3756410038A 75643BUMBLE B.
669775 8787679372C 98676BUMBLE B.
669781 6453649898A 00274LATER C. U.
669781 3746320387B 07823LATER C. U.
```

Figure 9–3

&&&&&&&&&&&&&&&&&&&&&&&&&&&&&&&&&&&&&&&&&&&&&&&&&&&&&&&&&&&&&&&&&&&&&&&&&&&&&&&&&&&&&&&&&&&&&&&

REG NO.	BR NO.	SMAN NO.	PRODUCT NO.	QTY	PRICE	RATE	AMOUNT SOLD	COMMISSION	SALESPERSON	PAGE 1

&&&&&&&&&&&&&&&&&&&&&&&&&&&&&&&&&&&&&&&&&&&&&&&&&&&&&&&&&&&&&&&&&&&&&&&&&&&&&&&&&&&&&&&&&&&&&&&

REG NO.	BR NO.	SMAN NO.	PRODUCT NO.	QTY	PRICE	RATE	AMOUNT SOLD	COMMISSION	SALESPERSON
01	04	13	328204	300	$20.00	5%	$6,000.00	$300.00	SMYTH J.
01	04	13	591823	10	$150.00	7%	$1,500.00	$105.00	SMYTH J.
01	04	23	291823	1000	$5.00	5%	$5,000.00	$250.00	COLBY S.
01	04	23	391028	400	$10.00	10%	$4,000.00	$400.00	COLBY S.
01	04	23	391781	3	$150.00	5%	$450.00	$22.50	COLBY S.
01	04	25	394883	20	$50.00	7%	$1,000.00	$70.00	HOE A.
01	11	14	928323	40	$60.00	7%	$2,400.00	$168.00	JACKSON J.
01	11	14	372819	100	$100.00	10%	$10,000.00	$1,000.00	JACKSON J.
01	11	14	958492	300	$22.00	7%	$6,600.00	$462.00	JACKSON J.
14	05	17	765381	15	$3.41	5%	$51.15	$2.56	SAMUELS S.
14	05	17	128455	100	$203.81	7%	$20,381.00	$1,426.67	SAMUELS S.
14	05	17	222222	5666	$0.22	5%	$1,246.52	$62.33	SAMUELS S.
14	05	17	121212	3	$293.17	10%	$879.51	$87.95	SAMUELS S.
14	05	25	447715	581	$4.50	7%	$2,614.50	$183.02	BABBAGE C.
14	05	25	618903	21	$146.83	10%	$3,083.43	$308.34	BABBAGE C.
14	05	45	444228	956	$3.51	5%	$3,355.56	$167.78	NORAD D.
14	05	45	118645	1111	$291.90	7%	$324,300.90	$22,701.06	NORAD D.
14	05	45	637100	6716	$1.23	10%	$8,260.68	$826.07	NORAD D.
14	05	61	950143	4	$0.11	10%	$0.44	$0.04	DEMKINS S.
14	05	61	000013	381	$2.34	7%	$891.54	$62.41	DEMKINS S.
14	05	77	037185	31	$0.32	5%	$9.92	$0.50	LEMONHEAD D.
14	55	01	652961	378	$83.12	7%	$31,419.36	$2,199.36	BIRDIE B.
14	55	01	408500	371	$1.73	10%	$641.83	$64.18	BIRDIE B.
14	55	01	301740	2874	$108.92	5%	$313,036.08	$15,651.80	BIRDIE B.
14	55	37	555555	28	$23.98	7%	$671.44	$47.00	TAMERLIN T.
14	55	37	432901	9999	$999.99	5%	$9,998,900.01	$499,945.00	TAMERLIN T.
14	55	45	213975	12	$8.27	10%	$99.24	$9.92	TUT K.
14	55	45	390127	871	$0.13	7%	$113.23	$7.93	TUT K.
14	55	45	883917	5	$38.21	10%	$191.05	$19.11	TUT K.
14	87	15	673017	987	$111.73	7%	$110,277.51	$7,719.43	DEETLE D.
14	87	15	333336	771	$1.53	5%	$1,179.63	$58.98	DEETLE D.
14	87	15	228361	1738	$0.24	7%	$417.12	$29.20	DEETLE D.
14	87	31	392744	831	$28.71	5%	$23,858.01	$1,192.90	TANNY V.
14	87	31	397581	1183	$0.37	7%	$437.71	$30.64	TANNY V.
14	87	31	777111	31	$0.02	5%	$0.62	$0.03	TANNY V.
14	87	59	662098	2	$887.54	10%	$1,775.08	$177.51	WILKE T.
14	87	59	221593	38	$748.61	10%	$28,447.18	$2,844.72	WILKE T.
14	87	63	002842	204	$0.23	5%	$46.92	$2.35	DURAN D.
14	87	63	893762	14	$38.51	7%	$539.14	$37.74	DURAN D.
14	87	63	382948	5612	$1.83	5%	$10,269.96	$513.50	DURAN D.
66	20	18	829000	381	$0.12	7%	$45.72	$3.20	DUWOP D.
66	20	18	382900	1821	$28.45	10%	$51,807.45	$5,180.75	DUWOP D.
66	20	27	564763	284	$2.84	7%	$806.56	$56.46	CARNIGIE D.
66	20	27	769023	9999	$999.34	5%	$9,992,400.66	$499,620.03	CARNIGIE D.
66	20	27	562940	9999	$992.74	7%	$9,926,407.26	$694,848.51	CARNIGIE D.
66	20	27	826731	9999	$999.27	10%	$9,991,700.73	$999,170.07	CARNIGIE D.
66	37	05	737289	12	$0.12	5%	$1.44	$0.07	PEABRAIN D.
66	37	05	729487	0	$0.02	10%	$0.00	$0.00	PEABRAIN D.
66	37	18	543823	283	$38.72	5%	$10,957.76	$547.89	DAPPER V.

Figure 9–4

PSYCHO PRODUCTS QUARTERLY SALES REPORT
10/14/84

| REG BR SMAN PRODUCT | QTY | PRICE | RATE | AMOUNT | COMMISSION SALESPERSON | PAGE 2 |

REG NO.	BR NO.	SMAN NO.	PRODUCT NO.	QTY	PRICE	RATE	AMOUNT SOLD	COMMISSION	SALESPERSON
66	37	18	780263	28	$0.12	7%	$3.36	$0.24	DAPPER V.
66	37	18	888888	274	$937.21	10%	$256,795.54	$25,679.55	DAPPER V.
66	37	18	364531	26	$73.82	5%	$1,919.32	$95.97	DAPPER V.
66	37	29	927483	123	$0.28	7%	$34.44	$2.41	GRAUER R.
66	37	29	828219	57	$28.47	10%	$1,622.79	$162.28	GRAUER R.
66	37	51	738215	382	$937.21	7%	$358,014.22	$25,061.00	LULU P.
66	97	37	892737	12	$82.74	5%	$992.88	$49.64	TRIPP U.
66	97	37	367301	8392	$0.12	10%	$1,007.04	$100.70	TRIPP U.
66	97	37	228701	3284	$12.74	7%	$41,838.16	$2,928.67	TRIPP U.
66	97	43	294652	35	$2.74	7%	$95.90	$6.71	WHIZ G.
66	97	43	003721	3	$234.72	10%	$704.16	$70.42	WHIZ G.
66	97	75	000234	28	$2.64	5%	$73.92	$3.70	BUMBLE B.
66	97	75	937583	372	$0.27	10%	$100.44	$10.04	BUMBLE B.
66	97	75	375641	38	$756.43	5%	$28,744.34	$1,437.22	BUMBLE B.
66	97	75	878767	9372	$986.76	10%	$9,247,914.72	$924,791.47	BUMBLE B.
66	97	81	645364	9898	$2.74	5%	$27,120.52	$1,356.03	LATER C. U.
66	97	81	374632	387	$78.23	7%	$30,275.01	$2,119.25	LATER C. U.

FINAL TOTALS: $50,895,730.61 SALES, $3,742,459.81 COMMISSIONS FOR PSYCHO PRODUCTS
****

Figure 9-4   (*continued*)

9.3 ADDITIONAL PROCEDURE DIVISION OPTIONS

Examine line 181 of the above program. One could have substituted:

PERFORM 100-INITIALIZATION.

in place of:

PERFORM 100-INITIALIZATION THRU 100-EXIT.

and have gotten the same results. Some say the latter gives a clearer picture of the range of the PERFORM statement; however, an additional paragraph with only the EXIT statement is required (some IBM compilers occasionally give a warning or information error stating "exit from performed procedure assumed" if the THRU option is not used). The general form can be found, of course, in Appendix D.

If one wants to perform more than one paragraph by using only one PERFORM statement, then the THRU option must be used. Consider:

                    PERFORM PAR-A THRU PAR-B-END.
                        .
                        .
                        .
        PAR-A.
                statement 1
                statement 2
                statement 3
                statement 4
        PAR-B.
                statement 5
                statement 6
        PAR-B-END.
                EXIT.

With one PERFORM, statements 1–6 are executed before control is passed back to the next statement following the PERFORM. Of course, one could have used:

                    PERFORM PAR-A.
                    PERFORM PAR-B.

to accomplish the same thing!!

The ACCEPT verb allows one to get information without having to "read" an entire record. The general form is as follows:

ACCEPT data-name FROM mnemonic-name [AT END declarative
                            statement(s)]

If the mnemonic name is not used, the system expects a field of information to be entered via the terminal. This will be used extensively in the chapter dealing with on-line updates of files. In line 191 of the above program the DATE (a six-digit numeric field in the form yymmdd) is put into WS-WORK-DATE. In this way the system can give us two digits for the year, followed by two for the month, followed by two for the day. If DAY were specified as the mnemonic name, one would get a five-digit field; the first two digits being the year and the last three the day of the year, numbered from 1 to 366. July 4, 1983, would be 83184, but July 4, 1984, would be 83185 (leap year). Finally, TIME returns an eight-digit numeric field. 9:30 AM is represented by 09300000 (the last four represent seconds and hundreths of seconds). 11:44 PM is represented by 23440000. One must make sure that the identifier receiving this information is large enough!!

The ON SIZE ERROR option can be used in arithmetic statements if one wants to know if the result of an arithmetic operation was too large for the receiving field. If it is not used, then truncation will occur without any error message. Suppose a salesman had a good month. He sold 100 items each with a price of $90. His commission rate, let's say, is 12%. What would his commission be if:

COMMISSION-RATE	PIC V99
QUANTITY-SOLD	PIC 999
PRICE-ITEM	PIC 999V99

SALESMAN-COMMISSION-AMOUNT	PIC $$$$.99

and the following statement were used:

> COMPUTE SALESMAN-COMMISSION-AMOUNT =
> QUANTITY-SOLD * PRICE-ITEM * COMMISSION-RATE.

The poor salesman would get $80.00 instead of $1080.00. The picture clause for SALESMAN-COMMISSION-AMOUNT is too small—it needs at least one more dollar sign!! The programmer should have used (or the angry salesman will tell him):

COMPUTE SALESMAN-COMISSION-AMOUNT =
QUANTITY-SOLD * PRICE-ITEM * COMMISSION-RATE
ON SIZE ERROR DISPLAY "FIX PAYROLL FOR " SALESMAN-IN.

The Rounded option is necessary in decimal multiplication or division. Consider:

AFIELD	PIC 9V99
BFIELD	PIC 9V99
CFIELD	PIC Z9.99

where AFIELD contains 1.27 and BFIELD contains 4.51. If one uses:

> COMPUTE CFIELD = AFIELD * BFIELD.

or:

> MULTIPLY AFIELD BY BFIELD GIVING CFIELD.

C-FIELD will contain 5.72 (internal 5.7277 truncated to 5.72). However if one uses:

> COMPUTE CFIELD ROUNDED = AFIELD * BFIELD.

or:

MULTIPLY AFIELD BY BFIELD GIVING CFIELD ROUNDED.

then CFIELD will contain 5.73.

9.4   A SINGLE CONTROL BREAK

The main intent of this chapter is to show how you can "add-on" to a program. In keeping with the philosophy of incremental design, code, and testing, one control break will be shown first—the salesman subtotal control break. The input data has all salesman numbers in ascending order. Subtotals showing total commissions for each salesman should be written to OUTLOOK.DAT every time there is a change in salesman number.

Examine the modified design and additional pseudocode [Figure 9–5]:

An additional module has been added below the "main loop" paragraph. This will require an additional nested PERFORM statement. Examine the related pseudocode to see if it fulfills the requirements of providing subtotals for salesman commission. What follows is the previous program with the additional module added, and the output data (from OUTLOOK.DAT) are located on Figure 9–6. As before, any additional code is in lower case:

```
 1      IDENTIFICATION DIVISION.
 2      PROGRAM-ID.           FIFTH.
 3      AUTHOR.               STEVE SAMUELS.
 4      INSTALLATION.         DEPAUL UNIVERSITY.
 5      DATE-WRITTEN.         10/3/83.
 6
 7      ************************************************************
 8      *****      INPUT:  THE INPUT TO THIS PROGRAM IS A FILE CALLED
 9      *****              "FIVE.DAT".  EACH RECORD IN
10      *****              THIS FILE CONSISTS OF ONE SALE AND INCLUDES
11      *****              REGION NUMBER, BRANCH NUMBER, SALESMAN
12      *****              NUMBER, PRODUCT NUMBER, QUANTITY, TYPE,
13      *****              PRICE AND SALESMAN NAME.  ALL THE RECORDS
14      *****              ARE SORTED BY SALESMAN NUMBER WITHIN BRANCH
15      *****              NUMBER WITHIN REGION NUMBER.
16      ************************************************************
17
18      ************************************************************
19      *****      OUTPUT:  THE OUTPUT FROM THIS PROGRAM CONSISTS OF
20      *****              A PRINTED REPORT WITH HEADING LINES CON-
21      *****              TAINING EDITED FIELDS FOR REGION NUMBER,
22      *****              BRANCH NUMBER, SALESMAN NUMBER, PRODUCT
23      *****              NUMBER, QUANTITY, PRICE, COMMISSION RATE,
24      *****              AMOUNT SOLD, COMMISSION AND SALESMAN NAME
25      *****              FOR EACH RECORD PROCESSED AS WELL AS
26      *****              subtotals for salesman total commission and
27      *****              final totals for amount sold and commissions.
28      ************************************************************
29
30      ************************************************************
31      *****      PROCESSING:  THE PROCESSING REQUIRED TO PREPARE
32      *****              THE REPORT CONSISTS OF READING AN INPUT
```

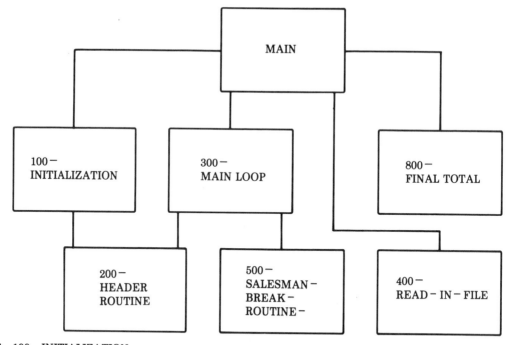

1. 100 — INITIALIZATION
   a. Open
   b. Get data record
   c. Transfer control to
      header routine

2. 200 — HEADER ROUTINE
   a. Header for report

3. 300 — MAIN – LOOP
   a. Check line count
   * b. Compare for salesman break
   c. Get commission
   * d. Calculations – include for salesman total
   e. Moves
   f. Write detail line
   g. Get data record

4. 400 — READ – IN FILE
   a. Read a record

* 5. 500 — SALESMAN – BREAK – ROUTINE
   a. Move temp – sales – total
   b. Write salesman line
   c. 0 out salesman total
   d. Move to compare area

6. 800 — FINAL – TOTAL
   a. Write totals
   b. Close
   c. Stop

Figure 9-5

```
33   *****        RECORD, FINDING THE CORRECT COMMISSION
34   *****        RATE, CALCULATING COMMISSION AND AMOUNT
35   *****        SOLD, MOVING EACH OF THE REQUIRED FIELDS
36   *****        FROM THE INPUT OR WORKING STORAGE AREA
37   *****        TO THE OUTPUT AREA, WRITING A REPORT LINE,
38   *****        AND ACCUMULATING FINAL TOTALS.
39   ***********************************************************
40
41   ENVIRONMENT DIVISION.
```

```
42
43        CONFIGURATION SECTION.
44
45        SOURCE-COMPUTER.      VAX-11-750.
46        OBJECT-COMPUTER.      VAX-11-750.
47
48        INPUT-OUTPUT SECTION.
49
50        FILE-CONTROL.
51            SELECT IN-FILE ASSIGN TO FIVE.
52            SELECT OUT-FILE ASSIGN TO OUTLOOK.
53
54        DATA DIVISION.
55
56        FILE SECTION.
57
58        FD  IN-FILE
59            DATA RECORD IS IN-REC.
60        01  IN-REC.
61            05  REGION-IN               PIC XX.
62            05  BRANCH-IN               PIC XX.
63            05  SMAN-NUMBER-IN          PIC XX.
64            05  FILLER                  PIC X.
65            05  PROD-NUMBER-IN          PIC X(6).
66            05  QUANTITY-IN             PIC 9(4).
67            05  COMMISSION-TYPE-IN      PIC X.
68                88 COMMISSION-RATE-CODE-A          VALUE "A".
69                88 COMMISSION-RATE-CODE-B          VALUE "B".
70                88 COMMISSION-RATE-CODE-C          VALUE "C".
71            05  FILLER                  PIC X.
72            05  PRICE-IN                PIC 999V99.
73            05  SMAN-NAME-IN            PIC X(20).
74
75        FD  OUT-FILE
76            DATA RECORD IS OUT-REC.
77        01  OUT-REC                     PIC X(132).
78
79
80
81        WORKING-STORAGE SECTION.
82
83        01  FINISHED                PIC XXX VALUE SPACES.
84            88 THERE-ARE-NO-MORE-RECORDS    VALUE "YES".
85            88 first-time                   value "on".
86        01  COUNTERS.
87            05  WS-LINE-COUNT           PIC 99 VALUE 0.
88            05  WS-PAGE-NUMBER          PIC 99 VALUE 0.
89
90        01  WS-DATE-WORK-AREA.
91            05  TODAY-YEAR              PIC 99      VALUE ZEROS.
92            05  TODAY-MONTH             PIC 99      VALUE ZEROS.
93            05  TODAY-DAY               PIC 99      VALUE ZEROS.
94
95        01  temp-sman-number           pic xx.
96        01  WS-CALCULATION-REGISTERS.
97            05  WS-AMT-SOLD             PIC 9(7)V99  VALUE ZEROS.
98            05  WS-COMMISS-RATE         PIC 99       VALUE ZEROS.
99            05  WS-COMMISSION           PIC 9(9)V99  VALUE ZEROS.
100           05  ws-sman-tot-commissions pic 9(10)v99 value zeros.
101           05  WS-TOTAL-COMMISSIONS    PIC 9(11)V99 VALUE ZEROS.
102           05  WS-TOTAL-SALES          PIC 9(11)V99 VALUE ZEROS.
```

```
103
104    01  WS-TITLE-LINE.
105        05  FILLER                    PIC X(29)     VALUE SPACES.
106        05  FILLER                    PIC X(38)     VALUE
                   "PSYCHO PRODUCTS QUARTERLY SALES REPORT".
107        05  FILLER                    PIC X(65)     VALUE SPACES.
108
109    01  WS-DATE-LINE.
110        05  FILLER                    PIC X(44)     VALUE SPACES.
111        05  DATE-OUT.
112            10  MONTH-OUT             PIC Z9        VALUE ZEROS.
113            10  FILLER                PIC X         VALUE "/".
114            10  DAY-OUT               PIC Z9        VALUE ZEROS.
115            10  FILLER                PIC X         VALUE "/".
116            10  YEAR-OUT              PIC 99        VALUE ZEROS.
117        05  FILLER                    PIC X(80)     VALUE SPACES.
118
119    01  WS-HEADING-LINE-FILLER.
120        05  FILLER                    PIC X(96)     VALUE ALL "&".
121        05  FILLER                    PIC X(36)     VALUE SPACES.
122
123    01  WS-HEADING-LINE-ONE.
124        05  FILLER                    PIC X(4)      VALUE "REG ".
125        05  FILLER                    PIC X(3)      VALUE "BR ".
126        05  FILLER                    PIC X(5)      VALUE "SMAN ".
127        05  FILLER                    PIC X(8)      VALUE "PRODUCT ".
128        05  FILLER                    PIC X(6)      VALUE " QTY  ".
129        05  FILLER                    PIC X(6)      VALUE " PRICE ".
130        05  FILLER                    PIC X(7)      VALUE " RATE  ".
131        05  FILLER                    PIC X(12)     VALUE "  AMOUNT    ".
132        05  FILLER                    PIC X(12)     VALUE "  COMMISSION".
133        05  FILLER                    PIC X(14)     VALUE " SALESPERSON  ".
134        05  FILLER                    PIC X(10)     VALUE SPACES.
135        05  FILLER                    PIC X(5)      VALUE "PAGE ".
136        05  PAGE-NUMBER-OUT           PIC ZZZ9      VALUE ZEROS.
137        05  FILLER                    PIC X(36)     VALUE SPACES.
138
139    01  WS-HEADING-LINE-TWO.
140        05  FILLER                    PIC X(4)      VALUE "NO. ".
141        05  FILLER                    PIC X(3)      VALUE "NO.".
142        05  FILLER                    PIC X(5)      VALUE " NO. ".
143        05  FILLER                    PIC X(8)      VALUE "  NO.   ".
144        05  FILLER                    PIC X(19)     VALUE SPACES.
145        05  FILLER                    PIC X(10)     VALUE "    SOLD  ".
146        05  FILLER                    PIC X(83)     VALUE SPACES.
147
148    01  WS-DATA-LINE.
149        05  REGION-OUT                PIC XX.
150        05  FILLER                    PIC XX  VALUE SPACES.
151        05  BRANCH-OUT                PIC XX.
152        05  FILLER                    PIC XX  VALUE SPACES.
153        05  SMAN-NUMBER-OUT           PIC XX.
154        05  FILLER                    PIC XX  VALUE SPACES.
155        05  PROD-NUMBER-OUT           PIC X(6).
156        05  FILLER                    PIC XX  VALUE SPACES.
157        05  QUANTITY-OUT              PIC ZZZ9.
158        05  FILLER                    PIC X  VALUE SPACES.
159        05  PRICE-OUT                 PIC $$$9.99.
160        05  FILLER                    PIC X  VALUE SPACES.
161        05  COMMISS-RATE-OUT          PIC Z9.
162        05  PERCENT-SIGN              PIC X  VALUE "%".
```

```
163        05  FILLER                     PIC X  VALUE SPACES.
164        05  AMT-SOLD-OUT               PIC $$,$$$,$$9.99.
165        05  FILLER                     PIC X  VALUE SPACES.
166        05  COMMISSION-OUT             PIC $$,$$$,$$9.99.
167        05  FILLER                     PIC X  VALUE SPACES.
168        05  SMAN-NAME-OUT              PIC X(20).
169        05  FILLER                      PIC X(20).
170    01  ws-smn-total-line.
171        05  filler                     pic x(10) value spaces.
172        05  filler                     pic x(22) value
173            "FOR SALESMAN NUMBER ".
174        05  sman-tot-num-out           pic xx.
175        05  filler                     pic x(1) value spaces.
176        05  filler                     pic x(25) value
177            " THE TOTAL COMMISSIONS = ".
178        05  sman-tot-comm-out          pic $$,$$$,$$$,$$$.99.
179
180    01  WS-TOTAL-LINE.
181        05  FILLER                     PIC X(16)   VALUE "FINAL TOTALS:   ".
182        05  TOTAL-SALES-OUT            PIC $$$$,$$$,$$$,$$9.99  VALUE ZEROS.
183        05  FILLER                     PIC X(10)   VALUE " SALES, ".
184        05  TOTAL-COMMISSIONS-OUT      PIC $$$,$$$,$$$,$$9.99 VALUE ZEROS.
185        05  FILLER                     PIC X(13)   VALUE " COMMISSIONS".
186        05  FILLER                  PIC X(56)   VALUE " FOR PSYCHO PRODUCTS".
187
188    01  WS-UNDERLINE.
189        05  FILLER                     PIC X(132)  VALUE "************".
190
191    PROCEDURE DIVISI
192
193    000-MAINLINE.
194        PERFORM 100-INITIALIZATION THRU 100-EXIT.
195        PERFORM 200-HEADING-ROUTINE THRU 200-EXIT.
196        PERFORM 400-READ-IN-FILE THRU 400-EXIT.
197        PERFORM 300-MAIN-LOOP THRU 300-EXIT
198            UNTIL THERE-ARE-NO-MORE-RECORDS.
199        PERFORM 800-FINAL-TOTAL THRU 800-EXIT.
200
201    100-INITIALIZATION.
202        OPEN INPUT  IN-FILE
203             OUTPUT OUT-FILE.
204        ACCEPT WS-DATE-WORK-AREA FROM DATE.
205            MOVE TODAY-MONTH TO MONTH-OUT.
206            MOVE TODAY-DAY   TO   DAY-OUT.
207            MOVE TODAY-YEAR  TO   YEAR-OUT.
208        Move "on" to finished.
209    100-EXIT.
210        EXIT.
211
212    200-HEADING-ROUTINE.
213        ADD 1 TO WS-PAGE-NUMBER.
214        MOVE WS-PAGE-NUMBER TO PAGE-NUMBER-OUT.
215        WRITE OUT-REC FROM WS-TITLE-LINE AFTER PAGE.
216        WRITE OUT-REC FROM WS-DATE-LINE AFTER 1.
217        WRITE OUT-REC FROM WS-HEADING-LINE-FILLER AFTER 2.
218        WRITE OUT-REC FROM WS-HEADING-LINE-ONE AFTER 1.
219        WRITE OUT-REC FROM WS-HEADING-LINE-TWO AFTER 1.
220        WRITE OUT-REC FROM WS-HEADING-LINE-FILLER AFTER 1.
221        MOVE 6 TO WS-LINE-COUNT.
222    200-EXIT.
223        EXIT.
```

```
224
225    300-MAIN-LOOP.
226        IF WS-LINE-COUNT > 54
227            PERFORM 200-HEADING-ROUTINE THRU 200-EXIT.
228
229        If first-time move spaces to finished.
230          If sman-number-in not = temp-sman-number
231            perform 500-salesman-break-routine thru 500-end.
232
233            IF COMMISSION-RATE-CODE-A
234                  MOVE 05 TO WS-COMMISS-RATE
235            ELSE IF COMMISSION-RATE-CODE-B
236                    MOVE 07 TO WS-COMMISS-RATE
237              ELSE MOVE 10 TO WS-COMMISS-RATE.
238
239        COMPUTE WS-AMT-SOLD = QUANTITY-IN * PRICE-IN.
240        COMPUTE WS-COMMISSION ROUNDED =
                  WS-AMT-SOLD * WS-COMMISS-RATE / 100.
241        ADD WS-COMMISSION TO WS-TOTAL-COMMISSIONS
242                           ws-sman-tot-commissions
243          ON SIZE ERROR DISPLAY "COMMISSION TOTAL FIELD TOO SMALL".
244        ADD WS-AMT-SOLD TO WS-TOTAL-SALES
245          ON SIZE ERROR DISPLAY "TOTAL COMPANY SALES FIELD TOO SMALL".
246
247        MOVE REGION-IN TO REGION-OUT.
248        MOVE BRANCH-IN TO BRANCH-OUT.
249        MOVE SMAN-NUMBER-IN TO SMAN-NUMBER-OUT.
250        MOVE PROD-NUMBER-IN   TO PROD-NUMBER-OUT.
251        MOVE QUANTITY-IN      TO QUANTITY-OUT.
252        MOVE PRICE-IN         TO PRICE-OUT.
253        MOVE WS-COMMISS-RATE   TO COMMISS-RATE-OUT.
254        MOVE WS-AMT-SOLD       TO AMT-SOLD-OUT.
255        MOVE WS-COMMISSION     TO COMMISSION-OUT.
256        MOVE SMAN-NAME-IN TO SMAN-NAME-OUT.
257        WRITE OUT-REC FROM WS-DATA-LINE  AFTER 1.
258        ADD 1 TO WS-LINE-COUNT.
259        PERFORM 400-READ-IN-FILE THRU 400-EXIT.
260        If there-are-no-more-records
261            perform 500-salesman-break-routine.
262    300-EXIT.
263        EXIT.
264
265    400-READ-IN-FILE.
266        READ IN-FILE
267            AT END MOVE "YES" TO FINISHED.
268        If first-time move sman-number-in to temp-sman-number.
269    400-EXIT.
270        EXIT.
271
272    500-salesman-break-routine.
273        move ws-sman-tot-commissions to sman-tot-comm-out.
274        move temp-sman-number to sman-tot-num-out.
275        write out-rec from ws-sman-total-line after 2.
276        move spaces to out-rec.
277        write out-rec after 2.
278        add 4 to ws-line-count.
279        move 0 to ws-sman-tot-commissions.
280        move sman-number-in to temp-sman-number.
281    500-end.
282        exit.
283    800-FINAL-TOTAL.
284        MOVE WS-TOTAL-COMMISSIONS TO TOTAL-COMMISSIONS-OUT.
```

```
285          MOVE WS-TOTAL-SALES TO TOTAL-SALES-OUT.
286
287          WRITE OUT-REC FROM WS-TOTAL-LINE AFTER 5.
288          WRITE OUT-REC FROM WS-UNDERLINE.
289
290          CLOSE IN-FILE OUT-FILE.
291          STOP RUN.
292      800-EXIT.
293          EXIT.
294
```

As you can see, the salesman subtotals were produced successfully. The beauty of the modular design approach is that, in many cases such as this, additional code can be added WITHOUT CHANGING ANY PREVIOUS CODE WHATSOEVER!!

The most important additions were:

a. Lines 26–27: Extra addition to documentation. This is very important.

b. Line 95: A temporary salesman number area used for comparison to the next number read in.

c. Line 100: A temporary area for total salesman commissions.

d. Lines 170–178: The formatted salesman total line.

e. Lines 230–231: The comparison is made. If the new number is not equal to the existing number the new module is performed.

f. Line 242: Logic provided to add each sales commission to a total salesman commission.

g. Lines 272–282: The logic for producing the salesman subtotal line.

The above information was added to the program with the intent of producing that nice report with subtotals for salesman commissions. Additional "patchwork" code was added:

Lines 85, 208, 229, and 268 were added to avoid a control break before the first record was processed. Take these lines out and the first entry of the report was as follows:

FOR SALESMAN NUMBER 0 THE TOTAL COMMISSION = $0.00

If lines 260–261 were not added, the last subtotal would never be produced.

The term "patchwork" coding implies adding a line here and there to produce desired results. One tries to avoid this kind of coding; however, few COBOL programs have been written without it. This type of coding is, at least, minimized if the algorithm is well thought out, modules are carefully added, related pseudocode makes sense, and the majority of code adheres to structured principles.

PSYCHO PRODUCTS QUARTERLY SALES REPORT
10/14/84

&&&&&&&&&&&&&&&&&&&&&&&&&&&&&&&&&&&&&&&&&&&&&&&&&&&&&&&&&&&&&&&&&&&&&&&&&&&&&&&&&&&&&&&&&&&&&&&&&

```
REG BR SMAN PRODUCT   QTY   PRICE   RATE    AMOUNT      COMMISSION SALESPERSON              PAGE   1
NO. NO. NO.   NO.                            SOLD
```
&&&&&&&&&&&&&&&&&&&&&&&&&&&&&&&&&&&&&&&&&&&&&&&&&&&&&&&&&&&&&&&&&&&&&&&&&&&&&&&&&&&&&&&&&&&&&&&&&
```
01  04  13  328204    300  $20.00   5%    $6,000.00        $300.00 SMYTH J.
01  04  13  591823     10 $150.00   7%    $1,500.00        $105.00 SMYTH J.

            FOR SALESMAN NUMBER   13  THE TOTAL COMMISSIONS =        $405.00


01  04  23  291823   1000   $5.00   5%    $5,000.00        $250.00 COLBY S.
01  04  23  391028    400  $10.00  10%    $4,000.00        $400.00 COLBY S.
01  04  23  391781      3 $150.00   5%      $450.00         $22.50 COLBY S.

            FOR SALESMAN NUMBER   23  THE TOTAL COMMISSIONS =        $672.50


01  04  25  394883     20  $50.00   7%    $1,000.00         $70.00 HOE A.

            FOR SALESMAN NUMBER   25  THE TOTAL COMMISSIONS =         $70.00


01  11  14  928323     40  $60.00   7%    $2,400.00        $168.00 JACKSON J.
01  11  14  372819    100 $100.00  10%   $10,000.00      $1,000.00 JACKSON J.
01  11  14  958492    300  $22.00   7%    $6,600.00        $462.00 JACKSON J.

            FOR SALESMAN NUMBER   14  THE TOTAL COMMISSIONS =      $1,630.00


14  05  17  765381     15   $3.41   5%       $51.15          $2.56 SAMUELS S.
14  05  17  128455    100 $203.81   7%   $20,381.00      $1,426.67 SAMUELS S.
14  05  17  222222   5666   $0.22   5%    $1,246.52         $62.33 SAMUELS S.
14  05  17  121212      3 $293.17  10%      $879.51         $87.95 SAMUELS S.

            FOR SALESMAN NUMBER   17  THE TOTAL COMMISSIONS =      $1,579.51


14  05  25  447715    581   $4.50   7%    $2,614.50        $183.02 BABBAGE C.
14  05  25  618903     21 $146.83  10%    $3,083.43        $308.34 BABBAGE C.

            FOR SALESMAN NUMBER   25  THE TOTAL COMMISSIONS =        $491.36


14  05  45  444228    956   $3.51   5%    $3,355.56        $167.78 NORAD D.
14  05  45  118645   1111 $291.90   7%  $324,300.90     $22,701.06 NORAD D.
14  05  45  637100   6716   $1.23  10%    $8,260.68        $826.07 NORAD D.

            FOR SALESMAN NUMBER   45  THE TOTAL COMMISSIONS =     $23,694.91


14  05  61  950143      4   $0.11  10%        $0.44          $0.04 DEMKINS S.
14  05  61  000013    381   $2.34   7%      $891.54         $62.41 DEMKINS S.

            FOR SALESMAN NUMBER   61  THE TOTAL COMMISSIONS =         $62.45


14  05  77  037185     31   $0.32   5%        $9.92          $0.50 LEMONHEAD D.
```

Figure 9-6

&&&&&&&&&&&&&&&&&&&&&&&&&&&&&&&&&&&&&&&&&&&&&&&&&&&&&&&&&&&&&&&&&&&&&&&&&&&&&&&&&&&&&&&&&&&&&&&&&&

| REG BR SMAN PRODUCT | QTY | PRICE | RATE | AMOUNT | COMMISSION SALESPERSON | PAGE 2 |
| NO. NO. NO. NO. | | | | SOLD | | |

&&&&&&&&&&&&&&&&&&&&&&&&&&&&&&&&&&&&&&&&&&&&&&&&&&&&&&&&&&&&&&&&&&&&&&&&&&&&&&&&&&&&&&&&&&&&&&&&&&

```
                FOR SALESMAN NUMBER   77  THE TOTAL COMMISSIONS =          $.50


14  55  01  652961    378 $83.12  7%    $31,419.36    $2,199.36 BIRDIE B.
14  55  01  408500    371  $1.73 10%       $641.83       $64.18 BIRDIE B.
14  55  01  301740   2874 $108.92  5%   $313,036.08   $15,651.80 BIRDIE B.

                FOR SALESMAN NUMBER   01  THE TOTAL COMMISSIONS =     $17,915.34

14  55  37  555555     28 $23.98  7%       $671.44       $47.00 TAMERLIN T.
14  55  37  432901   9999 $999.99  5% $9,998,900.01  $499,945.00 TAMERLIN T.

                FOR SALESMAN NUMBER   37  THE TOTAL COMMISSIONS =    $499,992.00


14  55  45  213975     12  $8.27 10%        $99.24        $9.92 TUT K.
14  55  45  390127    871  $0.13  7%       $113.23        $7.93 TUT K.
14  55  45  883917      5 $38.21 10%       $191.05       $19.11 TUT K.

                FOR SALESMAN NUMBER   45  THE TOTAL COMMISSIONS =        $36.96


14  87  15  673017    987 $111.73  7%   $110,277.51    $7,719.43 DEETLE D.
14  87  15  333336    771  $1.53  5%     $1,179.63       $58.98 DEETLE D.
14  87  15  228361   1738  $0.24  7%       $417.12       $29.20 DEETLE D.

                FOR SALESMAN NUMBER   15  THE TOTAL COMMISSIONS =     $7,807.61


14  87  31  392744    831 $28.71  5%    $23,858.01    $1,192.90 TANNY V.
14  87  31  397581   1183  $0.37  7%       $437.71       $30.64 TANNY V.
14  87  31  777111     31  $0.02  5%         $0.62        $0.03 TANNY V.

                FOR SALESMAN NUMBER   31  THE TOTAL COMMISSIONS =     $1,223.57


14  87  59  662098      2 $887.54 10%     $1,775.08      $177.51 WILKE T.
14  87  59  221593     38 $748.61 10%    $28,447.18    $2,844.72 WILKE T.

                FOR SALESMAN NUMBER   59  THE TOTAL COMMISSIONS =     $3,022.23


14  87  63  002842    204  $0.23  5%        $46.92        $2.35 DURAN D.
14  87  63  893762     14 $38.51  7%       $539.14       $37.74 DURAN D.
14  87  63  382948   5612  $1.83  5%    $10,269.96      $513.50 DURAN D.

                FOR SALESMAN NUMBER   63  THE TOTAL COMMISSIONS =       $553.59


66  20  18  829000    381  $0.12  7%        $45.72        $3.20 DUWOP D.
```

Figure 9-6 (*continued*)

&&&&&&&&&&&&&&&&&&&&&&&&&&&&&&&&&&&&&&&&&&&&&&&&&&&&&&&&&&&&&&&&&&&&&&&&&&&&&&&&&&&&&&&&&&&&&&&&&&

REG NO.	BR NO.	SMAN NO.	PRODUCT NO.	QTY	PRICE	RATE	AMOUNT SOLD	COMMISSION	SALESPERSON	PAGE 3

&&&&&&&&&&&&&&&&&&&&&&&&&&&&&&&&&&&&&&&&&&&&&&&&&&&&&&&&&&&&&&&&&&&&&&&&&&&&&&&&&&&&&&&&&&&&&&&&&&

| 66 | 20 | 18 | 382900 | 1821 | $28.45 | 10% | $51,807.45 | $5,180.75 | DUWOP D. | |

FOR SALESMAN NUMBER   18 THE TOTAL COMMISSIONS = $5,183.95

66	20	27	564763	284	$2.84	7%	$806.56	$56.46	CARNIGIE D.	
66	20	27	769023	9999	$999.34	5%	$9,992,400.66	$499,620.03	CARNIGIE D.	
66	20	27	562940	9999	$992.74	7%	$9,926,407.26	$694,848.51	CARNIGIE D.	
66	20	27	826731	9999	$999.27	10%	$9,991,700.73	$999,170.07	CARNIGIE D.	

FOR SALESMAN NUMBER   27 THE TOTAL COMMISSIONS = $2,193,695.07

| 66 | 37 | 05 | 737289 | 12 | $0.12 | 5% | $1.44 | $0.07 | PEABRAIN D. | |
| 66 | 37 | 05 | 729487 | 0 | $0.02 | 10% | $0.00 | $0.00 | PEABRAIN D. | |

FOR SALESMAN NUMBER   05 THE TOTAL COMMISSIONS = $.07

66	37	18	543823	283	$38.72	5%	$10,957.76	$547.89	DAPPER V.	
66	37	18	780263	28	$0.12	7%	$3.36	$0.24	DAPPER V.	
66	37	18	888888	274	$937.21	10%	$256,795.54	$25,679.55	DAPPER V.	
66	37	18	364531	26	$73.82	5%	$1,919.32	$95.97	DAPPER V.	

FOR SALESMAN NUMBER   18 THE TOTAL COMMISSIONS = $26,323.65

| 66 | 37 | 29 | 927483 | 123 | $0.28 | 7% | $34.44 | $2.41 | GRAUER R. | |
| 66 | 37 | 29 | 828219 | 57 | $28.47 | 10% | $1,622.79 | $162.28 | GRAUER R. | |

FOR SALESMAN NUMBER   29 THE TOTAL COMMISSIONS = $164.69

| 66 | 37 | 51 | 738215 | 382 | $937.21 | 7% | $358,014.22 | $25,061.00 | LULU P. | |

FOR SALESMAN NUMBER   51 THE TOTAL COMMISSIONS = $25,061.00

66	97	37	892737	12	$82.74	5%	$992.88	$49.64	TRIPP U.	
66	97	37	367301	8392	$0.12	10%	$1,007.04	$100.70	TRIPP U.	
66	97	37	228701	3284	$12.74	7%	$41,838.16	$2,928.67	TRIPP U.	

FOR SALESMAN NUMBER   37 THE TOTAL COMMISSIONS = $3,079.01

| 66 | 97 | 43 | 294652 | 35 | $2.74 | 7% | $95.90 | $6.71 | WHIZ G. | |
| 66 | 97 | 43 | 003721 | 3 | $234.72 | 10% | $704.16 | $70.42 | WHIZ G. | |

FOR SALESMAN NUMBER   43 THE TOTAL COMMISSIONS = $77.13

| 66 | 97 | 75 | 000234 | 28 | $2.64 | 5% | $73.92 | $3.70 | BUMBLE B. | |

Figure 9-6   (*continued*)

```
                    PSYCHO PRODUCTS QUARTERLY SALES REPORT
                                  10/14/84

&&&&&&&&&&&&&&&&&&&&&&&&&&&&&&&&&&&&&&&&&&&&&&&&&&&&&&&&&&&&&&&&&&&&&&&&&&&&&&&&&&&&&&&&&&&&&&&&
REG BR SMAN PRODUCT  QTY  PRICE  RATE    AMOUNT     COMMISSION SALESPERSON           PAGE   4
NO. NO. NO.   NO.                         SOLD
&&&&&&&&&&&&&&&&&&&&&&&&&&&&&&&&&&&&&&&&&&&&&&&&&&&&&&&&&&&&&&&&&&&&&&&&&&&&&&&&&&&&&&&&&&&&&&&&
66  97  75  937583   372  $0.27 10%      $100.44       $10.04 BUMBLE B.
66  97  75  375641    38 $756.43  5%   $28,744.34   $1,437.22 BUMBLE B.
66  97  75  878767  9372 $986.76 10% $9,247,914.72 $924,791.47 BUMBLE B.

       FOR SALESMAN NUMBER   75  THE TOTAL COMMISSIONS =       $926,242.43


66  97  81  645364  9898  $2.74  5%   $27,120.52   $1,356.03 LATER C. U.
66  97  81  374632   387 $78.23  7%   $30,275.01   $2,119.25 LATER C. U.

       FOR SALESMAN NUMBER   81  THE TOTAL COMMISSIONS =        $3,475.28




FINAL TOTALS:      $50,895,730.61  SALES,      $3,742,459.81  COMMISSIONS FOR PSYCHO PRODUCTS
************
```

Figure 9-6   *(continued)*

9.5 MULTIPLE CONTROL BREAKS

Our modular design can now be enhanced to include subtotals for branch
and region. It is quite easy to do this because the algorithm is identical to that
of the salesman total routine. Examine the completed modular design and
related pseudocode [Figure 9–7]. The program, with additional code in lower
case, follows immediately. The final report can be found in Figure 9–8: (the
code for salesman subtotals remains in lower case for comparison purposes).

```
 1      IDENTIFICATION DIVISION.
 2      PROGRAM-ID.              FIFTH.
 3      AUTHOR.                  STEVE SAMUELS.
 4      INSTALLATION.            DEPAUL UNIVERSITY.
 5      DATE-WRITTEN.            10/3/83.
 6
 7      ************************************************************
 8      *****    INPUT:  THE INPUT TO THIS PROGRAM IS A FILE CALLED
 9      *****            "FIVE.DAT".  EACH RECORD IN
10      *****            THIS FILE CONSISTS OF ONE SALE AND INCLUDES
11      *****            REGION NUMBER, BRANCH NUMBER, SALESMAN
12      *****            NUMBER, PRODUCT NUMBER, QUANTITY, TYPE,
13      *****            PRICE AND SALESMAN NAME.  ALL THE RECORDS
14      *****            ARE SORTED BY SALESMAN NUMBER WITHIN BRANCH
15      *****            NUMBER WITHIN REGION NUMBER.
16      ************************************************************
17
18      ************************************************************
```

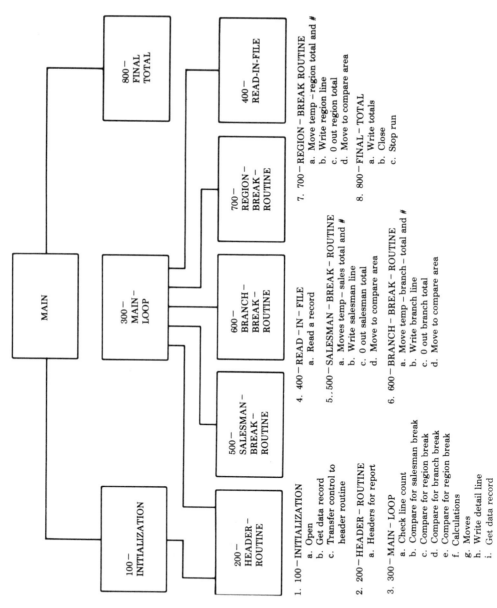

MAIN

100 – INITIALIZATION

800 – FINAL TOTAL

200 – HEADER – ROUTINE

500 – SALESMAN – BREAK – ROUTINE

300 – MAIN – LOOP

600 – BRANCH – BREAK – ROUTINE

700 – REGION – BREAK – ROUTINE

400 – READ-IN-FILE

1. 100 – INITIALIZATION
   a. Open
   b. Get data record
   c. Transfer control to header routine

2. 200 – HEADER – ROUTINE
   a. Headers for report

3. 300 – MAIN – LOOP
   a. Check line count
   b. Compare for salesman break
   c. Compare for region break
   d. Compare for branch break
   e. Compare for region break
   f. Calculations
   g. Moves
   h. Write detail line
   i. Get data record

4. 400 – READ – IN – FILE
   a. Read a record

5. 500 – SALESMAN – BREAK – ROUTINE
   a. Moves temp – sales total and #
   b. Write salesman line
   c. 0 out salesman total
   d. Move to compare area

6. 600 – BRANCH – BREAK – ROUTINE
   a. Move temp – branch – total and #
   b. Write branch line
   c. 0 out branch total
   d. Move to compare area

7. 700 – REGION – BREAK ROUTINE
   a. Move temp – region total and #
   b. Write region line
   c. 0 out region total
   d. Move to compare area

8. 800 – FINAL – TOTAL
   a. Write totals
   b. Close
   c. Stop run

Figure 9-7

```
19   *****      OUTPUT: THE OUTPUT FROM THIS PROGRAM CONSISTS OF
20   *****              A PRINTED REPORT, WITH HEADING LINES, CON-
21   *****              TAINING EDITED FIELDS FOR REGION NUMBER,
22   *****              BRANCH NUMBER, SALESMAN NUMBER, PRODUCT
23   *****              NUMBER, QUANTITY, PRICE, COMMISSION RATE,
24   *****              AMOUNT SOLD, COMMISSION AND SALESMAN NAME
25   *****              FOR EACH RECORD PROCESSED AS WELL AS
26   *****              subtotals for salesman total commission, branch
27                      total commission, region total commission,
28                      and final totals for amount sold and commissions
29   *********************************************************************
30
31   *********************************************************************
32   *****      PROCESSING:  THE PROCESSING REQUIRED TO PREPARE
33   *****              THE REPORT CONSISTS OF READING AN INPUT
34   *****              RECORD, FINDING THE CORRECT COMMISSION
35   *****              RATE, CALCULATING COMMISSION AND AMOUNT
36   *****              SOLD, MOVING EACH OF THE REQUIRED FIELDS
37   *****              FROM THE INPUT OR WORKING STORAGE AREA
38   *****              TO THE OUTPUT AREA, WRITING A REPORT LINE,
39   *****              AND ACCUMULATING FINAL TOTALS.
40   *********************************************************************
41
42   ENVIRONMENT DIVISION.
43
44   CONFIGURATION SECTION.
45
46   SOURCE-COMPUTER.     VAX-11-750.
47   OBJECT-COMPUTER.     VAX-11-750.
48
49   INPUT-OUTPUT SECTION.
50
51   FILE-CONTROL.
52       SELECT IN-FILE ASSIGN TO FIVE.
53       SELECT OUT-FILE ASSIGN TO OUTLOOK.
54
55   DATA DIVISION.
56
57   FILE SECTION.
58
59   FD  IN-FILE
60       DATA RECORD IS IN-REC.
61   01  IN-REC.
62       05  REGION-IN                PIC XX.
63       05  BRANCH-IN                PIC XX.
64       05  SMAN-NUMBER-IN           PIC XX.
65       05  FILLER                   PIC X.
66       05  PROD-NUMBER-IN           PIC X(6).
67       05  QUANTITY-IN              PIC 9(4).
68       05  COMMISSION-TYPE-IN       PIC X.
69           88 COMMISSION-RATE-CODE-A          VALUE "A".
70           88 COMMISSION-RATE-CODE-B          VALUE "B".
71           88 COMMISSION-RATE-CODE-C          VALUE "C".
72       05  FILLER                   PIC X.
73       05  PRICE-IN                 PIC 999V99.
74       05  SMAN-NAME-IN             PIC X(20).
75
76   FD  OUT-FILE
77       DATA RECORD IS OUT-REC.
78   01  OUT-REC                      PIC X(132).
79
```

```
80
81
82      WORKING-STORAGE SECTION.
83
84      01   FINISHED                    PIC XXX VALUE SPACES.
85           88 THERE-ARE-NO-MORE-RECORDS     VALUE "YES".
86           88 FIRST-TIME                    VALUE "on".
87      01   COUNTERS.
88           05   WS-LINE-COUNT          PIC 99 VALUE 0.
89           05   WS-PAGE-NUMBER         PIC 99 VALUE 0.
90
91      01   WS-DATE-WORK-AREA.
92           05   TODAY-YEAR             PIC 99      VALUE ZEROS.
93           05   TODAY-MONTH            PIC 99      VALUE ZEROS.
94           05   TODAY-DAY              PIC 99      VALUE ZEROS.
95
96      01   TEMP-SMAN-NUMBER            PIC XX.
97      01   temp-branch-number          pic xx.
98      01   temp-region-number          pic xx.
99      01   WS-CALCULATION-REGISTERS.
100          05   WS-AMT-SOLD            PIC 9(7)V99  VALUE ZEROS.
101          05   WS-COMMISS-RATE        PIC 99       VALUE ZEROS.
102          05   WS-COMMISSION          PIC 9(9)V99  VALUE ZEROS.
103          05   WS-SMAN-TOT-COMMISSIONS     PIC 9(10)V99 VALUE ZEROS.
104          05   ws-branch-tot-commissions   pic 9(10)v99 value zeros.
105          05   ws-region-tot-commissions   pic 9(10)v99 value zeros.
106          05   WS-TOTAL-COMMISSIONS   PIC 9(11)V99 VALUE ZEROS.
107          05   WS-TOTAL-SALES         PIC 9(11)V99 VALUE ZEROS.
108
109     01   WS-TITLE-LINE.
110          05   FILLER                PIC X(29)    VALUE SPACES.
111          05   FILLER                PIC X(38)    VALUE
                      "PSYCHO PRODUCTS QUARTERLY SALES REPORT".
112          05   FILLER                PIC X(65)    VALUE SPACES.
113
114     01   WS-DATE-LINE.
115          05   FILLER                PIC X(44)    VALUE SPACES.
116          05   DATE-OUT.
117               10 MONTH-OUT          PIC Z9       VALUE ZEROS.
118               10 FILLER             PIC X        VALUE "/".
119               10 DAY-OUT            PIC Z9       VALUE ZEROS.
120               10 FILLER             PIC X        VALUE "/".
121               10 YEAR-OUT           PIC 99       VALUE ZEROS.
122          05   FILLER                PIC X(80)    VALUE SPACES.
123
124     01   WS-HEADING-LINE-FILLER.
125          05   FILLER                PIC X(96)    VALUE ALL "&".
126          05   FILLER                PIC X(36)    VALUE SPACES.
127
128     01   WS-HEADING-LINE-ONE.
129          05   FILLER                PIC X(4)     VALUE "REG ".
130          05   FILLER                PIC X(3)     VALUE "BR ".
131          05   FILLER                PIC X(5)     VALUE "SMAN ".
132          05   FILLER                PIC X(8)     VALUE "PRODUCT ".
133          05   FILLER                PIC X(6)     VALUE " QTY  ".
134          05   FILLER                PIC X(6)     VALUE "PRICE ".
135          05   FILLER                PIC X(7)     VALUE " RATE   ".
136          05   FILLER                PIC X(12)    VALUE "  AMOUNT   ".
137          05   FILLER                PIC X(12)    VALUE " COMMISSION".
138          05   FILLER                PIC X(14)    VALUE " SALESPERSON  ".
139          05   FILLER                PIC X(10)    VALUE SPACES.
140          05   FILLER                PIC X(5)     VALUE "PAGE ".
```

```
141        05  PAGE-NUMBER-OUT          PIC ZZZ9     VALUE ZEROS.
142        05  FILLER                   PIC X(36)    VALUE SPACES.
143
144    01  WS-HEADING-LINE-TWO.
145        05  FILLER                   PIC X(4)     VALUE "NO. ".
146        05  FILLER                   PIC X(3)     VALUE "NO.".
147        05  FILLER                   PIC X(5)     VALUE " NO. ".
148        05  FILLER                   PIC X(8)     VALUE " NO.     ".
149        05  FILLER                   PIC X(19)    VALUE SPACES.
150        05  FILLER                   PIC X(10)    VALUE "   SOLD   ".
151        05  FILLER                   PIC X(83)    VALUE SPACES.
152
153    01  WS-DATA-LINE.
154        05  REGION-OUT               PIC XX.
155        05  FILLER                   PIC XX  VALUE SPACES.
156        05  BRANCH-OUT               PIC XX.
157        05  FILLER                   PIC XX  VALUE SPACES.
158        05  SMAN-NUMBER-OUT          PIC XX.
159        05  FILLER                   PIC XX  VALUE SPACES.
160        05  PROD-NUMBER-OUT          PIC X(6).
161        05  FILLER                   PIC XX  VALUE SPACES.
162        05  QUANTITY-OUT             PIC ZZZ9.
163        05  FILLER                   PIC X  VALUE SPACES.
164        05  PRICE-OUT                PIC $$$9.99.
165        05  FILLER                   PIC X  VALUE SPACES.
166        05  COMMISS-RATE-OUT         PIC Z9.
167        05  PERCENT-SIGN             PIC X  VALUE "%".
168        05  FILLER                   PIC X  VALUE SPACES.
169        05  AMT-SOLD-OUT             PIC $$,$$$,$$9.99.
170        05  FILLER                   PIC X  VALUE SPACES.
171        05  COMMISSION-OUT           PIC $$,$$$,$$9.99.
172        05  FILLER                   PIC X  VALUE SPACES.
173        05  SMAN-NAME-OUT            PIC X(20).
174        05  FILLER                   PIC X(20).
175
176    01  WS-SMAN-TOTAL-LINE.
177        05  FILLER                   PIC X(10) VALUE SPACES.
178        05  FILLER                   PIC X(22) VALUE
179            "FOR SALESMAN NUMBER ".
180        05  SMAN-TOT-NUM-OUT         PIC XX.
181        05  FILLER                   PIC X(1) VALUE SPACES.
182        05  FILLER                   PIC X(25) VALUE
183            " THE TOTAL COMMISSIONS = ".
184        05  SMAN-TOT-COMM-OUT        PIC $$,$$$,$$$,$$$.99.
185    01  ws-branch-total-line.
186        05  filler                   pic x(10) value spaces.
187        05  filler                   pic x(22) value
188            "FOR BRANCH NUMBER   ".
189        05  branch-tot-num-out       pic xx.
190        05  filler                   pic x(1) value spaces.
191        05  filler                   pic x(25) value
192            " THE TOTAL COMMISSIONS = ".
193        05  branch-tot-comm-out      pic $$,$$$,$$$,$$$.99.
194    01  ws-region-total-line.
195        05  filler                   pic x(10) value spaces.
196        05  filler                   pic x(22) value
197            "FOR REGION NUMBER   ".
198        05  region-tot-num-out       pic xx.
199        05  filler                   pic x(1) value spaces.
200        05  filler                   pic x(25) value
201            " THE TOTAL COMMISSIONS = ".
```

```
202          05  region-tot-comm-out      pic $$,$$$,$$$,$$$.99.
203
204      01  WS-TOTAL-LINE.
205          05  FILLER                   PIC X(16)    VALUE "FINAL TOTALS:   ".
206          05  TOTAL-SALES-OUT          PIC $$$$,$$$,$$$,$$9.99  VALUE ZEROS.
207          05  FILLER                   PIC X(10)    VALUE " SALES, ".
208          05  TOTAL-COMMISSIONS-OUT    PIC $$$,$$$,$$$,$$9.99 VALUE ZEROS.
209          05  FILLER                   PIC    3)    VALUE "  COMMISSIONS".
210          05  FILLER                       PIC X(56)    VALUE " FOR PSYCHO PRODUCTS".
211
212      01  WS-UNDERLINE.
213          05  FILLER                       PIC X(132)  VALUE "************".
214
215      PROCEDURE DIVISION.
216
217      000-MAINLINE.
218          PERFORM 100-INITIALIZATION THRU 100-EXIT.
219          PERFORM 200-HEADING-ROUTINE THRU 200-EXIT.
220          PERFORM 400-READ-IN-FILE THRU 400-EXIT.
221          PERFORM 300-MAIN-LOOP THRU 300-EXIT
222              UNTIL THERE-ARE-NO-MORE-RECORDS.
223          PERFORM 800-FINAL-TOTAL THRU 800-EXIT.
224
225           100-INITIALIZATION.
226          OPEN INPUT  IN-FILE
227              OUTPUT OUT-FILE.
228          ACCEPT WS-DATE-WORK-AREA FROM DATE.
229              MOVE TODAY-MONTH TO MONTH-OUT.
230              MOVE TODAY-DAY   TO  DAY-OUT.
231              MOVE TODAY-YEAR  TO  YEAR-OUT.
232          MOVE "on" TO FINISHED.
233      100-EXIT.
234          EXIT.
235
236      200-HEADING-ROUTINE.
237          ADD 1 TO WS-PAGE-NUMBER.
238          MOVE WS-PAGE-NUMBER TO PAGE-NUMBER-OUT.
239          WRITE OUT-REC FROM WS-TITLE-LINE AFTER PAGE.
240          WRITE OUT-REC FROM WS-DATE-LINE AFTER 1.
241          WRITE OUT-REC FROM WS-HEADING-LINE-FILLER AFTER 2.
242          WRITE OUT-REC FROM WS-HEADING-LINE-ONE AFTER 1.
243          WRITE OUT-REC FROM WS-HEADING-LINE-TWO AFTER 1.
244          WRITE OUT-REC FROM WS-HEADING-LINE-FILLER AFTER 1.
245          MOVE 6 TO WS-LINE-COUNT.
246      200-EXIT.
247          EXIT.
248
249      300-MAIN-LOOP.
250          IF WS-LINE-COUNT > 54
251              PERFORM 200-HEADING-ROUTINE THRU 200-EXIT.
252
253          IF FIRST-TIME MOVE SPACES TO FINISHED.
254          IF SMAN-NUMBER-IN NOT = TEMP-SMAN-NUMBER
255              PERFORM 500-SALESMAN-BREAK-ROUTINE THRU 500-END.
256          If branch-in not = temp-branch-number
257              perform 600-branch-break-routine thru 600-end.
258          If region-in not = temp-region-number
259              perform 700-region-break-routine thru 700-end.
260
261              IF COMMISSION-RATE-CODE-A
262                     MOVE 05 TO WS-COMMISS-RATE
263              ELSE IF COMMISSION-RATE-CODE-B
```

```
264                        MOVE 07 TO WS-COMMISS-RATE
265                     ELSE MOVE 10 TO WS-COMMISS-RATE.
266
267         COMPUTE WS-AMT-SOLD = QUANTITY-IN * PRICE-IN.
268         COMPUTE WS-COMMISSION ROUNDED =
                         WS-AMT-SOLD * WS-COMMISS-RATE / 100.
269         ADD WS-COMMISSION TO WS-TOTAL-COMMISSIONS
270                              WS-SMAN-TOT-COMMISSIONS
271                              ws-branch-tot-commissions
272                              ws-region-tot-commissions
273            ON SIZE ERROR DISPLAY "COMMISSION TOTAL FIELD TOO SMALL".
274
275         ADD WS-AMT-SOLD TO WS-TOTAL-SALES
276             ON SIZE ERROR DISPLAY "TOTAL COMPANY SALES FIELD TOO SMALL".
277
278         MOVE REGION-IN TO REGION-OUT.
279         MOVE BRANCH-IN TO BRANCH-OUT.
280         MOVE SMAN-NUMBER-IN TO SMAN-NUMBER-OUT.
281         MOVE PROD-NUMBER-IN   TO PROD-NUMBER-OUT.
282         MOVE QUANTITY-IN      TO QUANTITY-OUT.
283         MOVE PRICE-IN         TO PRICE-OUT.
284         MOVE WS-COMMISS-RATE  TO COMMISS-RATE-OUT.
285         MOVE WS-AMT-SOLD      TO AMT-SOLD-OUT.
286         MOVE WS-COMMISSION    TO COMMISSION-OUT.
287         MOVE SMAN-NAME-IN TO SMAN-NAME-OUT.
288         WRITE OUT-REC FROM WS-DATA-LINE  AFTER 1.
289         ADD 1 TO WS-LINE-COUNT.
290         PERFORM 400-READ-IN-FILE THRU 400-EXIT.
291         iF THERE-ARE-NO-MORE-RECORDS
292             PERFORM 500-SALESMAN-BREAK-ROUTINE
293             perform 600-branch-break-routine
294             perform 700-region-break-routine.
295     300-EXIT.
296         EXIT.
297
298     400-READ-IN-FILE.
299         READ IN-FILE
300             AT END MOVE "YES" TO FINISHED.
301         iF FIRST-TIME MOVE SMAN-NUMBER-IN TO TEMP-SMAN-NUMBER
302                       move branch-in to temp-branch-number
303                       move region-in to temp-region-number.
304     400-EXIT.
305         EXIT.
306
307     ************************************************************
308     *            CONTROL BREAK MODULES                        *
309     ************************************************************
310
311     500-SALESMAN-BREAK-ROUTINE.
312         MOVE WS-SMAN-TOT-COMMISSIONS TO SMAN-TOT-COMM-OUT.
313         MOVE TEMP-SMAN-NUMBER TO SMAN-TOT-NUM-OUT.
314         WRITE OUT-REC FROM WS-SMAN-TOTAL-LINE AFTER 2.
315         MOVE SPACES TO OUT-REC.
316         WRITE OUT-REC AFTER 1.
317         ADD 3 TO WS-LINE-COUNT.
318         MOVE 0 TO WS-SMAN-TOT-COMMISSIONS.
319         MOVE SMAN-NUMBER-IN TO TEMP-SMAN-NUMBER.
320     500-end.
321         exit.
322     600-branch-break-routine.
323         move ws-branch-tot-commissions to branch-tot-comm-out.
324         move temp-branch-number to branch-tot-num-out.
```

```
325        write out-rec from ws-branch-total-line after 1.
326        move spaces to out-rec.
327        write out-rec after 1.
328        add 2 to ws-line-count.
329        move 0 to ws-branch-tot-commissions.
330        move branch-in to temp-branch-number.
331    600-end.
332        exit.
333    700-region-break-routine.
334        move ws-region-tot-commissions to region-tot-comm-out.
335        move temp-region-number to region-tot-num-out.
336        write out-rec from ws-region-total-line after 1.
337        move spaces to out-rec.
338        write out-rec after 1.
339        add 2 to ws-line-count.
340        move 0 to ws-region-tot-commissions.
341        move region-in to temp-region-number.
342    700-end.
343        exit.
346    800-FINAL-TOTAL.
347        MOVE WS-TOTAL-COMMISSIONS TO TOTAL-COMMISSIONS-OUT.
348        MOVE WS-TOTAL-SALES TO TOTAL-SALES-OUT.
349
350        WRITE OUT-REC FROM WS-TOTAL-LINE AFTER 5.
351        WRITE OUT-REC FROM WS-UNDERLINE.
352
353        CLOSE IN-FILE OUT-FILE.
354        STOP RUN.
```

Two additional control breaks were manufactured without eliminating any code from the program that produced only one control break. The branch and region control break look almost identical to the salesman control break. Additional storage areas, used for the last two breaks, were added directly underneath the data-names and control lines used for the salesman control break.

More documentation was added to the Procedure Division to highlight these control break modules. It is most important to understand that although the algorithms are the same for three control breaks, one should try one break first—CODE, COMPILE, LINK, AND RUN IN SMALL INCREMENTS!!

SUMMARY

By now you should be solving more complex problems by continuing to write a basic four-module program, testing it with a complete data set, adding modules, retesting, and so on.

Additional syntax that was learned is:

1. IDENTIFICATION DIVISION
    a. INSTALLATION
    b. DATE-WRITTEN

```
&&&&&&&&&&&&&&&&&&&&&&&&&&&&&&&&&&&&&&&&&&&&&&&&&&&&&&&&&&&&&&&&&&&&&&&&&&&&&&&&&&&&&&&&&&&&&&&&&&&&&&&&&&
REG BR SMAN PRODUCT  QTY  PRICE  RATE    AMOUNT     COMMISSION SALESPERSON              PAGE   1
NO. NO. NO.  NO.                         SOLD
&&&&&&&&&&&&&&&&&&&&&&&&&&&&&&&&&&&&&&&&&&&&&&&&&&&&&&&&&&&&&&&&&&&&&&&&&&&&&&&&&&&&&&&&&&&&&&&&&&&&&&&&&&
01  04  13  328204   300  $20.00  5%    $6,000.00      $300.00 SMYTH J.
01  04  13  591823    10 $150.00  7%    $1,500.00      $105.00 SMYTH J.

            FOR SALESMAN NUMBER   13  THE TOTAL COMMISSIONS =          $405.00

01  04  23  291823  1000   $5.00  5%    $5,000.00      $250.00 COLBY S.
01  04  23  391028   400  $10.00 10%    $4,000.00      $400.00 COLBY S.
01  04  23  391781     3 $150.00  5%      $450.00       $22.50 COLBY S.

            FOR SALESMAN NUMBER   23  THE TOTAL COMMISSIONS =          $672.50

01  04  25  394883    20  $50.00  7%    $1,000.00       $70.00 HOE A.

            FOR SALESMAN NUMBER   25  THE TOTAL COMMISSIONS =           $70.00

            FOR BRANCH NUMBER     04  THE TOTAL COMMISSIONS =        $1,147.50

01  11  14  928323    40  $60.00  7%    $2,400.00      $168.00 JACKSON J.
01  11  14  372819   100 $100.00 10%   $10,000.00    $1,000.00 JACKSON J.
01  11  14  958492   300  $22.00  7%    $6,600.00      $462.00 JACKSON J.

            FOR SALESMAN NUMBER   14  THE TOTAL COMMISSIONS =        $1,630.00

            FOR BRANCH NUMBER     11  THE TOTAL COMMISSIONS =        $1,630.00

            FOR REGION NUMBER     01  THE TOTAL COMMISSIONS =        $2,777.50

14  05  17  765381    15   $3.41  5%       $51.15        $2.56 SAMUELS S.
14  05  17  128455   100 $203.81  7%   $20,381.00    $1,426.67 SAMUELS S.
14  05  17  222222  5666   $0.22  5%    $1,246.52       $62.33 SAMUELS S.
14  05  17  121212     3 $293.17 10%      $879.51       $87.95 SAMUELS S.

            FOR SALESMAN NUMBER   17  THE TOTAL COMMISSIONS =        $1,579.51

14  05  25  447715   581   $4.50  7%    $2,614.50      $183.02 BABBAGE C.
14  05  25  618903    21 $146.83 10%    $3,083.43      $308.34 BABBAGE C.

            FOR SALESMAN NUMBER   25  THE TOTAL COMMISSIONS =          $491.36

14  05  45  444228   956   $3.51  5%    $3,355.56      $167.78 NORAD D.
14  05  45  118645  1111 $291.90  7%  $324,300.90   $22,701.06 NORAD D.
14  05  45  637100  6716   $1.23 10%    $8,260.68      $826.07 NORAD D.

            FOR SALESMAN NUMBER   45  THE TOTAL COMMISSIONS =       $23,694.91

14  05  61  950143     4   $0.11 10%        $0.44        $0.04 DEMKINS S.
14  05  61  000013   381   $2.34  7%      $891.54       $62.41 DEMKINS S.

            FOR SALESMAN NUMBER   61  THE TOTAL COMMISSIONS =           $62.45

14  05  77  037185    31   $0.32  5%        $9.92        $0.50 LEMONHEAD D.
```

Figure 9–8

```
&&&&&&&&&&&&&&&&&&&&&&&&&&&&&&&&&&&&&&&&&&&&&&&&&&&&&&&&&&&&&&&&&&&&&&&&&&&&&&&&&&&&&&&&&&&&&&&&&&&&&&&
REG BR SMAN PRODUCT  QTY  PRICE  RATE     AMOUNT     COMMISSION SALESPERSON              PAGE   2
NO. NO. NO.  NO.                          SOLD
&&&&&&&&&&&&&&&&&&&&&&&&&&&&&&&&&&&&&&&&&&&&&&&&&&&&&&&&&&&&&&&&&&&&&&&&&&&&&&&&&&&&&&&&&&&&&&&&&&&&&&&

        FOR SALESMAN NUMBER   77  THE TOTAL COMMISSIONS =              $.50

        FOR BRANCH NUMBER     05  THE TOTAL COMMISSIONS =        $25,828.73

14  55  01  652961   378  $83.12  7%    $31,419.36    $2,199.36 BIRDIE B.
14  55  01  408500   371   $1.73 10%       $641.83       $64.18 BIRDIE B.
14  55  01  301740  2874 $108.92  5%   $313,036.08   $15,651.80 BIRDIE B.

        FOR SALESMAN NUMBER   01  THE TOTAL COMMISSIONS =        $17,915.34

14  55  37  555555    28  $23.98  7%       $671.44       $47.00 TAMERLIN T.
14  55  37  432901  9999 $999.99  5% $9,998,900.01  $499,945.00 TAMERLIN T.

        FOR SALESMAN NUMBER   37  THE TOTAL COMMISSIONS =       $499,992.00

14  55  45  213975    12   $8.27 10%        $99.24        $9.92 TUT K.
14  55  45  390127   871   $0.13  7%       $113.23        $7.93 TUT K.
14  55  45  883917     5  $38.21 10%       $191.05       $19.11 TUT K.

        FOR SALESMAN NUMBER   45  THE TOTAL COMMISSIONS =            $36.96

        FOR BRANCH NUMBER     55  THE TOTAL COMMISSIONS =       $517,944.30

14  87  15  673017   987 $111.73  7%   $110,277.51    $7,719.43 DEETLE D.
14  87  15  333336   771   $1.53  5%     $1,179.63       $58.98 DEETLE D.
14  87  15  228361  1738   $0.24  7%       $417.12       $29.20 DEETLE D.

        FOR SALESMAN NUMBER   15  THE TOTAL COMMISSIONS =         $7,807.61

14  87  31  392744   831  $28.71  5%    $23,858.01    $1,192.90 TANNY V.
14  87  31  397581  1183   $0.37  7%       $437.71       $30.64 TANNY V.
14  87  31  777111    31   $0.02  5%         $0.62        $0.03 TANNY V.

        FOR SALESMAN NUMBER   31  THE TOTAL COMMISSIONS =         $1,223.57

14  87  59  662098     2 $887.54 10%     $1,775.08      $177.51 WILKE T.
14  87  59  221593    38 $748.61 10%    $28,447.18    $2,844.72 WILKE T.

        FOR SALESMAN NUMBER   59  THE TOTAL COMMISSIONS =         $3,022.23

14  87  63  002842   204   $0.23  5%        $46.92        $2.35 DURAN D.
14  87  63  893762    14  $38.51  7%       $539.14       $37.74 DURAN D.
14  87  63  382948  5612   $1.83  5%    $10,269.96      $513.50 DURAN D.

        FOR SALESMAN NUMBER   63  THE TOTAL COMMISSIONS =           $553.59

        FOR BRANCH NUMBER     87  THE TOTAL COMMISSIONS =        $12,607.00

        FOR REGION NUMBER     14  THE TOTAL COMMISSIONS =       $556,380.03

66  20  18  829000   381   $0.12  7%        $45.72        $3.20 DUWOP D.
```

Figure 9-8 (*continued*)

```
&&&&&&&&&&&&&&&&&&&&&&&&&&&&&&&&&&&&&&&&&&&&&&&&&&&&&&&&&&&&&&&&&&&&&&&&&&&&&&&&&&&&&&&&&&&&&&&&&&&&&&&&&&
REG BR SMAN PRODUCT  QTY  PRICE  RATE    AMOUNT     COMMISSION SALESPERSON            PAGE   3
NO. NO. NO.   NO.                         SOLD
&&&&&&&&&&&&&&&&&&&&&&&&&&&&&&&&&&&&&&&&&&&&&&&&&&&&&&&&&&&&&&&&&&&&&&&&&&&&&&&&&&&&&&&&&&&&&&&&&&&&&&&&&&
66  20  18  382900  1821 $28.45 10%    $51,807.45    $5,180.75 DUWOP D.

            FOR SALESMAN NUMBER   18  THE TOTAL COMMISSIONS =       $5,183.95

66  20  27  564763   284  $2.84  7%       $806.56       $56.46 CARNIGIE D.
66  20  27  769023  9999 $999.34  5% $9,992,400.66 $499,620.03 CARNIGIE D.
66  20  27  562940  9999 $992.74  7% $9,926,407.26 $694,848.51 CARNIGIE D.
66  20  27  826731  9999 $999.27 10% $9,991,700.73 $999,170.07 CARNIGIE D.

            FOR SALESMAN NUMBER   27  THE TOTAL COMMISSIONS =   $2,193,695.07

            FOR BRANCH NUMBER     20  THE TOTAL COMMISSIONS =   $2,198,879.02

66  37  05  737289    12  $0.12  5%         $1.44        $0.07 PEABRAIN D.
66  37  05  729487     0  $0.02 10%         $0.00        $0.00 PEABRAIN D.

            FOR SALESMAN NUMBER   05  THE TOTAL COMMISSIONS =         $.07

66  37  18  543823   283 $38.72  5%    $10,957.76      $547.89 DAPPER V.
66  37  18  780263    28  $0.12  7%         $3.36        $0.24 DAPPER V.
66  37  18  888888   274 $937.21 10%  $256,795.54   $25,679.55 DAPPER V.
66  37  18  364531    26 $73.82  5%     $1,919.32       $95.97 DAPPER V.

            FOR SALESMAN NUMBER   18  THE TOTAL COMMISSIONS =      $26,323.65

66  37  29  927483   123  $0.28  7%        $34.44        $2.41 GRAUER R.
66  37  29  828219    57 $28.47 10%     $1,622.79      $162.28 GRAUER R.

            FOR SALESMAN NUMBER   29  THE TOTAL COMMISSIONS =        $164.69

66  37  51  738215   382 $937.21  7%   $358,014.22   $25,061.00 LULU P.

            FOR SALESMAN NUMBER   51  THE TOTAL COMMISSIONS =      $25,061.00

            FOR BRANCH NUMBER     37  THE TOTAL COMMISSIONS =      $51,549.41

66  97  37  892737    12 $82.74  5%       $992.88       $49.64 TRIPP U.
66  97  37  367301  8392  $0.12 10%     $1,007.04      $100.70 TRIPP U.
66  97  37  228701  3284 $12.74  7%    $41,838.16    $2,928.67 TRIPP U.

            FOR SALESMAN NUMBER   37  THE TOTAL COMMISSIONS =       $3,079.01

66  97  43  294652    35  $2.74  7%        $95.90        $6.71 WHIZ G.
66  97  43  003721     3 $234.72 10%      $704.16       $70.42 WHIZ G.

            FOR SALESMAN NUMBER   43  THE TOTAL COMMISSIONS =         $77.13

66  97  75  000234    28  $2.64  5%        $73.92        $3.70 BUMBLE B.
66  97  75  937583   372  $0.27 10%       $100.44       $10.04 BUMBLE B.
```

Figure 9-8 *(continued)*

PSYCHO PRODUCTS QUARTERLY SALES REPORT
10/14/84

&&&&&&&&&&&&&&&&&&&&&&&&&&&&&&&&&&&&&&&&&&&&&&&&&&&&&&&&&&&&&&&&&&&&&&&&&&&&&&&&&&&&&&&&&&&&&&&&&&&&&&&&&&&&&&&
| REG BR SMAN PRODUCT | QTY | PRICE | RATE | AMOUNT | COMMISSION | SALESPERSON | | PAGE | 4 |
| NO. NO. NO.   NO. | | | | SOLD | | | | | |

&&&&&&&&&&&&&&&&&&&&&&&&&&&&&&&&&&&&&&&&&&&&&&&&&&&&&&&&&&&&&&&&&&&&&&&&&&&&&&&&&&&&&&&&&&&&&&&&&&&&&&&&&&&&&&&

```
66  97  75  375641     38 $756.43  5%    $28,744.34      $1,437.22 BUMBLE B.
66  97  75  878767   9372 $986.76 10% $9,247,914.72    $924,791.47 BUMBLE B.

            FOR SALESMAN NUMBER   75  THE TOTAL COMMISSIONS =       $926,242.43

66  97  81  645364   9898   $2.74  5%    $27,120.52      $1,356.03 LATER C. U.
66  97  81  374632    387  $78.23  7%    $30,275.01      $2,119.25 LATER C. U.

            FOR SALESMAN NUMBER   81  THE TOTAL COMMISSIONS =        $3,475.28

            FOR BRANCH NUMBER     97  THE TOTAL COMMISSIONS =      $932,873.85

            FOR REGION NUMBER     66  THE TOTAL COMMISSIONS =    $3,183,302.28


FINAL TOTALS:       $50,895,730.61  SALES,      $3,742,459.81  COMMISSIONS FOR PSYCHO PRODUCTS
************
```

Figure 9-8   (*continued*)

2. ENVIRONMENT DIVISION
   a. CONFIGURATION SECTION

3. PROCEDURE DIVISION
   a. ACCEPT
   b. PERFORM. . . . . THRU
   c. ON SIZE ERROR
   d. ROUNDED

QUESTIONS

1. Provide the additional code necessary to suppress the salesman, branch, and region number so that they only appear for the first output record and each one appear only after their respective control breaks. A sample of the output would look like Figure 9-9.

2. Examine the following:

```
PROCEDURE DIVISION.
BEGIN.
        PERFORM PAR-A.
        PERFORM PAR-B THRU PAR-C.
```

```
&&&&&&&&&&&&&&&&&&&&&&&&&&&&&&&&&&&&&&&&&&&&&&&&&&&&&&&&&&&&&&&&&&&&&&&&&&&&&&&&&&&&&&&&
REG BR SMAN PRODUCT  QTY  PRICE  RATE    AMOUNT      COMMISSION SALESPERSON          PAGE    1
NO. NO. NO.  NO.                         SOLD
&&&&&&&&&&&&&&&&&&&&&&&&&&&&&&&&&&&&&&&&&&&&&&&&&&&&&&&&&&&&&&&&&&&&&&&&&&&&&&&&&&&&&&&&
01  04  13  328204  300 $20.00   5%    $6,000.00       $300.00 SMYTH J.
            591823   10 $150.00  7%    $1,500.00       $105.00 SMYTH J.
            FOR SALESMAN NUMBER   13  THE TOTAL COMMISSIONS =        $405.00

        23  291823 1000  $5.00   5%    $5,000.00       $250.00 COLBY S.
            391028  400 $10.00  10%    $4,000.00       $400.00 COLBY S.
            391781    3 $150.00  5%      $450.00        $22.50 COLBY S.
            FOR SALESMAN NUMBER   23  THE TOTAL COMMISSIONS =        $672.50

        25  394883   20 $50.00   7%    $1,000.00        $70.00 HOE A.
            FOR SALESMAN NUMBER   25  THE TOTAL COMMISSIONS =         $70.00

            FOR BRANCH NUMBER     04  THE TOTAL COMMISSIONS =      $1,147.50

    11  14  928323   40 $60.00   7%    $2,400.00       $168.00 JACKSON J.
            372819  100 $100.00 10%   $10,000.00     $1,000.00 JACKSON J.
            958492  300 $22.00   7%    $6,600.00       $462.00 JACKSON J.
            FOR SALESMAN NUMBER   14  THE TOTAL COMMISSIONS =      $1,630.00

            FOR BRANCH NUMBER     11  THE TOTAL COMMISSIONS =      $1,630.00

            FOR REGION NUMBER     01  THE TOTAL COMMISSIONS =      $2,777.50

14  05  17  765381   15  $3.41   5%       $51.15         $2.56 SAMUELS S.
            128455  100 $203.81  7%   $20,381.00     $1,426.67 SAMUELS S.
```

Figure 9–9

PERFORM PAR-B THRU PAR-D.
PERFORM PAR-E UNTIL Q > 3.
PERFORM PAR-D.
STOP RUN.
PAR-A.
MOVE 0 TO X Y Z.
COMPUTE Q = 1.
PAR-B.
ADD 3 TO X Y.
COMPUTE Z = X * Y.
MOVE Z TO P.
PAR-C.
COMPUTE P = X + Z.
COMPUTE M = P − Y.
PAR-D.
COMPUTE Z = Z + P.
COMPUTE M = M + Z.
PAR-E.
COMPUTE Z = Z − 4.
COMPUTE Q = Q + 1.

a. How many times is each paragraph executed?
b. What is in X,Y,Q,Z,P, and M after termination?

3. Rearrange (provide proper indentation) so that the following makes more sense:

IF A < B AND X = 0 IF Q = 1 DISPLAY "LIVER" ELSE DISPLAY "ONIONS" ELSE IF M = P DISPLAY "CATSUP" ELSE DISPLAY "MUSTARD".

a. Draw a respectable flowchart for the above.
b. If B = 3, A = 0, Q = 1, M = 9, P = 9, and X = 0 what should occur?
c. If M = 4, P = 4, Q = 1, B = 5, X = 0, and A = 6 what should occur?

PROGRAMMING PROBLEMS

1. A university has prepared input records, each with the following information:

Field	Columns
College code	1–2
Department name	3–22
# of undergraduates	24–27
# of graduates	28–30

You have been given a Graduate Assistantship. Part of your "slave labor" is to write a program that will produce the total undergraduate and graduate enrollment for each college and for the entire university.
    Example of output:

[Commerce]	01ACCOUNTING	0400250
"	01MARKETING	0300100
.	. .	. .
.		
[Science]	03CHEMISTRY	0100020
"	03BIOLOGY	0150050
"	03PHYSICS	0030008
etc.	etc.	etc.

Format of report is up to you!

*2. An airline wants to find some specific information:
    a. Which airport carried the most customers?
    b. Which airport carried the fewest number of passengers per week?

Examine the following input records:

Field	Columns
Airport	1–3 (1st three letters of airport name)
Week	4–5 (1st week through 52nd week)
Day	6 (1 through 7)
# of passengers	7–11

You will need to produce a report that has control breaks for week and airport (records are sorted day within week within airport).

Single-Level Tables

10.1 INTRODUCTION TO TABLE HANDLING TECHNIQUES

Some problems can be solved more efficiently through the use of tables. A table is really nothing more than a series of contiguous memory positions into which data are placed for quick and easy access. Suppose you were given a problem where student records, each containing a name and major number, were read and output records containing a name and major were produced. In other words:

JOE SMITH 03—would produce—JOE SMITH CHEMISTRY
AL UNGER 14—would produce—AL UNGER ECONOMICS
    etc.   etc.

After a record was read, the following could be an example of some Procedure Division code:

```
IF MAJOR-NUMBER = 1 MOVE "BIOLOGY" TO MAJOR-OUT
ELSE IF MAJOR-NUMBER = 2 MOVE "ACCOUNTING" TO MAJOR-OUT
ELSE IF MAJOR-NUMBER = 3 MOVE "CHEMISTRY"  TO MAJOR-OUT
      etc.                  etc.              etc.
```

With thirty-five or so majors, this gets a little ridiculous! Is there an easier way? Examine the following program (input data precedes it—output data follows it):

```
                    JOE SAMUELS        11
                    FRAN FRAZZLE       08
                    JANE JARDINE       01
                    STU BLATZ          04
```

```
 1      IDENTIFICATION DIVISION.
 2      PROGRAM-ID. SL-TABLE-PRACTICE.
 3      AUTHOR. SAMUELS.
 4      ENVIRONMENT DIVISION.
 5      CONFIGURATION SECTION.
 6      SOURCE-COMPUTER. VAX-750.
 7      OBJECT-COMPUTER. VAX-750.
 8      INPUT-OUTPUT SECTION.
 9      FILE-CONTROL.
10          SELECT INFILE ASSIGN TO STU10A.
11          SELECT OUTFILE ASSIGN TO REPORT10A.
12      DATA DIVISION.
13      FILE SECTION.
14      FD  INFILE
15          DATA RECORD IS INREC.
16      01  INREC.
17          02 STU-NAME-IN        PIC X(20).
18          02 MAJOR-NUM-IN        PIC 99.
19      FD  OUTFILE
20          DATA RECORD IS OUTREC.
21      01  OUTREC          PIC X(80).
22      WORKING-STORAGE SECTION.
23      01  OUTLINE.
24          02  STU-NAME-OUT       PIC X(20).
25          02  FILLER            PIC X(40) VALUE SPACES.
26          02  MAJOR-NAME-OUT    PIC X(20).
27      01  SWITCH               PIC XXX VALUE SPACES.
28          88 NO-MORE-RECS          VALUE "YES".
29      01  MAJOR-VALUES.
30          02  FILLER        PIC X(20) VALUE "BIOLOGY".
31          02  FILLER        PIC X(20) VALUE "ECONOMICS".
32          02  FILLER        PIC X(20) VALUE "CHEMISTRY".
33          02  FILLER        PIC X(20) VALUE "ACCOUNTING".
34          02  FILLER        PIC X(20) VALUE "PRE-LAW".
35          02  FILLER        PIC X(20) VALUE "EDUCATION".
36          02  FILLER        PIC X(20) VALUE "PHILOSOPHY".
37          02  FILLER        PIC X(20) VALUE "MARKETING".
38          02  FILLER        PIC X(20) VALUE "COMPUTER SCIENCE".
39          02  FILLER        PIC X(20) VALUE "PSYCHOLOGY".
40          02  FILLER        PIC X(20) VALUE "PHYSICS".
41          02  FILLER        PIC X(20) VALUE "MATHEMATICS".
42      01  MAJOR-TABLE REDEFINES MAJOR-VALUES.
43          02 MAJOR-NAME  OCCURS 12 TIMES PIC X(20).
44      PROCEDURE DIVISION.
45      BEGIN.
46          PERFORM 100-HSKP.
47          PERFORM 200-OVERANOVER UNTIL NO-MORE-RECS.
48          PERFORM 300-FINALE.
49      100-HSKP.
```

Declaration of Array

```
50          OPEN INPUT INFILE OUTPUT OUTFILE.
51          READ INFILE AT END MOVE "YES" TO SWITCH.
52      200-OVERANOVER.
53          MOVE STU-NAME-IN TO STU-NAME-OUT.
54          MOVE MAJOR-NAME (MAJOR-NUM-IN) TO MAJOR-NAME-OUT.
55          WRITE OUTREC FROM OUTLINE.
56          READ INFILE AT END MOVE "YES" TO SWITCH.
57      300-FINALE.
58          CLOSE INFILE OUTFILE.
59          STOP RUN.
```

JOE SAMUELS	PHYSICS
FRAN FRAZZLE	MARKETING
JANE JARDINE	BIOLOGY
STU BLATZ	ACCOUNTING

A few things are apparent. Much less Procedure Division code is necessary (absence of twelve "if" statements). Even with more majors, the same Procedure Division code could be used. No error routine was set up to handle a 0 or number greater than 12 in the MAJOR-NUM-IN field, although this could have been accomplished with one compound condition statement:

```
IF MAJOR-NUM-IN = 0 OR MAJOR-NUM-IN > 12
    DISPLAY "BAD NUMBER"
ELSE
    MOVE MAJOR-NAME (MAJOR-NUM-IN) TO MAJOR-NAME-OUT.
```

Also, there is no fancy report. What is new in the above program are:

a. Redefines

b. Occurs

c. COBOL subscripts (or table pointers)

As we define these terms, the code in the above example will be more easily understood.

10.2 REDEFINES CLAUSE

In some cases it becomes necessary to define the same data storage area with more than one name. Consider:

```
02 SAL-OUT                         PIC $$$$.99.
02 SAL-STATUS REDEFINES SAL-OUT    PIC X(7).
```

In this case, one can move an unedited salary amount with a definition of 9(3)V99 to SAL-OUT or move "FIRED" or some other non-numeric entity to

SAL-STATUS. The same 7-byte field is used! A report using this type of code may look something like this:

JONES	$150.00
SMITH	FIRED
KLANTON	$540.50
etc.	etc.

It is impossible to move "FIRED" to SAL-OUT just as it is unacceptable to move a numeric quantity 9(3)V99 to SAL-STATUS. The REDEFINES clause eliminates this dilemma by allowing both data-names with totally different picture descriptions.

In the above program (line 42) the REDEFINES clause gave us the opportunity to substitute another name for MAJOR-VALUES—the other being MAJOR-TABLE. This was necessary because of the language restriction in COBOL. The table (or array) name is MAJOR and the OCCURS and REDEFINES clause cannot appear on the same statement. Also, a VALUE clause cannot be used in the same statement as an OCCURS clause. The general form of the REDEFINES statement is as follows:

level number data-name REDEFINES preceding-data-name

Here is another example of the REDEFINES clause:

```
03   BRANCHER                PIC X(8).
03   WORK-BRANCH REDEFINES BRANCHER.
     04 BR-NUM               PIC 999.
     04 DEPT-NUM             PIC 9(5).
```

Both BRANCHER and WORK-BRANCH reference an 8-byte field.

10.3 OCCURS CLAUSE

The OCCURS clause defines the table by specifying the number of entries. In the above program (line 43) MAJOR-NAME is a "dimensionalized" data-name, or table. It really consists of twelve major names. Here are some other examples:

```
02   SALES OCCURS 30 TIMES      PIC 9(4)V99.


02   TAB-INFO OCCURS 5 TIMES.
     03   ITEM-NUM      PIC 99.
     03   ITEM-PRICE    PIC 99V99.
     03   ITEM-DESC     PIC X(10).
```

Sales	Sales
Sales (1)	400000
Sales (2)	250000
Sales (3)	325000
Sales (4)	810000
Sales (30)	090000

TAB – INFO

TAB – INFO (1)	23	0400	Widgets
TAB – INFO (2)	37	1200	Snurfs
TAB – INFO (3)	41	0850	Paint Set
TAB – INFO (4)	48	3150	C.P. Dolls
TAB – INFO (5)	61	0725	Laser Toy

Figure 10–1

In the first example SALES is a table of 30 elements, each element containing 6 numeric bytes. In the second example TAB-INFO is a table of 5 elements, each element containing 16 bytes (2 for the item number, 4 for the item prices, and 10 for the item description). The above are represented pictorially—see Figure 10–1.

The general form of the OCCURS clause is:

level number data-name OCCURS integer TIMES

10.4 SUBSCRIPTS

In order to reference particular elements of a table one needs to use a pointer or subscript. Let us suppose you were cooking your favorite fancy meal and were using a table of fifteen ingredients. Would the cookbook say to "add the ingredient and stir well." I think not! Which ingredient should one add—the fourth, sixth—what?

In the above program (line 54) a specific MAJOR-NAME was moved to another area. If MAJOR-NUM-IN, which is the pointer in this case, is five, then the fifth MAJOR-NAME is moved. The following rules for subscripts must be followed:

a. The subscript must appear in parentheses to the right of any array item (a data-name that has been "tableized or dimensionalized" by the use of the OCCURS clause). One space should be between the array item and left parenthesis although it is not mandatory on this system.

b. No space should precede the right parenthesis or follow the left parenthesis.

c. The subscript must be a positive nonzero integer or be a data-name containing a positive nonzero integer.

Examine the following program:

```
1     IDENTIFICATION DIVISION.
2     PROGRAM-ID. SL-TABLE-PRACTICE.
3     ENVIRONMENT DIVISION.
4     DATA DIVISION.
5     WORKING-STORAGE SECTION.
6     01  SUBX      PIC 99 COMP.
7     01  TABLE-VALUES.
8         02  FILLER    PIC X(15)      VALUE "523968102938572".
9         02  FILLER    PIC X(15)      VALUE "395849203847693".
10        02  FILLER    PIC X(15)      VALUE "501948603948692".
11        02  FILLER    PIC X(15)      VALUE "693947102948672".
12        02  FILLER    PIC X(15)      VALUE "602948693847693".
13        02  FILLER    PIC X(15)      VALUE "104920496748493".
14    01  REAL-TABLE REDEFINES TABLE-VALUES.
15        02  TABLE-SALARY    OCCURS 15 TIMES      PIC 9999V99.
16    PROCEDURE DIVISION.
17    GO-AHEAD.
18        PERFORM DISPLAY-SAL-ROUTINE VARYING SUBX FROM 1 BY 1
19        UNTIL SUBX > 15.
20        STOP RUN.
21    DISPLAY-SAL-ROUTINE.
22        DISPLAY TABLE-SALARY (SUBX).
```

Execution of this program results in all 15 elements of TABLE-SALARY being displayed one at a time:

```
                    $RUN DISPTAB
                    523968
                    102938
                    572395
                    849203
                    847693
                    501948
                    603948
                    692693
                    947102
                    948672
                    602948
                    693847
                    693104
                    920496
                    748493
```

The PERFORM statement (line 18) is a powerful one. It initializes the pointer (SUBX) to 1, checks to see if it is over 15, and since 1 is not greater than 15, TABLE-SALARY (1) is put out to the terminal. Control passes back to this PERFORM statement that increments SUBX by 1, checks to see if it is over 15, and since 2 is not greater than 15, TABLE-SALARY (2) is displayed.

This process continues until SUBX = 16. Notice that 15 6-byte elements = 90 bytes, the same number of characters in TABLE-VALUES!!

SUBX has a picture that includes COMP (or USAGE is COMPUTATIONAL), which makes this data-name binary (base-2). This does not change the output whatsoever, but the efficiency of the program execution increases dramatically since no conversion is necessary from decimal (base-10) to binary during incrementation. It is an excellent practice to define subscripts in Working-Storage as COMP.

The general form of the above PERFORM Statement is as follows:

PERFORM paragraph (section) name VARYING data-name
FROM integer BY integer UNTIL condition.

QUESTIONS

1. Suppose TABLE-VALUES were redefined as follows:

```
01   REAL-TABLEY REDEFINES TABLE-VALUES.
   02   TAB-INFO OCCURS 10 TIMES.
      03   TAB-ITEM-NUM          PIC 9999.
      03   TAB-ITEM-PRICE        PIC 9(3)V99.
```

a. What is the value of TAB-ITEM-NUM (6)?
b. What is the value of TAB-ITEM-PRICE (8)?
c. Write the Procedure Division code necessary to display the first, third, fifth, seventh and ninth TAB-ITEM-NUM.

2. Write a Working-Storage entry that contains twenty occupations. Redefine these values as a table of twenty occupations.

10.5   LOADING AND PROCESSING SINGLE-LEVEL TABLES

On many occasions it is unnecessary and rather time consuming to put values in Working-Storage and redefine them. Tables can be loaded by reading files and "loading" the records or parts of these records into a table.

Suppose an instructor had given a fifty-question multiple choice test. Each student record would consist of a student name, and fifty answers. Instead of using one hundred different data-names and fifty condition statements such as:

IF CORR-ANS-5 = STU-ANS-5

or

IF CORR-ANS-36 = STU-ANS-36

etc.

two tables could be set up and only one pointer needed. Examine the following input data, program, and output. The program follows the simple three-module design developed in previous chapters. All that will be required at this point is to show how to use tables to add up the correct answers and give each student a percentage.

Correct answer record (ANSKEY.DAT):

14253311342355543212123345211243211234221122454321

Student answer records (STUKEY.DAT):

MCCARTHY A	14253311344455543211123322112432112342211224542221
MARSTEIN P	14253311342355543212123345211243211235221122454321
DUMBELL M	21342314523123452344211111132345223223415323412 3232
DUDLEY D	34142331324333321344321113223221333345112324252132
ALUCARD E	45323111223432211342214223214323232342155554221223
CULT C	54313232414432432434243424321342324532131233233333
SUMMERS S	54312232323211434443321155532321121222123445443223
SAMUELS M	14253311344454543212123322112432112342211224542221
BYRNE J	15253311344455541211123322112432112342211224542221
ALARM F	14253311342355543212223345211243211235221122454321
BACH W	14253311342353543222123345211243211235221122454321
HALL M	14253211342355543212121345211243211235221122454321
CARTER B	23123123231454311322132334421444323233443224423332

```
 1      IDENTIFICATION DIVISION.
 2      PROGRAM-ID. SL-TABLE-PRACTICE.
 3      AUTHOR. SAMUELS.
 4      ENVIRONMENT DIVISION.
 5      CONFIGURATION SECTION.
 6      SOURCE-COMPUTER. VAX-750.
 7      OBJECT-COMPUTER. VAX-750.
 8      INPUT-OUTPUT SECTION.
 9      FILE-CONTROL.
10          SELECT CORR-FILE ASSIGN TO ANSKEY.
11          SELECT STU-FILE ASSIGN TO STUKEY.
12          SELECT GRADE-FILE ASSIGN TO GREPORT.
13      DATA DIVISION.
14      FILE SECTION.
15      FD  CORR-FILE
16          DATA RECORD IS CORR-REC.
17      01  CORR-REC      PIC X(50).
18      FD  STU-FILE
19          DATA RECORD IS STU-REC.
20      01  STU-REC       PIC X(75).
21      FD  GRADE-FILE
22          DATA RECORD IS GRADE-REC.
23      01  GRADE-REC     PIC X(80).
24      WORKING-STORAGE SECTION.
25      01  ENDITALL      PIC XXXX.
26      01  POINTX        PIC 99 COMP.
27      01  TEMP-SCORE    PIC 999 VALUE 0.
28      01  WS-CORR-REC.
29          02 CORR-ANS  OCCURS 50 TIMES  PIC X.
```

```
30    01  WS-STU-REC.
31        02 STU-NAME   PIC X(25).
32        02 STU-ANS    OCCURS 50 TIMES   PIC X.
33    01  HEADER-ONE.
34        02 FILLER      PIC X(80) VALUE  ALL "*".
35    01  HEADER-TWO.
36        02 FILLER       PIC X(50) VALUE "    NAME".
37        02 FILLER       PIC X(30) VALUE "PERCENTAGE CORRECT".
38    01  DETAIL-LINE.
39        02 STU-NAME-OUT  PIC X(25).
40        02 FILLER        PIC X(35) VALUE SPACES.
41        02 SCORE-OUT     PIC ZZ9.
42        02 FILLER        PIC X VALUE "%".
43        02 FILLER        PIC X(16) VALUE SPACES.
44    PROCEDURE DIVISION.
45    BEGINIT.
46        PERFORM 100-HSKP.
47        PERFORM 200-LOOPER UNTIL ENDITALL = "DONE".
48        PERFORM 400-SO-LONG.
49    100-HSKP.
50        OPEN INPUT CORR-FILE STU-FILE OUTPUT GRADE-FILE.
51        WRITE GRADE-REC FROM HEADER-ONE AFTER 1.
52        WRITE GRADE-REC FROM HEADER-TWO AFTER 1.
53        WRITE GRADE-REC FROM HEADER-ONE AFTER 1.
54        READ CORR-FILE INTO WS-CORR-REC AT END MOVE "DONE" TO ENDITALL.
55        READ STU-FILE INTO WS-STU-REC AT END MOVE "DONE" TO ENDITALL.
56    200-LOOPER.
57        MOVE 0 TO TEMP-SCORE.
58        MOVE STU-NAME TO STU-NAME-OUT.
59        PERFORM 300-CALC-SCORE VARYING POINTX FROM 1 BY 1
60            UNTIL POINTX > 50.
61        MOVE TEMP-SCORE TO SCORE-OUT.
62        WRITE GRADE-REC FROM DETAIL-LINE AFTER 1.
63        READ STU-FILE INTO WS-STU-REC AT END MOVE "DONE" TO ENDITALL.
64    300-CALC-SCORE.
65        IF CORR-ANS (POINTX) = STU-ANS (POINTX) ADD 2 TO TEMP-SCORE.
66    400-SO-LONG.
67        CLOSE CORR-FILE STU-FILE GRADE-FILE.
68        STOP RUN.
```

```
************************************************************************
```

NAME	PERCENTAGE CORRECT

```
************************************************************************
```

NAME	PERCENTAGE CORRECT
MCCARTHY A	56%
MARSTEIN P	98%
DUMBELL M	12%
DUDLEY D	20%
ALUCARD E	18%
CULT C	16%
SUMMERS S	18%
SAMUELS M	56%
BYRNE J	52%
ALARM F	96%
BACH W	94%
HALL M	94%
CARTER B	24%

Some things of interest should be stressed about the program:

1. Two tables are present—CORR-ANS (line 29) and STU-ANS (line 32).

2. A new type of READ statement is present. Instead of just reading the file, the READ. . . . .INTO option reads the file and puts or moves the record to a Working-Storage entry. Instead of using line 55, one could have substituted:

> READ STUFILE AT END MOVE "YES" TO SWITCH.
> MOVE STU-REC TO WS-STU-REC.

to accomplish the same thing. THE READ. . . . INTO option is analogous to the WRITE. . . . FROM option.

3. Line 59 is the all important PERFORM statement that initializes and auto-matically increments POINTX until POINTX becomes greater than 50.

4. The corresponding elements of both tables are compared in line 65 with POINTX being the subscript for both tables. See Figure 10–2 for a pictorial representation.

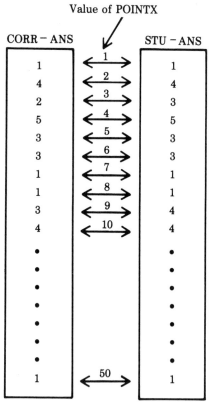

Figure 10-2

Life in "tableland" would not be complete if we couldn't load a table element by element. In the next program records will be read containing an item number, price, and description. Each item will be moved to the table. Processing stops when there are no more records so the table size may be larger than the amount of elements needed.

Input data [See Figure 10–3]:

```
1      IDENTIFICATION DIVISION.
2      PROGRAM-ID. SL-TABLE-LOAD-PRACTICE.
3      AUTHOR. SAMUELS.
4      ENVIRONMENT DIVISION.
5      CONFIGURATION SECTION.
6      SOURCE-COMPUTER. VAX-750.
7      OBJECT-COMPUTER. VAX-750.
8      INPUT-OUTPUT SECTION.
9      FILE-CONTROL.
10         SELECT RAW-FILE ASSIGN TO INVENTOR.
11     DATA DIVISION.
12     FILE SECTION.
13     FD  RAW-FILE
14         DATA RECORD IS RAW-REC.
15     01  RAW-REC            PIC X(30).
16     WORKING-STORAGE SECTION.
17     01  WS-RAW-REC.
18         02 INV-NUM-IN      PIC 99999.
19         02 INV-DESC-IN     PIC X(20).
20         02 INV-PRICE-IN    PIC 999V99.
21     01  SWITCH             PIC XXX VALUE SPACES.
22         88 ALL-DONE            VALUE "YES".
23     01  INVENTORY-TABLE.
24         02 INVENTORY-INFO OCCURS 0 TO 100 TIMES
25         DEPENDING ON COUNTX.
26             03 INV-NUM     PIC 9(5).
27             03 INV-DESC    PIC X(20).
28             03 INV-PRICE   PIC 999V99.
29     01  COUNTX             PIC 999 VALUE 0.
30     PROCEDURE DIVISION.
31     BEGIN.
32         PERFORM 100-START.
33         PERFORM 200-LOOPS UNTIL ALL-DONE.
34         PERFORM 300-BYE-BYE.
35     100-START.
36         OPEN INPUT RAW-FILE.
37         READ RAW-FILE INTO WS-RAW-REC AT END MOVE "YES" TO SWITCH.
38         ADD 1 TO COUNTX.
39     200-LOOPS.
40         MOVE INV-NUM-IN TO INV-NUM (COUNTX).
41         MOVE INV-DESC-IN TO INV-DESC (COUNTX).
42         MOVE INV-PRICE-IN TO INV-PRICE (COUNTX).
43         READ RAW-FILE INTO WS-RAW-REC AT END MOVE "YES" TO SWITCH.
44         IF NOT ALL-DONE ADD 1 TO COUNTX.
45     300-BYE-BYE.
46         CLOSE RAW-FILE.
47         STOP RUN.
```

In the above program, records are read, and each field is moved to a respective element of the table. In lines 24–25 a variable length table has been defined. If instead of lines 24–25 we wrote:

02 INVENTORY-INFO OCCURS 100 TIMES.

a 100-element table would be defined. It is possible that only forty or fifty records could have been read leaving a lot of wasted space. That is why the DEPENDING ON Option was used. The general form of this statement is:

Data-name OCCURS integer TO integer TIMES
DEPENDING ON data-name.

```
11235GENERATOR            04550
12345BATTER LEAD          01225
14555IGNITION COIL        02200
17893BRAKE LINING         00950
19823SHOCK ABSORBER       00250
21345HEADLAMP             00125
24567TRANSMISSION         19500
25675MASTER CYLINDER      03000
29832DIFFERENTIAL         12050
31243CLUTCH               05000
323244-AMP FUSE           00012
323253.5 AMP FUSE         00011
323262 AMP FUSE           00009
40032PISTON ASSEMBLY      02250
43678PWR STEERING FLUID   00220
45543ANTIFREEZE           00145
49823ALL WEATHER OIL      00035
56743EXHAUST SYSTEM       05600
56744MUFFLER              00995
63456RADIATOR             14000
67434RADIATOR HOSE        00450
67888WATER PUMP           01450
72345FAN ASSEMBLY         03300
75000GENERATOR BELT       00120
75001FAN BELT             00130
81234CARBURETOR           06660
82345GAS FILTER           00040
87483AIR FILTER           00100
89382OIL FILTER           00125
92345DISTRIBUTOR          00450
93456SPARK PLUG           00085
94784POINTS               00130
98734AIR CONDITIONER      15450
99936QUARTZ CLOCK         02400
```

Figure 10-3

QUESTIONS

1. How many bytes are in each of the following tables?

```
a.  01  HOME-TABLE.
        02  ROOMS OCCURS 25 TIMES.
            03  DRAWER-TYPE            PIC X(20).
            03  CLOSET-TYPE            PIC X(10).


b.  01  STATE-TABLE.
        02 ABRREV         OCCURS 50 TIMES PIC XX.
        02 GOV-NAME       OCCURS 50 TIMES PIC X(20).


c.  01  MONEY-TABLE.
        02  STOCK-PLAN  OCCURS 50 TIMES.
            03  PRICE                 PIC 999V99.
            03  FILLER                PIC X(4).
            03  NAME                  PIC X(15).
```

2. Write a program that will read records containing only a state name and population, and load them into a table.

10.6 TABLE LOOKUPS

There are two methods of finding out whether or not a particular value (numeric or otherwise) exists in a table. One method is by examining the table element by element ("linear search") until either the proper elemental value is found, or, after examining the entire table, the value does not exist.

Suppose someone wrote a number between one to one thousand on a piece of paper and you had to guess which number it was. If you went element by element, you would ask if the number was one, two, three, four, etc., until you guessed the number correctly. If you made your guess in a completely random fashion, it would take you an average of five hundred tries to guess each number. If you were looking for a phone number in a phone book, given the name, a linear search would have you start AT THE BEGIN-NING of the phone book until you came upon the correct name. For a search of this type the names would NOT have to be in alphabetic order. In guessing the number, the numbers would NOT have to be in ascending numerical order.

Examine the following program [execution on Figure 10-4]:

```
1    IDENTIFICATION DIVISION.
2    PROGRAM-ID. SL-TABLE-LOOKUP-PRACTICE.
3    AUTHOR. SAMUELS.
```

```
$ run prac10e
Enter inventory number
34254
INPUT NUMBER = 34254          TABLE-NUMBER = 11235
INPUT NUMBER = 34254          TABLE-NUMBER = 12345
INPUT NUMBER = 34254          TABLE-NUMBER = 14555
INPUT NUMBER = 34254          TABLE-NUMBER = 17893
INPUT NUMBER = 34254          TABLE-NUMBER = 19823
INPUT NUMBER = 34254          TABLE-NUMBER = 21345
INPUT NUMBER = 34254          TABLE-NUMBER = 24567
INPUT NUMBER = 34254          TABLE-NUMBER = 25675
INPUT NUMBER = 34254          TABLE-NUMBER = 29832
INPUT NUMBER = 34254          TABLE-NUMBER = 31243
INPUT NUMBER = 34254          TABLE-NUMBER = 32324
INPUT NUMBER = 34254          TABLE-NUMBER = 32325
INPUT NUMBER = 34254          TABLE-NUMBER = 32326
INPUT NUMBER = 34254          TABLE-NUMBER = 40032
INPUT NUMBER = 34254          TABLE-NUMBER = 43678
INPUT NUMBER = 34254          TABLE-NUMBER = 45543
INPUT NUMBER = 34254          TABLE-NUMBER = 49823
INPUT NUMBER = 34254          TABLE-NUMBER = 56743
INPUT NUMBER = 34254          TABLE-NUMBER = 56744
INPUT NUMBER = 34254          TABLE-NUMBER = 63456
INPUT NUMBER = 34254          TABLE-NUMBER = 67434
INPUT NUMBER = 34254          TABLE-NUMBER = 67888
INPUT NUMBER = 34254          TABLE-NUMBER = 72345
INPUT NUMBER = 34254          TABLE-NUMBER = 75000
INPUT NUMBER = 34254          TABLE-NUMBER = 75001
INPUT NUMBER = 34254          TABLE-NUMBER = 81234
INPUT NUMBER = 34254          TABLE-NUMBER = 82345
INPUT NUMBER = 34254          TABLE-NUMBER = 87483
INPUT NUMBER = 34254          TABLE-NUMBER = 89382
INPUT NUMBER = 34254          TABLE-NUMBER = 92345
INPUT NUMBER = 34254          TABLE-NUMBER = 93456
INPUT NUMBER = 34254          TABLE-NUMBER = 94784
INPUT NUMBER = 34254          TABLE-NUMBER = 98734
INPUT NUMBER = 34254          TABLE-NUMBER = 99936
number does not exist in table.
Enter inventory number
17893
INPUT NUMBER = 17893          TABLE-NUMBER = 11235
INPUT NUMBER = 17893          TABLE-NUMBER = 12345
INPUT NUMBER = 17893          TABLE-NUMBER = 14555
INPUT NUMBER = 17893          TABLE-NUMBER = 17893
        DESCRIPTION = BRAKE LINING
        PRICE = 00950
Enter inventory number
99999
```

[INPUT BY USER]

Figure 10-4

```
 4     ENVIRONMENT DIVISION.
 5     CONFIGURATION SECTION.
 6     SOURCE-COMPUTER. VAX-750.
 7     OBJECT-COMPUTER. VAX-750.
 8     INPUT-OUTPUT SECTION.
 9     FILE-CONTROL.
10         SELECT RAW-FILE ASSIGN TO INVENTOR.
11     DATA DIVISION.
12     FILE SECTION.
13     FD  RAW-FILE
14         DATA RECORD IS RAW-REC.
15     01  RAW-REC              PIC X(30).
16     WORKING-STORAGE SECTION.
17     01  WS-RAW-REC.
18         02 INV-NUM-IN        PIC 99999.
19         02 INV-DESC-IN       PIC X(20).
20         02 INV-PRICE-IN      PIC 999V99.
21     01  SWITCH               PIC XXX VALUE SPACES.
22         88 ALL-DONE            VALUE "YES".
23     01  FINDER-SWITCH        PIC XXX VALUE SPACES.
24         88  FOUND-IT           VALUE "YES".
25         88 NOT-IN-IT           VALUE "NO".
26     01  INVENTORY-TABLE.
27         02 INVENTORY-INFO OCCURS 0 TO 100 TIMES
28         DEPENDING ON COUNTX.
29             03 INV-NUM     PIC 9(5).
30             03 INV-DESC    PIC X(20).
31             03 INV-PRICE   PIC 999V99.
32     01  COUNTX               PIC 999 VALUE 0.
33     01  SUBX                 PIC 99 COMP VALUE 0.
34     PROCEDURE DIVISION.
35     BEGIN.
36         PERFORM 100-START.
37         PERFORM 200-LOOPS UNTIL ALL-DONE.
38         PERFORM 250-CLOSE.
39         PERFORM 300-RESTART.
40         PERFORM 400-RELOOP UNTIL INV-NUM-IN = 99999.
41         PERFORM 600-BYE-BYE.
42     100-START.
43         OPEN INPUT RAW-FILE.
44         READ RAW-FILE INTO WS-RAW-REC AT END MOVE "YES" TO SWITCH.
45         ADD 1 TO COUNTX.
46     200-LOOPS.
47         MOVE INV-NUM-IN TO INV-NUM (COUNTX).
48         MOVE INV-DESC-IN TO INV-DESC (COUNTX).
49         MOVE INV-PRICE-IN TO INV-PRICE (COUNTX).
50         READ RAW-FILE INTO WS-RAW-REC AT END MOVE "YES" TO SWITCH.
51         IF NOT ALL-DONE ADD 1 TO COUNTX.
52     250-CLOSE.
53         CLOSE RAW-FILE.
54     300-RESTART.
55         DISPLAY "Enter inventory number".
56         ACCEPT INV-NUM-IN.
57     400-RELOOP.
58         MOVE 1 TO SUBX.
59         MOVE SPACES TO FINDER-SWITCH.
60         PERFORM 500-LOCATE-STUFF UNTIL FOUND-IT OR NOT-IN-IT.
61         DISPLAY "Enter inventory number".
62         ACCEPT INV-NUM-IN.
63     500-LOCATE-STUFF.
64         DISPLAY "INPUT NUMBER = " INV-NUM-IN
```

```
65              "         TABLE-NUMBER = " INV-NUM (SUBX).
66          IF INV-NUM-IN = INV-NUM (SUBX)
67              DISPLAY "       DESCRIPTION = " INV-DESC (SUBX)
68              DISPLAY "        PRICE = " INV-PRICE (SUBX)
69              MOVE "YES" TO FINDER-SWITCH.
70          ADD 1 TO SUBX.
71          IF SUBX > COUNTX MOVE "NO" TO FINDER-SWITCH
72          DISPLAY "number does not exist in table.".
73      600-BYE-BYE.
74          STOP RUN.
```

Some important aspects of a table lookup program need to be explained:

a. Statements 42–53 "load" the table.

b. In statement 56, a number is entered from the terminal.

c. Statements 63–72 contain the logic for a linear search of the number. If it exists, the description and price are displayed. If the number does not exist, a message stating that the number is not in the table is displayed.

d. Notice the use of conditional data-names in statement 60.

Entering what number stops this program??

There is another way of doing a linear search. The following method employs the use of an index and the all important SEARCH verb. Observe the following program [execution in Figure 10–5]

```
 1      IDENTIFICATION DIVISION.
 2      PROGRAM-ID. SL-TABLE-LOOKUP-PRACTICE.
 3      AUTHOR. SAMUELS.
 4      ENVIRONMENT DIVISION.
 5      CONFIGURATION SECTION.
 6      SOURCE-COMPUTER. VAX-750.
 7      OBJECT-COMPUTER. VAX-750.
 8      INPUT-OUTPUT SECTION.
 9      FILE-CONTROL.
10          SELECT RAW-FILE ASSIGN TO INVENTOR.
11      DATA DIVISION.
12      FILE SECTION.
13      FD  RAW-FILE
14          DATA RECORD IS RAW-REC.
15      01  RAW-REC            PIC X(30).
16      WORKING-STORAGE SECTION.
17      01  WS-RAW-REC.
18          02 INV-NUM-IN      PIC 99999.
19          02 INV-DESC-IN     PIC X(20).
20          02 INV-PRICE-IN    PIC 999V99.
21      01  SWITCH             PIC XXX VALUE SPACES.
22          88 ALL-DONE            VALUE "YES".
23      01  INVENTORY-TABLE.
24          02 INVENTORY-INFO OCCURS 0 TO 100 TIMES
25          DEPENDING ON COUNTX INDEXED BY INV-IND.
26              03 INV-NUM     PIC 9(5).
27              03 INV-DESC    PIC X(20).
28              03 INV-PRICE   PIC 999V99.
29      01  COUNTX             PIC 999 VALUE 0.
30      PROCEDURE DIVISION.
```

```
                            $ run prac10f
                            Enter inventory number
                            89483
                            number not in table
                            Enter inventory number
                            89382
                            OIL FILTER
                            00125
                            Enter inventory number
                            99999
```

Figure 10-5

```
31    BEGIN.
32        PERFORM 100-START.
33        PERFORM 200-LOOPS UNTIL ALL-DONE.
34        PERFORM 250-CLOSE.
35        PERFORM 300-RESTART.
36        PERFORM 400-RELOOP UNTIL INV-NUM-IN = 99999.
37        PERFORM 600-BYE-BYE.
38    100-START.
39        OPEN INPUT RAW-FILE.
40        READ RAW-FILE INTO WS-RAW-REC AT END MOVE "YES" TO SWITCH.
41        ADD 1 TO COUNTX.
42    200-LOOPS.
43        MOVE INV-NUM-IN TO INV-NUM (COUNTX).
44        MOVE INV-DESC-IN TO INV-DESC (COUNTX).
45        MOVE INV-PRICE-IN TO INV-PRICE (COUNTX).
46        READ RAW-FILE INTO WS-RAW-REC AT END MOVE "YES" TO SWITCH.
47        IF NOT ALL-DONE ADD 1 TO COUNTX.
48    250-CLOSE.
49        CLOSE RAW-FILE.
50    300-RESTART.
51        DISPLAY "Enter inventory number".
52        ACCEPT INV-NUM-IN.
53    400-RELOOP.
54        SET INV-IND TO 1.
55        SEARCH INVENTORY-INFO AT END DISPLAY "number not in table"
56        WHEN INV-NUM-IN = INV-NUM (INV-IND)
57                DISPLAY INV-DESC (INV-IND)
58                DISPLAY INV-PRICE (INV-IND).
59        DISPLAY "Enter inventory number".
60        ACCEPT INV-NUM-IN.
61    600-BYE-BYE.
62        STOP RUN.
```

10.7 INDEXES

In statement 25, the clause:

INDEXED BY INV-IND

makes INV-IND the index for this table. Conceptually, indexes, such as

INV-IND, and subscripts, such as SUBX or COUNTX, act as "pointers" to the table. As far as a COBOL programmer is concerned, they do essentially the same thing; however, there are major advantages to using indexes.

a. Indexes do not require a picture clause because they represent a displacement. Notice that SUBX is absent from the above program. It is not needed. Each element in this table contains 30 bytes. The first element, referenced by SUBX = 1, is now referenced by INV-IND having a displacement value of 0. The second element, referenced by SUBX = 2, is now referenced by INV-IND having a displacement value of 30. If there are 50 elements in the table (each element containing a number, description, and price), then there are 50 displacement values. The fortieth displacement value for INV-IND = 1200. Internally, subscripts actually get converted to indexes; hence, indexing is more efficient for execution.

b. One can use the SEARCH verb for a linear search or the SEARCH ALL phrase for the more efficient binary search!! Examine lines 54–59. After the index is set to the "first displacement" (SET INV-IND TO 1), the SEARCH statement automatically increments the index until either the number is found or the search is unsuccessful. The logic is much simpler. An entire paragraph was eliminated plus there was no need for FINDER-SWITCH. See for yourself by comparing the last two programs listed above. The general form of that SEARCH statement is:

SEARCH table-item AT END declarative statement(s)
WHEN condition declarative statement(s).

c. Probably the best advantage to indexing is that one can use the binary search technique. Remember that number that was put down on a piece of paper for you to guess? This time ask if the number is greater than 500. If it is, ask if it is over 750. If it is not, ask if it is greater than 625 and so on. It will take you a lot less than 500 tries!! The binary search, therefore, eliminates half the table with every comparison and, in so doing, reduces the number of necessary comparisons.

Examine the following program:

```
1     IDENTIFICATION DIVISION.
2     PROGRAM-ID. SL-TABLE-LOOKUP-PRACTICE.
3     AUTHOR. SAMUELS.
4     ENVIRONMENT DIVISION.
5     CONFIGURATION SECTION.
6     SOURCE-COMPUTER. VAX-750.
7     OBJECT-COMPUTER. VAX-750.
.     INPUT-OUTPUT SECTION.
;     FILE-CONTROL.
10        SELECT RAW-FILE ASSIGN TO INVENTOR.
11    DATA DIVISION.
```

```
12    FILE SECTION.
13    FD  RAW-FILE
14        DATA RECORD IS RAW-REC.
15    01  RAW-REC            PIC X(30).
16    WORKING-STORAGE SECTION.
17    01  WS-RAW-REC.
18        02 INV-NUM-IN       PIC 99999.
19        02 INV-DESC-IN      PIC X(20).
20        02 INV-PRICE-IN     PIC 999V99.
21    01  SWITCH             PIC XXX VALUE SPACES.
22        88 ALL-DONE               VALUE "YES".
23    01  INVENTORY-TABLE.
24        02 INVENTORY-INFO OCCURS 0 TO 100 TIMES
25        DEPENDING ON COUNTX
26        ASCENDING KEY IS INV-NUM
27        INDEXED BY INV-IND.
28            03 INV-NUM       PIC 9(5).
29            03 INV-DESC      PIC X(20).
30            03 INV-PRICE     PIC 999V99.
31    01  COUNTX             PIC 999 VALUE 0.
32    PROCEDURE DIVISION.
33    BEGIN.
34        PERFORM 100-START.
35        PERFORM 200-LOOPS UNTIL ALL-DONE.
36        PERFORM 250-CLOSE.
37        PERFORM 300-RESTART.
38        PERFORM 400-RELOOP UNTIL INV-NUM-IN = 99999.
39        PERFORM 600-BYE-BYE.
40    100-START.
41        OPEN INPUT RAW-FILE.
42        READ RAW-FILE INTO WS-RAW-REC AT END MOVE "YES" TO SWITCH.
43        ADD 1 TO COUNTX.
44    200-LOOPS.
45        MOVE INV-NUM-IN TO INV-NUM (COUNTX).
46        MOVE INV-DESC-IN TO INV-DESC (COUNTX).
47        MOVE INV-PRICE-IN TO INV-PRICE (COUNTX).
48        READ RAW-FILE INTO WS-RAW-REC AT END MOVE "YES" TO SWITCH.
49        IF NOT ALL-DONE ADD 1 TO COUNTX.
50    250-CLOSE.
51        CLOSE RAW-FILE.
52    300-RESTART.
53        DISPLAY "Enter inventory number".
54        ACCEPT INV-NUM-IN.
55    400-RELOOP.
56        SET INV-IND TO 1.
57        SEARCH ALL INVENTORY-INFO AT END DISPLAY "number not in table"
58        WHEN INV-NUM (INV-IND) = INV-NUM-IN
59            DISPLAY INV-DESC (INV-IND)
60            DISPLAY INV-PRICE (INV-IND).
61        DISPLAY "Enter inventory number".
62        ACCEPT INV-NUM-IN.
63    600-BYE-BYE.
64        STOP RUN.
```

Notice that in order to use a binary search a new clause must be added to our table. Line 26 states that the INV-NUM is in ascending order. The ASCENDING or DESCENDING clause is required for one to use the SEARCH ALL phrase. The SEARCH ALL is substituted for SEARCH in line 57.

There are a couple of disadvantages to using indexes:

a. An index can reference only one table. In a previous program where we compared student answers with correct answers, only one "pointer" or sub-script was necessary. If each table was indexed, then both indexes would have to be used, causing additional code. Sometimes subscripting, although not as efficient for execution, is easier to code.

b. One must use the SET, SEARCH, or PERFORM statement to increment or decrement an index.

Also:

MOVE 3 TO INV-IND is not allowed.

use:

SET INV-IND TO 3.

And:

ADD 1 TO INV-IND is not allowed.

use:

SET INV-IND UP BY 1.

Or:

SUBTRACT 1 FROM INV-IND is not allowed.

use:

SET INV-IND DOWN BY 1.

One final note. Examine line 58. The items have been reversed from the previous program. If one uses:

INV-NUM-IN = INV-NUM (INV-IND)

one gets the following error message:

```
$cob inventab
  58                        WHEN INV-NUM-IN = INV-NUM (INV-IND)
                                 1
%COBOL-E-ERROR 302, (1) Condition must reference a key, and be in-
dexed by
   first index name
%COBOL-E-ENDDIAGS, UD2:[SAMUELS]INVENTAB.COB;4 completed
with 4 diagnostics
$
```

Well, at least this message made some sense. It states that the indexed item must be referenced first. This is necessary only for the binary search (SEARCH ALL), not the linear search (SEARCH).

QUESTIONS

1. Given the following definition in Working-Storage:

```
01  COURSE-NAME-VALUES.
    02  FILLER          PIC X(15) VALUE "0123CHEMISTRY".
    02  FILLER          PIC X(15) VALUE "1234BIOLOGY".
    02  FILLER          PIC X(15) VALUE "2421ECONOMICS".
    02  FILLER          PIC X(15) VALUE "3324ACCOUNTING".
    02  FILLER          PIC X(15) VALUE "4432PHYSICS".
    02  FILLER          PIC X(15) VALUE "4938EDUCATION".
    02  FILLER          PIC X(15) VALUE "6443PSYCHOLOGY".
    02  FILLER          PIC X(15) VALUE "8932PHILOSOPHY".
    02  FILLER          PIC X(15) VALUE "8999LAW".
    02  FILLER          PIC X(15) VALUE "9012COMP. SCI.".
```

Redefine the above values into a single-level table of course numbers and course names.

2. Redefine the above, again, to include the two clauses necessary if one wanted to do a binary search of the table.

3. Provide the Procedure Division code necessary to accept a number from the terminal and display the appropriate course name. If a number cannot be found, display an appropriate error message. Try doing this without indexes, and the binary search with indexes.

SUMMARY

This chapter, understandably, has some concepts that are rather difficult to comprehend. It is most important to remember that a table is really nothing more than an identifier (data-name) that can "hold" more than one value at a time. The number of items in the table is totally dependent on the OCCURS clause. To reference a particular item in a table, one needs to use a pointer of some kind (SUBSCRIPT or INDEX).

Additional table handling techniques includes:

1. The REDEFINES clause—a Data Division entry that allows one to describe an area in storage in a different way.

2. The PERFORM. . . . . .VARYING statement in the Procedure Division that allows one to load or process a table, usually element by element.

3. The SEARCH verb—a Procedure Division entry that allows one to look up a particular item in a table that has the INDEXED BY option.

PROGRAMMING PROBLEMS

A. Read into a table input records, each containing a name and salary.
   1. Print this table out backwards.
   2. Find the person with the highest salary.
   3. Find the person with the lowest salary.
   4. Find the average of all the salaries.

B. Suppose you were given the following payroll problem to solve for a particular trucking firm:

1. Truck drivers get paid biweekly—their pay is determined by how many miles they drive * their rate/mile * trips taken. Although their pay/mile rate remains constant for one year their routes may change from pay period to pay period, and the routes themselves may change (extra stop, detour, etc., causing an increase or decrease in the number of miles per "run" or route).

2. The route information is to be loaded into a table every pay period, but the rates/mile for the various pay classes can be put into the program.
   a. The input format for the route data is as follows:

Field	Columns
Route #	1–2
Destination	3–22
# of miles	23–25

b. There are ten rate/mile pay classes (you can put these values in Working-Storage, then redefine them using a pic V9999):

Pay Class #	Rate per Mile
1	.3456
2	.3478
3	.3506
4	.3540
5	.3566
6	.3589
7	.3622
8	.3651
9	.3678
10	.3701

c. The employee payroll records have the following format:

Field	Columns
Name	1–20
Pay class #	21–22
Route #	30–31
# of trips	40–41

3. two reports are to be printed:
   a. Route information (from the route data)
   b. Payroll report

The following is the data for the routes:

12DETROIT	292
16ST. LOUIS	305
22CLEVELAND	347
37DES MOINES	350
44ST. LOUIS	299
56MILWAUKEE	091
78MADISON	146
79GREEN BAY	204
81DAVENPORT	166
88LIMA	231
92LOUISVILLE	405
96SPRINGFIELD	199

The following are the data for the drivers:

SAM JOHNSON	08	16	14	
PETE SMITH	06	10	15	
SARAH TRUESDALE	10	01	08	
MAX COOK	06	04	07	
STEVE SAMUELS	12	05	12	(invalid record)
HARRY STORM	09	07	11	
SUE WILKENS	04	02	AB	(invalid record)

If you include an error report, you will need five SELECT statements (two for the input records and three for the output records).

Example:

To get the biweekly salary for HARRY STORM we know the following:

a. he gets .3678/mile (from table in Working-Storage)

b. he went to DES MOINES (from a table lookup of routes)

c. he made 11 trips

his salary = .3678 times 11 times 350

The format of the route information should include the destination, number, and miles. The format of the payroll report should include the driver's name, destination, number of trips, total mileage, and salary. The error report is up to you.

*C. Put a table of income tax rates into Working-Storage. Do this for single persons only [see any IRS Tax Brochure—use Table XYZ]. Write a program to accept a person's name and adjusted gross income from the terminal and display the federal tax.

Multilevel Tables

11.1 TWO-LEVEL TABLES

In the previous chapter, single-level tables were discussed. In order to find a data element in a one-dimensional array, one pointer (subscript or index) was required. With two- or three-level tables, two or three pointers are required.

Examine the following:

```
01 TABLE-VALUES.
    02 FILLER PIC X(20) VALUE "14329581736271827394".
    02 FILLER PIC X(20) VALUE "43293049182930594830".
    02 FILLER PIC X(20) VALUE "10594382930591820392".
    02 FILLER PIC X(20) VALUE "20930492039682473932".
    02 FILLER PIC X(20) VALUE "49203941929305948392".
```

Let us redefine this as a two dimensional table of Car Insurance Rates (the rate—999V99 is based on sex and location).

```
01   CAR-INSURANCE-TABLE REDEFINES TABLE-VALUES.
    02   SEX OCCURS 2 TIMES.
       03   LOCATION OCCURS 10 TIMES.
          04   RATE PIC 999V99.
```

One needs two pointers for the above table—assume male=1 and female=2. Schematically, the table could be represented as follows:

| | COLUMN | | | | | | | | | |
	1	2	3	4	5	6	7	8	9	10
R O	1 14329	58173	62718	27394	43293	04918	29305	54830	10594	38293
W	2 05918	20392	20930	49203	96824	73932	49203	94192	93059	48392

Rate (x y) = Rate (Row Column)

where X and Y are pointers to row and column. If $X = 1$ and $Y = 3$, then RATE (X Y) would point to the 1st row and 3rd column.
What is the value for:

a. RATE (1 3) ?

b. RATE (2 9) ?

c. RATE (3 3) ?

To answer the above questions one should understand that:

1. The redefinition (CAR-INSURANCE-TABLE) requires 100 characters because there are ten locations WITHIN each sex. Since there are two sexes this makes twenty combinations, each combination containing 5 characters (999V99)—20 times 5 = 100.

2. The first pointer references the sex. If it is 1, then one must look at the first 50 characters and if 2, then the last 50 characters are referenced. The second pointer references one of the ten locations within the 50 characters—each location containing 5-byte (5-character) rates.

So for (a), concern yourself with only the first 50 numbers since the sex pointer = 1. Now you should divide these 50 numbers up into ten 5-byte sections and find the 3rd section (location). The answer = 62718. For (b) the second 50 bytes are referenced.
We want the ninth location so that we obtain a rate = 93059. The third question is invalid. There is no possibility of a third sex!!
It is important to understand that if we had redefined TABLE-VALUES as follows:

```
01   CAR-INSURANCE-TABLE.
     02   LOCATION OCCURS 10 TIMES.
          03   SEX OCCURS 2 TIMES.
               04   RATE PIC 999V99.
```

the values of RATE (1 3) and RATE (2 9) would be different. In this redefinition, there are two sexes WITHIN ten locations. That is, one divides the table of numbers up into 10 sections, each section containing 10 characters. Then each section (location) is divided up into two 5-byte sections, one for each sex. Try to find the values for RATE (9 1) and RATE (6 2) with this redefinition.

If commas are used to separate these pointers then always follow a comma with a space: RATE (1,3) and RATE (1 ,3) are illegal: use RATE (1, 3).

11.2   THREE-LEVEL TABLES

Now let us try to redefine TABLE-VALUES in three dimensions. We will use two sexes, five locations, and two driver-types (good and bad) in our redefinition.

```
01   CAR-INSURANCE-TABLE REDEFINES TABLE-VALUES.
   02   SEX OCCURS 2 TIMES.
      03   LOCATION OCCURS 5 TIMES.
       04   DRIVER-TYPE OCCURS 2 TIMES.
       05   RATE PIC 999V99.
```

A diagram for the above redefinition is shown in Figure 11–1.

You will notice that there are still twenty combinations of 5-byte insurance rates. There are two driver-types WITHIN five locations WITHIN two sexes.

NOW—what is the car insurance rate for:

a. A bad female driver living in location three?

b. A good male driver living in location four?

To answer (a) we must look at the second 50 characters because female = 2. Then we divide these 50 characters five times and look for the third occurrence of 10 characters because location = 3. Finally we divide those 10 characters into two 5-byte rates because bad = 2. Hence the value for RATE (2 3 2) = 73932.

Now try to figure out (b)!!

Is it possible to write a routine (in COBOL, of course) that would compute and display what these rates would be with a 5% increase? Of course it is—see below:

PROCEDURE DIVISION.

.

.

.

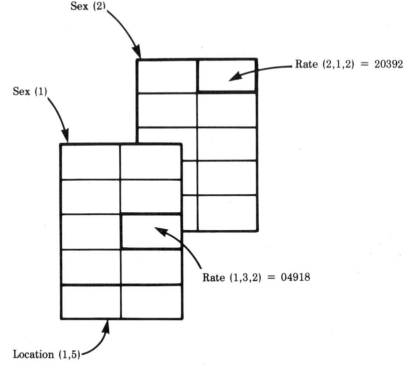

Sex (2)

Rate (2,1,2) = 20392

Sex (1)

Rate (1,3,2) = 04918

Location (1,5)

Figure 11–1

PERFORM COMPUTE-N-DISPLAY-RATES VARYING SEX-SUB
   FROM 1 BY 1 UNTIL SEX-SUB > 2
      AFTER LOCATION-SUB FROM 1 BY 1 UNTIL
      LOCATION-SUB > 5
         AFTER TYPE-SUB FROM 1 BY 1 UNTIL TYPE-SUB > 2.

.
.
.

COMPUTE-N-DISPLAY-RATES.
   COMPUTE NEW-RATE ROUNDED = RATE (SEX-SUB
      LOCATION-SUB TYPE-SUB) * 1.05.
   DISPLAY NEW-RATE.

It is assumed, of course, that the data-names introduced above are properly described in the DATA DIVISION.

Notice that the VARYING option of the PERFORM statement can be
extended for two- and three-dimensional tables with the addition of the

AFTER option. The general format is as follows:

PERFORM paragraph-name VARYING identifier FROM integer BY integer
    [AFTER identifier FROM integer BY integer]
        [AFTER identifier FROM integer BY integer]

In the above example using this type of PERFORM, SEX-SUB, LOCATION-SUB, AND TYPE-SUB are all initialized to 1. The first rate [RATE (1 1 1)] is multiplied by 1.05 giving NEW-RATE. NEW-RATE is then displayed on the terminal. Then, TYPE-SUB is incremented to 2 and RATE (1 1 2) is acted upon. TYPE-SUB is incremented to 3, but since that makes TYPE-SUB > 2, action by the PERFORM does not take place. Rather, LOCATION-SUB is incremented to 2 and TYPE-SUB is re-initialized to 1. RATE (1 2 1) is acted upon and so on. See Figure 11-1 for a complete illustration.

    Most tables are so large that it is ridiculous to put them all into Working-Storage and redefine them. It is better to read these values into a table. Examine the following table entry in Working-Storage:

```
01  INTERESTING-TABLE.
    02   BLOOD-TYPE OCCURS 4 TIMES INDEXED BY BL.
      03   RH-FACTOR OCCURS 2 TIMES INDEXED BY RH.
        04   WEIGHT-RANGE OCCURS 80 TIMES INDEXED BY WE.
          05  NUM-OF-PEOPLE                          PIC 9(4).
```

You should be able to answer the following questions:

1. How many bytes does this table hold?

2. Which pointer references the largest amount of data—how much for each occurrence?

Now let us load this table from a file containing records that each have only a 4-byte number. i.e.,

```
        FD   INFILE
             DATA RECORD IS IN-REC.
             01 NUM-IN                PIC 9(4).
```

The following represents the code to do the above:

```
PROCEDURE DIVISION.
        .
        .

        READ INFILE AT END MOVE "YES" TO SWITCH.
        PERFORM LOAD-GORY-TABLE VARYING BL FROM 1 BY 1
```

> UNTIL BL > 4
>   AFTER RH FROM 1 BY 1 UNTIL RH > 2
>   AFTER WE FROM 1 BY 1 UNTIL WE > 80.
>
> .
> .

> LOAD-GORY-TABLE.
>   MOVE NUM-IN TO NUM-OF-PEOPLE (BL RH WE).
>   READ INFILE AT END MOVE "YES" TO SWITCH.

The paragraph, LOAD-GORY-TABLE, will be "performed" or executed 640 times. Remember that there are eighty weight ranges within two Rh-factors within four blood types. Each time it is executed a 4-byte move to the three-dimensional table takes place. NUM-OF-PEOPLE (2 2 35) means refers to the thirty-fifth weight class with Rh-factor = 2 and blood-type = 2.

With three-level tables one has the capability of referencing one- or two-level tables. For example, BLOOD-TYPE (3) references everyone with the third blood type that represents 640 bytes. RH-FACTOR (1 2) references all those with Rh-factor = 2 and blood-type = 1 that represents 320 bytes in the table.

11.3   A PROBLEM

Multidimensional tables can be further clarified if we write a program to solve the following problem:

Four candidates for office are running in a primary political race. Besides wanting to find out who the winner will be, the party also wants to know how many votes each candidate got from each sex in six age groups (21–30, 31–40, etc.). The input file consists of records containing:

a. a two digit number that represents the number of voter information fields.

b. voter information fields with the age, sex, and candidate voted for.

An example of input data as follows:

0540132521552432224214

05 = 5 voter information fields

where: field one has a voter 40 years old, male, who voted for the third candidate. Field two has a 25-year-old female who voted for the first candidate, and so on.

Output should have the following format:

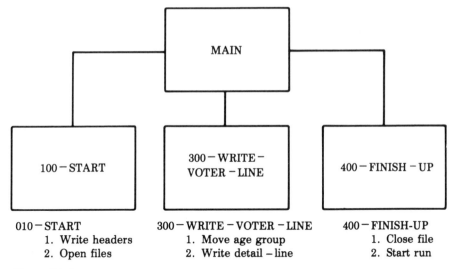

010 – START	300 – WRITE – VOTER – LINE	400 – FINISH-UP
1. Write headers	1. Move age group	1. Close file
2. Open files	2. Write detail – line	2. Start run

Figure 11-2

	CANDIDATE-ONE		CANDIDATE-TWO		CANDIDATE-THREE		CANDIDATE-FOUR	
	MALE	FEMALE	MALE	FEMALE	MALE	FEMALE	MALE	FEMALE
21–30	x	x	x	x	x	x	x	x
31–40	x	x	x	x	x	x	x	x
41–50	x	x	x	x	x	x	x	x
51–60	x	x	x	x	x	x	x	x
61–70	x	x	x	x	x	x	x	x
71–80	x	x	x	x	x	x	x	x

11.4 A SOLUTION

Let us begin by attacking the problem in our regular structured fashion, piece by piece. Examine Figure 11-2 that has the modular diagram and pseudo-code. We can begin by printing out the headers and the age groups of the six detail lines.

Examine the code below:

```
1    IDENTIFICATION DIVISION.
2    PROGRAM-ID. THREE-LEVEL-PRACTICE.
3    AUTHOR.  STEVE SAMUELS.
4    ENVIRONMENT DIVISION.
5    CONFIGURATION SECTION.
6    SOURCE-COMPUTER. VAX-750.
```

```
 7     OBJECT-COMPUTER. VAX-750.
 8     INPUT-OUTPUT SECTION.
 9     FILE-CONTROL.
10         SELECT OUTFILE ASSIGN TO TABREPORT.
11     DATA DIVISION.
12     FILE SECTION.
13     FD  OUTFILE
14         DATA RECORD IS TABREC.
15     01  TABREC        PIC X(80).
16     WORKING-STORAGE SECTION.
17     01  AGE-VALUES.
18         02  FILLER    PIC X(5) VALUE "21-30".
19         02  FILLER    PIC X(5) VALUE "31-40".
20         02  FILLER    PIC X(5) VALUE "41-50".
21         02  FILLER    PIC X(5) VALUE "51-60".
22         02  FILLER    PIC X(5) VALUE "61-70".
23         02  FILLER    PIC X(5) VALUE "71-80".
24     01  AGE-TABLE REDEFINES AGE-VALUES.
25         02 AGE-GROUP OCCURS 6 TIMES PIC X(5).
26     01  HEADER-ONE.
27         02  FILLER    PIC X(8) VALUE "AGE".
28         02  FILLER    PIC X(18) VALUE "CANDIDATE-ONE".
29         02  FILLER    PIC X(18) VALUE "CANDIDATE-TWO".
30         02  FILLER    PIC X(18) VALUE "CANDIDATE-THREE".
31         02  FILLER    PIC X(18) VALUE "CANDIDATE-FOUR".
32     01  HEADER-TWO.
33         02  FILLER    PIC X(8) VALUE "GROUP".
34         02  FILLER    PIC X(18) VALUE "MALE      FEMALE".
35         02  FILLER    PIC X(18) VALUE "MALE      FEMALE".
36         02  FILLER    PIC X(18) VALUE "MALE      FEMALE".
37         02  FILLER    PIC X(18) VALUE "MALE      FEMALE".
38     01  HEADER-THREE.
39         02  FILLER PIC X(80) VALUE ALL "*".
40     01  VOTER-LINE.
41         02  AGE-GROUP-OUT    PIC X(5).
42         02  FILLER           PIC X(75).
43     01  AGE-SUB          PIC 9 COMP.
44     PROCEDURE DIVISION.
45     BEGIN.
46         PERFORM 100-START.
47         PERFORM 300-WRITE-VOTER-LINE VARYING AGE-SUB
48             FROM 1 BY 1 UNTIL AGE-SUB > 6.
49         PERFORM 400-FINISH-UP.
50     100-START.
51         OPEN OUTPUT OUTFILE.
52         WRITE TABREC FROM HEADER-THREE AFTER PAGE.
53         WRITE TABREC FROM HEADER-ONE AFTER 1.
54         WRITE TABREC FROM HEADER-TWO AFTER 1.
55         WRITE TABREC FROM HEADER-THREE AFTER 1.
56     300-WRITE-VOTER-LINE.
57         MOVE AGE-GROUP (AGE-SUB) TO AGE-GROUP-OUT.
58         WRITE TABREC FROM VOTER-LINE AFTER 2.
59     400-FINISH-UP.
60         CLOSE OUTFILE.
61         STOP RUN.
```

The following represents the output from the above program.

```
**********************************************************************************
AGE   CANDIDATE-ONE    CANDIDATE-TWO     CANDIDATE-THREE    CANDIDATE-FOUR
GROUP MALE     FEMALE   MALE      FEMALE  MALE      FEMALE  MALE      FEMALE
**********************************************************************************
```
21–30
31–40
41–50
51–60
61–70
71–80

Of course there is no voter information!! No records were read in and there was no three-level table set up in Working-Storage to accumulate these totals. Although the above is pretty straightforward, we now need to read a record, convert the age in each voter field to a subscript, and use sex and vote as subscripts before adding 1 to this table. Let's read in one record to see if we can load this table. Then let us add the code to move from this three-level table to the Voter-Line.

Examine the modified modular diagram and related pseudocode (Figure 11–3) for enhancing this program. The code follows below:

```
1       IDENTIFICATION DIVISION.
2       PROGRAM-ID. THREE-LEVEL-PRACTICE.
3       AUTHOR.  STEVE SAMUELS.
4       ENVIRONMENT DIVISION.
5       CONFIGURATION SECTION.
6       SOURCE-COMPUTER. VAX-750.
7       OBJECT-COMPUTER. VAX-750.
8       INPUT-OUTPUT SECTION.
9       FILE-CONTROL.
10          select infile assign to votes.
11          SELECT OUTFILE ASSIGN TO TABREPORT.
12      DATA DIVISION.
13      FILE SECTION.
14      fd  infile
15          data record is inrec.
16      01  inrec.
17          02 num-of-vote-fields     pic 99.
18          02 voter-info occurs 0 to 15 times
19          depending on num-of-vote-fields.
20              03 age-in    pic 99.
21              03 sex-in    pic 9.
22              03 choice-in pic 9.
23      FD  OUTFILE
24          DATA RECORD IS TABREC.
25      01  TABREC          PIC X(80).
26      WORKING-STORAGE SECTION.
27      01  AGE-VALUES.
28          02  FILLER   PIC X(5) VALUE "21-30".
29          02  FILLER   PIC X(5) VALUE "31-40".
30          02  FILLER   PIC X(5) VALUE "41-50".
31          02  FILLER   PIC X(5) VALUE "51-60".
32          02  FILLER   PIC X(5) VALUE "61-70".
33          02  FILLER   PIC X(5) VALUE "71-80".
```

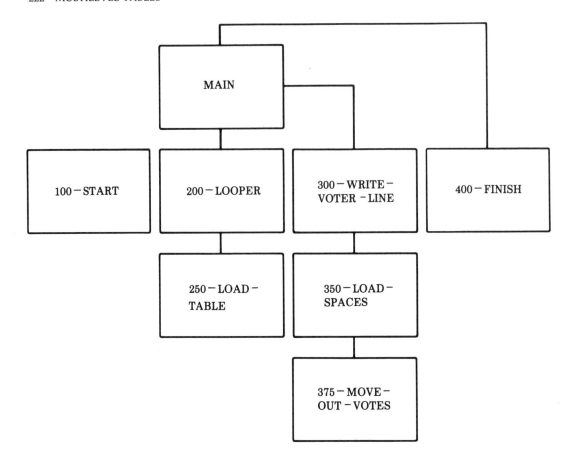

Additional Module in RED

1. 100 – START
    a. Open files
    b. Initialize table
    c. Headers
    d. Initial read

2. 200 – LOOPER
    a. Transfer control to load table
    b. Subsequent reads

3. 250 – LOAD – TABLE
    a. Ready subscripts
        1 1 to table

4. 300 – WRITE VOTER LINE
    a. Transfer control to next paragraph
        4 times (4 candidates)
    b. Move age sub
    c. Write detail line

5. 375 – MOVE – OUT – VOTES
    a. Move number of votes to detail line
        - 8 numbers!

6. 400 – FINISH
    a. Close file
    b. Stop run

Figure 11–3

```
34     01  AGE-TABLE REDEFINES AGE-VALUES.
35         02 AGE-GROUP OCCURS 6 TIMES PIC X(5).
36     01  HEADER-ONE.
37         02  FILLER   PIC X(8) VALUE "AGE".
38         02  FILLER   PIC X(18) VALUE "CANDIDATE-ONE".
39         02  FILLER   PIC X(18) VALUE "CANDIDATE-TWO".
40         02  FILLER   PIC X(18) VALUE "CANDIDATE-THREE".
41         02  FILLER   PIC X(18) VALUE "CANDIDATE-FOUR".
42     01  HEADER-TWO.
43         02  FILLER   PIC X(8) VALUE   "OUP".
44         02  FILLER   PIC X(18) VALUE "MALE     FEMALE".
45         02  FILLER   PIC X(18) VALUE "MALE     FEMALE".
46         02  FILLER   PIC X(18) VALUE "MALE     FEMALE".
47         02  FILLER   PIC X(18) VALUE "MALE     FEMALE".
48     01  HEADER-THREE.
49         02  FILLER PIC X(80) VALUE ALL "*".
50     01  VOTER-LINE.
51         02  AGE-GROUP-OUT    PIC X(5).
52         02  vote-info-out.
53             03 vote-out occurs 4 times.
54          04 spacer-one      pic x(4).
55          04 sex-out occurs 2 times.
56                05 votes-out pic zzzzzz9.
57     01  voter-table.
58         02  age occurs 6 times.
59           03  sex occurs 2 times.
60             04  vote occurs 4 times.
61           05 num-of-votes pic 99.
62     01  AGE-SUB            pic 9 comp.
63     01  sex-sub           pic 9 comp.
64     01  vote-sub          pic 9 comp.
65     01  switch     pic xxx value spaces.
66         88 there-are-no-more-recs   value "yes".
67     01  sub        pic 9 comp.
68     PROCEDURE DIVISION.
69     BEGIN.
70         PERFORM 100-START.
71         perform 200-looper until there-are-no-more-recs.
72         PERFORM 300-WRITE-VOTER-LINE VARYING AGE-SUB
73            FROM 1 BY 1 UNTIL AGE-SUB > 6.
74         PERFORM 400-FINISH-UP.
75     100-START.
76         open input infile output outfile.
77         move zeros to voter-table.
78         WRITE TABREC FROM HEADER-THREE AFTER PAGE.
79         WRITE TABREC FROM HEADER-ONE AFTER 1.
80         WRITE TABREC FROM HEADER-TWO AFTER 1.
81         WRITE TABREC FROM HEADER-THREE AFTER 1.
82         read infile at end move "yes" to switch.
83     200-looper.
84         perform 250-load-table varying sub from 1 by 1
85            until sub > num-of-vote-fields.
86         read infile at end move "yes" to switch.
87     250-load-table.
88         compute age-sub = (age-in (sub) - 11) / 10.
89         move sex-in (sub) to sex-sub.
90         move choice-in (sub) to vote-sub.
91         add 1 to num-of-votes (age-sub sex-sub vote-sub).
92     300-WRITE-VOTER-LINE.
93         perform 350-load-spaces varying
94            vote-sub from 1 by 1 until vote-sub > 4.
```

```
 95          MOVE AGE-GROUP (AGE-SUB) TO AGE-GROUP-OUT.
 96          WRITE TABREC FROM VOTER-LINE AFTER 2.
 97      350-load-spaces.
 98          if vote-sub not = 1 move spaces to spacer-one (vote-sub).
 99          perform 375-move-out-votes varying sex-sub
100             from 1 by 1 until sex-sub > 2.
101      375-move-out-votes.
102          move num-of-votes (age-sub sex-sub vote-sub) to
103             votes-out (vote-sub sex-sub).
104      400-FINISH-UP.
105          close infile outfile.
106          STOP RUN.
```

Before examining any output from test data it would be wise to examine and explain fully the additional code in this program.

Additions to the DATA DIVISION are as follows:

Line 10   Aassigns the logical name INFILE to the external data file (VOTES.DAT)

Lines 14:22   Represent the file description of INFILE. Notice that each record can vary in length because of the variable length data described in line 18. For example:

013314

represents 1 voter field (subrecord). This field has a 33-year-old male who voted for candidate four.

03222242233713

has three voter fields. How old are these voters? Who is male? Female? For whom did they vote?

Lines 52:56   Enhance the output line. SPACER-ONE is a one-dimensional array. It has four elements with each one providing four spaces to permit proper spacing between candidate fields in the output line. VOTES-OUT is a two-dimensional array. There are two sexes within four candidates. The large zero-suppressed picture description provides proper spacing between sex fields in the output line.

Lines 57:61   Represent the three-dimensional array to accumulate the votes. Additional subscripts are provided (lines 63 and 64).

Line 67   Shows a data element used as a counter for handling the variable length table of each input record.

Additions to the PROCEDURE DIVISION are as follows:

Line 71   Passes control to the loop that controls the processing of each record until there are no more records to be processed.

Line 76   Modifies the OPEN statement. We now have an input file.

Line 77   Zeros out the entire three-dimensional table. Note, however, that if one uses:

$$\text{MOVE 0 TO VOTER-TABLE.}$$

only the first element is initialized to zero. A stack dump results if one attempts to add to any other element (original contents unknown).

Line 82   Initial read. This and the read statement in line 86 are in keeping with the structured code developed in previous chapters.

Line 84   Controls processing of each record by passing control to a subordinate module that handles each subrecord. This control ceases after the number of subrecords in each record is exhausted.

Lines 87:91   Involve getting proper values in subscripts from the input subrecords so that votes can be added to the table.

Lines 93:94   Is a statement that transfers control to a module that provides an instruction to space between candidate fields 2, 3, and 4 (there is proper spacing before the candidate one field because of the age-group entry).

Lines 99:100   Is a statement that passes control to a module containing a complex MOVE statement that moves data from a three-dimensional array to the two-level table on the output line. If you think about it, it would be very difficult to print out a table in three dimensions!!!

11.5   INCREMENTAL TESTING

We shall use the concept of incremental testing on this program. First, the program will be tested with a file containing one record which has only one subrecord. This will show whether or not the proper calculation of the AGE-SUB is correct and whether or not the one vote is added to the proper area in the table and appropriate output line. In the second test, we will use a record that contains many subrecords. This will test whether or not the control statement (line 67) and associated module for handling the variable length record are working properly. Finally, the test will include a file with many records containing a variety of subrecords. This will test whether or not our main loop structure is correct.

Test 1

Input Data ———————————————————————————————————————

013314

Output Data ———————————————————————————————————————

****

AGE GROUP	CANDIDATE-ONE		CANDIDATE-TWO		CANDIDATE-THREE		CANDIDATE-FOUR	
	MALE	FEMALE	MALE	FEMALE	MALE	FEMALE	MALE	FEMALE

****

AGE GROUP	MALE	FEMALE	MALE	FEMALE	MALE	FEMALE	MALE	FEMALE
21–30	0	0	0	0	0	0	0	0
31–40	0	0	0	0	0	0	1	0
41–50	0	0	0	0	0	0	0	0
51–60	0	0	0	0	0	0	0	0
61–70	0	0	0	0	0	0	0	0
71–80	0	0	0	0	0	0	0	0

Well, it looks like this first test was successful. We had a 33-year-old male who voted for candidate 4.

Test 2

Input Date ———————————————————————————————————————

03222242233713

Output Data ———————————————————————————————————————

****

AGE GROUP	CANDIDATE-ONE		CANDIDATE-TWO		CANDIDATE-THREE		CANDIDATE-FOUR	
	MALE	FEMALE	MALE	FEMALE	MALE	FEMALE	MALE	FEMALE

****

AGE GROUP	MALE	FEMALE	MALE	FEMALE	MALE	FEMALE	MALE	FEMALE
21–30	0	0	0	1	0	0	0	0
31–40	0	0	0	0	1	0	0	0
41–50	0	0	0	0	0	1	0	0
51–60	0	0	0	0	0	0	0	0
61–70	0	0	0	0	0	0	0	0
71–80	0	0	0	0	0	0	0	0

Test #2 was successful. We had a file that contained one record with three subrecords. Look at the output above and see for yourself!

Test 3

Input Data ──

> 042224751370136221
> 0221134423
> 0553117712752235235021
> 013314
> 042322431156117223

Output Data ──

```
**************************************************************************
```

AGE GROUP	CANDIDATE-ONE MALE	FEMALE	CANDIDATE-TWO MALE	FEMALE	CANDIDATE-THREE MALE	FEMALE	CANDIDATE-FOUR MALE	FEMALE
21–30	0	0	0	1	1	0	0	1
31–40	0	0	0	0	0	1	1	0
41–50	1	1	0	0	0	1	0	0
51–60	2	0	0	0	0	0	0	0
61–70	0	1	0	0	1	0	0	0
71–80	0	0	1	1	1	1	0	0

Test #3 was successful. We had a total of sixteen vote fields in five records. All sixteen votes are accounted for in the report above. They are also in the proper areas. Yes, there were two males between 51–60 who voted for candidate one.

Should there be further testing? Absolutely. How about testing for non-numeric data in all fields? What would happen if a 95-year-old man voted? Our report does not take care of that. What about data that contain a sub-record with sex = 3? A vote for candidate eight? Maybe there should also be a test for a record that is supposed to have five subrecords, but only has four. The reverse of that is also possible.

Further modules should be added along with more extensive test data. This will be left up to you.

SUMMARY

In this chapter, the concept of table handling was expanded to show additional logic and syntax required to solve multilevel table problems. There was expansion of the PERFORM .... VARYING statement.

Most importantly, however, was the concept of incremental testing. This is a technique that is of primary importance. It makes no sense to test an entire data set on a multilevel table program the first time. If a stack dump results, it is difficult to determine at which point the execution error occurred. It is easier to add data in relatively small amounts so that modules and the syntax involved can be easily tested.

QUESTIONS

1. Write the COBOL entries (DATA DIVISION) for setting up the following tables:

a. A two-dimensional table consists of 50 rows and 20 columns with each element having a PIC X(5).

b. A three-dimensional table that is based on six branches within five districts within three regions with each element having a PIC 999.

2. Redefine the following numbers as a three-level table of three account-types within two sexes within twelve age groups and each element containing a PIC 99V99.

```
01   INSURANCE-VALUES.
     02   FILLER   PIC 9(12)   VALUE 303055756690.
     02   FILLER   PIC 9(12)   VALUE 307056756810.
     02   FILLER   PIC 9(12)   VALUE 310057506900.
     02   FILLER   PIC 9(12)   VALUE 313058256990.
     02   FILLER   PIC 9(12)   VALUE 315058757050.
     02   FILLER   PIC 9(12)   VALUE 319059757170.
     02   FILLER   PIC 9(12)   VALUE 322060507260.
     02   FILLER   PIC 9(12)   VALUE 325061257350.
     02   FILLER   PIC 9(12)   VALUE 329062257470.
     02   FILLER   PIC 9(12)   VALUE 333063257590.
     02   FILLER   PIC 9(12)   VALUE 338064507740.
     02   FILLER   PIC 9(12)   VALUE 345066257950.
     02   FILLER   PIC 9(12)   VALUE 284051006120.
     02   FILLER   PIC 9(12)   VALUE 291052756330.
     02   FILLER   PIC 9(12)   VALUE 298054506540.
     02   FILLER   PIC 9(12)   VALUE 303055756690.
     02   FILLER   PIC 9(12)   VALUE 307056756810.
     02   FILLER   PIC 9(12)   VALUE 310057506900.
     02   FILLER   PIC 9(12)   VALUE 313058256990.
     02   FILLER   PIC 9(12)   VALUE 315058757050.
     02   FILLER   PIC 9(12)   VALUE 319059757170.
     02   FILLER   PIC 9(12)   VALUE 322060507260.
     02   FILLER   PIC 9(12)   VALUE 325061257350.
     02   FILLER   PIC 9(12)   VALUE 329062257470.
```

3. Suppose we redefined the values above as follows:

```
01   INSURANCE-TABLE REDEFINES INSURANCE-VALUES.
    02   LOCATION OCCURS 6 TIMES.
        03   BRANCH OCCURS 4 TIMES.
            04   RISK-FACTOR OCCURS 2 TIMES.
                05   RATE 9(4)V99.
```

What is the value of:

    a. RATE (5 2 2)?
    b. RATE (2 4 1)?
    c. RATE (3 4 3)?

4. Modify the program in this chapter to include modules and resulting code to:
    a. Accumulate total votes for each candidate.
    b. Find who won.
    c. Include invalid data and write an error report.

PROGRAMMING PROBLEMS

1. Samuels, Inc. is a large corporation that consists of two subsidiaries, Flintstone with four stores east of the Mississippi River and Siliconer with four stores west of the Mississippi River. Each store is made up of six departments (video, cosmetics, toys, gardening, hardware, and clothing). Each day the corporation receives information on the amount of sales for each department within each store in each subsidiary. An input file consists of records that contain:

    a. the subsidiary (A or B)
    b. the store (1,2,3, or 4)
    c. the department (1,2,3,4,5, or 6)
    d. the amount (7 digits—assumed decimal)

Example of input:

A240150000

Create two acceptable output reports (one for Flintstone and one for Siliconer) that will show sales totals for each department within each store. Include invalid data and create a third report (Error Report) listing the appropriate errors and error messages. Also:

    a. Which subsidiary sold the most?
    b. Which department in which store sold the least (heads will roll!)?
    c. Which store sold the most?
    d. What is the percentage of erroneous records?

*2. Commercial airlines used by QUICK-N-SAFE-GLOBE have a capacity of one hundred twenty passengers each. The seats are arranged in twenty rows with six seats per row. A seat numbered 15–5 is in the fifteenth row, fifth seat. An input file of 120 records, each consisting of a passenger's last name and seat request, is to be processed. Write a program that will read this file and assign seats on a first-come first-served basis (the 1st record gets the 1st choice and the 120th record gets the 120th choice). If a seat a person wants is already filled, assign that person any other seat in the same row. If this is not possible, assign a seat in the nearest row moving toward the back of the airplane. If all the seats in the requested row and all rows behind are filled, try to find a seat for the person by starting at row #1 and moving toward the rear of the airplane. After all the seats are filled, print out a seating chart in table form that shows each person's name in the proper seating arrangement (six names per row, twenty rows).

Sorting

The objective in sorting is to rearrange records in a file according to the requirements of a particular application. This can be accomplished by:

1. Having the programmer create his own algorithm and resulting code to accomplish the sort.

2. Invoking a utility sort by using the appropriate DCL command [$SORT command].

3. Invoking a utility sort by calling it directly from a COBOL program [use of SORT statement].

Method one is usually reserved for other programming languages. The reader is encouraged to consult VAX/VMS Command Language User's Guide for the second method. We shall concentrate on the third method that employs the following general form of the SORT verb:

SORT sortfile ⟨ ON ASCENDING ⟩
⟨DESCENDING KEY⟩ sortkey

⟨INPUT PROCEDURE sect-name⟩
⟨USING filename⟩

⟨OUTPUT PROCEDURE sect-name⟩
⟨GIVING filename⟩.

The different parts of this SORT statement will be explained as we proceed through this chapter.

12.1   SORT STATEMENT WITH "USING" AND "GIVING" OPTIONS

When records are sorted, one or more fields (keys) are used to order the records—the collating sequence can be either ascending (low to high) or descending (high to low). If more than one key is used, the first key is the major key and the other key(s) are sorted within the sequence of the major key.

We can show how the SORT verb can help us out given the following situation:

A small company, comprising of a few sales departments, wants to run a sales contest. The salesman with the highest commission amount in each department wins an all expense-paid trip to Alsip, Illinois for a day. The company wants to sort the departments in ascending order and the commission amounts in decreasing order WITHIN each department (department is the major key and commission is the minor key). Examine the following input data:

JONES	12	040000
SMITH	09	030000
COLBY	14	060000
FRANZEN	06	100000
PETERSON	14	080000
GRATES	12	030000
MEYERS	14	050000
OVERMAN	06	030000
JACKSON	09	120000
MARRS	03	110000
BERNOT	06	040000
BELSON	06	060000
ARTURO	14	020000
WALTERS	09	050000
ZERNO	09	130000
SLADE	14	150000
LEVIN	06	001000
FLODIN	12	140000
BUSHNELL	03	030000
FEUER	09	100000

And now the program to accomplish this:

```
1    IDENTIFICATION DIVISION.
2    PROGRAM-ID. HELPSORT.
```

```
3      AUTHOR.   STEVE SAMUELS.
4
5      ENVIRONMENT DIVISION.
6      CONFIGURATION SECTION.
7      INPUT-OUTPUT SECTION.
8      FILE-CONTROL.
9          SELECT INFILE ASSIGN TO UNSORT.
10         SELECT SORT-FILE ASSIGN TO TEMPO.
11         SELECT OUTFILE ASSIGN TO SORTED.
12
13     DATA DIVISION.
14     FILE SECTION.
15     FD  INFILE
16         DATA RECORD IS INREC.
17     01  INREC.
18         02 NAME-IN          PIC X(10).
19         02 DEPT-IN          PIC XX.
20         02 FILLER           PIC X.
21         02 AMOUNT-IN         PIC 9(4)V99.
22     SD  SORT-FILE
23         DATA RECORD IS SORT-REC.
24     01  SORT-REC.
25         02 SORT-NAME         PIC X(10).
26         02 SORT-DEPT         PIC XX.
27         02 FILLER            PIC X.
28         02 SORT-AMOUNT        PIC 9(4)V99.
29     FD  OUTFILE
30         DATA RECORD IS OUTREC.
31     01  OUTREC.
32         02 NAME-OUT          PIC X(10).
33         02 DEPT-OUT          PIC XX.
34         02 FILLER            PIC X.
35         02 AMOUNT-OUT         PIC 9(4)V99.
36     WORKING-STORAGE SECTION.
37
38     PROCEDURE DIVISION.
39     BEGIN.
40         SORT SORT-FILE ASCENDING KEY SORT-DEPT
41             DESCENDING KEY SORT-AMOUNT
42           USING INFILE
43           GIVING OUTFILE.
44         STOP RUN.
```

And the resulting output data follows:

MARRS	03	110000
BUSHNELL	03	030000
FRANZEN	06	100000
BELSON	06	060000
BERNOT	06	040000
OVERMAN	06	030000
LEVIN	06	001000
ZERNO	09	130000
JACKSON	09	120000
FEUER	09	100000
WALTERS	09	050000

SMITH	09	030000
FLODIN	12	140000
JONES	12	040000
GRATES	12	030000
SLADE	14	150000
PETERSON	14	080000
COLBY	14	060000
MEYERS	14	050000
ARTURO	14	020000

In order to successfully accomplish this sort, the programmer must make provisions for a sort-work area. Notice line 10 in the above listing. Although UNSORT.DAT is present in the user directory before execution and both UNSORT.DAT and SORTED.DAT appear after execution, TEMPO.DAT is only temporarily created. It represents the sort-work area. We also need a new type of description for the sort-file—the SD.

Notice lines 22–28 that represent the SORT-FILE description. The sort keys must be present HERE. The sort keys CANNOT be present in input and output record descriptions.

Lines 40–43 give the simplest form of the SORT statement (there are 3 other types to be explained later).

The output data (SORTED.DAT) is properly sorted with highest commissions first WITHIN departments with lowest number first.

The USING option does the following:

a. opens the input file.

b. reads the entire file and passes it to the sort-work area.

The GIVING option does the following:

a. writes to the output file.

b. closes this file.

Examine Figure 12–1 for a schematic file diagram for further clarification.

12.2 SORT STATEMENT WITH "INPUT PROCEDURE" AND "GIVING" OPTIONS

What if some invalid data were present? We need a separate validation section, so that each record can be examined first before its release to the sort-work area. This requires two new COBOL coding considerations:

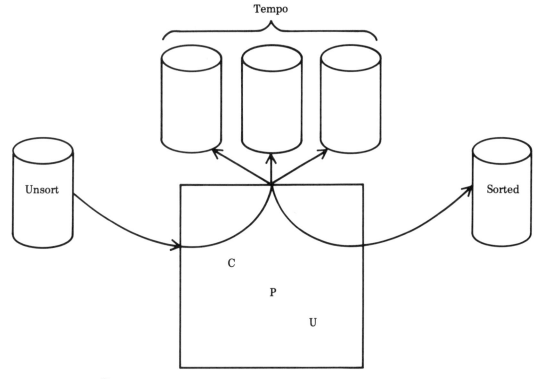

Figure 12–1

a. The INPUT PROCEDURE option.

b. The RELEASE verb.

Assume that invalid data are present (non-numeric entries for department number and/or amount fields).

Examine the following program that represents the second way a SORT verb can be used:

```
1       IDENTIFICATION DIVISION.
2       PROGRAM-ID. HELPSORT.
3       AUTHOR.   STEVE SAMUELS.
4
5       ENVIRONMENT DIVISION.
6       CONFIGURATION SECTION.
7       INPUT-OUTPUT SECTION.
8       FILE-CONTROL.
9           SELECT INFILE ASSIGN TO UNSORT.
10          SELECT SORT-FILE ASSIGN TO TEMPO.
11          SELECT OUTFILE ASSIGN TO SORTED.
12
13      DATA DIVISION.
```

```
14      FILE SECTION.
15      FD   INFILE
16           DATA RECORD IS INREC.
17      01   INREC.
18           02 NAME-IN            PIC X(10).
19           02 DEPT-IN            PIC XX.
20           02 FILLER             PIC X.
21           02 AMOUNT-IN          PIC 9(4)V99.
22      SD   SORT-FILE
23           DATA RECORD IS SORT-REC.
24      01   SORT-REC.
25           02 SORT-NAME          PIC X(10).
26           02 SORT-DEPT          PIC XX.
27           02 FILLER             PIC X.
28           02 SORT-AMOUNT        PIC 9(4)V99.
29      FD   OUTFILE
30           DATA RECORD IS OUTREC.
31      01   OUTREC.
32           02 NAME-OUT           PIC X(10).
33           02 DEPT-OUT           PIC XX.
34           02 FILLER             PIC X.
35           02 AMOUNT-OUT         PIC 9(4)V99.
36      WORKING-STORAGE SECTION.
37      01   switch          pic xxx value spaces.
38           88 no-more-records    value "yes".
39
40      PROCEDURE DIVISION.
41      begin section.
42      here-we-go.
43          SORT SORT-FILE ASCENDING KEY SORT-DEPT
44               DESCENDING KEY SORT-AMOUNT
45               input procedure check-it-out
46               GIVING OUTFILE.
47          STOP RUN.
48      check-it-out section.
49      100-start.
50          perform 200-first-part.
51          perform 300-loops until no-more-records.
52          go to 400-exit.
53      200-first-part.
54          open input infile.
55          read infile at end move "yes" to switch.
56      300-loops.
57          if dept-in not numeric or amount-in not numeric
58              next sentence
59          else
60             move name-in to sort-name
61             move dept-in to sort-dept
62             move amount-in to sort-amount
63             release sort-rec.
64          read infile at end move "yes" to switch.
65      400-exit.
66         exit.
```

As you can see, quite a lot of additional code is necessary if one wants to examine each record before releasing it to the sort-work area. The USING option cannot be used since the entire file would be moved, and that would include invalid records. In place of the USING option, the INPUT PROCE-DURE option is used (line 45). This requires that the entire Procedure Division be sectioned. Each section requires a paragraph name (lines 42 and 49).

The CHECK-IT-OUT section appears to have the same modular framework as previous programs. Obviously the modified program is more complicated in the fact that:

a. An OPEN statement is required (line 54).

b. Each statement must be read and checked (validated).

c. Good records are released to the sort-work area. The RELEASE verb used in line 63 acts like a WRITE statement. Notice that you must release the record name—NOT the file name. The general format is as follows:

RELEASE record-name [FROM work-rec]

(where record-name = an 01 level description in the SD and work-rec is an 01 level description in Working-Storage).

Look at statement 52. The GO TO statement, which is rarely used, is required to branch to the EXIT statement so that control passes back to the SORT statement. If it is not used, then after the last record is read, statement 54 will be executed again. You cannot open a file that is already opened!! When the CHECK-IT-OUT section is exited, the actual sort takes place and control is passed back to the GIVING option of the SORT statement.

12.3   SORT STATEMENT WITH "INPUT PROCEDURE" AND "OUTPUT PROCEDURE" OPTIONS

As was stated earlier, the salesman with the highest commission total in each department will get rewarded. Also, the amount should be edited so that the output data looks more presentable. In order to examine each record after the sort, the OUTPUT PROCEDURE must replace the GIVING option. Examine the following program:

```
 1     IDENTIFICATION DIVISION.
 2     PROGRAM-ID. HELPSORT.
 3     AUTHOR.   STEVE SAMUELS.
 4
 5     ENVIRONMENT DIVISION.
 6     CONFIGURATION SECTION.
 7     INPUT-OUTPUT SECTION.
 8     FILE-CONTROL.
 9         SELECT INFILE ASSIGN TO UNSORT.
10         SELECT SORT-FILE ASSIGN TO TEMPO.
11         SELECT OUTFILE ASSIGN TO SORTED.
12
13     DATA DIVISION.
14     FILE SECTION.
15     FD  INFILE
```

```
16          DATA RECORD IS INREC.
17      01  INREC.
18          02 NAME-IN           PIC X(10).
19          02 DEPT-IN           PIC XX.
20          02 FILLER            PIC X.
21          02 AMOUNT-IN         PIC 9(4)V99.
22      SD  SORT-FILE
23          DATA RECORD IS SORT-REC.
24      01  SORT-REC.
25          02 SORT-NAME         PIC X(10).
26          02 SORT-DEPT         PIC XX.
27          02 FILLER            PIC X.
28          02 SORT-AMOUNT       PIC 9(4)V99.
29      FD  OUTFILE
30          DATA RECORD IS OUTREC.
31      01  OUTREC.
32          02 NAME-OUT          PIC X(10).
33          02 filler            pic x(5).
34          02 DEPT-OUT          PIC XX.
35          02 filler            pic x(5).
36          02 amount-out        pic $$,$$$.99.
37          02 filler            pic x(5).
38          02 message-out       pic x(10).
39      WORKING-STORAGE SECTION.
40      01  SWITCH               PIC XXX VALUE SPACES.
41          88 NO-MORE-RECORDS       VALUE "YES".
42      01  temp-dept            pic xx value "00".
43
44      PROCEDURE DIVISION.
45      BEGIN SECTION.
46      HERE-WE-GO.
47          SORT SORT-FILE ASCENDING KEY SORT-DEPT
48              DESCENDING KEY SORT-AMOUNT
49            INPUT PROCEDURE CHECK-IT-OUT
50            output procedure give-a-bonus.
51          close outfile.
52          STOP RUN.
53      CHECK-IT-OUT SECTION.
54      100-START.
55          PERFORM 200-FIRST-PART.
56          PERFORM 300-LOOPS UNTIL NO-MORE-RECORDS.
57          GO TO 400-EXIT.
58      200-FIRST-PART.
59          OPEN INPUT INFILE.
60          READ INFILE AT END MOVE "YES" TO SWITCH.
61      300-LOOPS.
62          IF DEPT-IN NOT NUMERIC OR AMOUNT-IN NOT NUMERIC
63            NEXT SENTENCE
64          ELSE
65            MOVE NAME-IN TO SORT-NAME
66            MOVE DEPT-IN TO SORT-DEPT
67            MOVE AMOUNT-IN TO SORT-AMOUNT
68            RELEASE SORT-REC.
69          READ INFILE AT END MOVE "YES" TO SWITCH.
70      400-EXIT.
71          EXIT.
72      give-a-bonus section.
73      one-more-time.
74          perform 500-second-part.
75          perform 600-reloop until no-more-records.
76          go to 700-exit.
```

```
77      500-second-part.
78          close infile.
79          open output outfile.
80          move spaces to switch.
81          return sort-file at end move "YES" to switch.
82      600-reloop.
83          move spaces to outrec.
84          move sort-name to name-out.
85          move sort-dept to dept-out.
86          move sort-amount to amount-out.
87          if dept-out not = temp-dept
88              move "ATTABOY" to message-out
89              move dept-out to temp-dept
90          else
91              move spaces to message-out.
92          write outrec.
93          return sort-file at end move "YES" to switch.
94      700-exit.
95          exit.
```

The output records (SORTED.DAT) are as follows:

MARRS	03	$1,100.00	ATTABOY
BUSHNELL	03	$300.00	
FRANZEN	06	$1,000.00	ATTABOY
BELSON	06	$600.00	
BERNOT	06	$400.00	
OVERMAN	06	$300.00	
LEVIN	06	$10.00	
ZERNO	09	$1,300.00	ATTABOY
JACKSON	09	$1,200.00	
FEUER	09	$1,000.00	
WALTERS	09	$500.00	
SMITH	09	$300.00	
FLODIN	12	$1,400.00	ATTABOY
JONES	12	$400.00	
GRATES	12	$300.00	
SLADE	14	$1,500.00	ATTABOY
PETERSON	14	$800.00	
COLBY	14	$600.00	
MEYERS	14	$500.00	
ARTURO	14	$200.00	

The output file created looks somewhat like a decent report. In order to do this the output file description was expanded (lines 31–38). Also, the OUTPUT PROCEDURE option replaced the GIVING option in the SORT statement (line 50). Therefore, an entirely new section (GIVE-A-BONUS) was added to the Procedure Division. To examine each record from the sort file requires the RETURN verb (lines 81 and 93). The RETURN verb has the following general format:

RETURN sortfile [INTO work-rec] AT END declarative statement(s).

(where sortfile is the file name in the SD).

Notice that the RETURN statement is quite similar to the READ statement. You RETURN the file name. Also note that this new section has the same basic modular design as the CHECK-IT-OUT section. Statement 81 returns the initial record from the sort and statement 93 returns all the rest. When an end of file condition is reached, the loop (statements 82–93) is no longer executed. Since the file is sorted by highest commission first within ascending department number, statements 87–91 determine who gets the bonus (noted by ATTABOY on output record. Examine Figure 12–2 for a complete modular design of this program. It comprises two basic modular designs we have been seeing in most of the previous chapters.

Although one gets to examine each record after the sort, you pay for that with additional code. By replacing the GIVING option with the OUTPUT PROCEDURE option, you must:

a. Open the output file.

b. Use the RETURN verb.

c. Write to the output file.

d. Close the output file.

Three out of four different versions of the SORT statement have been discussed. The fourth one would employ the USING option and the OUTPUT PROCEDURE option. This would be less complicated than the last program listed above. One would use this version if no special processing were necessary before records were sent to the sort (USING), but that each record would be examined after the sort (OUTPUT PROCEDURE). The RETURN verb would also be required, not the RELEASE verb!

12.4   THE MERGE STATEMENT

One can also merge two or more files, identically sequenced on a set of key values, into one file. The MERGE statement has the following general format:

```
MERGE merge-file ON (ASCENDING)
                    (DESCENDING KEY) merge-key
        USING file-one, file-two. . . . .
            (OUTPUT PROCEDURE sect-name)
            (GIVING file-name).
```

(where mergefile and merge key appear in the SD).

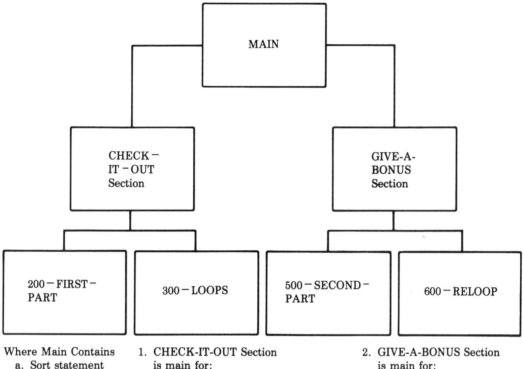

	MAIN	
CHECK–IT–OUT Section		GIVE-A-BONUS Section
200–FIRST–PART	300–LOOPS	500–SECOND–PART	600–RELOOP

Where Main Contains
a. Sort statement
b. Stop run

1. CHECK-IT-OUT Section
   is main for:
   a. 200 – FIRST – PART
      i. Open
      ii. Initial read
   b. 300 – LOOPS
      i. Check for errors
      ii. Release to sort (good read)
      iii. Subsequent reads

2. GIVE-A-BONUS Section
   is main for:
   a. 500 – SECOND – PART
      i. Close infile
      ii. Open outfile
      iii. Initial return
   b. 600 – RELOOP
      i. Checks for "winner"
      ii. Write record
      iii. Subsequent returns

Figure 12–2

Notice that the Input Procedure is not allowed. The files are merged according to a key or keys that are ascending or descending. Files that are to be merged should first be sorted on the keys in question.

The following example shows the use of the MERGE statement on two files. The input files will be given first, followed by the program, followed by the output file created:

FILEC.DAT

012SAMUELS

314COLBY
426JONES
885MARKIN
944BAILEY

FILEE.DAT

323UPSS
402KLUTZ
446YULD
623SCHNOOK
923PETERSON
993SHARONS

The MERGE Program Listing

```
8    1        IDENTIFICATION DIVISION.
     2        PROGRAM-ID. MERGER.
     3        ENVIRONMENT DIVISION.
     4        INPUT-OUTPUT SECTION.
     5        FILE-CONTROL.
     6            SELECT INFILE-C ASSIGN TO FILEC.
     7            SELECT SORTFILE ASSIGN TO TEMPO.
     8            SELECT INFILE-E ASSIGN TO FILEE.
     9            SELECT OUTFILE ASSIGN TO FILEF.
    10        DATA DIVISION.
    11        FILE SECTION.
    12        FD  INFILE-C
    13            DATA RECORD IS INREC-C.
    14        01  INREC-C      PIC X(15).
    15        SD  SORTFILE
    16            DATA RECORD IS SORTREC.
    17        01  SORTREC.
    18            02 ID        PIC 999.
    19            02 NAME      PIC X(12).
    20        FD  INFILE-E
    21            DATA RECORD IS INREC-E.
    22        01  INREC-E      PIC X(15).
    23        FD  OUTFILE
    24            DATA RECORD IS OUTREC.
    25        01  OUTREC.
    26            02 MAST-NUM  PIC 999.
    27            02 MAST-NAME PIC X(12).
    28        WORKING-STORAGE SECTION.
    29        PROCEDURE DIVISION.
    30        BEGIN.
    31            MERGE SORTFILE ASCENDING KEY ID
    32                USING INFILE-C INFILE-E GIVING OUTFILE.
    33            STOP RUN.
```

FILE-F

012SAMUELS
314COLBY

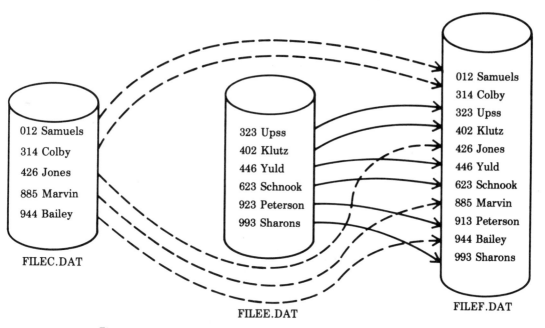

Figure 12-3

```
323UPSS
402KLUTZ
426JONES
446YULD
623SCHNOOK
885MARKIN
923PETERSON
944BAILEY
993SHARONS
```

Notice that the last data file is merged and it is sorted on the first 3 bytes or ID number. Examine Figure 12-3 for a schematic representation of this merge procedure.

SUMMARY

We have demonstrated three of the four possible combinations of the SORT statement for arranging records in ascending or descending sequences based on a key or series of key fields. It is important to note that the RELEASE statement must appear if the INPUT PROCEDURE is used and the RETURN statement must appear if the OUTPUT PROCEDURE is used. The Using and Giving options are the easiest because the files are automatically opened, read, written, and closed; however, USING and GIVING cannot be used if there is any further processing to be done before or after the sort.

Finally, the MERGE statement was also demonstrated.

QUESTIONS

1. Given the following input data:

Name	Major	Department no.
MONROE	CHEMISTRY	300
JACKSON	HISTORY	600
OBRIEN	EDUCATION	300
PETERSON	PHYSICS	300
JOHNSON	PSYCHOLOGY	300
MURDOCK	PHYSICS	300
LABBIE	EDUCATION	300
ENGEL	BIOLOGY	300
PRICE	HISTORY	600
GAWELL	CHEMISTRY	600
SMITH	EDUCATION	300
PARSON	CHEMISTRY	300
HYDE	HISTORY	600
WHITE	PHYSICS	300
MEYER	CHEMISTRY	600
ALLISON	EDUCATION	600
KANTER	BIOLOGY	300
SIMS	HISTORY	300
KILCON	HISTORY	600
JARDIN	CHEMISTRY	600
MILTON	PSYCHOLOGY	300
SAMUELS	BIOLOGY	600
ERWIN	CHEMISTRY	300

a. Provide a SORT statement that will rearrange the above so that the student names are ascending WITHIN descending departments (300=undergraduate and 600=graduate).

b. Provide a SORT statement that will rearrange the above so that the student names are ascending WITHIN ascending majors WITHIN ascending departments.

c. Write acceptable file descriptions for (a) and (b).

2. Given the statement:

SORT FILER ASCENDING KEY VENDOR
ASCENDING KEY AMOUNT
USING IN-FILE
OUTPUT PROCEDURE ELIMINATE-SOME.

a. What is the major key? The minor key?
b. Could you write this statement using less code? How?
c. Which file contains VENDOR and AMOUNT?
d. Where is the output file opened?
e. Is there special processing to occur with the input file? How?
f. Which file is specified in the SD?

PROGRAMMING PROBLEMS

1. Write a program that will sort the data in Question 1 according to Question 1a so that a report will show all undergraduates on one page and all graduates on another page. The program should also provide the totals of majors in each department.

2. Include invalid data for (1) and include an error report. [This will involve four files—one for input, one for sort, and two for output.]

*3. Write a program that will read a file containing the following five records:

YOU MUST REMEMBER THIS
A KISS IS STILL A KISS
A SIGH IS JUST A SIGH
THE FUNDAMENTAL THINGS APPLY
AS TIME GOES BY.

The output from this program lists all the words in ascending order—vertically!

A
A
A
A
APPLY
AS
BY
etc.

## 13

Character Manipulation

In some cases it becomes necessary to:

a. Separate characters in a field into two or more fields.

b. Bring together characters in separate fields into one field.

c. Do character translation—convert one character into one or more characters.

d. Manipulate words or strings of words within fields or strings of data.

To do this we will discuss three COBOL character manipulation statements—STRING, UNSTRING, and INSPECT.

13.1 THE STRING STATEMENT

The STRING statement has the following format:

STRING data-source-name DELIMITED BY ⟨delimiter-name⟩
⟨SIZE⟩
INTO data-destination-name [WITH POINTER]
[ON OVERFLOW declarative statement(s) [END-STRING]].

One of the best examples of using the STRING statement is to use it to convert a date given by the system (YYMMDD) to an English date. For example, 811205 becomes December 5, 1981. Or 770513 becomes May 13, 1977.

Examine the program below that accepts the date from the system and displays the English date through the use of the STRING statement.

```
 1    IDENTIFICATION DIVISION.
 2    PROGRAM-ID. STRINGER.
 3    ENVIRONMENT DIVISION.
 4    DATA DIVISION.
 5    WORKING-STORAGE SECTION.
 6    01  ENGLISH-DATE-POINTER        PIC 99.
 7    01  DATER                       PIC X(18).
 8    01  MONTH-VALUES.
 9        02 FILLER      PIC X(10) VALUE "JANUARY".
10        02 FILLER      PIC X(10) VALUE "FEBRUARY".
11        02 FILLER      PIC X(10) VALUE "MARCH".
12        02 FILLER      PIC X(10) VALUE "APRIL".
13        02 FILLER      PIC X(10) VALUE "MAY".
14        02 FILLER      PIC X(10) VALUE "JUNE".
15        02 FILLER      PIC X(10) VALUE "JULY".
16        02 FILLER      PIC X(10) VALUE "AUGUST".
17        02 FILLER      PIC X(10) VALUE "SEPTEMBER".
18        02 FILLER      PIC X(10) VALUE "OCTOBER".
19        02 FILLER      PIC X(10) VALUE "NOVEMBER".
20        02 FILLER      PIC X(10) VALUE "DECEMBER".
21    01 MONTH-TABLE REDEFINES MONTH-VALUES.
22        02 MONTHER   OCCURS 12 TIMES  PIC X(10).
23    01 CAL-DATE.
24       02  CAL-YEAR            PIC 99.
25       02  CAL-MONTH           PIC 99.
26       02  CAL-DAY.
27          03 TENS-PLACE        PIC 9.
28          03 UNITS-PLACE       PIC 9.
29    01  COMMA-SPACE-CENTURY   PIC X(4) VALUE ", 19".
30    PROCEDURE DIVISION.
31    BEGIN.
32        MOVE SPACES TO DATER.
33        ACCEPT CAL-DATE FROM DATE.
34        MOVE 1 TO ENGLISH-DATE-POINTER.
35        STRING MONTHER (CAL-MONTH) DELIMITED BY SPACE
36            SPACE          DELIMITED BY SIZE
37            INTO DATER
38            POINTER ENGLISH-DATE-POINTER.
39        DISPLAY "        Pointer = " ENGLISH-DATE-POINTER.
40        DISPLAY DATER.
41        IF TENS-PLACE = 0
42            STRING UNITS-PLACE DELIMITED BY SIZE
43                INTO DATER
44                POINTER ENGLISH-DATE-POINTER
45        ELSE
46            STRING CAL-DAY  DELIMITED BY SIZE
47                INTO DATER
48                POINTER ENGLISH-DATE-POINTER.
49        DISPLAY "        Pointer = " ENGLISH-DATE-POINTER.
50        DISPLAY DATER.
51        STRING COMMA-SPACE-CENTURY  CAL-YEAR
52            DELIMITED BY SIZE
```

```
53              INTO DATER
54              POINTER ENGLISH-DATE-POINTER.
55      DISPLAY "        Pointer = " ENGLISH-DATE-POINTER.
56      DISPLAY DATER.
57      STOP RUN.
```

The output is as follows:

Pointer = 10

DECEMBER

Pointer = 12

DECEMBER 27

Pointer = 18

DECEMBER 27, 1983

Let us examine this program step by step.

a. Line 33   CAL-DATE, a six-byte field, receives the date from the system in the form YYMMDD.

b. Line 34   ENGLISH-DATE-POINTER is set to 1 to indicate the first position in the date string.

c. Lines 35–38   The proper month, MONTHER, from the table is put into DATER, an 18-byte field, from left to right followed by a space. The month, DECEMBER, is 8 bytes long although it was originally in a 10-byte field. DE-LIMITED BY SPACE means to transfer DECEMBER without the trailing spaces into DATER. The second SPACE is to be strung after DECEMBER. The delimiter, itself, is not transferred.

d. At this point the ENGLISH-DATE-POINTER located in the byte adjacent to DECEMBER and the space is given the value of 10. The program displays this value along with what DATER contains up to this point. Diagrammatically speaking:

DECEMBER
^^^^^^^^^^

123456789"
         ^

10th byte of DATER

e. Lines 40–47   String the day after DECEMBER. If the number were less than ten, then only the units position would be "attached" or strung. [Just stringing CAL-DAY to the month without checking to see if the number is greater than 9 could result in producing JANUARY 04 or JULY 09, etc.] Now the pointer and DATER are displayed and we get, diagrammatically speaking:

DECEMBER 27
^^^^^^^^^

^

12th byte of DATER

f. Lines 50–53   String the century (19,) and year (83) into DATER. We'll leave it you to figure out why ENGLISH-DATE-POINTER = 18.

The On Overflow option can be added and assume control if the receiving field is too small to receive data.

The next program spruces things up a bit and includes a loop structure to continue accepting and converting dates until 000000 is entered. Any reasonable date can be entered. For this program the dates will be entered by the user.

```
1    IDENTIFICATION DIVISION.
2    PROGRAM-ID. STRINGER.
3    ENVIRONMENT DIVISION.
4    DATA DIVISION.
5    WORKING-STORAGE SECTION.
6    01  ENGLISH-DATE-POINTER        PIC 99 comp.
7    01  DATER                       PIC X(18).
8    01  MONTH-VALUES.
9        02 FILLER      PIC X(10) VALUE "JANUARY".
10       02 FILLER      PIC X(10) VALUE "FEBRUARY".
11       02 FILLER      PIC X(10) VALUE "MARCH".
12       02 FILLER      PIC X(10) VALUE "APRIL".
13       02 FILLER      PIC X(10) VALUE "MAY".
14       02 FILLER      PIC X(10) VALUE "JUNE".
15       02 FILLER      PIC X(10) VALUE "JULY".
16       02 FILLER      PIC X(10) VALUE "AUGUST".
17       02 FILLER      PIC X(10) VALUE "SEPTEMBER".
18       02 FILLER      PIC X(10) VALUE "OCTOBER".
19       02 FILLER      PIC X(10) VALUE "NOVEMBER".
20       02 FILLER      PIC X(10) VALUE "DECEMBER".
21   01 MONTH-TABLE REDEFINES MONTH-VALUES.
22       02 MONTHER   OCCURS 12 TIMES  PIC X(10).
23   01 CAL-DATE.
24       02  CAL-YEAR            PIC 99.
25       02  CAL-MONTH           PIC 99.
26       02  CAL-DAY.
27           03 TENS-PLACE       PIC 9.
28           03 UNITS-PLACE      PIC 9.
29   01  COMMA-SPACE-CENTURY   PIC X(4) VALUE ", 19".
30   PROCEDURE DIVISION.
31   BEGIN.
32       perform 100-start.
33       perform 200-looper until cal-date = 000000.
34       perform 300-end.
35   100-start.
36       display "Please enter 6 digits".
37       accept cal-date.
38   200-looper.
39       move spaces to dater.
```

```
40          MOVE 1 TO ENGLISH-DATE-POINTER.
41          STRING MONTHER (CAL-MONTH) DELIMITED BY SPACE
42             SPACE          DELIMITED BY SIZE
43             INTO DATER
44             POINTER ENGLISH-DATE-POINTER.
45          IF TENS-PLACE = 0
46             STRING UNITS-PLACE DELIMITED BY SIZE
47                INTO DATER
48                POINTER ENGLISH-DATE-POINTER
49          ELSE
50                STRING CAL-DAY   DELIMITED BY SIZE
51                INTO DATER
52                POINTER ENGLISH-DATE-POINTER.
53          STRING COMMA-SPACE-CENTURY   CAL-YEAR
54             DELIMITED BY SIZE
55                INTO DATER
56          POINTER ENGLISH-DATE-POINTER.
57          display "Here is the English date".
58          display dater.
59          display " ".
60          display "Please enter 6 digits".
61          accept cal-date.
62       300-end.
63          display "Run terminated".
64          stop run.
```

A sample of output as follows:

Please enter 6 digits
781003 (input by user)
Here is the English date
OCTOBER 3, 1978

Please enter 6 digits
830709
Here is the English date
JULY 9, 1983

Please enter 6 digits
810430
Here is the English date
APRIL 30, 1981

Please enter 6 digits
000000
Run terminated

The picture clause of ENGLISH-DATE-POINTER has been modified to binary. This will increase efficiency in execution since no conversion from decimal to binary occurs. Also, we have been able to utilize our basic three-paragraph (modular) structure again!!

13.2   THE UNSTRING STATEMENT

What if the date was entered in this fashion: MM/DD/YY. Switching the numbers around won't cause much difficulty because all one has to do is switch around CAL-DATE. But how does one get rid of those "/"? I'm glad you asked! The UNSTRING statement is used for this purpose. It has the following general format:

UNSTRING data-source-string
    [DELIMTED BY [ALL] delimiter-name [OR [ALL] delimiter-name2]]
       INTO data-destination-string1 data destination-string2. . . . .
         [DELIMITER IN delimiter-destination-name]
           [COUNT IN data-count-name]
             [WITH POINTER data-pointer-name]
               [TALLYING IN data-tallying-name
                  [ON OVERFLOW declarative statement(s) [END-
                    STRING]].

Examine the following program that unstrings those "/" from the date entered and uses previous code to convert to (string) the English date.

```
1     IDENTIFICATION DIVISION.
2     PROGRAM-ID. UNSTRING-STRING.
3     ENVIRONMENT DIVISION.
4     DATA DIVISION.
5     WORKING-STORAGE SECTION.
6     01  ENGLISH-DATE-POINTER         PIC 99 COMP.
7     01  DATER                        PIC X(18).
8     01  MONTH-VALUES.
9         02 FILLER     PIC X(10) VALUE "JANUARY".
10        02 FILLER     PIC X(10) VALUE "FEBRUARY".
11        02 FILLER     PIC X(10) VALUE "MARCH".
12        02 FILLER     PIC X(10) VALUE "APRIL".
13        02 FILLER     PIC X(10) VALUE "MAY".
14        02 FILLER     PIC X(10) VALUE "JUNE".
15        02 FILLER     PIC X(10) VALUE "JULY".
16        02 FILLER     PIC X(10) VALUE "AUGUST".
17        02 FILLER     PIC X(10) VALUE "SEPTEMBER".
18        02 FILLER     PIC X(10) VALUE "OCTOBER".
19        02 FILLER     PIC X(10) VALUE "NOVEMBER".
20        02 FILLER     PIC X(10) VALUE "DECEMBER".
21    01 MONTH-TABLE REDEFINES MONTH-VALUES.
22        02 MONTHER   OCCURS 12 TIMES  PIC X(10).
23    01 CAL-DATE.
24        02  CAL-MONTH             PIC 99.
25        02  CAL-DAY.
26            03 TENS-PLACE         PIC 9.
27            03 UNITS-PLACE        FIC 9.
28        02  CAL-YEAR              PIC 99.
29    01  WHOLE-DATE               PIC X(8).
30    01  COMMA-SPACE-CENTURY      PIC X(4) VALUE ", 19".
31    PROCEDURE DIVISION.
32    BEGIN.
```

```
33          PERFORM 010-FIRST-PART.
34          PERFORM 020-LOOPER UNTIL WHOLE-DATE = "00/00/00".
35          PERFORM 300-END.
36      010-FIRST-PART.
37          DISPLAY "Please enter 8 characters for date ".
38          accept whole-date.
39      020-LOOPER.
40          MOVE SPACES TO DATER.
41
42          unstring whole-date delimited by all "/"
43              into cal-month cal-day cal-year.
44          MOVE 1 TO ENGLISH-DATE-POINTER.
45
46          STRING MONTHER (CAL-MONTH) DELIMITED BY SPACE
47              SPACE           DELIMITED BY SIZE
48              INTO DATER
49              POINTER ENGLISH-DATE-POINTER.
50
51          IF TENS-PLACE = 0
52              STRING UNITS-PLACE DELIMITED BY SIZE
53                  INTO DATER
54                  POINTER ENGLISH-DATE-POINTER
55          ELSE
56              STRING CAL-DAY   DELIMITED BY SIZE
57                  INTO DATER
58                  POINTER ENGLISH-DATE-POINTER.
59
60          STRING COMMA-SPACE-CENTURY   CAL-YEAR
61              DELIMITED BY SIZE
62                INTO DATER
63                POINTER ENGLISH-DATE-POINTER.
64
65          DISPLAY "Here is the English date ".
66          DISPLAY DATER.
67          DISPLAY " ". DISPLAY " ".
68
69          Display "Please enter 8 characters for date".
70          accept whole-date.
71      300-END.
72          Display "Run terminated".
73          STOP RUN.
```

Output from the above is as follows:

> Please enter 8 characters for date
> 10/13/66 (input from user)
> Here is the English date
> OCTOBER 13, 1966
>
> Please enter 8 characters for date
> 07/08/81
> Here is the English date
> JULY 8, 1981
>
> Please enter 8 characters for date
> 00/00/00
> Run terminated

In examining the above program we find:

a. Line 29   Describes an 8-byte alphanumeric string.

b. Line 38   Accepts input and places it in WHOLE-DATE.

c. Lines 42–44   Unstrings WHOLE-DATE (MM/DD/YY) and moves MM to CAL-MONTH, YY to CAL-DAY, and YY to CAL-YEAR. The delimiter, "/", goes nowhere!

d. Line 70   Accepts all further input and the program ceases when 00/00/00 is entered.

The simplest form of the UNSTRING statement was used. What if the following was entered:

$$10/15/62\&12/09/77\&09/07/82\&03/27/51\&\%$$

The UNSTRING statement would have to contain those options necessary to remove part of this entire string (created a substring) and unstring this substring.

Examine the following program:

```
1      IDENTIFICATION DIVISION.
2      PROGRAM-ID. UNSTRING-STRING.
3      ENVIRONMENT DIVISION.
4      DATA DIVISION.
5      WORKING-STORAGE SECTION.
6      01  ENGLISH-DATE-POINTER       PIC 99 COMP.
7      01  DATER                      PIC X(18).
8      01  MONTH-VALUES.
9          02 FILLER       PIC X(10) VALUE "JANUARY".
10         02 FILLER       PIC X(10) VALUE "FEBRUARY".
11         02 FILLER       PIC X(10) VALUE "MARCH".
12         02 FILLER       PIC X(10) VALUE "APRIL".
13         02 FILLER       PIC X(10) VALUE "MAY".
14         02 FILLER       PIC X(10) VALUE "JUNE".
15         02 FILLER       PIC X(10) VALUE "JULY".
16         02 FILLER       PIC X(10) VALUE "AUGUST".
17         02 FILLER       PIC X(10) VALUE "SEPTEMBER".
18         02 FILLER       PIC X(10) VALUE "OCTOBER".
19         02 FILLER       PIC X(10) VALUE "NOVEMBER".
20         02 FILLER       PIC X(10) VALUE "DECEMBER".
21     01 MONTH-TABLE REDEFINES MONTH-VALUES.
22         02 MONTHER   OCCURS 12 TIMES   PIC X(10).
23     01 CAL-DATE.
24         02  CAL-MONTH              PIC 99.
25         02  CAL-DAY.
26             03 TENS-PLACE          PIC 9.
27             03 UNITS-PLACE         PIC 9.
28         02  CAL-YEAR               PIC 99.
29     01  WHOLE-DATE                 PIC X(8).
30     01  COMMA-SPACE-CENTURY   PIC X(4) VALUE ", 19".
```

```
31     01   terminator        pic x value spaces.
32     01   CHAR-COUNT        PIC 99 VALUE 0.
33     01   CHAR-POINTER      PIC 99.
34     01   ENTIRE-THING      PIC X(80).
35
36     PROCEDURE DIVISION.
37     BEGIN.
38         PERFORM 010-FIRST-PART.
39         PERFORM 020-LOOPER UNTIL TERMINATOR = "%".
40         PERFORM 300-END.
41
42     010-FIRST-PART.
43         DISPLAY "Please enter the entire string!!".
44         ACCEPT ENTIRE-THING.
45         MOVE 1 TO CHAR-COUNT.
46         MOVE 1 TO CHAR-POINTER.
47         unstring entire-thing delimited by "&" or "%"
48             into whole-date
49             delimiter terminator
50             count char-count
51             pointer char-pointer.
52     020-LOOPER.
53         UNSTRING WHOLE-DATE DELIMITED BY ALL "/"
54             INTO CAL-MONTH CAL-DAY CAL-YEAR.
55         MOVE SPACES TO DATER.
56         MOVE 1 TO ENGLISH-DATE-POINTER.
57         STRING MONTHER (CAL-MONTH) DELIMITED BY SPACE
58             SPACE         DELIMITED BY SIZE
59              INTO DATER
60               POINTER ENGLISH-DATE-POINTER.
61
62         IF TENS-PLACE = 0
63             STRING UNITS-PLACE DELIMITED BY SIZE
64                 INTO DATER
65                 POINTER ENGLISH-DATE-POINTER
66         ELSE
67             STRING CAL-DAY  DELIMITED BY SIZE
68                 INTO DATER
69                 POINTER ENGLISH-DATE-POINTER.
70
71         STRING COMMA-SPACE-CENTURY  CAL-YEAR
72           DELIMITED BY SIZE
73             INTO DATER
74             POINTER ENGLISH-DATE-POINTER.
75
76         DISPLAY "Here is the English date ".
77         DISPLAY DATER.
78         DISPLAY " ". DISPLAY " ".
79
80         unstring entire-thing delimited by "&" or "%"
81             into whole-date
82             delimiter terminator
83             count char-count
84             pointer char-pointer.
85     300-END.
86         DISPLAY " ".  DISPLAY " ".
87         DISPLAY "Run terminated".
```

The output is as follows:

Please enter the entire string!!
05/13/66&12/12/77&09/29/81&06/08/54&%
Here is the English date
MAY 13, 1966

Here is the English date
DECEMBER 12, 1977

Here is the English date
SEPTEMBER 29, 1981

Here is the English date
JUNE 8, 1954

Run terminated

Besides additional entries in the Data Division, options were added to one of the UNSTRING statements.

a. Line 44   The original string entered by the user, containing four substrings, is entered and placed in ENTIRE-THING.

b. Lines 47–51 represent the new UNSTRING statement. The Delimiter option causes "&" to be moved into TERMINATOR. The Count option causes 8 to be moved into CHAR-COUNT (the number of bytes removed up to the "&"). The Pointer option causes 10 to be placed into CHAR-POINTER (the next byte after the first "&"). So, the first execution of this statement puts the first 8 bytes into WHOLE-DATE.

c. Lines 80–84 are identical to lines 47–51. This statement continues to remove 8-byte substrings—the start of the next substring determined by CHAR-POINTER. When the delimiter "%" is moved into terminator, execution of the loop ceases.

13.3   THE INSPECT STATEMENT

The INSPECT statement has two general forms:

a. INSPECT with the Replacing option as follows:

```
INSPECT data-source-string REPLACING
        ⟨CHARACTERS BY replace-char [⟨BEFORE⟩
                                    ⟨AFTER⟩ INITIAL delim-val]
        ⟨ALL
        ⟨LEADING compare-value BY replace-char
        ⟨FIRST
```

⟨BEFORE⟩
⟨AFTER⟩ INITIAL delim-val].

b. INSPECT with the Tallying option as follows:

INSPECT data-source-string TALLYING
⟨data-tally-name FOR CHARACTERS⟩
⟨ALL
⟨LEADING compare-value⟩
[⟨BEFORE⟩
⟨AFTER⟩   initial delimiter-value].

The INSPECT statement with the Replacing option is typically used for character translation and editing of fields. Following are some examples using the INSPECT statement with the Replacing phrase:

	Contents of Identifier	
Statement	Before Execution	After Execution
INSPECT SOC-SEC-OUT		
REPLACING ALL SPACES BY "–".	324b23b5232	324–23–5232
INSPECT TEMP-AREA		
REPLACING FIRST "A" BY "*".	BANANA	B*NANA
INSPECT PRICE-IN		
REPLACING LEADING SPACES		
BY ZEROS.	bbb93243	00093243
INSPECT QUANTITY		
REPLACING CHARACTERS BY 0		
AFTER INITIAL ".".	24921.53	24921.00

The picture clause for the identifiers in the above examples can be alphanumeric, numeric, or numeric-edited. What follows are examples of the INSPECT statement using the Tallying phrase:

Statement	Contents of Identifier	Value of XCOUNT After Execution
INSPECT WIDGET TALLYING		
XCOUNT FOR ALL "–".	234–533–423–423	3
INSPECT QUAN-IN TALLYING		
XCOUNT FOR ALL LEADING ZEROS.	000023125	4
INSPECT NAMER TALLYING		
XCOUNT FOR ALL CHARACTERS		
BEFORE INITIAL "R".	INTRODUCTORY	3

It is best to include COMP in the data description of XCOUNT for maximum efficiency.

SUMMARY

The following new syntax was used to show how to manipulate character strings:

a. STRING

b. UNSTRING

c. INSPECT

The reserved word DATE was also used to bring in the date in the form yymmdd from the system.

QUESTIONS

1. Write INSPECT statements necessary to covert:

FRIBBLE	to	FRABBLE
bbbb321	to	0000321
S783LSM	to	QQQQQQQ
0232.32	to	0000.32

(Use appropriate identifiers or data-names.)

2. Write an UNSTRING statement to break apart:

23124,50,89.32,WIDGETS

into four fields. (Use appropriate data-names.)

3. Write a STRING statement to form KERMIT THE FROG from three identifiers (data-names) containing:

KERMITbbbb
THEbbbbbbb
FROGbbbbbb

(Use appropriate data-names.)

PROGRAMMING PROBLEMS

1. Write a program that will: read in a file whose records contain

last name, first name/address/city/zip

and make labels like this:

> first name   last name
> address
> city
> zip

For example:

SAMUELS, STEPHEN/243 S. WABASH/CHICAGO/60604
                    becomes
STEPHEN SAMUELS
243 S. WABASH
CHICAGO
60604

DOG, HOUND/1234 W. SOUTH ST./SACRAMENTO/95825
                    becomes
HOUND DOG
1234 W. SOUTH ST.
SACRAMENTO
95825

2. Examine programming problem #3 of the previous chapter. Write a program, using the UNSTRING statement to accomplish this.

*3. Write a program that will read a file containing a name and edited salary. Output should be the name and the amount in words!!
    For example:

MR. MONEYBAGS $2,345.45

becomes

MR. MONEYBAGS   TWO THOUSAND THREE HUNDRED FORTY FIVE AND FORTY FIVE CENTS

14

Report Writer

It is possible to generate very fancy reports that include headings, subtotals, and final totals without writing detailed Procdure Division logic.

This chapter deals with the REPORT WRITER, a feature that can automatically generate the following report elements:

1. A report header—printed once at the beginning of the report.

2. Page headers—printed on the top of each page.

3. Detail lines—more than one kind.

4. Control headings and footings—printed when there is a change in a control group.

5. Page footings—printed at the bottom of each page.

6. Report footings—printed at the end of the report.

In addition, subtotals and page counters are facilitated. Modular design can be kept very simple since the amount of Procedure Division code is drastically reduced.

14.1   A REPORT WRITER PROGRAM

At the end of chapter 9 a program was developed to produce a report including not only detail lines but also three control breaks plus a total or
summary line. The program was over 350 lines long with the Procedure Division representing over one-third of the COBOL code.

Here we will show an alternate method of producing that report (see
Figure 9-8) by using the REPORT WRITER feature. After examining the
listing, you should have a clear picture of how this feature operates. Specific
rules of syntax will, of course, follow this listing:

```
 1      IDENTIFICATION DIVISION.
 2      PROGRAM-ID.  REPORT-WRITER.
 3      AUTHOR. STEVE SAMUELS.
 4      ENVIRONMENT DIVISION.
 5      CONFIGURATION SECTION.
 6      SOURCE-COMPUTER. VAX-750.
 7      OBJECT-COMPUTER. VAX-750.
 8      INPUT-OUTPUT SECTION.
 9      FILE-CONTROL.
10          SELECT IN-FILE ASSIGN TO FIVE.
11          SELECT OUT-FILE ASSIGN TO REPT.
12      DATA DIVISION.
13      FILE SECTION.
14      COPY "PREVIOUS.LIB".
31      FD  OUT-FILE
32          REPORT IS SALES-REPORT.
33      WORKING-STORAGE SECTION.
34      01  SWITCH                    PIC XXX VALUE SPACES.
35          88  THERE-ARE-NO-MORE-RECORDS    VALUE "YES".
36      01  DATEX.
37          02 YEAR-IN      PIC XX.
38          02 MONTH-IN     PIC XX.
39          02 DAY-IN       PIC XX.
40      01  AMOUNT                    PIC 9(7)V99.
41      01  RATE                      PIC 99.
42      01  COMMISSION                PIC 9(6)V99.
43
44      REPORT SECTION.
45      RD  SALES-REPORT
46          PAGE LIMIT 66
47          HEADING 1
48          FIRST DETAIL 6
49          LAST DETAIL 45
50          CONTROLS ARE FINAL  REGION-IN  BRANCH-IN  SMAN-NUMBER-IN.
51
52      01  REPORT-HEADER TYPE IS RH NEXT GROUP NEXT PAGE.
53          02  LINE 10.
54              03  COLUMN 20    PIC X(6) VALUE "PSYCHO".
55          02  LINE 11.
56              03  COLUMN 22    PIC X(8) VALUE "PRODUCTS".
57          02  LINE 12.
58              03  COLUMN 24    PIC X(10) VALUE "QUARTERLY".
59          02  LINE 13.
60              03  COLUMN 26    PIC X(5) VALUE "SALES".
61          02  LINE 14.
62              03  COLUMN 28    PIC X(6) VALUE "REPORT".
```

```
63        02  LINE 45.
64            03  COLUMN 60    PIC XX SOURCE MONTH-IN.
65            03  COLUMN 62    PIC X  VALUE "/".
66            03  COLUMN 63    PIC XX SOURCE DAY-IN.
67            03  COLUMN 65    PIC X  VALUE "/".
68            03  COLUMN 66    PIC XX SOURCE YEAR-IN.
69
70   01  HEADINGS  TYPE IS PH.
71        02  LINE 1.
72            03  COLUMN 1     PIC X(132) VALUE ALL "&".
73        02  LINE 2.
74            03  COLUMN 1     PIC X(3) VALUE "REG".
75            03  COLUMN 5     PIC XX VALUE "BR".
76            03  COLUMN 8     PIC XXXX VALUE "SMAN".
77            03  COLUMN 13    PIC X(7) VALUE "PRODUCT".
78            03  COLUMN 22    PIC XXX VALUE "QTY".
79            03  COLUMN 27    PIC X(5) VALUE "PRICE".
80            03  COLUMN 34    PIC X(4) VALUE "RATE".
81            03  COLUMN 43    PIC X(6) VALUE "AMOUNT".
82            03  COLUMN 54    PIC X(10) VALUE "COMMISSION".
83            03  COLUMN 65    PIC X(11) VALUE "SALESPERSON".
84            03  COLUMN 88    PIC X(4) VALUE "PAGE".
85            03  COLUMN 95    PIC Z9 SOURCE PAGE-COUNTER.
86        02  LINE 3.
87            03  COLUMN 1     PIC X(3) VALUE "NO.".
88            03  COLUMN 5     PIC X(3) VALUE "NO.".
89            03  COLUMN 9     PIC X(3) VALUE "NO.".
90            03  COLUMN 15    PIC X(3) VALUE "NO.".
91            03  COLUMN 44    PIC X(4) VALUE "SOLD".
92        02  LINE 4.
93            03  COLUMN 1     PIC X(132) VALUE ALL "&".
94
95   01  DETAIL-LINE TYPE IS DETAIL  LINE PLUS 1.
96        02 COLUMN 1   GROUP INDICATE    PIC XX SOURCE REGION-IN.
97        02 COLUMN 5   GROUP INDICATE    PIC XX SOURCE BRANCH-IN.

98        02 COLUMN 9   GROUP INDICATE    PIC XX SOURCE SMAN-NUMBER-IN.
99        02 COLUMN 14           PIC X(6) SOURCE PROD-NUMBER-IN.
100       02 COLUMN 22           PIC ZZ9 SOURCE QUANTITY-IN.
101       02 COLUMN 26           PIC $$$$.99 SOURCE PRICE-IN.
102       02 COLUMN 33           PIC Z9 SOURCE RATE.
103       02 COLUMN 35           PIC X VALUE "%".
104       02 COLUMN 38           PIC $$,$$$,$$$.99 SOURCE AMOUNT.
105       02 COLUMN 53           PIC $$$$,$$$.99 SOURCE COMMISSION.
106       02 COLUMN 66           PIC X(10) SOURCE SMAN-NAME-IN.
107
108  01  SALESMAN-LINE    TYPE IS CF  SMAN-NUMBER-IN  LINE PLUS 2
                           NEXT GROUP PLUS 1.
109       02 COLUMN 12          PIC X(22) VALUE "FOR SALESMAN NUMBER".
110       02 COLUMN 35          PIC XX SOURCE SMAN-NUMBER-IN.
111       02 COLUMN 39          PIC X(24) VALUE "THE TOTAL COMMISSIONS = ".
112       02 COLUMN 64          PIC $$,$$$,$$$.99 SUM COMMISSION.
113
114  01  BRANCH-LINE      TYPE IS CF  BRANCH-IN  LINE PLUS 2
                           NEXT GROUP PLUS 1.
115       02 COLUMN 12          PIC X(22) VALUE " FOR BRANCH NUMBER".
116       02 COLUMN 35          PIC XX SOURCE BRANCH-IN.
117       02 COLUMN 39          PIC X(24) VALUE "THE TOTAL COMMISSIONS = ".
118       02 COLUMN 64          PIC $$,$$$,$$$.99 SUM COMMISSION.
119
120  01  REGION-LINE      TYPE IS CF  REGION-IN
```

```
                            LINE PLUS 2 NEXT GROUP PLUS 1.
121            02 COLUMN 12      PIC X(22) VALUE " FOR REGION NUMBER".
122            02 COLUMN 35      PIC XX SOURCE REGION-IN.
123            02 COLUMN 39      PIC X(24) VALUE "THE TOTAL COMMISSIONS = ".
124            02 COLUMN 64      PIC $$,$$$,$$$.99 SUM COMMISSION.
125
126    01  FINAL-LINE    TYPE IS CF  FINAL        LINE IS PLUS 6.
127            02 COLUMN 1       PIC X(14) VALUE "FINAL TOTALS:".
128            02 COLUMN 17      PIC $$$,$$$,$$$.99 SUM AMOUNT.
129            02 COLUMN 33      PIC X(5) VALUE "SALES".
130            02 COLUMN 45      PIC $$,$$$,$$$.99 SUM COMMISSION.
131            02 COLUMN 60      PIC X(30) VALUE "COMMISSIONS FOR PSYCO PRODUCTS".
132
133    PROCEDURE DIVISION.
134    BEGIN.
135        PERFORM 100-FIRST.
136        PERFORM 200-LOOPER UNTIL THERE-ARE-NO-MORE-RECORDS.
137        PERFORM 300-END.
138    100-FIRST.
139        ACCEPT DATEX FROM DATE.
140        OPEN INPUT IN-FILE OUTPUT OUT-FILE.
141        INITIATE SALES-REPORT.
142        READ IN-FILE AT END MOVE "YES" TO SWITCH.
143    200-LOOPER.
144        MULTIPLY PRICE-IN BY QUANTITY-IN IN GIVING AMOUNT.
145        IF COMMISSION-RATE-CODE-A
146           COMPUTE COMMISSION ROUNDED = AMOUNT * .05
147            MOVE 5 TO RATE
148        ELSE IF COMMISSION-RATE-CODE-B
149              COMPUTE COMMISSION ROUNDED = AMOUNT * .07
150             MOVE 7 TO RATE
151            ELSE IF COMMISSION-RATE-CODE-C
152                 COMPUTE COMMISSION ROUNDED = AMOUNT * .10
153                MOVE 10 TO RATE.
154        GENERATE DETAIL-LINE.
155        READ IN-FILE AT END MOVE "YES" TO SWITCH.
156    300-END.
157        TERMINATE SALES-REPORT.
158        CLOSE IN-FILE OUT-FILE.
159        STOP RUN.
```

The output data is shown in Figure 14–1. The report is a little fancier because:

1. The report has a title with a date on a separate page.

2. The salesman, branch, and region numbers are printed at the beginning and only after a control break.

14.2   EXPLANATION OF THE REPORT WRITER PROGRAM

Even with these enhancements this program is less that one-half the size of the last program presented in chapter 9. The output is almost identical!
Important syntax considerations are as follows:

a. Line 14   The COPY clause has nothing to do with the REPORT WRITER. It was added because there is no need to write all that code over again, since we have used a program with the same input format. A separate library file was created by using the following editor techniques:

1. EDT the program in chapter 9.

2. Locate the range (beginning and ending lines) of the input file description (in this case lines 59–74).

3. Write (create) this new file with the WRITE editor command:

```
$EDT PROG9.COB
     1       IDENTIFICATION DIVISION (editor response)
*write previous.lib 59:74
UD2:[SAMUELS]PREVIOUS.LIB;1 16 lines (editor response)
*quit
$
```

The file, PREVIOUS.LIB, is 16 lines long and is in the directory.

$

```
            PSYCHO
             PRODUCTS
              QUARTERLY
               SALES
                REPORT
```

12/29/83

Figure 14–1

```
01  04  13   328204  300  $20.00 5%      $6,000.00     $300.00  SMYTH J.
             591823   10 $150.00 7%      $1,500.00     $105.00  SMYTH J.

             FOR SALESMAN NUMBER   13  THE TOTAL COMMISSIONS =      $405.00

01  04  23   291823    0   $5.00 5%      $5,000.00     $250.00  COLBY S.
             391028  400  $10.0010%      $4,000.00     $400.00  COLBY S.
             391781    3 $150.00 5%        $450.00      $22.50  COLBY S.


             FOR SALESMAN NUMBER   23  THE TOTAL COMMISSIONS =      $672.50

01  04  25   394883   20  $50.00 7%      $1,000.00      $70.00  HOE A.

             FOR SALESMAN NUMBER   25  THE TOTAL COMMISSIONS =       $70.00

             FOR BRANCH NUMBER     04  THE TOTAL COMMISSIONS =    $1,147.50

01  11  14   928323   40  $60.00 7%      $2,400.00     $168.00  JACKSON J.
             372819  100 $100.0010%     $10,000.00   $1,000.00  JACKSON J.
             958492  300  $22.00 7%      $6,600.00     $462.00  JACKSON J.

             FOR SALESMAN NUMBER   14  THE TOTAL COMMISSIONS =    $1,630.00

             FOR BRANCH NUMBER     11  THE TOTAL COMMISSIONS =    $1,630.00

             FOR REGION NUMBER     01  THE TOTAL COMMISSIONS =    $2,777.50

14  05  17   765381   15   $3.41 5%         $51.15       $2.56  SAMUELS S.
             128455  100 $203.81 7%     $20,381.00   $1,426.67  SAMUELS S.
             222222  666    $.22 5%      $1,246.52      $62.33  SAMUELS S.
             121212    3 $293.1710%        $879.51      $87.95  SAMUELS S.

             FOR SALESMAN NUMBER   17  THE TOTAL COMMISSIONS =    $1,579.51

14  05  25   447715  581   $4.50 7%      $2,614.50     $183.02  BABBAGE C.
             618903   21 $146.8310%      $3,083.43     $308.34  BABBAGE C.

             FOR SALESMAN NUMBER   25  THE TOTAL COMMISSIONS =      $491.36

14  05  45   444228  956   $3.51 5%      $3,355.56     $167.78  NORAD D.
```

Figure 14-1 (*continued*)

```
&&&&&&&&&&&&&&&&&&&&&&&&&&&&&&&&&&&&&&&&&&&&&&&&&&&&&&&&&&&&&&&&&&&&&&&&&&&&&&&&&&&&&&&&&&&&&&&&&&&&&&
REG BR SMAN PRODUCT  QTY  PRICE  RATE     AMOUNT     COMMISSION SALESPERSON            PAGE    3
NO. NO. NO.   NO.                          SOLD
&&&&&&&&&&&&&&&&&&&&&&&&&&&&&&&&&&&&&&&&&&&&&&&&&&&&&&&&&&&&&&&&&&&&&&&&&&&&&&&&&&&&&&&&&&&&&&&&&&&&&&

14  05  45   118645  111 $291.90 7%   $324,300.90  $22,701.06 NORAD D.
             637100  716   $1.2310%      $8,260.68     $826.07 NORAD D.

        FOR SALESMAN NUMBER    45  THE TOTAL COMMISSIONS =    $23,694.91

14  05  61   950143    4   $.1110%           $.44        $.04 DEMKINS S.
             000013  381   $2.34 7%        $891.54      $62.41 DEMKINS S.

        FOR SALESMAN NUMBER    61  THE TOTAL COMMISSIONS =       $62.45

14  05  77   037185   31   $.32 5%           $9.92        $.50 LEMONHEAD

        FOR SALESMAN NUMBER    77  THE TOTAL COMMISSIONS =         $.50

        FOR BRANCH NUMBER      05  THE TOTAL COMMISSIONS =    $25,828.73

14  55  01   652961  378  $83.12 7%    $31,419.36   $2,199.36 BIRDIE B.
             408500  371   $1.7310%       $641.83      $64.18 BIRDIE B.
             301740  874 $108.92 5%   $313,036.08  $15,651.80 BIRDIE B.

        FOR SALESMAN NUMBER    01  THE TOTAL COMMISSIONS =    $17,915.34

14  55  37   555555   28  $23.98 7%       $671.44      $47.00 TAMERLIN T
             432901  999 $999.99 5% $9,998,900.01 $499,945.00 TAMERLIN T

        FOR SALESMAN NUMBER    37  THE TOTAL COMMISSIONS =   $499,992.00

14  55  45   213975   12   $8.2710%        $99.24       $9.92 TUT K.
             390127  871   $.13 7%        $113.23       $7.93 TUT K.
             883917    5  $38.2110%       $191.05      $19.11 TUT K.
```

Figure 14-1   (continued)

```
&&&&&&&&&&&&&&&&&&&&&&&&&&&&&&&&&&&&&&&&&&&&&&&&&&&&&&&&&&&&&&&&&&&&&&&&&&&&&&&&&&&&&&&&&&&&&&&&&&&&&&&
REG BR SMAN PRODUCT  QTY   PRICE  RATE   AMOUNT    COMMISSION SALESPERSON           PAGE    4
NO. NO. NO.  NO.                          SOLD
&&&&&&&&&&&&&&&&&&&&&&&&&&&&&&&&&&&&&&&&&&&&&&&&&&&&&&&&&&&&&&&&&&&&&&&&&&&&&&&&&&&&&&&&&&&&&&&&&&&&&&&

14  87  31   392744  831  $28.71 5%    $23,858.01   $1,192.90 TANNY V.
             397581  183   $.37  7%       $437.71      $30.64 TANNY V.
             777111   31   $.02  5%         $.62        $.03 TANNY V.

             FOR SALESMAN NUMBER   31  THE TOTAL COMMISSIONS =    $1,223.57

14  87  59   662098    2 $887.5410%    $1,775.08     $177.51 WILKE T.
             221593   38 $748.6110%   $28,447.18   $2,844.72 WILKE T.

             FOR SALESMAN NUMBER   59  THE TOTAL COMMISSIONS =    $3,022.23

14  87  63   002842  204   $.23  5%       $46.92       $2.35 DURAN D.
             893762   14 $38.51  7%      $539.14      $37.74 DURAN D.
             382948  612  $1.83  5%   $10,269.96     $513.50 DURAN D.

             FOR SALESMAN NUMBER   63  THE TOTAL COMMISSIONS =      $553.59

             FOR BRANCH NUMBER     87  THE TOTAL COMMISSIONS =   $12,607.00

             FOR REGION NUMBER     14  THE TOTAL COMMISSIONS =  $556,380.03

66  20  18   829000  381   $.12  7%       $45.72       $3.20 DUWOP D.
             382900  821 $28.4510%    $51,807.45   $5,180.75 DUWOP D.

             FOR SALESMAN NUMBER   18  THE TOTAL COMMISSIONS =    $5,183.95

66  20  27   564763  284  $2.84  7%      $806.56      $56.46 CARNIGIE D
             769023  999 $999.34 5%  $9,992,400.66 $499,620.03 CARNIGIE D
             562940  999 $992.74 7%  $9,926,407.26 $694,848.51 CARNIGIE D
             826731  999 $999.2710%  $9,991,700.73 $999,170.07 CARNIGIE D

             FOR SALESMAN NUMBER   27  THE TOTAL COMMISSIONS = $2,193,695.07

             FOR BRANCH NUMBER     20  THE TOTAL COMMISSIONS = $2,198,879.02

66  37  05   737289   12   $.12  5%        $1.44        $.07 PEABRAIN D
             729487    0   $.0210%          $.00        $.00 PEABRAIN D

             FOR SALESMAN NUMBER   05  THE TOTAL COMMISSIONS =        $.07
```

Figure 14-1 (*continued*)

```
66  37  18   543823  283 $38.72  5%    $10,957.76      $547.89  DAPPER V.
             780263   28   $.12  7%         $3.36         $.24  DAPPER V.
             888888  274 $937.21 10%   $256,795.54   $25,679.55  DAPPER V.
             364531   26 $73.82  5%     $1,919.32       $95.97  DAPPER V.

         FOR SALESMAN NUMBER    18  THE TOTAL COMMISSIONS =     $26,323.65

66  37  29   927483  123   $.28  7%        $34.44        $2.41  GRAUER R.
             828219   57 $28.47 10%     $1,622.79      $162.28  GRAUER R.

         FOR SALESMAN NUMBER    29  THE TOTAL COMMISSIONS =       $164.69

66  37  51   738215  382 $937.21 7%    $358,014.22   $25,061.00  LULU P.

         FOR SALESMAN NUMBER    51  THE TOTAL COMMISSIONS =     $25,061.00

         FOR BRANCH NUMBER      37  THE TOTAL COMMISSIONS =     $51,549.41

66  97  37   892737   12 $82.74  5%       $992.88       $49.64  TRIPP U.
             367301  392   $.12 10%     $1,007.04      $100.70  TRIPP U.
             228701  284 $12.74  7%    $41,838.16    $2,928.67  TRIPP U.

         FOR SALESMAN NUMBER    37  THE TOTAL COMMISSIONS =      $3,079.01

66  97  43   294652   35  $2.74  7%        $95.90        $6.71  WHIZ G.
             003721    3 $234.72 10%       $704.16       $70.42  WHIZ G.

         FOR SALESMAN NUMBER    43  THE TOTAL COMMISSIONS =        $77.13

66  97  75   000234   28  $2.64  5%        $73.92        $3.70  BUMBLE B.
             937583  372   $.27 10%       $100.44       $10.04  BUMBLE B.
             375641   38 $756.43 5%     $28,744.34    $1,437.22  BUMBLE B.
             878767  372 $986.76 10%  $9,247,914.72 $924,791.47  BUMBLE B.

         FOR SALESMAN NUMBER    75  THE TOTAL COMMISSIONS =    $926,242.43

66  97  81   645364  898  $2.74  5%    $27,120.52    $1,356.03  LATER C. U
             374632  387 $78.23  7%    $30,275.01    $2,119.25  LATER C. U

         FOR SALESMAN NUMBER    81  THE TOTAL COMMISSIONS =      $3,475.28
```

Figure 14-1 (continued)

```
&&&&&&&&&&&&&&&&&&&&&&&&&&&&&&&&&&&&&&&&&&&&&&&&&&&&&&&&&&&&&&&&&&&&&&&&&&&&&&&&&&&&&&&&&&&&&&&&&
REG BR SMAN PRODUCT  QTY  PRICE  RATE     AMOUNT      COMMISSION SALESPERSON              PAGE   6
NO. NO. NO.   NO.                          SOLD
&&&&&&&&&&&&&&&&&&&&&&&&&&&&&&&&&&&&&&&&&&&&&&&&&&&&&&&&&&&&&&&&&&&&&&&&&&&&&&&&&&&&&&&&&&&&&&&&&

        FOR BRANCH NUMBER      97  THE TOTAL COMMISSIONS =    $932,873.85

        FOR REGION NUMBER      66  THE TOTAL COMMISSIONS =  $3,183,302.28
```

Figure 14-1 (*continued*)

The COPY statement is quite useful. With it, you can include parts of other programs in new programs. It is especially useful for large file descriptions. The general form is as follows:

COPY "filename".

If one wanted the listing of PREVIOUS.LIB written out in the listing file it would be necessary to call for the COPY_LIST qualifier during compilation. NO_COPY_LIST is the default (the one assumed until another is specified) qualifier on most VAX systems.

$COB/LIS/COPY_LIST REPORTER   (REPORTER = external .COB file)

and the listing is expanded, as follows (only a portion is shown here):

```
 1      IDENTIFICATION DIVISION.
 2      PROGRAM-ID.  REPORT-WRITER.
 3      AUTHOR. STEVE SAMUELS.
 4      ENVIRONMENT DIVISION.
 5      CONFIGURATION SECTION.
 6      SOURCE-COMPUTER. VAX-750.
 7      OBJECT-COMPUTER. VAX-750.
 8      INPUT-OUTPUT SECTION.
 9      FILE-CONTROL.
10          SELECT IN-FILE ASSIGN TO FIVE.
11          SELECT OUT-FILE ASSIGN TO REPT.
12      DATA DIVISION.
13      FILE SECTION.
14      COPY "PREVIOUS.LIB".
15L         FD   IN-FILE
16L         DATA RECORD IS IN-REC.
17L         01   IN-REC.
18L             05   REGION-IN        PIC XX.
19L             05   BRANCH-IN        PIC XX.
20L             05   SMAN-NUMBER-IN   PIC XX.
21L             05   FILLER           PIC X.
22L             05   PROD-NUMBER-IN   PIC X(6).
```

```
23L              05  QUANTITY-IN          PIC 9(4).
24L              05  COMMISSION-TYPE-IN PIC X.
25L                  88 COMMISSION-RATE-CODE-A      VALUE "A".
26L                  88 COMMISSION-RATE-CODE-B      VALUE "B".
27L                  88 COMMISSION-RATE-CODE-C      VALUE "C".
28L              05  FILLER        PIC X.
29L              05  PRICE-IN            PIC 999V99.
30L              05  SMAN-NAME-IN        PIC X(20).
31     FD  OUT-FILE
32         REPORT IS SALES-REPORT.
33     WORKING-STORAGE SECTION.
34     01  SWITCH               PIC XXX VALUE SPACES.
35         88  THERE-ARE-NO-MORE-RECORDS     VALUE "YES".
36     01  DATEX.
37         02 YEAR-IN      PIC XX.
38         02 MONTH-IN     PIC XX.
39         02 DAY-IN       PIC XX.
40     01  AMOUNT             PIC 9(7)V99.
41     01  RATE               PIC 99.
42     01  COMMISSION         PIC 9(6)V99.
43
44     REPORT SECTION.
45     RD  SALES-REPORT
46          PAGE LIMIT 66
```

Notice the "L" next to some of the line numbers after the COPY "PRE-VIOUS.LIB" statement. Our listing has been expanded.

b. Lines 31–32   Represent the output file description, but there is no record name (DATA RECORD IS IN-REC, for example). Instead, line 32 assigns a name to the report, SALES-REPORT, and serves as link to the RD entry of the REPORT SECTION.

c. Line 44   This new section must be present if one is to use the REPORT WRITER feature.

d. Lines 45–50   Contain information pertaining to the entire report. As you can see, 66 lines per page are allowed with each page, printing header lines starting at line 1, and the first detail line starting at line 6. According to these specifications, detail lines cannot be printed after line 45 but rather start on the next page on line 6 under the header lines. The CONTROLS ARE clause determines the relative order of control breaks from highest to lowest. FINAL, a reserved word, gives the final break or final totals. The general format of the REPORT SECTION entry is as follows:

```
RD report name
    [⟨CONTROL IS ⟨control name⟩
     ⟨CONTROLS ARE ⟨FINAL control name1 control name2 . . . ⟩]
    [PAGE [LIMIT IS] page size [LINE]
    [PAGE [LIMITS ARE]        [LINES]
    [HEADING heading line]
    [FIRST DETAIL first detail line]
```

[LAST DETAIL last detail line]
[FOOTING footing line].

The REPORT WRITER allows the programmer to specify three types of headings: the report heading, which is printed at the beginning of the report, page headings printed at the top of each page, and control headings that are printed when there is a control break. One or more detail lines can be printed. In addition, three types of footings can be printed: the control footing is printed after each control break, the page footing is printed at the bottom of the page, and a report footing can be printed at the end of the report.

The report listed in Figure 14–1 and produced by the program listed above has a report header, page headings, a detail line, and control footings. Each line must be specified in the report section (first to last). The general form of the 01 level report group descriptions is shown below:

01 [group data name]

$$\text{LINE NUMBER IS} \begin{Bmatrix} \text{line num[ON NEXT PAGE]} \\ \text{PLUS line-num-plus} \end{Bmatrix}$$

$$\text{NEXT GROUP IS} \begin{Bmatrix} \text{next-group-line-num} \\ \text{PLUS next-group-line-num-plus} \\ \text{NEXT PAGE} \end{Bmatrix}$$

$$\text{TYPE IS} \begin{Bmatrix} \text{REPORT HEADING} \\ \text{RH} \\ \text{PAGE HEADING} \\ \text{PH} \\ \text{CONTROL FOOTING} \qquad \text{control-head-name} \\ \text{CF} \qquad\qquad \text{FINAL} \\ \text{DETAIL} \\ \text{DE} \\ \text{CONTROL FOOTING} \qquad \text{control-foot-name} \\ \text{CF} \\ \text{PAGE FOOTING} \\ \text{PF} \\ \text{REPORT FOOTING} \\ \text{RF} \end{Bmatrix}$$

e. Lines 52–68   Specify the report heading [TYPE IS RH]. REPORT-HEADER, the identifier used to name this description, is optional. NEXT GROUP NEXT PAGE makes the next group (page headers) print on the next page. Line numbers and columns are specified rather than the AFTER option (the WRITE statement is noticeably absent from the Procedure Division) and

FILLER clauses are noticeably missing from the Data Division. LINE represents vertical spacing and COLUMN represents horizontal spacing.
SOURCE is a clause that moves information into a specific field. The date,
MONTH-IN, DAY-IN, and YEAR-IN are moved to the respective columns
because of this clause. Hence, this eliminates the need for MOVE statements
in the Procedure Division.

f. Lines 70–93 represent the syntax for the header lines. HEADINGS is optional. TYPE IS PH is required, of course. Line 85 contains the reserved word
PAGE-COUNTER. This is automatically initialized to 1 and incremented as
each page is produced. The programmer need not provide special code in the
Procedure Division nor define it in the Data Division. The rest of the code
appears to be straightfoward and four header lines are accounted for.

g. Lines 95–106 format the detail line along with specific field entries. Again,
the SOURCE clause removes the need for additional MOVE statements in
the Procedure Division. LINE PLUS 1 specifies single spacing. GROUP IN-
DICATE causes salesman number, branch number, and region number to be
printed at the beginning and only after control breaks. The identifier, DE-
TAIL-LINE, or other programmer supplied data-name, must be present. It is
used in the GENERATE statement in the Procedure Division.

h. Lines 108–131 are the control footing lines for salesman, branch region,
and final [TYPE IS CF]. The identifiers SALESMAN-LINE, BRANCH-LINE,
etc., are optional. The SUM clause causes automatic accumulation of specified data items. It can only be used on lines of type CONTROL FOOTING.
The identifier (COMMISSION) in the first three footings is automatically
reset to 0 after each one is printed. Since there are three different totals, the
Report Writer feature automatically sets up separate, temporary fields to accumulate these sums.

*Note that the footings are from smallest total (salesman) to largest (final).
This is exactly the opposite of the order used in the "controls are" clause of
the RD section.*

The Procedure Division looks quite simple. It still retains a basic three-
modular structure but three new statements have been added:

1. The INITIATE statement initializes counters and totals.

2. The GENERATE statement automatically causes the production of the
various report groups.

3. The TERMINATE statement completes the processing of the report.

The REPORT WRITER feature is very easy to use because cumbersome logic is simplified. Essentially, the major characteristics of the report are present in the REPORT SECTION that eliminates much of the detailed instructions in the Procedure Division. The REPORT WRITER feature lends itself to those reports that accumulate sums and may or may not have control breaks. It is not intended to be used all the time. There are situations where the mechanics of this feature would be too cumbersome and not produce the desired result.

There are some additional features that should be mentioned. If it is desired to do some processing outside of the REPORT WRITER feature, the use of DECLARATIVES affords this possibility. For example, if we added to the Procedure Division as follows:

```
PROCEDURE DIVISION.
DECLARATIVES.
A-1 SECTION.
      USE BEFORE REPORTING REPORT-HEADER.
A-2.
      DISPLAY "HI FOLKS".
END DECLARATIVES.
MAIN SECTION.
BEGIN.
      PERFORM etc.

         .

         .
```

HI FOLKS would be displayed before the report header would be printed. This is a very simple case, but one could add further statements as needed. You must use sections with DECLARATIVES and you must use END DECLARATIVES before starting a new section.

The use of the RESET clause in the REPORT SECTION cancels automatic reinitialization of certain sums. For example, in the SALESMAN-LINE one could state:

```
02 COLUMN 64      PIC $$$,$$$,$$$.99 SUM COMMISSION RESET ON
                                                 BRANCH-IN.
```

This would cause a control break to accumulate a total until there was a change in branch number, not salesman number. The total would invariably be higher.

SUMMARY

The use of the REPORT WRITER feature facilitates the production of many types of reports. It is best used with reports that contain control breaks.

The addition of the COPY clause was demonstrated to enable one to include code from an external file.

QUESTIONS

1. Write the RD for a report that would have the following specifications:
   a. Header lines—start on line 2.
   b. Detail lines start on line 8 and end on line 38.
   c. Control fields—department number and final totals.
   d. Footings on every page—line 50.
   e. 68 lines/page.
Use appropriate identifiers for control fields.

2. Write a page header that will do the following:

NUMBER OF STUDENTS   NUMBER OF FAILURES
^   ^

^   ^

(col. 5)   (col. 60)

PROGRAMMING PROBLEMS

1. Write a program that will read in records with the following format:

Field	Columns
Name	1–20
City code	21–23
Salary	31–36 (assumed decimal)

Use the REPORT WRITER feature to print out:
   a. A report header.
   b. Appropriate page headers.
   c. Detail line.
   d. Control footing containing totals for city and final.

Use the following data:

JONES, AMY	003	030000
PETERSON, SAM	003	400000
JOHNSON, JUNE	003	150000
KLINGER, JOHN	005	040000

BRUDER, BARBARA	007	200000
STANTON, HAROLD	007	120000
DRUCKER, LANDRA	010	050000
RITTER, CALVIN	010	990000
WALTERS, RICHARD	010	020000
ZYCH, ROBERT	010	005000
ADAMS, SANDRA	020	040000

*2. Include invalid data and create an error report along with the report produced in problem #1. Include not only non-numeric data but also a record or two with the city code out of sequence!

15

Subprogramming

Up to now, this text has demonstrated how to use modular design and coding techniques for writing logically correct and understandable COBOL programs. Each program consisted of "modules" or paragraphs. These paragraphs were meant to be as distinct from one another as possible. This is a structured concept called LOW COUPLING. If the instructions in the paragraphs are interrelated, then an error (stack dump) in one module may cause problems in another module. Hence, the more highly coupled these modules are, the more difficult the program becomes to debug and maintain.

The instructions within each paragraph should be closely related. This is another very important concept called HIGH COHESION. Instructions in a paragraph should do more than just follow one another—they should, taken together, perform a specific task.

As problems become more complex, modular designs and the programs themselves become longer and more complicated. Also, the ability to adhere to LOW COUPLING and HIGH COHESION principles becomes much more difficult as the program acquires additional modules and, of course, much more code. The ability to write subprograms enables us to break down a large, complex problem into smaller and easier to understand units that can be independently programmed. Writing subprograms to solve these smaller tasks, thereby solving the original large problem, is just an extension of writing separate paragraphs in one program. Instead of "performing" a module, you "call" a subprogram.

The entire concept of subprogramming can be thoroughly demonstrated by writing a series of programs, one a calling program (main) and the others called programs (subprograms), to solve the following problem.

15.1   A PROBLEM

A hardware store receives information about its inventory with records made up of subrecords containing the inventory number, quantity on hand, price, and description. The original input file is as follows:

```
26392,15,10.50,RED-PAINT*28426,15,10.50,GREEN-PAINT*91241,5,80.00,POWER-RAKE*%
84321,10,4.60,PIPES*26437,5,20.00,BREAKERS*39462,100,2.00,SWITCHES*%
342A3,9,2.50,LAMP-CORD*21682,2,146.20,MOWER*33826,B7,6.00,LAWN-SEED*%
39924,10,17.20,WINDOWS*64643,100,4.50,NAILS*60203,50,.50,E-COVERS*%
13846,8,45.00,DOORS*38880,12,C.B4,HAMMERS*88332,6C,12.00,SAWS*%
26392,15,10.50,RED-PAINT*28426,15,10.50,GRN-PAINT*91241,5,80.00,POWER-RAKE*%
44445,10,8.60,BRACKETS*77468,1B,11.00,HOSES*80001,230,6.50,FERTILIZER*%
99326,14,BB.13,FRAMES*88113,12,1.50,TACKS*91130,100,1.50,JIFFIES*%
18307,10,15.50,COOLERS*10308,10,130.00,GRILLS*73736,6,140.00,BENCHES*%
8B6A3,3,143.50,LAMPPOSTS*21111,1,650.00,BLOWERS*%
```

From this input data, three files must be created:

1. An inventory report—for the Big Boss

2. An error report

3. A master file capable of being updated

The reports have the following general format:

Report 1

	ERROR ANALYSIS		
INVENTORY NUMBER	QUAN	PRICE	MESSAGE
33826	B7	6.00	Invalid quantity
342A3	9	2.50	Invalid account number

Report 2

<u>INVENTORY REPORT</u>
<u>DECEMBER 30, 1983</u>
<u>INVENTORY NAME INVENTORY NUMBER QUAN PRICE AMOUNT</u>

INVENTORY NAME	INVENTORY NUMBER	QUAN	PRICE	AMOUNT
MOWERS	21682	2	146.20	292.40
BREAKERS	26437	5	20.00	100.00
SWITCHES	39462	100	2.00	200.00
PIPES	84321	10	4.60	46.00

TOTAL INVENTORY = $638.40

Report 3

MASTER FILE

21682MOWERS	0002	014620
26437BREAKERS	0005	002000
39462SWITCHES	0100	000200
84321PIPES	0010	000460

Well, we certainly have our work cut out for us. Fortunately, UN-STRING, STRING, SORT, and REPORT WRITER have just been discussed. We will certainly need to UNSTRING the input data. We will need a program identical to the one in Chapter 13 to STRING the English date. We need to use a sort to put the inventory numbers in ascending sequence so that the file created could be updated. Finally, we need a couple of nice reports.

15.2 MODULAR DESIGN SOLUTION

Figure 15-1 shows the modular design representing the logic to solve this problem. The file representation in Figure 15-2 details what file we start with and what files we end with, including intermediate files. It appears as if the UNSTRING module can be a program, and the SORT module can be a program, producing an error report and master file through the use of the OUTPUT PROCEDURE. The inventory report can be produced by the REPORT module. Including the date-conversion program this totals four programs. Actually, there is a fifth program, the one for the MAIN module. It will "call" the other four programs, thereby making them subprograms.

Some would argue that there are just too many programs to solve this problem—that it could be done in one larger program. The intent of this chapter, as well as the previous ones, is to implement module designs by coding COBOL programs in small discrete steps. In this way, the student has

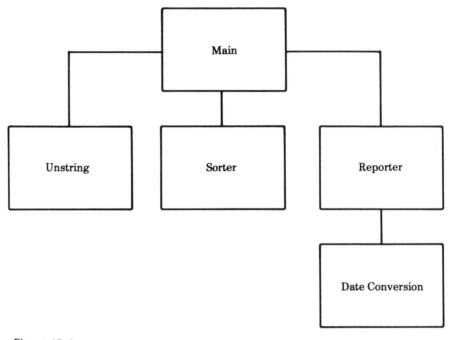

Figure 15–1

a greater appreciation of the flexibility of the COBOL language and spends most of his or her time solving problems rather than devoting enormous blocks of time to debugging a large, unwieldy program. It has been this author's experience that students complete most or all of the programming assignment in COBOL courses if they adhere to the principle of "doing it in small steps"!!! Conversely, students who must write 2000 line programs to solve a problem invariably become frustrated.

One has to feel sorry for that student who gets a stack dump or has output data that makes no sense and asks an instructor to find the problem in a 2000 line program. Actually, I feel sorrier for the instructor. The student who is solving a problem in steps and runs into a snag can, at the very least, show the instructor a previous program with some correct output and the current program with some additions (maybe 20–40 lines or so). The errors should be easier to detect. To emphasize this point to my students, I give absolutely no credit for a 2000 line program that produces no output or totally invalid output, but I will give partial credit to a 200 line program that may only provide headers and scant, but correct, detail lines. I think you get the point of all this. Let us get back to solving the problem at hand.

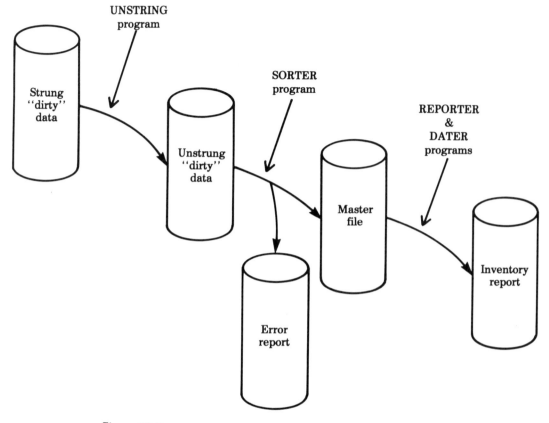

Figure 15–2

15.3 A PARTIAL SOLUTION—THE UNSTRING PROGRAM

The UNSTRING subprogram, like all the other subprograms, is a separate and complete program that must be compiled independently. Then, if compilation is successful, it can be linked to the MAIN program that has also had a successful compilation. The UNSTRING subprogram has the modular design shown in Figure 15–3. Instead of coding the entire UNSTRING subprogram, I will attempt to code it in steps. First, a routine should be developed to unstring one subrecord. In other words, write the code and execute a program to convert:

14353,210,1.34,BASKETS

to

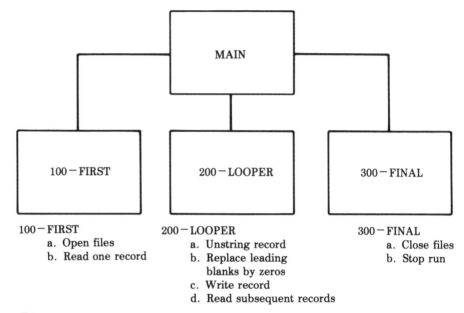

100 – FIRST
  a. Open files
  b. Read one record

200 – LOOPER
  a. Unstring record
  b. Replace leading
     blanks by zeros
  c. Write record
  d. Read subsequent records

300 – FINAL
  a. Close files
  b. Stop run

Figure 15-3

14352 0201 001.34 BASKETS

We will assume that there are no more than 9999 items of one kind in the store. Also, the maximum price of any item will equal 999.99. Examine the code below to do this:

```
 1      IDENTIFICATION DIVISION.
 2      PROGRAM-ID. UNSTRING-IT.
 3      AUTHOR. STEVE SAMUELS.
 4      ENVIRONMENT DIVISION.
 5      CONFIGURATION SECTION.
 6      INPUT-OUTPUT SECTION.
 7      FILE-CONTROL.
 8          SELECT INFILE ASSIGN TO STRUNG.
 9          SELECT OUTFILE ASSIGN TO UNSTRUNG.
10      DATA DIVISION.
11      FILE SECTION.
12      FD  INFILE
13          DATA RECORD IS INREC.
14      01  INREC       PIC X(80).
15      FD  OUTFILE
16          DATA RECORD IS OUTREC.
17      01  OUTREC.
18          02 INV-NO-OUT   PIC X(5).
19          02 FILLER       PIC X.
20          02 QUAN-OUT     PIC X(4) JUSTIFIED RIGHT.
21          02 FILLER       PIC X.
22          02 PRICE-OUT    PIC X(6) JUST RIGHT.
23          02 FILLER       PIC X.
```

```
24          02 DESC-OUT      PIC X(10).
25     WORKING-STORAGE SECTION.
26     01   SWITCH            PIC XXX VALUE SPACES.
27          88 NO-MORE-RECS      VALUE "YES".
28     PROCEDURE DIVISION.
29     BEGINNER.
30          PERFORM 100-FIRST.
31          PERFORM 200-LOOPER UNTIL NO-MORE-RECS.
32          PERFORM 300-FINAL.
33     100-FIRST.
34          OPEN INPUT INFILE OUTPUT OUTFILE.
35          READ INFILE AT END MOVE "YES" TO SWITCH.
36     200-LOOPER.
37          MOVE SPACES TO OUTREC.
38          UNSTRING INREC
39            DELIMITED BY ALL "," INTO
40              INV-NO-OUT
41              QUAN-OUT
42              PRICE-OUT
43              DESC-OUT.
44          INSPECT QUAN-OUT REPLACING LEADING " " BY "0".
45          INSPECT PRICE-OUT REPLACING LEADING " " BY "0".
46          WRITE OUTREC.
47          READ INFILE AT END MOVE "YES" TO SWITCH.
48     300-FINAL.
49          CLOSE INFILE OUTFILE.
50          STOP RUN.
```

The program listed above has the JUSTIFIED RIGHT (or JUST RIGHT) clause next to the QUAN-OUT and PRICE-OUT field. This enables the data to be pushed as far right as possible so that leading blanks on the left, if any, can be replaced by zeros with the INSPECT statement (lines 44 and 45). I knew I'd find a reason to use that verb!!

The logic in the loop to unstring a subrecord will now be placed in a subordinate module. Examine the modified design in Figure 15-4 and the code below to unstring an entire record of subrecords:

```
 1     IDENTIFICATION DIVISION.
 2     PROGRAM-ID. UNSTRING-IT.
 3     AUTHOR. STEVE SAMUELS.
 4     ENVIRONMENT DIVISION.
 5     CONFIGURATION SECTION.
 6     INPUT-OUTPUT SECTION.
 7     FILE-CONTROL.
 8          SELECT INFILE ASSIGN TO STRUNG.
 9          SELECT OUTFILE ASSIGN TO UNSTRUNG.
10     DATA DIVISION.
11     FILE SECTION.
12     FD   INFILE
13          DATA RECORD IS INREC.
14     01   INREC      PIC X(80).
15     FD   OUTFILE
16          DATA RECORD IS OUTREC.
17     01   OUTREC.
18          02 INV-NO-OUT  PIC X(5).
19          02 FILLER      PIC X.
20          02 QUAN-OUT    PIC X(4) JUSTIFIED RIGHT.
21          02 FILLER      PIC X.
```

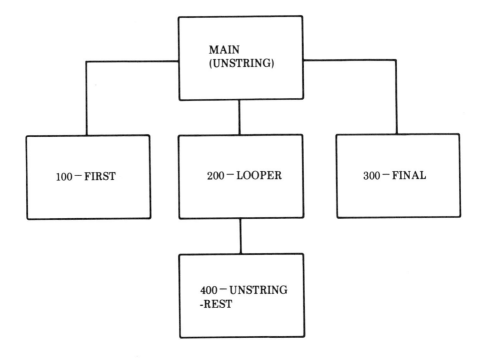

100 – FIRST
  a. Open
  b. Initial read

200 – LOOPER
  a. Unstring record into a subrecord
  b. Transfer control to 400 – UNSTRING-REST
  c. Subsequent reads

300 – FINAL
  a. Close
  b. Exit

400 – UNSTRING – REST
  a. Unstring subrecord into component field
  b. Write an unstring record

Figure 15-4

```
22          02 PRICE-OUT    PIC X(6) JUST RIGHT.
23          02 FILLER       PIC X.
24          02 DESC-OUT     PIC X(10).
25      WORKING-STORAGE SECTION.
26      01  SWITCH          PIC XXX VALUE SPACES.
27          88 NO-MORE-RECS     VALUE "YES".
28      01  holder    pic x.
29      01  xpoint    pic 99 value 1 comp.
30      01  xcount    pic 99.
31      01  subrec    pic x(30) value spaces.
32      PROCEDURE DIVISION.
33      BEGINNER.
34          PERFORM 100-FIRST.
35          PERFORM 200-LOOPER UNTIL NO-MORE-RECS.
36          PERFORM 300-FINAL.
37      100-FIRST.
38          OPEN INPUT INFILE OUTPUT OUTFILE.
39          READ INFILE AT END MOVE "YES" TO SWITCH.
```

```
40      200-LOOPER.
41          MOVE SPACES TO OUTREC.
42          unstring inrec
43            delimited by "*" or "%"
44            into subrec
45            delimiter holder
46            count xcount
47            pointer xpoint.
48          perform 400-unstring-rest until holder = "%".
49          move 1 to xpoint.
50          READ INFILE AT END MOVE "YES" TO SWITCH.
51      300-FINAL.
52          CLOSE INFILE OUTFILE.
53          STOP RUN.
54      400-UNSTRING-REST.
55          UNSTRING subrec
56            DELIMITED BY ALL ","
57            INTO
58            INV-NO-OUT
59            QUAN-OUT
60            PRICE-OUT
61            DESC-OUT.
62          WRITE OUTREC.
63          move spaces to subrec.
64          unstring inrec
65            delimited by "*" or "%"
66            into subrec
67            delimiter holder
68            count xcount
69            pointer xpoint.
```

The output is as follows:

84321	10	4.60	PIPES
26437	5	20.00	BREAKERS
39462	100	2.00	SWITCHES
342A3	9	2.50	LAMP-CORD
21682	2	146.20	MOWER
33826	B7	6.00	LAWN-SEED
39924	10	17.20	WINDOWS
64643	100	4.50	NAILS
60203	50	.50	E-COVERS
13846	8	45.00	DOORS
38880	12	C.B4	HAMMERS
88332	6C	12.00	SAWS
26392	15	10.50	RED-PAINT
28426	15	10.50	GRN-PAINT
91241	5	80.00	POWER-RAKE
44445	10	8.60	BRACKETS
77468	1B	11.00	HOSES
80001	230	6.50	FERTILIZER
99326	14	BB.13	FRAMES
88113	12	1.50	TACKS

91130	100	1.50	JIFFIES
18307	10	15.50	COOLERS
10308	10	130.00	GRILLS
73736	6	140.00	BENCHES
8B6A3	3	143.50	LAMPPOSTS
21111	1	650.00	BLOWERS

15.4   THE MAIN OR CALLING PROGRAM

The main module, or the superordinate of modules UNSTRING, SORT, DATE, and REPORT, is also the calling program. Since we have one subprogram (UNSTRING-IT) completed, the main program, DRIVER, can "call" it. Examine this main program below:

```
1       IDENTIFICATION DIVISION.
2       PROGRAM-ID. DRIVER.
3       AUTHOR. STEVE SAMUELS.
4       ENVIRONMENT DIVISION.
5       DATA DIVISION.
6       WORKING-STORAGE SECTION.
7       PROCEDURE DIVISION.
8       BEGIN.
9           CALL "UNSTRING-IT".
10          STOP RUN.
```

Line 9 acts like a PERFORM statement. It transfers control over to the UNSTRING program and control is returned to the main program when EXIT PROGRAM is executed in UNSTRING. In order to make UNSTRING a subprogram you must first replace STOP RUN (line 53) with EXIT PROGRAM. The CALL statement must use the PROGRAM-ID name of the subprogram. The general format of the CALL statement is as follows:

CALL "program-id-name" [USING indentifier1, identifier2. . . . .].

To successfully run this on the VAX, you do the following:

$COB MAIN   (external file—MAIN.COB of main program)
$COB UNSTRING   (external file—UNSTRING.COB of unstring program)
$LINK MAIN,UNSTRING (links up both programs into one file—
                                    MAIN.EXE)
$RUN MAIN   (executes MAIN.EXE)

15.5   A PARTIAL SOLUTION—THE SORT PROGRAM

The output data is the same. It looks unstrung but does not have the inventory numbers in ascending order and there are invalid records! An output file

(UNSTRUNG.DAT) was created by the program UNSTRING-IT. The SORTER program listed below uses UNSTRUNG.DAT as an input file creating a sorted output file called SORTED.DAT.

```
1      IDENTIFICATION DIVISION.
2      PROGRAM-ID. SORTER.
3      AUTHOR. STEVE SAMUELS.
4      ENVIRONMENT DIVISION.
5      CONFIGURATION SECTION.
6      INPUT-OUTPUT SECTION.
7      FILE-CONTROL.
8          SELECT INFILE ASSIGN TO UNSTRUNG.
9          SELECT SORTFILE ASSIGN TO TEMPO.
10         SELECT OUTFILE ASSIGN TO SORTED.
11     DATA DIVISION.
12     FILE SECTION.
13     FD  INFILE
14         DATA RECORD IS INREC.
15     01  INREC       PIC X(28).
16     SD  SORTFILE
17         DATA RECORD IS SORTREC.
18     01  SORTREC.
19         02 INV-NUM      PIC X(5).
20         02 REST-OF-REC PIC X(23).
21     FD  OUTFILE
22         DATA RECORD IS OUTREC.
23     01  OUTREC      PIC X(28).
24     WORKING-STORAGE SECTION.
25     PROCEDURE DIVISION.
26     BEGIN.
27         SORT SORTFILE
28           ASCENDING KEY INV-NUM
29             USING INFILE
30               GIVING OUTFILE.
31         EXIT PROGRAM.
```

Actually, this program was called from the main program. The main program now contains two CALL statements:

```
1      IDENTIFICATION DIVISION.
2      PROGRAM-ID. DRIVER.
3      AUTHOR. STEVE SAMUELS.
4      ENVIRONMENT DIVISION.
5      DATA DIVISION.
6      WORKING-STORAGE SECTION.
7      PROCEDURE DIVISION.
8      BEGIN.
9          CALL "UNSTRING-IT".
10         CALL "SORTER".
11         STOP RUN.
```

After UNSTRING-IT (the program-id name of one of the subprograms) is executed, control passes back to the main program that now transfers control to the SORT program (CALL "SORTER" statement).

The output data (SORTED.DAT) looks like this:

10308	10	130.00	GRILLS
13846	8	45.00	DOORS
18307	10	15.50	COOLERS
21111	1	650.00	BLOWERS
21682	2	146.20	MOWER
26392	15	10.50	RED-PAINT
26437	5	20.00	BREAKERS
28426	15	10.50	GRN-PAINT
33826	B7	6.00	LAWN-SEED
342A3	9	2.50	LAMP-CORD
38880	12	C.B4	HAMMERS
39462	100	2.00	SWITCHES
39924	10	17.20	WINDOWS
44445	10	8.60	BRACKETS
60203	50	.50	E-COVERS
64643	100	4.50	NAILS
73736	6	140.00	BENCHES
77468	1B	11.00	HOSES
80001	230	6.50	FERTILIZER
84321	10	4.60	PIPES
88113	12	1.50	TACKS
88332	6C	12.00	SAWS
8B6A3	3	143.50	LAMPPOSTS
91130	100	1.50	JIFFIES
91241	5	80.00	POWER-RAKE
99326	14	BB.13	FRAMES

On the command level, another compile was necessary, plus an addition to the link command:

```
$COB SORTER (takes SORTER.COB and makes SORTER.OBJ)
$LINK MAIN,UNSTRING,SORTER
$RUN MAIN
```

15.6   A PARTIAL SOLUTION—AN ENHANCED SORT PROGRAM (WITH OUTPUT PROCEDURE)

The data, although sorted by inventory number, have some invalid records. If we removed the invalid records, we could create a master file. These invalid records could be written to an error file. It appears that a good place to do this would be in the sort program. Examine Figure 15–5. Since each record would have to be examined after the sort, the OUTPUT PROCEDURE would be required; hence, our SORTER.COB file will have to be modified. Examine this modified SORT program that follows:

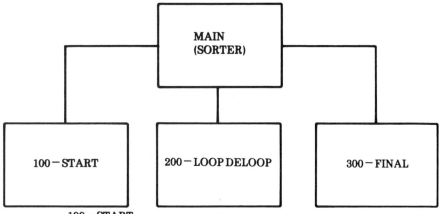

100 – START
- a. Open
- b. Headers for error report are written
- c. Initial return

200 – LOOP DELOOP
- a. Check fields for errors
- b. If error – switch is on then write error report record
   else write master file record
- c. Subsequent returns

300 – FINAL
- a. Close
- b. Exit

Figure 15-5

```
 1     IDENTIFICATION DIVISION.
 2     PROGRAM-ID. SORTER.
 3     AUTHOR. STEVE SAMUELS.
 4     ENVIRONMENT DIVISION.
 5     CONFIGURATION SECTION.
 6     INPUT-OUTPUT SECTION.
 7     FILE-CONTROL.
 8         SELECT INFILE ASSIGN TO UNSTRUNG.
 9         SELECT SORTFILE ASSIGN TO TEMPO.
10         SELECT MASTFILE ASSIGN TO MASTER.
11         SELECT ERRORFILE ASSIGN TO ERRORS.
12     DATA DIVISION.
13     FILE SECTION.
14     FD  INFILE
15         DATA RECORD IS INREC.
16     01  INREC            PIC X(28).
17     SD  SORTFILE
18         DATA RECORD IS SORTREC.
19     01  SORTREC.
20         02 SORT-INV-NO    PIC X(5).
21         02 FILLER         PIC X(1).
22         02 SORT-QUAN      PIC X(4)   JUST RIGHT.
23         02 FILLER         PIC X.
24         02 SORT-PRICE     PIC X(6)   JUST RIGHT.
```

```
25          02 REAL-PRICE REDEFINES SORT-PRICE.
26             03 SORT-DOLLARS    PIC 999.
27             03 FILLER          PIC X.
28             03 SORT-CENTS      PIC V99.
29          02 FILLER          PIC X.
30          02 SORT-DESC       PIC X(10).
31     FD  MASTFILE
32         DATA RECORD IS MASTREC.
33     01  MASTREC             PIC X(24).
34     FD  ERRORFILE
35         DATA RECORD IS ERRORREC.
36     01  ERRORREC            PIC X(75).
37     WORKING-STORAGE SECTION.
38     01  ERROR-SWITCH    PIC XXX.
39     01  SWITCHER        PIC XXX VALUE SPACES.
40         88  BALL-GAME-IS-OVER VALUE "YES".
41     01  HEADER-ONE.
42         02 FILLER       PIC X(20) VALUE SPACES.
43         02 FILLER       PIC X(40) VALUE "ERROR REPORT".
44         02 FILLER       PIC X(15) VALUE SPACES.
45     01  HEADER-TWO.
46         02 FILLER       PIC X(10) VALUE "INV-NUM".
47         02 FILLER       PIC X(10) VALUE "QUAN".
48         02 FILLER       PIC X(10) VALUE "PRICE".
49         02 FILLER       PIC X(15) VALUE "DESCRIPTION".
50         02 FILLER       PIC X(30) VALUE "     ERROR MESSAGE".
51     01  HEADER-THREE.
52         02 FILLER       PIC X(75) VALUE ALL "*".
53     01  WORK-MAST-REC.
54         02 MAST-INV-NO      PIC X(5).
55         02 MAST-QUAN        PIC 9(4).
56         02 MAST-PRICE       PIC 999V99.
57         02 MAST-DESC        PIC X(10).
58     01  ERROR-LINE.
59         02 ERROR-INV-NO     PIC X(5).
60         02 FILLER           PIC X(5) VALUE SPACES.
61         02 ERROR-QUAN       PIC X(4).
62         02 FILLER           PIC X(5) VALUE SPACES.
63         02 ERROR-PRICE      PIC X(6).
64         02 FILLER           PIC X(5) VALUE SPACES.
65         02 ERROR-DESC       PIC X(10).
66         02 FILLER           PIC X(5) VALUE SPACES.
67         02 ERROR-MESSAGE    PIC X(30).
68     PROCEDURE DIVISION.
69     BEGINNER SECTION.
70     BEGIN.
71         SORT SORTFILE
72            ASCENDING KEY SORT-INV-NO
73             USING INFILE
74             OUTPUT PROCEDURE REPORT-N-MASTER.
75     REPORT-N-MASTER SECTION.
76     STARTER.
77         PERFORM 100-START.
78         PERFORM 200-LOOPDELOOP UNTIL BALL-GAME-IS-OVER.
79         PERFORM 300-FINAL.
80     100-START.
81         OPEN OUTPUT MASTFILE ERRORFILE.
82         WRITE ERRORREC FROM HEADER-ONE AFTER 1.
83         WRITE ERRORREC FROM HEADER-TWO AFTER 5.
84         WRITE ERRORREC FROM HEADER-THREE AFTER 1.
85         RETURN SORTFILE AT END MOVE "YES" TO SWITCHER.
```

```
86    200-LOOPDELOOP.
87        INSPECT SORT-QUAN REPLACING LEADING SPACES BY "0".
88        INSPECT SORT-PRICE REPLACING LEADING SPACES BY "0".
89        MOVE SPACES TO ERROR-SWITCH.
90        MOVE SPACES TO ERROR-MESSAGE.
91        IF SORT-INV-NO IS NOT NUMERIC MOVE "YES" TO ERROR-SWITCH
92            MOVE "INVALID INVENTORY NUMBER" TO ERROR-MESSAGE
93        ELSE
94            IF SORT-QUAN IS NOT NUMERIC MOVE "YES" TO ERROR-SWITCH
95               MOVE "INVALID QUANTITY" TO ERROR-MESSAGE
96            ELSE
97          IF SORT-DOLLARS NOT NUMERIC OR SORT-CENTS NOT NUMERIC
98             MOVE "YES" TO ERROR-SWITCH
99             MOVE "INVALID PRICE" TO ERROR-MESSAGE.
100       IF ERROR-SWITCH = "YES"
101           MOVE SORT-INV-NO TO ERROR-INV-NO
102           MOVE SORT-QUAN    TO ERROR-QUAN
103           MOVE SORT-PRICE   TO ERROR-PRICE
104           MOVE SORT-DESC    TO ERROR-DESC
105           WRITE ERRORREC FROM ERROR-LINE AFTER 2
106       ELSE
107           MOVE SORT-INV-NO TO MAST-INV-NO
108           MOVE SORT-QUAN    TO MAST-QUAN
109           COMPUTE MAST-PRICE = SORT-DOLLARS + SORT-CENTS
110           MOVE SORT-DESC    TO MAST-DESC
111           WRITE MASTREC FROM WORK-MAST-REC.
112       RETURN SORTFILE AT END MOVE "YES" TO SWITCHER.
113   300-FINAL.
114       CLOSE ERRORFILE MASTFILE.
115       EXIT PROGRAM.
```

The error report follows:

ERROR REPORT

INV-NUM	QUAN	PRICE	DESCRIPTION	ERROR MESSAGE
****
33826	00B7	006.00	LAWN-SEED	INVALID QUANTITY
342A3	0009	002.50	LAMP-CORD	INVALID INVENTORY NUMBER
38880	0012	00C.B4	HAMMERS	INVALID PRICE
77468	001B	011.00	HOSES	INVALID QUANTITY
88332	006C	012.00	SAWS	INVALID QUANTITY
8B6A3	0003	143.50	LAMPPOSTS	INVALID INVENTORY NUMBER
99326	0014	0BB.13	FRAMES	INVALID PRICE

And now the master file:

```
10308001013000GRILLS
13846000804500DOORS
18307001001550COOLERS
21111000165000BLOWERS
21682000214620MOWER
26392001501050RED-PAINT
```

```
26437000502000BREAKERS
28426001501050GRN-PAIN
39462010000200SWITCHES
39924001001720WINDOWS
44445001000860BRACKETS
60203005000050E-COVERS
64643010000450NAILS
73736000614000BENCHES
80001023000650FERTILIZER
84321001000460PIPES
88113001200150TACKS
91130010000150JIFFIES
91241000508000POWER-RAKE
```

We have accomplished the task of separating the file that was produced in the UNSTRING program into two acceptable files, an error report and a master file. Notice that the master file need not contain spaces between fields. The extra blanks just take up extra disk space. This is especially inefficient with a very large master file. The error file is not the best one that can be produced. The logic to handle duplicate inventory numbers and records that have more than one invalid field is not present. The intent here is solely to show how subprogramming facilitates solving complex programming problems.

In examining the newer SORT program we find:

1. Lines 25–28 are necessary, in conjunction with line number 109 (COMPUTE statement), to have the master file contain an unedited price necessary for calculations and updating.

2. Line 74 causes the entire Procedure Division to be "sectioned." There is much more code because the program does so much more.

3. Line 89 must be present, otherwise every record after the first invalid record will be written to the error file. The switch (ERROR-SWITCH) must be reset each time.

15.7   A PARTIAL SOLUTION—THE REPORT WRITER PROGRAM

We have this marvelously clean master file that can be used as input for a nice INVENTORY REPORT. This, and a date program developed in a previous program, will be the last two subprograms. Examine the inventory report and date subprograms below:

```
1     IDENTIFICATION DIVISION.
2     PROGRAM-ID. REPORTER.
3     AUTHOR. STEVE SAMUELS.
```

```
4    ENVIRONMENT DIVISION.
5    CONFIGURATION SECTION.
6    INPUT-OUTPUT SECTION.
7    FILE-CONTROL.
8        SELECT INFILE ASSIGN TO MASTER.
9        SELECT OUTFILE ASSIGN TO INVREPT.
10   DATA DIVISION.
11   FILE SECTION.
12   FD  INFILE
13       DATA RECORD IS INREC.
14   01  INREC.
15       02 MAST-INV-NO    PIC X(5).
16       02 MAST-QUAN      PIC 9999.
17       02 MAST-PRICE     PIC 999V99.
18       02 MAST-DESC      PIC X(10).
19   FD  OUTFILE
20       REPORT IS INVENTORY-REPORT.
21   WORKING-STORAGE SECTION.
22   01  SWITCH           PIC XXX VALUE SPACES.
23       88 NO-MORE-RECS VALUE "YES".
24   01  AMOUNT           PIC 99999V99.
25   01  ENGLISH-DATE     PIC X(18).
26   REPORT SECTION.
27   RD  INVENTORY-REPORT
28       PAGE LIMIT 68
29       HEADING 2
30       FIRST DETAIL 9
31       LAST DETAIL 50
32       CONTROL IS FINAL.
33   01  TYPE IS PH.
34       02 LINE 2.
35          03 COLUMN 30     PIC X(20) VALUE "INVENTORY REPORT".
36       02 LINE 3.
37          03 COLUMN 30     PIC X(16) VALUE ALL "_".
38       02 LINE 4.
39          03 COLUMN 31     PIC X(18) SOURCE ENGLISH-DATE.
40       02 LINE 6.
41          03 COLUMN 2      PIC X(16) VALUE "INVENTORY NUMBER".
42          03 COLUMN 22     PIC X(8)  VALUE "QUANTITY".
43          03 COLUMN 35     PIC X(5)  VALUE "PRICE".
44          03 COLUMN 45     PIC X(7)  VALUE "AMOUNT".
45          03 COLUMN 57     PIC X(11) VALUE "DESCRIPTION".
46       02 LINE 7.
47          03 COLUMN 1      PIC X(69) VALUE ALL "-".
48   01  DETAILER TYPE IS DETAIL LINE PLUS 1.
49       02 COLUMN 4    PIC X(5) SOURCE MAST-INV-NO.
50       02 COLUMN 24   PIC ZZZ9 SOURCE MAST-QUAN.
51       02 COLUMN 34   PIC $$$$.99 SOURCE MAST-PRICE.
52       02 COLUMN 43   PIC $$$,$$$.99 SOURCE AMOUNT.
53       02 COLUMN 58   PIC X(10) SOURCE MAST-DESC.
54   01  TYPE IS CF FINAL LINE PLUS 4.
55       02 COLUMN 20   PIC X(25) VALUE "FINAL INVENTORY TOTAL = ".
56       02 COLUMN 46   PIC $$$$,$$$.99 SUM AMOUNT.
57   PROCEDURE DIVISION.
58   BEGIN.
59       PERFORM 100-START.
60       PERFORM 200-LOOPS UNTIL NO-MORE-RECS.
61       PERFORM 300-FINAL.
62   100-START.
63       CALL "DATE-GETTER" USING ENGLISH-DATE.
64       OPEN INPUT INFILE OUTPUT OUTFILE.
```

```
65          INITIATE INVENTORY-REPORT.
66          READ INFILE AT END MOVE "YES" TO SWITCH.
67      200-LOOPS.
68          MULTIPLY MAST-QUAN BY MAST-PRICE GIVING AMOUNT.
69          GENERATE DETAILER.
70          READ INFILE AT END MOVE "YES" TO SWITCH.
71      300-FINAL.
72          TERMINATE INVENTORY-REPORT.
73          CLOSE INFILE OUTFILE.
74          EXIT PROGRAM.


1       IDENTIFICATION DIVISION.
2       PROGRAM-ID. DATE-GETTER.
3       ENVIRONMENT DIVISION.
4       DATA DIVISION.
5       WORKING-STORAGE SECTION.
6       01  ENGLISH-DATE-POINTER        PIC 99.
7       01  MONTH-VALUES.
8           02 FILLER PIC X(10)      VALUE "JANUARY".
9           02 FILLER PIC X(10)      VALUE "FEBRUARY".
10          02 FILLER PIC X(10)      VALUE "MARCH".
11          02 FILLER PIC X(10)      VALUE "APRIL".
12          02 FILLER PIC X(10)      VALUE "MAY".
13          02 FILLER PIC X(10)      VALUE "JUNE".
14          02 FILLER PIC X(10)      VALUE "JULY".
15          02 FILLER PIC X(10)      VALUE "AUGUST".
16          02 FILLER PIC X(10)      VALUE "SEPTEMBER".
17          02 FILLER PIC X(10)      VALUE "OCTOBER".
18          02 FILLER PIC X(10)      VALUE "NOVEMBER".
19          02 FILLER PIC X(10)      VALUE "DECEMBER".
20      01 MONTH-TABLE REDEFINES MONTH-VALUES.
21          02 MONTHER  OCCURS 12 TIMES  PIC X(10).
22      01 CAL-DATE.
23          02  CAL-YEAR      PIC 99.
24          02  CAL-MONTH     PIC 99.
25          02  CAL-DAY.
26              03 TENS-PLACE   PIC 9.
27              03 UNITS-PLACE  PIC 9.
28      01  COMMA-SPACE-CENTURY   PIC X(4) VALUE ", 19".
29      LINKAGE SECTION.
30      01  DATER           PIC X(18).
31      PROCEDURE DIVISION
32          USING DATER.
33      BEGIN.
34          ACCEPT CAL-DATE FROM DATE.
35          MOVE 1 TO ENGLISH-DATE-POINTER.
36          STRING MONTHER (CAL-MONTH) DELIMITED BY SPACE
37              SPACE         DELIMITED BY SIZE
38              INTO DATER
39              POINTER ENGLISH-DATE-POINTER.
40          IF TENS-PLACE = 0
41              STRING UNITS-PLACE DELIMITED BY SIZE
42                  INTO DATER
43                  POINTER ENGLISH-DATE-POINTER
44          ELSE
45              STRING CAL-DAY  DELIMITED BY SIZE
46                  INTO DATER
47                  POINTER ENGLISH-DATE-POINTER.
48          STRING COMMA-SPACE-CENTURY  CAL-YEAR
```

```
49                    DELIMITED BY SIZE
50                    INTO DATER
51                    POINTER ENGLISH-DATE-POINTER.
52          EXIT PROGRAM.
```

. . . and the final report, produced by the REPORTER program:

INVENTORY REPORT

JANUARY 2, 1984

INVENTORY NUMBER	QUANTITY	PRICE	AMOUNT	DESCRIPTION
10308	10	$130.00	$1,300.00	GRILLS
13846	8	$45.00	$360.00	DOORS
18307	10	$15.50	$155.00	COOLERS
21111	1	$650.00	$650.00	BLOWERS
21682	2	$146.20	$292.40	MOWER
26392	15	$10.50	$157.50	RED-PAINT
26437	5	$20.00	$100.00	BREAKERS
28426	15	$10.50	$157.50	GRN-PAINT
39462	100	$2.00	$200.00	SWITCHES
39924	10	$17.20	$172.00	WINDOWS
44445	10	$8.60	$86.00	BRACKETS
60203	50	$.50	$25.00	E-COVERS
64643	100	$4.50	$450.00	NAILS
73736	6	$140.00	$840.00	BENCHES
80001	230	$6.50	$1,495.00	FERTILIZER
84321	10	$4.60	$46.00	PIPES
88113	12	$1.50	$18.00	TACKS
91130	100	$1.50	$150.00	JIFFIES
91241	5	$80.00	$400.00	POWER-RAKE

FINAL INVENTORY TOTAL = $7,054.40

REPORTER not only is a subprogram, it also calls another subprogram, DATE-GETTER. Both these programs have one common data field, the English date. This date is named ENGLISH-DATE in REPORTER and DATER in the DATE-GETTER program.

In order to have two or more programs access the same data field, the USING option of the CALL statement must be used. Line 63 of the REPORTER program calls the DATE-GETTER program and the address of the argument (data-name), ENGLISH-DATE, is passed to the called program, referenced in DATE-GETTER by DATER. These two data-names could have been the same since they are technically in separate programs. The USING option of PROCEDURE DIVISION must also be used. Finally, a Linkage Section must be set up in the subprogram with a description of the data-name in question.

So there are some general rules one must follow for "calling" subprograms and for the "called" subprograms themselves. The rules are clarified if we use a specific example [also see Figure 15–6]:

Calling Program	Called Program
CALL "FEDERAL-TAX" USING ADJUSTED-GROSS EXEMPTIONS FED-TAX.	PROCEDURE DIVISION USING ADJUSTED-GROSS EXEMPTIONS CAL-FED-TAX.

1. FEDERAL-TAX is the Program-Id name of the subprogram, a separate COBOL program that must to be compiled and linked with the calling program.

2. The addresses of ADJUSTED-GROSS, EXEMPTIONS, AND FED-TAX are passed to the subprogram. The data-names are the same for the first two arguments, but different for the third.

3. The arguments' order of appearance in the phrases of the above CALL statement and the called program's Procedure Division header determine the correspondence between the data-names used by the calling and called program.

4. The arguments (data-names) in the subprogram must appear in the Linkage Section of the Data Division of Federal-Tax. The picture clauses in both programs should be the same although their level numbers and data-names need not be the same.

5. When the subprogram is exited the contents of the data-names whose addresses were passed are now the contents of the data names in the calling program. If, for example, a field was originally initialized to 0 in a calling program and its contents change in a subprogram, it is the programmer's responsibility to reinitialize that field, if the need arises, in the calling program or before exiting the subprogram.

6. Group items, tables, and identifiers embedded in "copy" clauses can be passed.

7. A maximum of 255 arguments are allowed.

8. BY CONTENT option of Using passes the address of a temporary data item containing the contents of the argument to the subprogram. The called program can change this temporary item but not the original contents of the argument.

15.8 COMMAND FILES

In order to successfully run the main program along with the four subprograms, each program had to be compiled and then "linked" as follows:

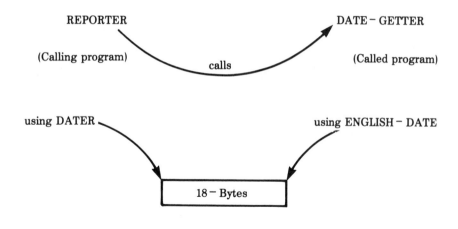

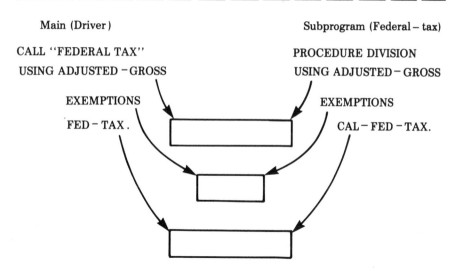

Note: Data – names need not be the same, but the order
in which they appear in the CALL statement
and corresponding PROCEDURE DIVISION statement
is very important.

Figure 15–6

$LINK MAIN,UNSTRING,SORTER,REPORTER,DATER

and then:

$RUN MAIN

Every time a modification is made to one or more of the above programs, those modified programs have to be recompiled and the above LINK statement used again. This can become quite cumbersome so a command file was set up. A command file is nothing more than a file of commands. We can create a command file through the use of the Editor as follows:

```
$EDT SAM.COM
Input file does not exist
*I
        $LINK MAIN,UNSTRING,SORTER,REPORTER,DATER
        $RUN MAIN
*EX
UD2:[SAMUELS]SAM.COM;1 2 lines.
```

To execute this command file, the following is used:

```
$@SAM        (the @ symbol is used to execute command files)
```

This is certainly shorter than entering the entire LINK command. As long as modified programs are compiled first ($COB filename) to create an .OBJ file, execution of the command file causes execution of the $LINK and $RUN commands. For whatever reason the command file can be extended as follows:

```
$COB MAIN
$COB UNSTRINGER
$COB SORTER
$COB REPORTER
$COB DATER
$LINK MAIN,UNSTRING,SORTER,REPORTER,DATER
$RUN MAIN
$PUR
$DELETE MAIN.OBJ;*
$DELETE UNSTRINGER.OBJ;*
$DELETE SORTER.OBJ;*
$DELETE REPORTER.OBJ;*
$DELETE DATER.OBJ;*
$DELETE MAIN.EXE;*
$DELETE UNSTRING.EXE;*
$DELETE SORTER.EXE;*
$DELETE REPORTER.EXE;*
$DELETE DATER.EXE;*
```

Of course, upon execution of this command file (@SAM), all COBOL programs are compiled, linked, and executed. Extra (lower number) versions are "purged," and object and executable modules are deleted to save disk space. This is NOT a recommended procedure when the entire system is being heavily used, for it takes far too much time. Further information on command files can be found in the *VAX/VMS Command User's Guide*.

SUMMARY

The beauty of the subprogramming process is that many programmers, participating in a large group project, can still work fairly independently. If Programmer-A needs some information from a program written by Programmer-B, all both really need to know is what fields and/or records are common to each program, their size, and the order in which they appear in the USING statement.

A fairly complex problem was stated in the beginning of this chapter and solved through the use of the subprogramming process. Files produced from one program were used by other programs. One superordinate program, the DRIVER, controlled the order of execution of the subordinate or subprograms. The following additional syntax was used:

1. CALL subprogram [USING identifier–1, identifier–2. . . . .].

2. PROCEDURE DIVISION [USING identifier–2, identifier –2 . . .].

3. EXIT PROGRAM.

Additionally, the concept of command files was explained and used to show how compilation, linking, and execution of a multiprogramming project could be accomplished.

QUESTIONS

Assume the following entries in the Working-Storage section of a main program:

```
01   WORK-REC.
     02   NAME            PIC X(20).
     02   STAT            PIC 9.
01   CUST-REF-NUM         PIC 9(5).
01   RATE-TAB.
     02   RATE OCCURS 7 TIMES PIC 99V99.
```

Assume the Program-Id name of a subprogram = SUBBER.

1. Write the statement necessary to pass the address of these fields to the subprogram.

2. Write the corresponding statement in the subprogram.

3. Write the necessary section in the Data Division of the subprogram.

PROGRAMMING PROBLEMS

1. A company (UCHEATUM TAX SERVICE) wants to figure out the 1983 income tax for their clients. They have commissioned you to write a main program to read in records containing the following information:

Field	Columns
name	1–20
annual salary	21–27 (assumed decimal)
tax status	30
total deductions	32–38 (assumed decimal)
number of exemptions	40

You should also write a subprogram that can calculate the federal tax for these clients.

Tax status = 1 (use Schedule X values on page 30 of 1983 tax return booklet)
       = 2 (use Schedule Y—married, filing jointly)
       = 3 (use Schedule Z)

Example of input:

    JOHN D. JACKSON   3600000   3   0700000 3

Example of output:

NAME	GROSS SALARY	TAX TABLE	FEDERAL TAX
JOHN D. JACKSON	$36,000.00	Z	$4,722.00

To obtain the tax of $4,722.00 the following was done:

a. Subract deductions from gross salary. [36,000 − 7,000] This give $29,000 for adjusted gross.

b. Multiply exemptions by $1000. Subtract from adjusted gross to give taxable amount. [$29,000 − 3000 in this case]. Taxable amount = $26,000.

c. You might want to set up a single level table for each status type. Below is an example of Tax Table Z:

```
01   TAX-Z-VALUES.
     02 FILLER PIC    9(12) VALUE 023000000011.
     02 FILLER PIC    9(12) VALUE 044000023113.
     02 FILLER PIC    9(12) VALUE 065000050415.
     02 FILLER PIC    9(12) VALUE 087000083418.
     02 FILLER PIC    9(12) VALUE 118000139219.
     02 FILLER PIC    9(12) VALUE 150000200021.
     02 FILLER PIC    9(12) VALUE 182000267225.
     02 FILLER PIC    9(12) VALUE 235000399729.
     02 FILLER PIC    9(12) VALUE 288000553434.
     02 FILLER PIC    9(12) VALUE 341000733637.
     02 FILLER PIC    9(12) VALUE 447001125844.
     02 FILLER PIC    9(12) VALUE 606001825448.
     02 FILLER PIC    9(12) VALUE 818002843050.
01   TAX-Z-TABLE REDEFINES TAX-Z-VALUES.
     02   TAX-Z-INFO OCCURS 13 TIMES INDEXED BY TZ.
          03 MIN-Z-AMOUNT    PIC 9(5).
          03 MIN-Z-TAX       PIC 9(5).
          03 Z-PERC          PIC V99.
```

d. Search table until taxable income $<$ min-z-amount. You now have the right area (indexed)—minimum tax $= \$3,997 + .29 * (\$26,000 - \$23,500) = \$4,722$.

You might want to combine all three tax tables into one two dimensional table. Whatever tables you use should be in the subprogram. The subprogram returns the federal tax!!

Provide appropriate test data.

*2. A number of institutions (banks, credit card companies, etc.) use account numbers that are self-checking. A self-checking number is a code number with an additional calculated digit called the "check digit."

Six-digit self-checking code numbers (five basic numbers + one check digit) are to be validated.

a. A main program will read in input records containing the following information:

Field	Columns
Number	1–6
type of number (code) validation	7–9 (M10 or M11)

b. A subprogram is to be written for each of the validation techniques (M10 and M11). If the number is a valid code the number is returned and no error message is printed and no correct check digit written. If the number is invalid, an error message is printed along with the correct check digit.

Example of input:

341248M10
269241M10
222127M11
34124XM11
154267M11

Modulus–10 Checking System [Rules]

1. Each number is made up of a code plus one check digit (rightmost digit). A six-digit number contains 5 numbers for code + 1 check digit.

2. Assign a weight factor of 2 to the units position of the code (the fifth number) and every second position going from right to left. The other digits (except the check digit) are assigned a weight factor of 1.

3. Multiply weight factor by appropriate digit.

4. Add the results of the multiplication in (3).

5. Divide sum by 10.

6. Subtract the remainder from 10.

7. Check the result in (6) with check digit. If they match, the number (six-digit in this case) is valid.

The first number using M10 (modulus–10) is valid. Proof:

Rule #1	3	4	1	2	4	8(check digit)
Rule #2	2	1	2	1	2	
Rule #3	6	4	2	2	8	

Rule #4   SUM = 6+4+2+2+8 = 22

Rule #5   22/10 = 2 with a remainder of 2

Rule #6   10 − 2 = 8

Rule #7   8 = 8 (check digit). Number is valid.

The second number (269241) is invalid. Proof gives value of 2. Check digit is 1.

Modulus–11 Checking System [Rules]

1. See modulus-10.

2. Start with units position. Assign a weight factor of 2. Go from right to left and increase the weight factor by 1 each time.

3. Multiply digits by weight factor.

4. Add results of multiplication.

5. Divide sum by 11.

6. Subtract remainder from 11.

7. Check number from (6) against check digit. If they are the same, the original number is valid. [A remainder of 10 causes a check digit = X. This is one variation of this checking system.]

The third number with M–11 (modulus–11) is valid. Proof:

Rule #1   2   2   2   1   2   7 (check digit)
Rule #2   6   5   4   3   2

Rule #3   12   10   8   3   4

Rule #4   Sum = 12+10+8+3+4 = 37

Rule #5   37/11 = 3 with a remainder of 4

Rule #6   11 − 4 = 7

Rule #7   The calculated number, 7, equals the check digit.

The fourth number (34124X) is also valid. A remainder of 1 is subtracted from 11 giving 10, which = X according to our rules.

The fifth number (154267) is invalid. The check digit should be 1.

Use your own test data. The subprograms should return the check digit if valid, or an error message with the corrected check digit.
Example of output:

NUMBER	CHECKING METHOD	ERROR MESSAGE	CORRECTED DIGIT
341248	modulus 10		
269241	modulus 10	invalid	2
221224	modulus 11		
34124X	modulus 11		
154267	modulus 11	invalid	1

Sequential File Processing

16.1 THE DETAILS OF SEQUENTIAL PROCESSING

The whole idea of creating a master file in the previous chapter was to enable us to update it in this chapter. Sequential file updating, or processing, is one of the two main methods used today. The other is random processing, which is discussed in the next chapter. Sequential access always means the processing of each record in a file, one after another, from first to last. The file used to update a master file is called a transaction file. To sequentially update a master file the following is required:

1. The master and transaction file must be in ascending or descending order according to some key field.

2. This key field must be present in both files.

3. Updating consists of adding, deleting, or changing records, thereby producing a new master file. Examine Figure 6–1.

You are encouraged to read Appendix B: Magnetic Disk File Concepts, to understand how sequential files are organized on magnetic disk devices.

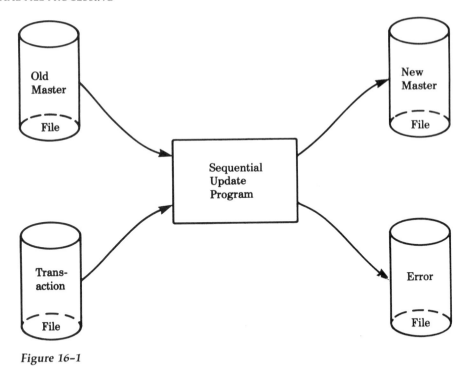

Figure 16-1

Notice that an error file is produced. This should be used if the transaction file contains invalid transaction records. Not only might there be, for example, non-numeric data in numeric fields, but the transaction itself might be invalid. It is possible that a transaction will attempt to change a master record that doesn't exist. It is also possible that a transaction cannot be added to a master file because it already exists there. Or perhaps an attempt is made to delete a master record that doesn't exist!! That is why an error file is set up!

16.2 THE DELETION PROCESS

We will try to update that master file produced in the previous chapter. Examine Figure 16-2 for a modular design that shows sequential updating using only transactions that delete master records. We will add modules to add and change the master file later. Step by step is the best method!

Assume the master and transaction files are to be sorted. Examine the transaction records below (the master records can be examined in the previous chapter):

26437	D
80001	D

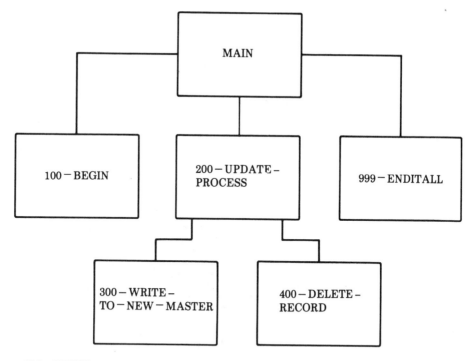

100 – BEGIN
 a. Open files
 b. Read master & transaction records (INITIAL READS)

200 – UPDATE – PROCESS
 a. Move master record to work area
 b. Test master & transaction #'s
  1. If master < transaction transfer control to routine that writes new master from work – area
  2. If master = transaction AND it is a delete transfer control to routine that reads another master and transaction record

300 – WRITE – NEW – MASTER
 a. Write new master from work – area
 b. Read another master

400 – DELETE RECORD
 a. Read another master
 b. Read another transaction

500 – ENDITALL
 a. Close
 b. Stop

Figure 16-2

If our sequential update program works, a new master file should be created that does not have the above two items. Examine the program below:

```
1     IDENTIFICATION DIVISION.
2     PROGRAM-ID. SEQUENTIAL-UPDATE.
3     AUTHOR. SAMUELS.
4     ENVIRONMENT DIVISION.
5     CONFIGURATION SECTION.
6     SOURCE-COMPUTER. VAX-750.
7     OBJECT-COMPUTER. VAX-750.
8     INPUT-OUTPUT SECTION.
9     FILE-CONTROL.
10        SELECT OLDMASTFILE ASSIGN TO OLDMAST.
11        SELECT TRANSFILE ASSIGN TO TRANS.
12        SELECT NEWMASTFILE ASSIGN TO NEWMAST.
13    DATA DIVISION.
14    FILE SECTION.
15    FD  OLDMASTFILE
16        DATA RECORD IS OLDMAST-REC.
17    01  OLDMAST-REC.
18        02 OLDMAST-INV-NO      PIC X(5).
19        02 OLDMAST-QUAN        PIC 9999.
20        02 OLDMAST-PRICE       PIC 999V99.
21        02 OLDMAST-DESC        PIC X(10).
22    FD  TRANSFILE
23        DATA RECORD IS TRANS-REC.
24    01  TRANS-REC.
25        02 TRANS-INV-NO        PIC X(5).
26        02 TRANS-QUAN          PIC 9999.
27        02 TRANS-PRICE         PIC 999V99.
28        02 TRANS-DESC          PIC X(10).
29        02 FILLER              PIC X.
30        02 TRANS-CODE          PIC X.
31    FD  NEWMASTFILE
32        DATA RECORD IS NEWMAST-REC.
33    01  NEWMAST-REC            PIC X(24).
34    WORKING-STORAGE SECTION.
35    01  OLDMAST-SWITCH            PIC XXX VALUE SPACES.
36        88  NO-MORE-OLD-MASTERS      VALUE "YES".
37    01  TRANS-SWITCH             PIC XXX VALUE SPACES.
38        88  NO-MORE-TRANSACTIONS    VALUE "YES".
39    01  WORK-REC.
40        02 WORK-INV-NO         PIC X(5).
41        02 WORK-QUAN           PIC 9999.
42        02 WORK-PRICE          PIC 999V99.
43        02 WORK-DESC           PIC X(10).
44    PROCEDURE DIVISION.
45    START-HERE.
46        PERFORM 100-BEGIN.
47        PERFORM 200-UPDATE-PROCESS UNTIL
48             NO-MORE-OLD-MASTERS AND NO-MORE-TRANSACTIONS.
49        PERFORM 999-ENDITALL.
50    100-BEGIN.
51        OPEN INPUT OLDMASTFILE TRANSFILE OUTPUT NEWMASTFILE.
52        READ OLDMASTFILE AT END MOVE "YES" TO OLDMAST-SWITCH.
53        READ TRANSFILE AT END MOVE "YES" TO TRANS-SWITCH.
54    200-UPDATE-PROCESS.
55        MOVE OLDMAST-REC TO WORK-REC.
56        IF OLDMAST-INV-NO < TRANS-INV-NO
57            PERFORM 300-WRITE-TO-NEW-MASTER
```

```
58          ELSE
59              IF (OLDMAST-INV-NO = TRANS-INV-NO) AND (TRANS-CODE = "D")
60                  PERFORM 400-DELETE-RECORD.
61      300-WRITE-TO-NEW-MASTER.
62          WRITE NEWMAST-REC FROM WORK-REC.
63          READ OLDMASTFILE AT END MOVE "YES" TO OLDMAST-SWITCH.
64      400-DELETE-RECORD.
65          READ OLDMASTFILE AT END MOVE "YES" TO OLDMAST-SWITCH.
66          READ TRANSFILE AT END
67            MOVE "YES" TO TRANS-SWITCH
68            MOVE HIGH-VALUES TO TRANS-INV-NO.
69      999-ENDITALL.
70          CLOSE OLDMASTFILE TRANSFILE NEWMASTFILE.
71          STOP RUN.
```

Some important points about this program must be considered:

1. Statement 47 controls the loop process. When there aren't any more transactions or master records, the program stops.

2. Statement 56 is a conditional statement which, when true, passes control to a module that writes the new master from a Working-Storage area. This area was created because some transactions will change master records. Then, when a transaction record is read having an inventory number greater than a master inventory number, this work area can be written to the new master file.

3. The 400–DELETE-RECORD module only needs two statements. The deletion process should not permit one to write to a new master file. Line 68 (MOVE HIGH-VALUES TO TRANS-INV-NO) is very important. This moves the highest value (all binary ones) that can be represented by the computer for this field. Without this addition to the READ statement, this program goes into an infinite loop because statement 56 or statement 59 is not satisfied [no value is put into TRANS-INV-NO when the end of file is reached!].

Examine the new master file:

```
10308001013000GRILLS
13846000804500DOORS
18307001001550COOLERS
21111000165000BLOWERS
21682000214620MOWER
26392001501050RED-PAINT
28426001501050GRN-PAINT
39462010000200SWITCHES
39924001001720WINDOWS
44445001000860BRACKETS
60203005000050E-COVERS
```

64643010000450NAILS
73736000614000BENCHES
84321001000460PIPES
88113001200150TACKS
91130010000150JIFFIES
91241000508000POWER-RAKE

Two items are obviously not present. To fully understand the deletion process, one should "walk through" the Procedure Division using the old master file and transaction file. The first comparison shows the old master inventory number to be less than the transaction inventory number. Hence, the module that writes the new master record is entered. Since the old master is in WORK-REC, it is written to the new master file. Another master record is read, and again the old master inventory number is less so the same process occurs.

A situation is finally reached when both the master inventory number and transaction inventory number are equal. In this case a module is entered that causes another master record AND another transaction record to be read. The comparison shows that the master is less than the transaction and so on.

You should finish this "walk-through" before attempting to go any further.

16.3   THE ADDITION PROCESS

An attempt will now be made to add records. Examine the modified design in Figure 16–32. Examine the transaction records listed below:

09382000615000LANTERNS   A
26437   D
29411006000125ACETONE   A
67722100000010WASHERS   A
80001   D

Now examine the modified sequential update program with the the additional "add" module:

```
1    IDENTIFICATION DIVISION.
2    PROGRAM-ID. SEQUENTIAL-UPDATE.
3    AUTHOR. SAMUELS.
4    ENVIRONMENT DIVISION.
5    CONFIGURATION SECTION.
6    SOURCE-COMPUTER. VAX-750.
7    OBJECT-COMPUTER. VAX-750.
8    INPUT-OUTPUT SECTION.
9    FILE-CONTROL.
```

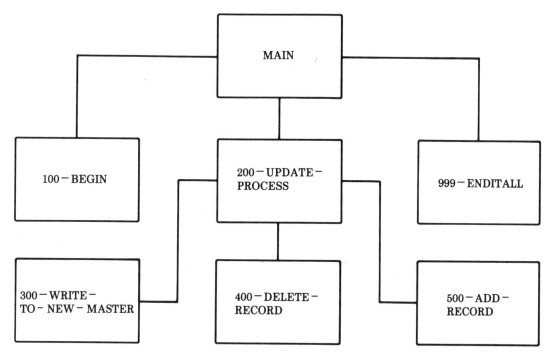

100 – BEGIN
      No change from 16 – 1

200 – UPDATE – PROCESS
      Add the condition if master > transaction;
      then transfer control to 500 – ADD – RECORD

300 – WRITE – TO – NEW – MASTER
      No change from 16 – 1

400 – DELETE – RECORD
      No change from 16 – 1

500 – ADD – RECORD
      Move transaction record to work – area
      Write new master from this area
      Read another transaction

999 – ENDITALL
      No change from 16 – 1

Figure 16-3

```
10        SELECT OLDMASTFILE ASSIGN TO OLDMAST.
11        SE  CT TRANSFILE ASSIGN TO TRANS.
12        SELECT NEWMASTFILE ASSIGN TO NEWMAST.
13    DATA DIVISION.
14    FILE SECTION.
```

```
15    FD   OLDMASTFILE
16         DATA RECORD IS OLDMAST-REC.
17    01   OLDMAST-REC.
18         02 OLDMAST-INV-NO      PIC X(5).
19         02 OLDMAST-QUAN        PIC 9999.
20         02 OLDMAST-PRICE       PIC 999V99.
21         02 OLDMAST-DESC        PIC X(10).
22    FD   TRANSFILE
23         DATA RECORD IS TRANS-REC.
24    01   TRANS-REC.
25         02 TRANS-INV-NO        PIC X(5).
26         02 TRANS-QUAN          PIC 9999.
27         02 TRANS-PRICE         PIC 999V99.
28         02 TRANS-DESC          PIC X(10).
29         02 FILLER              PIC X.
30         02 TRANS-CODE          PIC X.
31    FD   NEWMASTFILE
32         DATA RECORD IS NEWMAST-REC.
33    01   NEWMAST-REC            PIC X(24).
34    WORKING-STORAGE SECTION.
35    01   OLDMAST-SWITCH         PIC XXX VALUE SPACES.
36         88  NO-MORE-OLD-MASTERS     VALUE "YES".
37    01   TRANS-SWITCH           PIC XXX VALUE SPACES.
38         88  NO-MORE-TRANSACTIONS    VALUE "YES".
39    01   WORK-REC.
40         02 WORK-INV-NO         PIC X(5).
41         02 WORK-QUAN           PIC 9999.
42         02 WORK-PRICE          PIC 999V99.
43         02 WORK-DESC           PIC X(10).
44    PROCEDURE DIVISION.
45    START-HERE.
46         PERFORM 100-BEGIN.
47         PERFORM 200-UPDATE-PROCESS UNTIL
48         NO-MORE-OLD-MASTERS AND NO-MORE-TRANSACTIONS.
49         PERFORM 999-ENDITALL.
50    100-BEGIN.
51         OPEN INPUT OLDMASTFILE TRANSFILE OUTPUT NEWMASTFILE.
52         READ OLDMASTFILE AT END MOVE "YES" TO OLDMAST-SWITCH.
53         READ TRANSFILE AT END MOVE "YES" TO TRANS-SWITCH.
54    200-UPDATE-PROCESS.
55         MOVE OLDMAST-REC TO WORK-REC.
56         IF OLDMAST-INV-NO ( TRANS-INV-NO
57            PERFORM 300-WRITE-TO-NEW-MASTER
58         ELSE
59            IF (OLDMAST-INV-NO = TRANS-INV-NO) AND (TRANS-CODE = "D")
60               PERFORM 400-DELETE-RECORD
61            else
62               perform 500-add-record.
63    300-WRITE-TO-NEW-MASTER.
64         WRITE NEWMAST-REC FROM WORK-REC.
65         READ OLDMASTFILE AT END MOVE "YES" TO OLDMAST-SWITCH.
66    400-DELETE-RECORD.
67         READ OLDMASTFILE AT END MOVE "YES" TO OLDMAST-SWITCH.
68         READ TRANSFILE AT END
69          MOVE "YES" TO TRANS-SWITCH
70          MOVE HIGH-VALUES TO TRANS-INV-NO.
71    500-add-record.
72         move trans-rec to work-rec.
73         write newmast-rec from work-rec.
74         read transfile at end
75          move "yes" to trans-switch
```

```
76              move high-values to trans-inv-no.
77      999-ENDITALL.
78          CLOSE OLDMASTFILE TRANSFILE NEWMASTFILE.
79          STOP RUN.
```

The new master, listed below, shows that we have been successful in deleting and adding records:

```
09382000615000LANTERNS
10308001013000GRILLS
13846000804500DOORS
18307001001550COOLERS
21111000165000BLOWERS
21682000214620MOWER
26392001501050RED-PAINT
28426001501050GRN-PAINT
29411006000125ACETONE
39462010000200SWITCHES
39924001001720WINDOWS
44445001000860BRACKETS
60203005000050E-COVERS
64643010000450NAILS
67722100000010WASHERS
73736000614000BENCHES
84321001000460PIPES
88113001200150TACKS
91130010000150JIFFIES
91241000508000POWER-RAKE
```

Three records were added. Do you know which ones? Did you "walk through" the program using both files? Did you follow the logic in the Procedure Division when the transaction number was less than the master number? If you answered NO to any of these, don't go any further until you understand the add record module thoroughly.

You cannot read this text like a novel. It stands to reason that you may have to go over certain parts again and again.

16.4 THE CHANGE PROCESS

Of course, no update is complete without a change module. Examine Figure 16–4 with the design modification. Examine the new transaction file below:

```
09382000615000LANTERNS    A
```

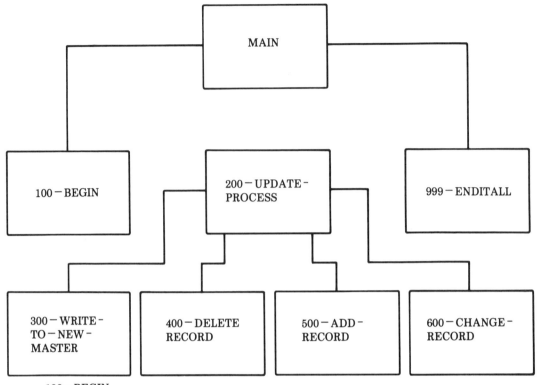

100 – BEGIN
    No change from 16 – 1

200 – UPDATE PROCESS
    Add condition where master = transaction and it is a change then transfer control
    to 600 – CHANGE – RECORD
    Initialize change – switch

300 – WRITE – TO – NEW – MASTER
    Reinitialize change – switch after new master record is written

400 – DELETE – RECORD
    No change from 16 – 2

500 – ADD – RECORD
    No change from 16 – 2

600 – CHANGE – RECORD
    Change word – rec depending on type of change
    Reset change – switch
    Read another transaction record

999 – ENDITALL
    No change from 16 – 1

Figure 16-4

18307	FREEZERS	1
26437		D
29411006000125ACETONE		A
39924 01850		2
67722100000010WASHERS		A
737360001		3
737360004		4
80001		D
881130009		3

Notice that there is more than one change to inventory item #73736. The following program should be able to delete, add, and change:

```
1      IDENTIFICATION DIVISION.
2      PROGRAM-ID. SEQUENTIAL-UPDATE.
3      AUTHOR. SAMUELS.
4      ENVIRONMENT DIVISION.
5      CONFIGURATION SECTION.
6      SOURCE-COMPUTER. VAX-750.
7      OBJECT-COMPUTER. VAX-750.
8      INPUT-OUTPUT SECTION.
9      FILE-CONTROL.
10         SELECT OLDMASTFILE ASSIGN TO OLDMAST.
11         SELECT TRANSFILE ASSIGN TO TRANS.
12         SELECT NEWMASTFILE ASSIGN TO NEWMAST.
13     DATA DIVISION.
14     FILE SECTION.
15     FD  OLDMASTFILE
16         DATA RECORD IS OLDMAST-REC.
17     01  OLDMAST-REC.
18         02 OLDMAST-INV-NO      PIC X(5).
19         02 OLDMAST-QUAN        PIC 9999.
20         02 OLDMAST-PRICE       PIC 999V99.
21         02 OLDMAST-DESC        PIC X(10).
22     FD  TRANSFILE
23         DATA RECORD IS TRANS-REC.
24     01  TRANS-REC.
25         02 TRANS-INV-NO        PIC X(5).
26         02 TRANS-QUAN          PIC 9999.
27         02 TRANS-PRICE         PIC 999V99.
28         02 TRANS-DESC          PIC X(10).
29         02 FILLER              PIC X.
30         02 TRANS-CODE          PIC X.
31             88 change-desc       value "1".
32             88 change-price      value "2".
33             88 add-quan          value "3".
34             88 sub-quan          value "4".
35     FD  NEWMASTFILE
36         DATA RECORD IS NEWMAST-REC.
37     01  NEWMAST-REC            PIC X(24).
38     WORKING-STORAGE SECTION.
39     01  OLDMAST-SWITCH          PIC XXX VALUE SPACES.
40         88 NO-MORE-OLD-MASTERS      VALUE "YES".
41     01  TRANS-SWITCH            PIC XXX VALUE SPACES.
42         88 NO-MORE-TRANSACTIONS     VALUE "YES".
```

```
43    01   change-switch          pic xx value "NO".
44    01   WORK-REC.
45         02 WORK-INV-NO          PIC X(5).
46         02 WORK-QUAN            PIC 9999.
47         02 WORK-PRICE           PIC 999V99.
48         02 WORK-DESC            PIC X(10).
49    PROCEDURE DIVISION.
50    START-HERE.
51        PERFORM 100-BEGIN.
52        PERFORM 200-UPDATE-PROCESS UNTIL
53           NO-MORE-OLD-MASTERS AND NO-MORE-TRANSACTIONS.
54        PERFORM 999-ENDITALL.
55    100-BEGIN.
56        OPEN INPUT OLDMASTFILE TRANSFILE OUTPUT NEWMASTFILE.
57        READ OLDMASTFILE AT END MOVE "YES" TO OLDMAST-SWITCH.
58        READ TRANSFILE AT END MOVE "YES" TO TRANS-SWITCH.
59    200-UPDATE-PROCESS.
60        if change-switch = "NO"
61           MOVE OLDMAST-REC TO WORK-REC.
62        IF OLDMAST-INV-NO < TRANS-INV-NO
63           PERFORM 300-WRITE-TO-NEW-MASTER
64        ELSE
65          IF (OLDMAST-INV-NO = TRANS-INV-NO) AND (TRANS-CODE = "D")
66           PERFORM 400-DELETE-RECORD
67          ELSE
68           if (oldmast-inv-no = trans-inv-no)
                   and (trans-code not = "D")
69             perform 600-change-record
70          ELSE
71               PERFORM 500-ADD-RECORD.
72    300-WRITE-TO-NEW-MASTER.
73        WRITE NEWMAST-REC FROM WORK-REC.
74        if change-switch = spaces
75           move "NO" to change-switch.
76        READ OLDMASTFILE AT END MOVE "YES" TO OLDMAST-SWITCH.
77    400-DELETE-RECORD.
78        READ OLDMASTFILE AT END MOVE "YES" TO OLDMAST-SWITCH.
79        READ TRANSFILE AT END
80          MOVE "YES" TO TRANS-SWITCH
81          MOVE HIGH-VALUES TO TRANS-INV-NO.
82    500-ADD-RECORD.
83        MOVE TRANS-REC TO WORK-REC.
84        WRITE NEWMAST-REC FROM WORK-REC.
85        READ TRANSFILE AT END
86          MOVE "YES" TO TRANS-SWITCH
87          MOVE HIGH-VALUES TO TRANS-INV-NO.
88    600-change-record.
89        If change-desc move trans-desc to work-desc
90        else
91          if change-price move trans-price to work-price
92          else
93            if add-quan add trans-quan to work-quan
94            else
95               if sub-quan subtract trans-quan from work-quan.
96          move spaces to change-switch.
97          read transfile at end
98            move "YES" to trans-switch
99            move high-values to trans-inv-no.
100   999-ENDITALL.
101       CLOSE OLDMASTFILE TRANSFILE NEWMASTFILE.
102       STOP RUN.
```

You may wonder at the addition and use of CHANGE-SWITCH in lines 43, 60, 74–75, and 96. It was put there so that a changed master record would be written to the new master file. If you take these statements out, the program still runs. The WORK-REC area actually contains the modified (changed) record; however, the old master record will be moved to the new master record area and written. These additional statements insure that the modified record will be written to the new master file.

In examining the new master file, listed below, we find that:

a. The name of COOLERS was changed to FREEZERS.

b. The price of WINDOWS was changed from 1720 to 1850.

c. 1 was added to the quantity of BENCHES and then 4 was subtracted.

d. 9 was added to the quantity of TACKS.

```
09382000615000LANTERNS
10308001013000GRILLS
13846000804500DOORS
18307001001550FREEZERS
21111000165000BLOWERS
21682000214620MOWER
26392001501050RED-PAINT
28426001501050GREEN-PAIN
29411006000125ACETONE
39462010000200SWITCHES
39924001001850WINDOWS
44445001000860BRACKETS
60203005000050E-COVERS
64643010000450NAILS
67722100000010WASHERS
73736000314000BENCHES
84321001000460PIPES
88113002100150TACKS
91130010000150JIFFIES
91241000508000POWER-RAKE
```

16.5   THE ADDITION OF A "BACK-ORDER" MODULE TO THE ENTIRE SEQUENTIAL PROCESS

There is one more module we could add, excluding the addition of modules and resulting code for invalid transaction records. It is possible that a transaction could have a quantity to be subtracted that is greater than the quantity listed in the old master file. In the real world, one processes this record by

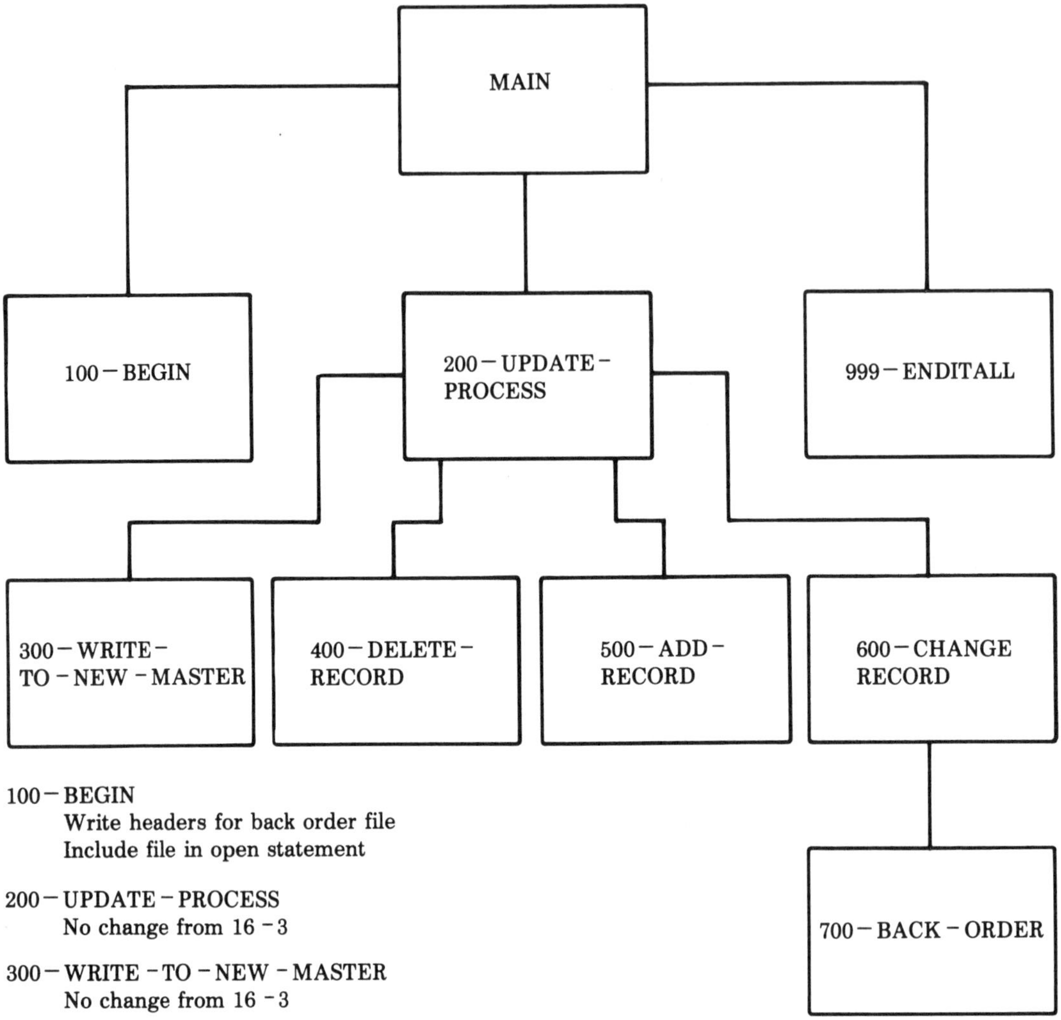

100 — BEGIN
    Write headers for back order file
    Include file in open statement

200 — UPDATE — PROCESS
    No change from 16 − 3

300 — WRITE — TO — NEW — MASTER
    No change from 16 − 3

400 — DELETE — RECORD
    No change from 16 − 2

500 — ADD — RECORD
    No change from 16 − 2

600 — CHANGE — RECORD
    If quan from transaction > quan for master
    and it is a subtraction change,
    transfer control to 700 − BACK − ORDER routine

700 — BACK − ORDER
    Compute backorder amount
    Change work − rec accordingly
    Write to backorder file

999 — ENDITALL
    Include backorder file on
    close statement

Figure 16-5

delivering all that is in stock and back ordering the remainder. One way this can be handled, in a programming sense, is to create a file containing records of those items that need to be back ordered. Let us add two transaction records having quantities to be subtracted that are greater than the "amount available." Examine Figure 16–5. Now look at the new transaction file below and the modified program that follows the file:

```
09382000615000LANTERNS      A
138460010                   4
18307           FREEZERS     1
26437                       D
29411006000125ACETONE        A
39924     01850              2
444450020                   4
67722100000010WASHERS        A
737360001                   3
737360004                   4
80001                       D
881130009                   3
```

```
 1    IDENTIFICATION DIVISION.
 2    PROGRAM-ID. SEQUENTIAL-UPDATE.
 3    AUTHOR. SAMUELS.
 4    ENVIRONMENT DIVISION.
 5    CONFIGURATION SECTION.
 6    SOURCE-COMPUTER. VAX-750.
 7    OBJECT-COMPUTER. VAX-750.
 8    INPUT-OUTPUT SECTION.
 9    FILE-CONTROL.
10        SELECT OLDMASTFILE ASSIGN TO OLDMAST.
11        SELECT TRANSFILE ASSIGN TO TRANS.
12        SELECT NEWMASTFILE ASSIGN TO NEWMAST.
13        Select backorderfile assign to back.
14    DATA DIVISION.
15     FILE SECTION.
16    FD  OLDMASTFILE
17        DATA RECORD IS OLDMAST-REC.
18    01  OLDMAST-REC.
19        02 OLDMAST-INV-NO          PIC X(5).
20        02 OLDMAST-QUAN            PIC 9999.
21        02 OLDMAST-PRICE           PIC 999V99.
22        02 OLDMAST-DESC            PIC X(10).
23    FD  TRANSFILE
24        DATA RECORD IS TRANS-REC.
25    01  TRANS-REC.
26        02 TRANS-INV-NO            PIC X(5).
27        02 TRANS-QUAN              PIC 9999.
28        02 TRANS-PRICE             PIC 999V99.
29        02 TRANS-DESC              PIC X(10).
30        02 FILLER                  PIC X.
31        02 TRANS-CODE              PIC X.
32           88 CHANGE-DESC             VALUE "1".
```

```
33              88 CHANGE-PRICE              VALUE "2".
34              88 ADD-QUAN                  VALUE "3".
35              88 SUB-QUAN                  VALUE "4".
36      FD  NEWMASTFILE
37          DATA RECORD IS NEWMAST-REC.
38      01  NEWMAST-REC                      PIC X(24).
39      fd  backorderfile
40          data record is back-rec.
41      01  back-rec        pic x(80).
42      WORKING-STORAGE SECTION.
43      01  OLDMAST-SWITCH                   PIC XXX VALUE SPACES.
44          88  NO-MORE-OLD-MASTERS          VALUE "YES".
45      01  TRANS-SWITCH                     PIC XXX VALUE SPACES.
46          88  NO-MORE-TRANSACTIONS         VALUE "YES".
47      01  CHANGE-SWITCH                    PIC XX VALUE "NO".
48      01  WORK-REC.
49          02 WORK-INV-NO                   PIC X(5).
50          02 WORK-QUAN                     PIC 9999.
51          02 WORK-PRICE                    PIC 999V99.
52          02 WORK-DESC                     PIC X(10).
53      01  header.
54          02 filler          pic x(11) value "DESCRIPTION".
55          02 filler          pic x(10) value spaces.
56          02 filler          pic x(20) value "INVENTORY NUMBER".
57          02 filler          pic x(10) value spaces.
58          02 filler          pic x(10) value "QUANTITY".
59          02 filler          pic x(10) value spaces.
60          02 filler          pic x(8) value "PRICE".
61      01  back-order-line.
62          02 back-desc       pic x(10).
63          02 filler          pic x(15) value spaces.
64          02 back-inv-no     pic x(5).
65          02 filler          pic x(21) value spaces.
66          02 back-quan       pic zzz9.
67          02 filler          pic x(14) value spaces.
68          02 back-price      pic $$$$.99.
69      PROCEDURE DIVISION.
70      START-HERE.
71          PERFORM 100-BEGIN.
72          PERFORM 200-UPDATE-PROCESS UNTIL
73              NO-MORE-OLD-MASTERS AND NO-MORE-TRANSACTIONS.
74          PERFORM 999-ENDITALL.
75      100-BEGIN.
76          OPEN INPUT OLDMASTFILE TRANSFILE OUTPUT NEWMASTFILE backorderfile.
77          write back-rec from header after page.
78          move all "-" to back-rec.
79          write back-rec after 1.
80          READ OLDMASTFILE AT END MOVE "YES" TO OLDMAST-SWITCH.
81          READ TRANSFILE AT END MOVE "YES" TO TRANS-SWITCH.
82      200-UPDATE-PROCESS.
83          IF CHANGE-SWITCH = "NO"
84              MOVE OLDMAST-REC TO WORK-REC.
85          IF OLDMAST-INV-NO < TRANS-INV-NO
86                  PERFORM 300-WRITE-TO-NEW-MASTER
87              ELSE
88                IF (OLDMAST-INV-NO = TRANS-INV-NO) AND (TRANS-CODE = "D")
89                  PERFORM 400-DELETE-RECORD
90                ELSE
91                  IF (OLDMAST-INV-NO = TRANS-INV-NO) AND (TRANS-CODE NOT = "D")
92                      PERFORM 600-CHANGE-RECORD
93                  ELSE
```

```
 94                    PERFORM 500-ADD-RECORD.
 95      300-WRITE-TO-NEW-MASTER.
 96          WRITE NEWMAST-REC FROM WORK-REC.
 97          IF CHANGE-SWITCH = SPACES
 98             MOVE "NO" TO CHANGE-SWITCH.
 99          READ OLDMASTFILE AT END MOVE "YES" TO OLDMAST-SWITCH.
100      400-DELETE-RECORD.
101          READ OLDMASTFILE AT END MOVE "YES" TO OLDMAST-SWITCH.
102          READ TRANSFILE AT END
103                   MOVE "YES" TO TRANS-SWITCH
104                   MOVE HIGH-VALUES TO TRANS-INV-NO.
105      500-ADD-RECORD.
106          MOVE TRANS-REC TO WORK-REC.
107          WRITE NEWMAST-REC FROM WORK-REC.
108          READ TRANSFILE AT END
109                   MOVE "YES" TO TRANS-SWITCH
110                   MOVE HIGH-VALUES TO TRANS-INV-NO.
111      600-CHANGE-RECORD.
112          IF CHANGE-DESC MOVE TRANS-DESC TO WORK-DESC
113          ELSE
114             IF CHANGE-PRICE MOVE TRANS-PRICE TO WORK-PRICE
115             ELSE
116                IF ADD-QUAN ADD TRANS-QUAN TO WORK-QUAN
117                ELSE
118                   IF SUB-QUAN
119                      if trans-quan > work-quan
120                              perform 700-back-order
121                              move 0 to work-quan
122                      else subtract trans-quan from work-quan.
123          MOVE SPACES TO CHANGE-SWITCH.
124          READ TRANSFILE AT END
125                   MOVE "YES" TO TRANS-SWITCH
126                   MOVE HIGH-VALUES TO TRANS-INV-NO.
127      700-back-order.
128          compute back-quan = work-quan - trans-quan.
129          move work-desc to back-desc.
130          move work-price to back-price.
131          move trans-inv-no to back-inv-no.
132          write back-rec from back-order-line after 2.
133      999-ENDITALL.
134          CLOSE OLDMASTFILE TRANSFILE NEWMASTFILE backorderfile.
135          STOP RUN.
```

And the new back-order file was created—see below:

DESCRIPTION	INVENTORY NUMBER	QUANTITY	PRICE
DOORS	13846	2	$45.00
BRACKETS	44445	10	$8.60

We can just keep adding modules to our design and additional syntax accordingly. The latest program cannot be considered complex since we have GRADUALLY worked up to it in little steps. Line 78 shows a modification to the MOVE statement.

A program, REPORTER, already exists along with DATER and MAIN.

We can replace the CALL "SORTER" with CALL "SEQUENTIAL-UP-DATE" in the MAIN to produce a nice inventory report of the new master. We should also change the external file name in REPORTER to NEWMAST (see SELECT statement in the REPORTER program in the previous chapter). The command file can be modified accordingly:

```
$LINK MAIN,UPDATER,REPORTER,DATER
$RUN MAIN
```

We execute the command file with @SAM to produce the following inventory report:

INVENTORY REPORT
JANUARY 28, 1984

INVENTORY NUMBER	QUANTITY	PRICE	AMOUNT	DESCRIPTION
09382	6	$150.00	$900.00	LANTERNS
10308	10	$130.00	$1,300.00	GRILLS
13846	0	$45.00	$.00	DOORS
18307	10	$15.50	$155.00	FREEZERS
21111	1	$650.00	$650.00	BLOWERS
21682	2	$146.20	$292.40	MOWER
26392	15	$10.50	$157.50	RED-PAINT
28426	15	$10.50	$157.50	GREEN-PAIN
29411	60	$1.25	$75.00	ACETONE
39462	100	$2.00	$200.00	SWITCHES
39924	10	$18.50	$185.00	WINDOWS
44445	0	$8.60	$.00	BRACKETS
60203	50	$.50	$25.00	E-COVERS
64643	100	$4.50	$450.00	NAILS
67722	1000	$.10	$100.00	WASHERS
73736	3	$140.00	$420.00	BENCHES
84321	10	$4.60	$46.00	PIPES
88113	21	$1.50	$31.50	TACKS
91130	100	$1.50	$150.00	JIFFIES
91241	5	$80.00	$400.00	POWER-RAKE

FINAL INVENTORY TOTAL = $5,694.90

SUMMARY

The importance of programming in steps was stressed again. A complex program to sequentially update a master file can be more easily accomplished if the the entire task is broken up into subtasks. Each subtask is incrementally tested before additional modules are added.

PROGRAMMING PROBLEMS

1. Include an error routine in the above update program by putting some invalid records in the transaction file. Include invalid data that will test for:
   a. Non-numeric conditions.
   b. Invalid add (attempt to add a record that is already in the master file).
   c. Invalid delete (attempt to delete a record that is not in the master file).
   d. Change in a record that was previously deleted.

2. UFLUNKOUT University has a master file containing tuition information on students. Each record in the file has the following format:

Field	Columns
NAME	1–20
SS#	21–29
# OF CREDIT HOURS	30–31
TUITION BALANCE	32–35 (9999)

Transaction records are used to update this file. Each transaction record contains, at the very least, a SS# and transaction code. Students can:
   a. be added to the file (code 1).
   b. be deleted from the file (code 2).
   c. have their tuition balance increased (code 3).
   d. have their tuition balance decreased (code 4).
   e. have their # of credit hours increased (code 5).
   f. have their # of credit hours decreased (code 6).

These transaction records have the following format:

Field	Columns
SS#	1–9
Transaction #	11
Name (if code 1)	13–32
# of credit hours (if code 1)	33–34
tuition balance (if code 1)	35–38
# of hours added or subtracted (if code 5 or 6)	13–14
tuition added or subtracted (if code 3 or 4)	13–16

Use this master file:

JONES SAM	111223333150800
PETERSON SARAH	132412231121200
KETTLES JANE	203943021150000
RYERSON STUART	244392012121000
LANDSBERG STANLEY	300021230160500
WILSON DERRICK	440329123160400
MEYERS JUDY	498291023131500
HOLTZER HAROLD	520123492192300
FLOME HERMAN	640493203000000
FOSTER SALLY	669302394120050
KEARNS URSULA	801928493121000
STOPLER AMY	899402938131000
ANDERSON GARY	911029392140900
MURDOCK ALAN	984930239150600

Use this transaction file for updating the above:

640493203	2		
772839123	1	EMERSON RYAN	131000
911029392	5	04	
498291023	3	0500	
300021230	4	0100	
200000321	1	PAULSON ROBERT	140500
911029392	3	1000	
520123492	6	07	

Create the following:
   a. An updated master file.
   b. A nice report with headers, detail lines, and totals for number of credit
      hours and total tuition owed (if a student overpays, so state on this re-
      port).

The transaction file has to be sorted on SS# first!!!

*3. The university, mentioned in the previous problem, also has a master file
containing course registration for its students. The records in this file are
variable in length since some students enroll for more courses than others.
This file has to be updated because students are dropping certain courses and
adding others.

   The master file contains records with the following format:

Field	Columns
STUDENT #	1–5
Number of courses	7 (max # = 6)
Course numbers (based on # of courses)	9–26 (maximum of 6 3-digit numbers)

Example of master file:

```
12332  5  124234354113246
34213  4  124335432154
88123  5  124335154246822
```

The transaction file contains records with the following format:

Field	Columns
STUDENT #	1–5
code (1=add course, 2=drop course)	7
Course #	9–11

Example of transaction file records:

```
34213  2  335
88123  1  665
34213  1  246
34213  1  665
```

As one can see, student 34213 added two courses and dropped one. Student 88123 added one course. An example of records in a new master file would be:

```
12332 5 124234356113256
34213 5 124432154246665
88123 6 124335154246822665
```

So, for example, if a student originally takes five courses (old master record) and then drops one (transaction record), his record in the new master file is actually smaller!!

Besides updating an appropriate master (use your own data) with transaction records (sorted on student #, of course) thereby producing a new master file, also produce a nice report as follows:

STUDENT NUMBER	NO. OF COURSES	COURSE NUMBER
12332	5	124
		234
		356
		113
		256
34213	5	124
		432
		154
		246
		665
88123	6	124
		335
		154
		246
		822
		655

You may want to include a COURSE LISTING column that would list the type of course to which a particular number corresponds. For example, course 822 may be CHEMISTRY.

You may also want to provide invalid data for an error file.

## 17

Random Processing

There is an easier way to update files. Instead of reading master records and transaction records, determining a low, equal, or high condition, and then updating, random access allows us to go directly to a particular record for deletion or change. No comparisons are necessary. The production of error messages is facilitated because of the Invalid Key option, which will be explained later.

You are encouraged to read Appendix-B, Magnetic Disk File Concepts, to understand how indexed files are organized on magnetic disk devices.

17.1 CREATION OF AN INDEXED FILE

As always, one doesn't get something for nothing. In order to randomly process records, the master file needs to be indexed (which requires additional disk space and additional cost). In any case, we will use the SORTER program developed in chapter 15 and modify it slightly so that we can create an indexed master file. Examine this procedure below:

```
1    IDENTIFICATION DIVISION.
2    PROGRAM-ID. SORTER.
3    AUTHOR. STEVE SAMUELS.
4    ENVIRONMENT DIVISION.
5    CONFIGURATION SECTION.
```

```
  6    INPUT-OUTPUT SECTION.
  7    FILE-CONTROL.
  8        SELECT INFILE ASSIGN TO UNSTRUNG.
  9        SELECT SORTFILE ASSIGN TO TEMPO.
 10        SELECT MASTFILE ASSIGN TO MASTER
 11            organization is indexed
 12            access is sequential
 13            record key is mast-num.
 14        SELECT ERRORFILE ASSIGN TO ERRORS.
 15    DATA DIVISION.
 16    FILE SECTION.
 17    FD  INFILE
 18        DATA RECORD IS INREC.
 19    01  INREC                PIC X(28).
 20    SD  SORTFILE
 21        DATA RECORD IS SORTREC.
 22    01  SORTREC.
 23        02 SORT-INV-NO     PIC X(5).
 24        02 FILLER          PIC X(1).
 25        02 SORT-QUAN       PIC X(4)  JUST RIGHT.
 26        02 FILLER          PIC X.
 27        02 SORT-PRICE      PIC X(6)  JUST RIGHT.
 28        02 REAL-PRICE REDEFINES SORT-PRICE.
 29            03 SORT-DOLLARS   PIC 999.
 30            03 FILLER         PIC X.
 31            03 SORT-CENTS     PIC V99.
 32        02 FILLER          PIC X.
 33        02 SORT-DESC       PIC X(10).
 34    FD  MASTFILE
 35        DATA RECORD IS MASTREC.
 36    01  MASTREC.
 37        02 mast-num          pic x(5).
 38        02 rest-of-rec       pic x(19).
 39    FD  ERRORFILE
 40        DATA RECORD IS ERRORREC.
 41    01  ERRORREC       PIC X(75).
 42    WORKING-STORAGE SECTION.
 43    01  ERROR-SWITCH   PIC XXX.
 44    01  SWITCHER       PIC XXX VALUE SPACES.
 45        88  BALL-GAME-IS-OVER VALUE "YES".
 46    01  HEADER-ONE.
 47        02 FILLER     PIC X(20) VALUE SPACES.
 48        02 FILLER     PIC X(40) VALUE "ERROR REPORT".
 49        02 FILLER     PIC X(15) VALUE SPACES.
 50    01  HEADER-TWO.
 51        02 FILLER     PIC X(10) VALUE "INV-NUM".
 52        02 FILLER     PIC X(10) VALUE "QUAN".
 53        02 FILLER     PIC X(10) VALUE "PRICE".
 54        02 FILLER     PIC X(15) VALUE "DESCRIPTION".
 55        02 FILLER     PIC X(30) VALUE "    ERROR MESSAGE".
 56    01  HEADER-THREE.
 57        02 FILLER     PIC X(75) VALUE ALL "*".
 58    01  WORK-MAST-REC.
 59        02 MAST-INV-NO    PIC X(5).
 60        02 MAST-QUAN      PIC 9(4).
 61        02 MAST-PRICE     PIC 999V99.
 62        02 MAST-DESC      PIC X(10).
 63    01  ERROR-LINE.
 64        02 ERROR-INV-NO    PIC X(5).
 65        02 FILLER          PIC X(5) VALUE SPACES.
 66        02 ERROR-QUAN      PIC X(4).
 67        02 FILLER          PIC X(5) VALUE SPACES.
```

```
68          02 ERROR-PRICE      PIC X(6).
69          02 FILLER           PIC X(5) VALUE SPACES.
70          02 ERROR-DESC       PIC X(10).
71          02 FILLER           PIC X(5) VALUE SPACES.
72          02 ERROR-MESSAGE    PIC X(30).
73      PROCEDURE DIVISION.
74      BEGINNER SECTION.
75      BEGIN.
76          SORT SORTFILE
77            ASCENDING KEY SORT-INV-NO
78              USING INFILE
79              OUTPUT PROCEDURE REPORT-N-MASTER.
80      REPORT-N-MASTER SECTION.
81      STARTER.
82          PERFORM 100-START.
83          PERFORM 200-LOOPDELOOP UNTIL BALL-GAME-IS-OVER.
84          PERFORM 300-FINAL.
85      100-START.
86          OPE N OUTPUT MASTFILE ERRORFILE.
87          WRITE ERRORREC FROM HEADER-ONE AFTER 1.
88          WRITE ERRORREC FROM HEADER-TWO AFTER 5.
89          WRITE ERRORREC FROM HEADER-THREE AFTER 1.
90          RETURN SORTFILE AT END MOVE "YES" TO SWITCHER.
91      200-LOOPDELOOP.
92          INSPECT SORT-QUAN REPLACING LEADING SPACES BY "0".
93          INSPECT SORT-PRICE REPLACING LEADING SPACES BY "0".
94          MOVE SPACES TO ERROR-SWITCH.
95          MOVE SPACES TO ERROR-MESSAGE.
96          IF SORT-INV-NO IS NOT NUMERIC MOVE "YES" TO ERROR-SWITCH
97              MOVE "INVALID INVENTORY NUMBER" TO ERROR-MESSAGE
98          ELSE
99              IF SORT-QUAN IS NOT NUMERIC MOVE "YES" TO ERROR-SWITCH
100                 MOVE "INVALID QUANTITY" TO ERROR-MESSAGE
101             ELSE
102                 IF SORT-DOLLARS NOT NUMERIC OR SORT-CENTS NOT NUMERIC
103                     MOVE "YES" TO ERROR-SWITCH
104                     MOVE "INVALID PRICE" TO ERROR-MESSAGE.
105         IF ERROR-SWITCH = "YES"
106             MOVE SORT-INV-NO TO ERROR-INV-NO
107             MOVE SORT-QUAN    TO ERROR-QUAN
108             MOVE SORT-PRICE  TO ERROR-PRICE
109             MOVE SORT-DESC    TO ERROR-DESC
110             WRITE ERRORREC FROM ERROR-LINE AFTER 2
111         ELSE
112             MOVE SORT-INV-NO TO MAST-INV-NO
113             MOVE SORT-QUAN    TO MAST-QUAN
114             COMPUTE MAST-PRICE = SORT-DOLLARS + SORT-CENTS
115             MOVE SORT-DESC    TO MAST-DESC
116             WRITE MASTREC FROM WORK-MAST-REC invalid key
117                 display "problem here".
118         RETURN SORTFILE AT END MOVE "YES" TO SWITCHER.
119     300-FINAL.
120         CLOSE ERRORFILE MASTFILE.
121         EXIT PROGRAM.
```

The SORTER program from chapter 15 has been changed to do the following:

a. Line 11 allows the master file to be indexed (ORGANIZATION IS IN-DEXED). To create this file, one writes to the file one record after another (line 12: ACCESS IS SEQUENTIAL) by using some field in each record as a primary key (line 13: RECORD KEY IS MAST-NUM).

b. This primary key has to be specified in the master file record description—line 37.

c. When writing to this file the INVALID KEY clause is required on the WRITE statement (line 116). This protects one against attempting to write a record with the same primary key that was present in a previous record. In this case "problem here" would be displayed on the terminal.

Now examine the transaction file to update this master file:

```
09382000615000LANTERNS      A
29411006000125JIFFIES        A
138460010                    4
444450020                    4
67722100000010WASHERS        A
737360004                    4
80001                        D
881130009                    3
18307           FREEZERS     D
39924      01850             2
7373600004                   4
26437                        D
```

17.2 UPDATE OF AN INDEXED FILE—THE DELETION PROCESS

Notice that these records are NOT sorted. They needn't be for random processing. What we will do is write a random update program, in steps of course, that will change the master file. With random updating, a new master is NOT created. Instead the old master BECOMES the new master. If one wants an old master file, then two versions should be kept—the latter being the one changed. A program will be developed that will delete records first; then an "add record" module will be added, and finally a "change module." The structured design for the sequential update program is essentially the same, except that one needs to write the pseudocode to determine if the master number is high, equal to, or lower than the transaction number. The random processing program to perform just deletions follows:

```
1    IDENTIFICATION DIVISION.
2    PROGRAM-ID. RANDOM-UPDATE.
3    ENVIRONMENT DIVISION.
4    CONFIGURATION SECTION.
5    SOURCE-COMPUTER. VAX-750
6    OBJECT-COMPUTER. VAX-750.
7    INPUT-OUTPUT SECTION.
```

```
 8     FILE-CONTROL.
 9         SELECT MASTERFILE ASSIGN TO MASTER
10             ORGANIZATION IS INDEXED
11             ACCESS IS RANDOM
12             RECORD KEY IS MAST-NUM.
13         SELECT TRANSFILE ASSIGN TO TRANS.
14     DATA DIVISION.
15     FILE SECTION.
16     FD  MASTERFILE
17         DATA RECORD IS MASTREC.
18     01  MASTREC.
19         02 MAST-NUM       PIC X(5).
20         02 MAST-QUAN      PIC 9999.
21         02 MAST-PRICE     PIC 999V99.
22         02 MAST-DESC      PIC X(10).
23     COPY "TRANS.LIB".
24L    FD  TRANSFILE
25L        DATA RECORD IS TRANS-REC.
26L    01  TRANS-REC.
27L        02 TRANS-INV-NO       PIC X(5).
28L        02 TRANS-QUAN         PIC 9999.
29L        02 TRANS-PRICE        PIC 999V99.
30L        02 TRANS-DESC         PIC X(10).
31L        02 FILLER             PIC X.
32L        02 TRANS-CODE         PIC X.
33L           88 CHANGE-DESC        VALUE "1".
34L           88 CHANGE-PRICE       VALUE "2".
35L           88 ADD-QUAN           VALUE "3".
36L           88 SUB-QUAN           VALUE "4".
37     WORKING-STORAGE SECTION.
38     01  SWITCH             PIC XXX.
39         88 THAT-IS-ALL-FOLKS    VALUE "YES".
40     PROCEDURE DIVISION.
41     BEGIN.
42         PERFORM 100-FIRST-PART.
43         PERFORM 200-LOOPS UNTIL THAT-IS-ALL-FOLKS.
44         PERFORM 900-LAST-PART.
45     100-FIRST-PART.
46         OPEN INPUT TRANSFILE I-O MASTERFILE.
47         READ TRANSFILE AT END MOVE "YES" TO SWITCH.
48     200-LOOPS.
49         IF TRANS-CODE = "D"
50             PERFORM 300-DELETE-ROUTINE.
51         READ TRANSFILE AT END MOVE "YES" TO SWITCH.
52     300-DELETE-ROUTINE.
53         MOVE TRANS-INV-NO TO MAST-NUM.
54         DELETE MASTERFILE INVALID KEY DISPLAY "CANNOT DELETE".
55     900-LAST-PART.
56         CLOSE TRANSFILE MASTERFILE.
57         STOP RUN.
```

The above looks quite simple, but there are some important considerations:

a. Line 11 allows us to update the master file in a random fashion.

b. Line 46 has the I-O option instead of INPUT or OUTPUT. This is absolutely necessary for random processing since we will be reading from and writing to the file.

c. Line 54 contains the DELETE verb. When the TRANS-INV-NO is moved to the MAST-NUM the next statement searches the indexed file for the appropriate number and deletes the record. If no record with that number exists, the INVALID KEY option takes over. The general form of this statement is as follows:

DELETE filename INVALID KEY declarative statement(s).

d. The COPY verb was used since the same file description was used in a previous program.

17.3 UPDATE OF AN INDEXED FILE—THE ADDITION PROCESS

What follows is the above program, with the addition of the "add" module.

```
1       IDENTIFICATION DIVISION.
2       PROGRAM-ID. RANDOM-UPDATE.
3       ENVIRONMENT DIVISION.
4       CONFIGURATION SECTION.
5       SOURCE-COMPUTER. VAX-750.
6       OBJECT-COMPUTER. VAX-750.
7       INPUT-OUTPUT SECTION.
8       FILE-CONTROL.
9           SELECT MASTERFILE ASSIGN TO MASTER
10              ORGANIZATION IS INDEXED
11              ACCESS IS RANDOM
12              RECORD KEY IS MAST-NUM.
13          SELECT TRANSFILE ASSIGN TO TRANS.
14      DATA DIVISION.
15      FILE SECTION.
16      FD  MASTERFILE
17          DATA RECORD IS MASTREC.
18      01  MASTREC.
19          02 MAST-NUM         PIC X(5).
20          02 MAST-QUAN        PIC 9999.
21          02 MAST-PRICE       PIC 999V99.
22          02 MAST-DESC        PIC X(10).
23      COPY "TRANS.LIB".
37      WORKING-STORAGE SECTION.
38      01  SWITCH              PIC XXX.
39          88 THAT-IS-ALL-FOLKS        VALUE "YES".
40      PROCEDURE DIVISION.
41      BEGIN.
42          PERFORM 100-FIRST-PART.
43          PERFORM 200-LOOPS UNTIL THAT-IS-ALL-FOLKS.
44          PERFORM 900-LAST-PART.
45      100-FIRST-PART.
46          OPEN INPUT TRANSFILE I-O MASTERFILE.
47          READ TRANSFILE AT END MOVE "YES" TO SWITCH.
48      200-LOOPS.
49          IF TRANS-CODE = "D"
50              PERFORM 300-DELETE-ROUTINE
51          else if trans-code = "A"
52              perform 400-add-routine.
53          READ TRANSFILE AT END MOVE "YES" TO SWITCH.
```

```
54    300-DELETE-ROUTINE.
55          MOVE TRANS-INV-NO TO MAST-NUM.
56          DELETE MASTERFILE INVALID KEY DISPLAY "CANNOT DELETE".
57    400-add-routine.
58          move trans-inv-no to mast-num.
59          move trans-quan to mast-quan.
60          move trans-price to mast-price.
61          move trans-desc to mast-desc.
62          write mastrec invalid key display "this is not possible".
63    900-LAST-PART.
64          CLOSE TRANSFILE MASTERFILE.
65          STOP RUN.
```

Notice the additional condition (lines 51–52) and the module that will add records to the master file (lines 57–62). Already you can see that this program is a lot shorter than the sequential update program. The INVALID KEY clause is required on the WRITE statement because this prohibits adding duplicate records to a master file—THE PRIMARY RECORD KEY (mast-num in this case) MUST BE UNIQUE. By examining the test transaction data and master file, we find that the above program works!

----

partial transaction file
to test delete and add

```
09382000615000LANTERNS        A
80001                         D
29411006000125JIFFIES         A
67722100000010WASHERS         A
26437                         D
```

----

master file containing
the three additions and minus
two records that were deleted

```
308001013000GRILLS
13846000804500DOORS
18307001001550COOLERS
21111000165000BLOWERS
21682000214620MOWER
26392001501050RED-PAINT
26437000502000BREAKERS
28426001501050GREEN-PAIN
39462010000200SWITCHES
39924001001720WINDOWS
44445001000860BRACKETS
60203005000050E-COVERS
64643010000450NAILS
```

```
73736000614000BENCHES
80001023000650FERTILIZER
84321001000460PIPES
88113001200150TACKS
91130010000150JIFFIES
91241000508000POWER-RAKE
```

Again, it is important to note that a new master file is NOT created. Rather, the original master file is changed. Constant (successful) updating does not result in additional versions of the master file accruing in the user's directory.

17.4 UPDATE OF AN INDEXED FILE—THE CHANGE PROCESS

Finally, the random processing program will be enhanced to include changes along with adds and deletions. Examine the final version below:

```
1        IDENTIFICATION DIVISION.
2        PROGRAM-ID. RANDOM-UPDATE.
3        ENVIRONMENT DIVISION.
4        CONFIGURATION SECTION.
5        SOURCE-COMPUTER. VAX-750.
6        OBJECT-COMPUTER. VAX-750.
7        INPUT-OUTPUT SECTION.
8        FILE-CONTROL.
9            SELECT MASTERFILE ASSIGN TO MASTER
10               ORGANIZATION IS INDEXED
11               ACCESS IS RANDOM
12               RECORD KEY IS MAST-NUM.
13           SELECT TRANSFILE ASSIGN TO TRANS.
14           select backorderfile assign to back.
15       DATA DIVISION.
16       FILE SECTION.
17       FD  MASTERFILE
18           DATA RECORD IS MASTREC.
19       01  MASTREC.
20           02 MAST-NUM          PIC X(5).
21           02 MAST-QUAN         PIC 9999.
22           02 MAST-PRICE        PIC 999V99.
23           02 MAST-DESC         PIC X(10).
24       COPY "TRANS.LIB".
25L      FD  TRANSFILE
26L          DATA RECORD IS TRANS-REC.
27L      01  TRANS-REC.
28L          02 TRANS-INV-NO       PIC X(5).
29L          02 TRANS-QUAN         PIC 9999.
30L          02 TRANS-PRICE        PIC 999V99.
31L          02 TRANS-DESC         PIC X(10).
32L          02 FILLER             PIC X.
33L          02 TRANS-CODE         PIC X.
34L              88 CHANGE-DESC        VALUE "1".
35L              88 CHANGE-PRICE       VALUE "2".
36L              88 ADD-QUAN           VALUE "3".
```

```
37L           88 SUB-QUAN           VALUE "4".
38    fd  backorderfile
39        data record is back-rec.
40    01  back-rec             pic x(80).
41    WORKING-STORAGE SECTION.
42    01  SWITCH               PIC XXX.
43        88 THAT-IS-ALL-FOLKS     VALUE "YES".
44    copy "back.lib".
45L   01  back-order-line.
46L       02  back-desc         pic x(10).
47L       02  filler           pic x(15) value spaces.
48L       02  back-inv-no       pic x(5).
49L       02  filler           pic x(21) value spaces.
50L       02  back-quan         pic zzz9.
51L       02  filler           pic x(14) value spaces.
52L       02  back-price        pic $$$$.99.
53    PROCEDURE DIVISION.
54    BEGIN.
55        PERFORM 100-FIRST-PART.
56        PERFORM 200-LOOPS UNTIL THAT-IS-ALL-FOLKS.
57        PERFORM 900-LAST-PART.
58    100-FIRST-PART.
59        OPEN INPUT TRANSFILE I-O MASTERFILE output backorderfile.
60        READ TRANSFILE AT END MOVE "YES" TO SWITCH.
61    200-LOOPS.
62        IF TRANS-CODE = "D"
63                PERFORM 300-DELETE-ROUTINE
64        ELSE IF TRANS-CODE = "A"
65                PERFORM 400-ADD-ROUTINE
66            else
67                perform 500-change-routine.
68        READ TRANSFILE AT END MOVE "YES" TO SWITCH.
69    300-DELETE-ROUTINE.
70        MOVE TRANS-INV-NO TO MAST-NUM.
71        DELETE MASTERFILE INVALID KEY DISPLAY "CANNOT DELETE".
72    400-ADD-ROUTINE.
73        MOVE TRANS-INV-NO TO MAST-NUM.
74        MOVE TRANS-QUAN TO MAST-QUAN.
75        MOVE TRANS-PRICE TO MAST-PRICE.
76        MOVE TRANS-DESC TO MAST-DESC.
77        WRITE MASTREC INVALID KEY DISPLAY "this is not possible".
78    500-change-routine.
79        move trans-inv-no to mast-num.
80        read masterfile invalid key display "cannot find it".
81        if change-desc move trans-desc to mast-desc
82        else if change-price move trans-price to mast-price
83            else if add-quan add trans-quan to mast-quan
84                else if trans-quan not > mast-quan
85                    subtract trans-quan from mast-quan
86                    else perform 600-back-order-routine.
87        rewrite mastrec invalid key display "oooooops".
88    600-back-order-routine.
89        move mast-num to back-inv-no.
90        move mast-desc to back-desc.
91        move mast-price to back-price.
92        compute back-quan = trans-quan - mast-quan.
93        write back-rec from back-order-line after 2.
94        move 0 to mast-quan.
95    900-LAST-PART.
96        CLOSE TRANSFILE MASTERFILE backorderfile.
97        STOP RUN.
```

In examining this final version, attention should be directed to the following:

a. Lines 14, 38–40, and 44–52 (from the copy of a portion of the sequential update program) involve file and record description for those items that must be back-ordered.

b. Line 79 moves a transaction number to the record key area so that a particular record can be found with the READ statement in line 80. If no record can be found, then the message "cannot find it" will be displayed on the user's terminal.

c. Lines 81–86 provide the logic for the various changes that may have to be made to the master file.

d. Line 87 is absolutely necessary to write the modified record back to the master file. If, somehow, the record key changes, the INVALID KEY clause takes over. The general form of this statement is as follows:

REWRITE filename INVALID KEY declarative statement(s).

e. Lines 88–94 are the additional code necessary for the module that handles the case of the transaction quantity (amount ordered) exceeding the master quantity (amount on hand).

A very nice inventory report can also be produced by a slight modification of the REPORT WRITER program (REPORTER.COB) used in the previous chapter for the sequential update problem. This modification, of course, will be in the SELECT statement since we are now using an indexed file. Rather than display the whole program, we modify the SELECT statement as follows:

```
SELECT INFILE ASSIGN TO MASTER
       ORGANIZATION IS INDEXED
       ACCESS IS SEQUENTIAL
       RECORD KEY IS MAST-NUM.
```

This file (INFILE) is opened as INPUT, not I-O since we want to process the records, first to last, sequentially. The nice part about indexed files is that we can access the records in the file randomly or serially (sequentially). If you make this modification to the report along with modifications to a main program and LINK statement, you will get the same inventory report as that which appeared at the end of the previous chapter (except for the date of the report).

SUMMARY

The logic and code for handling the update of indexed files is a lot easier than the sequential update method. If one compares the two programs (indexed from this chapter, and sequential from the previous chapter), two glaringly obvious differences are apparent. The sequential program is 40% longer and contains an additional file!

Nevertheless, sequential processing is preferred over random processing if more than 10% of the master file needs to be updated. For random processing, the access arm of the disk unit may have to move back and forth if the transactions are not sorted first. This requires more time than having the access arm remain stationary while the read-write heads are "reading from" or "writing to" a particular track on a particular cylinder. See Appendix B for a description of the hardware aspects of disk units.

Additional syntax considerations for random processing are as follows:

a. In the SELECT statement one needs to specify:

> ORGANIZATION IS INDEXED
> ACCESS IS SEQUENTIAL (or RANDOM)
> RECORD KEY IS key-name

b. For random processing the OPEN statement must be:

> OPEN I-O filename

c. For reading an indexed file one must use:

> READ filename INVALID KEY declarative statement(s)

d. For deleting a record from an indexed file one must use:

> DELETE filename INVALID KEY declarative statement(s)

e. For adding a record to an indexed file one must use:

> WRITE record-name INVALID KEY declarative statement(s)

f. For changing a record in an indexed file one must:
   1. Move the appropriate information to the key field.
   2. Read the indexed file (c).
   3. Perform the necessary change
   4. REWRITE record name INVALID KEY declarative statement(s).

PROGRAMMING PROBLEMS

Provide the code necessary to perform the problems in the previous chapter using indexed files this time.

## 18

Cursor Movement Programming with Random Processing

The actual coding of a program that randomly updates a master file is easier than the sequential update developed in chapter 16. This process can be enhanced by allowing the user to update a master file one record at a time with the use of a "displayed menu" and "update screen." The cursor can actually be positioned at certain points on the screen. The user then enters in information, and the cursor is moved somewhere else, enabling the user to enter more information. You have seen this procedure in banks, stores, hospitals, and other areas that require information to be processed from terminal entry. The operating system on the VAX–11 systems contain RTL (Run Time Library) procedures that can be "called" in the Procedure Division of COBOL programs to control cursor positioning. One needs, however, a VT–52 or VT–100 type terminal to be able to accomplish this type of cursor movement programming.

With the new release of Version 3, it is possible to use extensions of the ACCEPT and DISPLAY statements to accomplish screen cursor movement programming. If your Run Time Library (RTL) has been updated by your Systems Manager, it is easier to use these extensions rather than call special RTL functions that do the same thing. In order to use the ACCEPT and

DISPLAY extensions, one must use the following DCL statement that allows you to access the modified RTL object library:

$DEFINE LNK$LIBRARY SYS$LIBRARY:C79V3RTL.OLB

Actually, it is a good idea to put the above statement in your LOGIN.COM file. One should also use the /NOSYSSHR option with the $LINK command, otherwise you will incur multiple definition messages at link time, such as:

```
%LINK-W-MULDEF, symbol COB$DISPLAY multiple defined
    in module VMSRTL file SYS$SYSROOT:[SYSLIB]VMSRTL.EXE;1
%LINK-W-MULDEF, symbol COB$DIS_NO_ADV multiply defined
    in module VMSRTL file SYS$SYSROOT:[SYSLIB]VMSRTL.EXE;1
%LINK-W-MULDEF, symbol COB$ACCEPT multiply defined
    in module VMSRTL file SYS$SYSROOT:[SYSLIB]VMSRTL.EXT;1
```

Since these are just warning messages, they can be ignored. All the NO-SYSSHR option does is suppress these messages since your object program references a routine in the shared RTL image (VMSRTL.EXE).

It is possible, however, that you do not have Version 3 of VAX COBOL installed and/or the RTL library has not been updated. In this case, no extensions of the ACCEPT and DISPLAY statements are allowed and you will have to rely on direct calls to the RTL functions for screen cursor movements. [**Do NOT use $LINK/NOSYSSHR at the link step if you are using direct calls to the RTL functions. Use only $LINK. The $LINK/NOSSYSHR should only be used if you are using ACCEPT and DISPLAY extensions.**]

In section 18–1 and 18–3, programs using direct calls to RTL functions and programs using extensions of the ACCEPT and DISPLAY verbs are listed.

18.1 BASIC CURSOR MOVEMENTS AND SCREEN DISPLAYS

The following programs clear the screen and put the cursor at line 1, column 1. The first program (A) uses a call to a RTL function, and the second program (B) uses an extension of the DISPLAY statement. [The $LINK/NO-SYSSHR option was used after compilation of program B.]

A.

```
1    IDENTIFICATION DIVISION.
2    PROGRAM-ID. SCREEN-PRACTICE.
3    AUTHOR. THE GREAT ONE.
4    ENVIRONMENT DIVISION.
```

```
5    DATA DIVISION.
6    WORKING-STORAGE SECTION.
7    PROCEDURE DIVISION.
8    BEGIN.
9        CALL "SCR$ERASE_PAGE" USING BY VALUE 1,1.
10       STOP RUN.
```

B.

```
1    IDENTIFICATION DIVISION.
2    PROGRAM-ID.   SCREEN-PRACTICE.
3    AUTHOR.   THE GREAT ONE.
4    ENVIRONMENT DIVISION.
5    DATA DIVISION.
6    WORKING-STORAGE SECTION.
7    PROCEDURE DIVISION.
8    BEGIN.
9        DISPLAY "" AT LINE 1 COLUMN 1 ERASE TO END OF SCREEN.
10       STOP RUN.
```

The following programs clear the screen and paint a form on the screen (see Figure 18-1). The cursor is moved to line 3, column 20 and then INVENTORY CONTROL is displayed. The cursor is then moved to line 5, column 24 and so on. Program B uses extensions of the DISPLAY statement.

A.

```
1    IDENTIFICATION DIVISION.
2    PROGRAM-ID. SECOND-SCREEN.
3    AUTHOR. STEVE SAMUELS.
4    ENVIRONMENT DIVISION.
5    DATA DIVISION.
6    WORKING-STORAGE SECTION.
7    PROCEDURE DIVISION.
8    BEGIN.
9        CALL   "SCR$ERASE_PAGE" USING BY VALUE 1,1.
10       call "scr$set_cursor" using by value 3,20.
11       display "INVENTORY CONTROL" with no advancing.
12       call "scr$set_cursor" using by value 5,24.
13       display "TERMINAL SESSION" with no advancing.
14       call "scr$set_cursor" using by value 7,28.
15       display "FOR RANDOM UPDATES" with no advancing.
16       stop run.
```

The WITH NO ADVANCING clause used with the DISPLAY statement is absolutely necessary. Otherwise, the second line, "INVENTORY CONTROL," will be displayed on line 6. We wanted line 5. Notice the RTL function SCR$SET_CURSOR was called first to move the cursor to the appropriate position before anything was displayed on the screen. Now examine program B which does essentially the same thing:

```
                    INVENTORY CONTROL

                    TERMINAL SESSION

                    RANDOM DATES
```

Figure 18-1

B.

```
 1      IDENTIFICATION DIVISION.
 2      PROGRAM-ID.  SCREEN-PRACTICE.
 3      AUTHOR.  THE GREAT ONE.
 4      ENVIRONMENT DIVISION.
 5      DATA DIVISION.
 6      WORKING-STORAGE SECTION.
 7      PROCEDURE DIVISION.
 8      BEGIN.
 9          DISPLAY "" AT LINE 1 COLUMN 1 ERASE TO END OF SCREEN.
10          DISPLAY "INVENTORY CONTROL" REVERSED AT LINE 3 COLUMN 20.
11          DISPLAY "TERMINAL SESSION" BLINKING AT LINE 5 COLUMN 24.
12          DISPLAY "FOR RANDOM UPDATES" BOLD AT LINE 7 COLUMN 28.
13          STOP RUN.
```

As you can see, one can get fancy with the DISPLAY extensions. REVERSED means reversed video; that is, dark letters against a light background. Use of the BLINKING option shows bold-normal repeating on the displayed phrase, "TERMINAL SESSSION". The BOLD option makes "RANDOM UPDATES" come out brighter than the rest of the information. [One can do this with a third number (parameter) next to the line,column parameters of the RTL calls (1=BOLD, 2=REVERSED, 4=BLINKING, and 8=UNDERLINE). For example, "BY VALUE 7,28,2" means line 7, column 28, and reverse video.]

The following program (A) produces the same screen except that an RTL function (SCR$PUT_SCREEN) is now called to move the cursor and put the line on the screen. Program B, using the DISPLAY extensions, does the same thing. Examine both programs below:

A.

```
1       IDENTIFICATION DIVISION.
2       PROGRAM-ID. SECOND-SCREEN.
3       AUTHOR. STEVE SAMUELS.
4       ENVIRONMENT DIVISION.
5       DATA DIVISION.
6       WORKING-STORAGE SECTION.
7       01  first-line.
8           02 filler pic x(20) value "INVENTORY CONTROL".
9       01  second-line.
10          02 filler pic x(20) value "TERMINAL SESSION".
11      01  third-line.
12          02 filler pic x(20) value "RANDOM UPDATES".
13      PROCEDURE DIVISION.
14      BEGIN.
15          CALL  "SCR$ERASE_PAGE" USING BY VALUE 1,1.
16          call "scr$put_screen" using by descriptor first-line
17                          by value 3,20.
18          call "scr$put_screen" using by descriptor second-line
19                          by value 5,24.
20          call "scr$put_screen" using by descriptor third-line
21                          by value 7,28.
22          stop run.
```

With the BY DESCRIPTOR clause and the BY VALUE clause, the SCR$PUT_SCREEN function does the following:

1. Moves the cursor to an appropriate area on the screen.

2. Moves the appropriate data-name to that area.

3. Puts whatever is in the data-name on the screen.

B.

```
1       IDENTIFICATION DIVISION.
2       PROGRAM-ID.  SCREEN-PRACTICE.
3       AUTHOR.  THE GREAT ONE.
4       ENVIRONMENT DIVISION.
5       DATA DIVISION.
6       WORKING-STORAGE SECTION.
7       01  first-line.
8           02 filler   pic x(20) value "INVENTORY CONTROL".
9       01  second-line.
10          02 filler   pic x(20) value "TERMINAL SESSION".
11      01  third-line.
12          02 filler   pic x(20) value "RANDOM UPDATES".
13      PROCEDURE DIVISION.
14      BEGIN.
15          DISPLAY "" AT LINE 1 COLUMN 1 ERASE TO END OF SCREEN.
```

```
16          DISPLAY first-line REVERSED AT LINE 3 COLUMN 20.
17          DISPLAY second-line BLINKING AT LINE 5 COLUMN 24.
18          DISPLAY third-line BOLD AT LINE 7 COLUMN 28.
19          STOP RUN.
```

The following programs allow for one response from a user (terminal input). After the initial screen is displayed, or "painted," the user is asked if he/she wants to continue. If the user response is "Y", then a second screen is displayed (see Figure 18–2). Program B uses an extension of the ACCEPT statement.

A.

```
1     IDENTIFICATION DIVISION.
2     PROGRAM-ID. SECOND-SCREEN.
3     AUTHOR. STEVE SAMUELS.
4     ENVIRONMENT DIVISION.
5     DATA DIVISION.
6     WORKING-STORAGE SECTION.
7     01   FIRST-LINE.
8          02 FILLER       PIC X(20) VALUE "INVENTORY CONTROL".
9     01   SECOND-LINE.
10         02 FILLER       PIC X(20) VALUE "TERMINAL SESSION".
11    01   THIRD-LINE.
12         02 FILLER       PIC X(20) VALUE "RANDOM UPDATES".
13    01   crt-response    pic x.
14    01   inventory-line-one.
15         02 filler       pic x(22) value "INVENTORY NUMBER:_____".
16    01   inventory-line-two.
17         02 filler       pic x(13) value "QUANTITY:____".
18         02 filler       pic x(10) value spaces.
19         02 filler       pic x(12) value "PRICE:___.__".
20         02 filler       pic x(30) value "  (dollars-<ret>-cents)".
21    01   inventory-line-three.
22         02 filler       pic x(35) value "DESCRIPTION_____".
23    PROCEDURE DIVISION.
24    BEGIN.
25         CALL  "SCR$ERASE_PAGE" USING BY VALUE 1,1.
26         CALL "SCR$PUT_SCREEN" USING BY DESCRIPTOR FIRST-LINE
27                   BY VALUE 3,20.
28         CALL "SCR$PUT_SCREEN" USING BY DESCRIPTOR SECOND-LINE
29                   BY VALUE 5,24.
30         CALL "SCR$PUT_SCREEN" USING BY DESCRIPTOR THIRD-LINE
31                   BY VALUE 7,28.
32         call "scr$set_cursor" using by value 20,50.
33         display "do you want more?   (Y/N)" with no advancing.
34         accept crt-response.
35         if crt-response = "Y" perform main-screen-routine.
36         STOP RUN.
37    main-screen-routine.
38         call "scr$erase_page" using by value 1,1.
39         call "scr$put_screen" using by descriptor inventory-line-one
40                   by value 5,10.
41         call "scr$put_screen" using by descriptor inventory-line-two
42                   by value 10,10.
43         call "scr$put_screen" using by descriptor inventory-line-three
44                   by value 15,10.
```

INVENTORY NUMBER: _ _ _ _ _ _

QUANTITY: _ _ _ _   PRICE: _ _ _ _ . _ _   (dollars – < ret > – cents)

DESCRIPTION: _ _ _ _ _ _ _ _ _ _ _

Figure 18–2

B.

```
1     IDENTIFICATION DIVISION.
2     PROGRAM-ID.  SECOND-SCREEN.
3     AUTHOR.  THE GREAT ONE.
4     ENVIRONMENT DIVISION.
5     DATA DIVISION.
6     WORKING-STORAGE SECTION.
7     01  FIRST-LINE.
8         02  FILLER    PIC X(20) VALUE "INVENTORY CONTROL".
9     01  SECOND-LINE.
10        02  FILLER    PIC X(20) VALUE "TERMINAL SESSION".
11    01  THIRD-LINE.
12        02  FILLER    PIC X(20) VALUE "RANDOM UPDATES".
13    01  crt-response   pic x.
14    01  inventory-line-one.
15        02  filler    pic x(22) value "INVENTORY NUMBER:_____".
16    01  inventory-line-two.
17        02  filler    pic x(13) value "QUANTITY:____".
18        02  filler    pic x(10) value spaces.
19        02  filler    pic x(12) value "PRICE:___.__".
20        02  filler    pic x(30) value "  (dollars-<ret>-cents)".
21    01  inventory-line-three.
22        02  filler    pic x(35) value "DESCRIPTION_____".
23    PROCEDURE DIVISION.
24    BEGIN.
25        DISPLAY "" AT LINE 1 COLUMN 1 ERASE TO END OF SCREEN.
```

```
26          DISPLAY FIRST-LINE REVERSED AT LINE 3 COLUMN 20.
27          DISPLAY SECOND-LINE BLINKING AT LINE 5 COLUMN 24.
28          DISPLAY THIRD-LINE BOLD AT LINE 7 COLUMN 28.
29          display "do you want more?  (Y/N)" at line 20 column 50.
30          accept crt-response with bell from line 20 column 75.
31          if crt-response = "Y" perform main-screen-routine.
32          STOP RUN.
33    main-screen-routine.
34          display "" at line 1 column 1 erase to end of screen.
35          display inventory-line-one at line 5 column 10.
36          display inventory-line-two at line 10 column 10.
37          display inventory-line-three at line 15 column 10.
```

Here a screen was produced which, with proper cursor movement, could enable a user to input specific fields of information. [In the latter program (B) the WITH BELL option was used in the ACCEPT statement which sounds the bell and prompts the user for a response at line 20 and column 75.] After information was entered an indexed file could be updated. The same modular design used in the previous chapter could be used, but instead of reading in records in a batch mode to randomly update the file, on-line processing could be used. A user could be given a menu that would allow him/her to add, delete, or change a record. After the choice was made, the update screen (Figure 18–2) could be used for terminal input. The proper random update would, hopefully, take place and the user would be asked to either make another update or stop processing.

18.2   SCREEN DISPLAYS AND TERMINAL ENTRY

A common method for user input is to have a series of menus available to give a user a choice of what function he/she wishes to accomplish. The following program gives a user a choice of producing a report, updating, or terminating the session: [Only programs using calls to RTL functions are used in this section. A good exercise would be to code the programs in the section using extensions of ACCEPT and DISPLAY. The general format for all these extensions can be found in Appendix D.]

```
 1        IDENTIFICATION DIVISION.
 2        PROGRAM-ID. MAINLINE.
 3        AUTHOR. STEVE SAMUELS.
 4        ENVIRONMENT DIVISION.
 5        CONFIGURATION SECTION.
 6        SOURCE-COMPUTER. VAX-750.
 7        OBJECT-COMPUTER. VAX-750.
 8        DATA DIVISION.

 9        WORKING-STORAGE SECTION.
10        01  CHOICE          PIC 9 VALUE 0.

11        01  HEADING-LINE  PIC X(30) VALUE "RANDOM UPDATE - TERMINAL ENTRY".
12        01  LINE-1          PIC X(20) VALUE " 1. REPORT".
```

```
13        01  LINE-2        PIC X(20) VALUE " 2. UPDATE".
14        01  LINE-3        PIC X(20) VALUE " 3. EXIT".
15        01  LINE-4        PIC X(20) VALUE "please choose one".
16        PROCEDURE DIVISION.
17        BEGIN.
18            PERFORM MAIN-MENU-ROUTINE UNTIL CHOICE = 3.
19            PERFORM END-IT-ALL.
20        MAIN-MENU-ROUTINE.
21            CALL "SCR$ERASE_PAGE" USING BY VALUE 1,1.
22            CALL "SCR$PUT_SCREEN" USING BY DESCRIPTOR HEADING-LINE
23                                       BY VALUE 3,6.
24            CALL "SCR$PUT_SCREEN" USING BY DESCRIPTOR LINE-1
25                                       BY VALUE 10,20.
26            CALL "SCR$PUT_SCREEN" USING BY DESCRIPTOR LINE-2
27                                         BY VALUE 14,20.
28            CALL "SCR$PUT_SCREEN" USING BY DESCRIPTOR LINE-3
29                                         BY VALUE 18,20.
30            CALL "SCR$PUT_SCREEN" USING BY DESCRIPTOR LINE-4
31                                         BY VALUE 22,24.
32                ACCEPT CHOICE.
33                EVALUATE CHOICE
34                    WHEN 1 CALL "REPORTER"
35                    WHEN 2 CALL "UPDATER"
36                    WHEN 3 GO TO MENU-END
37                END-EVALUATE.
38        MENU-END.
39                EXIT.
40        END-IT-ALL.
41                STOP RUN.
```

The menu produced can be examined in Figure 18–3. The EVALUATE statement is used (lines 33–37) in place of IF statements to test the choice. Choice #1 produces a report from the same program used in the two previous chapters. Choice #3 is obvious, while choice #2 calls the UPDATER program which produces another menu (see Figure 18–4). Examine this latter program:

```
1     IDENTIFICATION DIVISION.
2     PROGRAM-ID. UPDATER.
3     AUTHOR. STEVE SAMUELS.
4     ENVIRONMENT DIVISION.
5     CONFIGURATION SECTION.
6     SOURCE-COMPUTER. VAX-750.
7     OBJECT-COMPUTER. VAX-750.
8     INPUT-OUTPUT SECTION.
9     FILE-CONTROL.
10        SELECT MASTERFILE ASSIGN TO MASTER
11            ORGANIZATION IS INDEXED
12            ACCESS IS RANDOM
13            RECORD KEY IS MAST-NUM.
14    DATA DIVISION.
15    FILE SECTION.
16    FD  MASTERFILE
17        DATA RECORD IS MASTREC.
18    01  MASTREC.
19        02 MAST-NUM        PIC X(5).
20        02 MAST-QUAN       PIC 9999.
21        02 MAST-PRICE      PIC 999V99.
```

```
┌─────────────────────────────────────────────────────────┐
│                                                         │
│        RANDOM UPDATE    -    TERMINAL ENTRY             │
│                                                         │
│                                                         │
│                                                         │
│                    1.  REPORT                           │
│                                                         │
│                    2.  UPDATE                           │
│                                                         │
│                    3.  EXIT                             │
│                                                         │
│                  please choose one                      │
│                                                         │
│                                                         │
│                                                         │
└─────────────────────────────────────────────────────────┘
```

Figure 18–3

```
┌─────────────────────────────────────────────────────────┐
│                                                         │
│                    UPDATE MENU                          │
│                                                         │
│         1. DELETE RECORD                                │
│         2. ADD RECORD                                   │
│         3. CHANGE RECORD (ADD AMOUNT)                   │
│         4. CHANGE RECORD (SUBTRACT AMOUNT)              │
│         5. CHANGE PRICE                                 │
│         6. CHANGE DESCRIPTION                           │
│         7. RETURN TO MAIN MENU                          │
│                                                         │
│                                                         │
│                   enter choice                          │
│                                                         │
│                                                         │
└─────────────────────────────────────────────────────────┘
```

Figure 18–4

```
22        02 MAST-DESC         PIC X(10).


23    WORKING-STORAGE SECTION.
24    01  UPDATE-CHOICE        PIC 9.
25        88 DELETE-REC        VALUE 1.
26        88 ADD-REC           VALUE 2.
27        88 ADD-AMOUNT         VALUE 3.
28        88 SUB-AMOUNT         VALUE 4.
29        88 CHANGE-PRICE       VALUE 5.
30        88 CHANGE-DESC        VALUE 6.
31    01  CRT-RESPONSE         PIC X.
32    01  inventory-line-one.
33        02 filler      pic x(22) value "INVENTORY NUMBER:_____".
34    01  inventory-line-two.
35        02 filler       pic x(13) value "QUANTITY:___".
36        02 filler       pic x(10) value spaces.
37        02 filler       pic x(12) value "PRICE:___.__".
38        02 filler       pic x(30) value "   (dollars-<ret>-cents)".
39    01  inventory-line-three.
40        02 filler       pic x(35) value "DESCRIPTION_____".
41    01  LINE-1   PIC X(11) VALUE "UPDATE MENU".
42    01  LINE-2   PIC X(17) VALUE " 1. DELETE RECORD".
43    01  LINE-3   PIC X(14) VALUE " 2. ADD RECORD".
44    01  LINE-4   PIC X(32) VALUE " 3. CHANGE RECORD (ADD AMOUNT)".
45    01  LINE-5   PIC X(35) VALUE " 4. CHANGE RECORD (SUBTRACT AMOUNT)".
46    01  LINE-6   PIC X(16) VALUE " 5. CHANGE PRICE".
47    01  LINE-7   PIC X(22) VALUE " 6. CHANGE DESCRIPTION".
48    01  LINE-8   PIC X(23) VALUE " 7. RETURN TO MAIN MENU".
49    01  LINE-9   PIC X(14) VALUE " enter choice".
50    PROCEDURE DIVISION.
51    BEGIN.
52        PERFORM 100-FIRST-PART.
53        PERFORM 200-LOOPS UNTIL UPDATE-CHOICE = 7.
54        PERFORM 900-LAST-PART.
55    100-FIRST-PART.
56        OPEN I-O MASTERFILE.
57        PERFORM 300-UPDATE-MENU.
58    200-LOOPS.
59        EVALUATE UPDATE-CHOICE
60            WHEN 1 PERFORM 400-DELETE-ROUTINE
61            WHEN 2 PERFORM 500-ADD-ROUTINE
62            WHEN 3 THRU 6 PERFORM 600-CHANGE-ROUTINE
63            WHEN 7 GO TO 200-LOOPS-END.
64        PERFORM 300-UPDATE-MENU.
65    200-LOOPS-END.
66        EXIT.
67    300-UPDATE-MENU.
68        CALL "SCR$ERASE_PAGE" USING BY VALUE 1,1.
69        CALL "SCR$PUT_SCREEN" USING BY DESCRIPTOR LINE-1
                    BY VALUE 5,28.
70        CALL "SCR$PUT_SCREEN" USING BY DESCRIPTOR LINE-2
                    BY VALUE 8,25.
71        CALL "SCR$PUT_SCREEN" USING BY DESCRIPTOR LINE-3
                    BY VALUE 9,25.
72        CALL "SCR$PUT_SCREEN" USING BY DESCRIPTOR LINE-4
                    BY VALUE 10,25.
73        CALL "SCR$PUT_SCREEN" USING BY DESCRIPTOR LINE-5
                    BY VALUE 11,25.

74        CALL "SCR$PUT_SCREEN" USING BY DESCRIPTOR LINE-6
```

```
                               BY VALUE 12,25.
      75         CALL "SCR$PUT_SCREEN" USING BY DESCRIPTOR LINE-7
                               BY VALUE 13,25.
      76         CALL "SCR$PUT_SCREEN" USING BY DESCRIPTOR LINE-8
                               BY VALUE 14,25.
      77         CALL "SCR$PUT_SCREEN" USING BY DESCRIPTOR LINE-9
                               BY VALUE 20,30.
      78         ACCEPT UPDATE-CHOICE.
      79     400-DELETE-ROUTINE.
      80     500-ADD-ROUTINE.
      81     600-CHANGE-ROUTINE.

      82     700-BACK-ORDER-ROUTINE.
      83         CALL "SCR$SET_CURSOR" USING BY VALUE 22,30.
      84         DISPLAY "not enough in stock - press <RET> to continue"
                               WITH NO ADVANCING.
      85         ACCEPT CRT-RESPONSE.
      86     900-LAST-PART.
      87           CLOSE MASTERFILE.
      88           EXIT PROGRAM.
```

The two programs above were linked together, along with the RE-
PORTER program. After the first menu was displayed, a second menu (Figure 18–4) was displayed if one chose the #2 function. None of the functions
in the UPDATE program work except #7, which returns control to the main
program, and the main menu is displayed again. This type of programming
and coding for displaying screens (menus) follows structured concepts. The
UPDATE program is a "stub" program—one that is called, displays a screen,
and exits back to the calling program. Once the highest-level modules are
tested and found to work properly, then the subordinate (lower) modules can
be coded and thoroughly tested. These modules will do the actual updating
(see 500–ADD-ROUTINE, 600–CHANGE-ROUTINE etc.).

The EVALUATE statement was used again in the last program above in
lines 59–63. The general format for this statement is as follows:

$$
\text{EVALUATE} \begin{Bmatrix} \text{subj-term} \\ \text{TRUE} \\ \text{FALSE} \end{Bmatrix}
$$

$$
\left\{ \left\{ \text{WHEN} \begin{Bmatrix} \text{ANY} \\ \text{cond} \\ \text{TRUE} \\ \text{FALSE} \\ [\text{NOT}] \begin{Bmatrix} \text{obj-term} \begin{bmatrix} \begin{Bmatrix} \text{THRU} \\ \text{THROUGH} \end{Bmatrix} \text{obj-term} \end{bmatrix} \end{Bmatrix} \dots \end{Bmatrix} \dots \text{st-1} \right\} \right.
$$

[WHEN OTHER st-2]
[END-EVALUATE]

where:

a. subj-item is an identifier, an arithmetic or conditional expression, or a literal other than the figurative constant ZERO.

b. cond is a conditional expression.

c. obj-item is a literal, an identifier, or an arithmetic expression.

d. st–1 and st–2 are imperative statements.

Here are two more examples of the EVALUATE statement:

1. using multiple conditions.

```
EVALUATE SALARY-STATUS HOURS-WORKED
      WHEN        "M"      41 THRU 48   PERFORM COMP-PAY
      WHEN        "H"      41 THRU 48   PERFORM OVERTIME-PAY
      WHEN        "M"      48 THRU 99   PERFORM BONUS-PAY
      WHEN        "H"      48 THRU 99   PERFORM DOUBLETIME-PAY
END-EVALUATE.
```

It appears, from the above example, that if one were in the managerial area (SALARY-STATUS = "M") and worked 46 hours (HOURS-WORKED = 46), there would be some sort of compensation (COMP-PAY). If one were an hourly worker and worked 55 hours, then double pay per hour would be invoked. Notice that both conditions must be true for a particular WHEN condition to be satisfied.

2. using relational conditions and arithmetic statements.

```
EVALUATE BRANCH-NO > 15, ITEM-NO,100 * PRICE
     WHEN           TRUE     6519     200000     PERFORM ROUTINE-UPDATE
     WHEN           FALSE    4483     300000     PERFORM AUDIT-ROUTINE
     WHEN           TRUE     4483     300000     PERFORM RECALL-ROUTINE
END-EVALUATE.
```

In this case if BRANCH-NO = 18 the first condition is TRUE. The ITEM-NO must equal 6519 and 100 * PRICE must equal 200000 for control of program to pass to ROUTINE-UPDATE. What happens when BRANCH-NO is equal to 25, ITEM-NO is equal to 4483, and 100 times PRICE is equal to 200000? In this case none of the WHEN conditions is satisfied and the next statement following END-EVALUATE is executed.

18.3 RANDOM UPDATES WITH SCREEN DISPLAY AND CURSOR MOVEMENT PROGRAMMING

We are at that point where we can modify the UPDATER program to include all functions for random updating. The Data Division contains the formatted items to be put on the screen. It is best to show you the entire UPDATER program and review it in sections. Program A uses calls to RTL functions and program B uses the extensions of ACCEPT and DISPLAY. Each program is followed by comments.

A.

```
1      IDENTIFICATION DIVISION.
2      PROGRAM-ID. UPDATER.
3      AUTHOR. STEVE SAMUELS.
4      ENVIRONMENT DIVISION.
5      CONFIGURATION SECTION.
6      SOURCE-COMPUTER. VAX-750.
7      OBJECT-COMPUTER. VAX-750.
8      INPUT-OUTPUT SECTION.
9      FILE-CONTROL.
10         SELECT MASTERFILE ASSIGN TO MASTER
11             ORGANIZATION IS INDEXED
12             ACCESS IS RANDOM
13             RECORD KEY IS MAST-NUM.
14     DATA DIVISION.
15     FILE SECTION.

16     FD  MASTERFILE
17         DATA RECORD IS MASTREC.
18     01  MASTREC.
19         02 MAST-NUM        PIC X(5).
20         02 MAST-QUAN        PIC 9999.
21         02 mast-price.
22             03 mast-dollars      pic 999.
23             03 mast-cents   pic v99.
24         02 MAST-DESC        PIC X(10).
25     WORKING-STORAGE SECTION.
26     01  UPDATE-CHOICE       PIC 9.
27         88 DELETE-REC       VALUE 1.
28         88 ADD-REC          VALUE 2.
29         88 ADD-AMOUNT       VALUE 3.
30         88 SUB-AMOUNT       VALUE 4.
31         88 CHANGE-PRICE     VALUE 5.
32         88 CHANGE-DESC      VALUE 6.

33     01  CRT-RESPONSE        PIC X.
34     01  inventory-line-one.
35         02 filler     pic x(22) value "INVENTORY NUMBER:_____".
36     01  inventory-line-two.
37         02 filler     pic x(13) value "QUANTITY:____".
38         02 filler     pic x(10) value spaces.
39         02 filler     pic x(12) value "PRICE:___.__".
40         02 filler     pic x(30) value "   (dollars-<ret>-cents)".
41     01  inventory-line-three.
42         02 filler     pic x(22) value "DESCRIPTION:_____".
```

```
43    01  LINE-1    PIC X(11) VALUE "UPDATE MENU".
44    01  LINE-2    PIC X(17) VALUE " 1. DELETE RECORD".
45    01  LINE-3    PIC X(14) VALUE " 2. ADD RECORD".
46    01  LINE-4    PIC X(32) VALUE " 3. CHANGE RECORD (ADD AMOUNT)".
47    01  LINE-5    PIC X(35) VALUE
                " 4. CHANGE RECORD (SUBTRACT AMOUNT)".
48    01  LINE-6    PIC X(16) VALUE " 5. CHANGE PRICE".
49    01  LINE-7    PIC X(22) VALUE " 6. CHANGE DESCRIPTION".
50    01  LINE-8    PIC X(23) VALUE " 7. RETURN TO MAIN MENU".
51    01  LINE-9    PIC X(14) VALUE " enter choice".
52    01  transrec.
53        02 trans-inv-no   pic x(5).
54        02 trans-quan     pic 9999.
55        02 trans-price.
56           03 trans-dollars    pic 999.
57           03 trans-cents      pic v99.
58        02 trans-desc     pic x(10).
59    PROCEDURE DIVISION.
60    BEGIN.
61        PERFORM 100-FIRST-PART.
62        PERFORM 200-LOOPS UNTIL UPDATE-CHOICE = 7.
63        PERFORM 900-LAST-PART.
64    100-FIRST-PART.
65        OPEN I-O MASTERFILE.
66        PERFORM 300-UPDATE-MENU.
67    200-LOOPS.
68        EVALUATE UPDATE-CHOICE
69            WHEN 1 PERFORM 400-DELETE-ROUTINE thru 400-end-delete
70            WHEN 2 PERFORM 500-ADD-ROUTINE thru 500-end-add
71            WHEN 3 THRU 6 PERFORM 600-CHANGE-ROUTINE
                    thru 600-end-cha:
72            WHEN 7 GO TO 200-LOOPS-END.

73        PERFORM 300-UPDATE-MENU.
74    200-LOOPS-END.
75        EXIT.
76    300-UPDATE-MENU.
77        CALL "SCR$ERASE_PAGE" USING BY VALUE 1,1.
78        CALL "SCR$PUT_SCREEN" USING BY DESCRIPTOR LINE-1
                    BY VALUE 5,28.
79        CALL "SCR$PUT_SCREEN" USING BY DESCRIPTOR LINE-2
                    BY VALUE 8,25.
80        CALL "SCR$PUT_SCREEN" USING BY DESCRIPTOR LINE-3
                    BY VALUE 9,25.
81        CALL "SCR$PUT_SCREEN" USING BY DESCRIPTOR LINE-4
                    BY VALUE 10,25.
82        CALL "SCR$PUT_SCREEN" USING BY DESCRIPTOR LINE-5
                    BY VALUE 11,25.
83        CALL "SCR$PUT_SCREEN" USING BY DESCRIPTOR LINE-6
                    BY VALUE 12,25.
84        CALL "SCR$PUT_SCREEN" USING BY DESCRIPTOR LINE-7
                    BY VALUE 13,25.
85        CALL "SCR$PUT_SCREEN" USING BY DESCRIPTOR LINE-8
                    BY VALUE 14,25.
86        CALL "SCR$PUT_SCREEN" USING BY DESCRIPTOR LINE-9
                    BY VALUE 20,30.
87        ACCEPT UPDATE-CHOICE.
88    400-DELETE-ROUTINE.
89        call "scr$erase_page" using by value 1,1.
90        call "scr$put_screen" using by descriptor inventory-line-one
91                    by value 7,15.
```

```
 92          call "scr$set_cursor" using by value 7,32.
 93          accept trans-inv-no.
 94          move trans-inv-no to mast-num.
 95          read masterfile invalid key
 96              call "scr$set_cursor" using by value 22,30
 97              display "RECORD NOT FOUND - PRESS <RET>"
 98                  with no advancing
 99              accept crt-response
100              go to 400-end-delete.
101          call "scr$put_screen" using by descriptor inventory-line-two
102                      by value 10,5.
103          call "scr$put_screen" using by descriptor mast-quan
104                      by value 10,14.
105          call "scr$put_screen" using by descriptor mast-dollars
106                      by value 10,34.
107          call "scr$put_screen" using by descriptor mast-cents
108                      by value 10,38.
109          call "scr$put_screen" using by descriptor
110              inventory-line-three  by value 13,20.
111          call "scr$put_screen" using by descriptor mast-desc
112                      by value 13,32.
113          call "scr$set_cursor" using by value 20,30.
114          display "DO YOU WANT TO DELETE THIS RECORD - (Y/N)?"
                     with no advancing.
115          accept crt-response.
116          call "scr$set_cursor" using by value 22,30
117          if crt-response = "Y" delete masterfile invalid key
118              go to 400-end-delete.
119          if crt-response = "Y"
120              display "RECORD DELETED - PRESS <RET>" with no advancing
121          else
122              display "RECORD NOT DELETED - PRESS <RET>"
                         with no advancing.

123          accept crt-response.
124      400-end-delete.
125          exit.
126      500-ADD-ROUTINE.
127          call "scr$erase_page" using by value 1,1.
128          call "scr$put_screen" using by descriptor inventory-line-one
129                      by value 7,15.
130          call "scr$put_screen" using by descriptor inventory-line-two
131                      by value 10,5.
132          call "scr$put_screen" using by descriptor
133              inventory-line-three by value 13,20.
134          call "scr$set_cursor" using by value 7,32.
135          accept trans-inv-no.
136          call "scr$set_cursor" using by value 10,14.
137          accept trans-quan.
138          call "scr$set_cursor" using by value 10,34.
139          accept trans-dollars.
140          call "scr$set_cursor" using by value 10,38.
141          accept trans-cents.
142          call "scr$set_cursor" using by value 13,32.
143          accept trans-desc.
144          write mastrec from transrec invalid key
145              call "scr$set_cursor" using by value 22,30
146              display "RECORD ALREADY EXISTS - PRESS <RET>"
147                      with no advancing
148              accept crt-response
149              go to 500-end-add.
```

```
150        call "scr$set_cursor" using by value 22,30.
151        display "RECORD ADDED - PRESS <RET>" with no advancing.
152        accept crt-response.

153    500-end-add.
154        exit.
155    600-CHANGE-ROUTINE.
156        call "scr$erase_page" using by value 1,1.
157        call "scr$put_screen" using by descriptor inventory-line-one
158                    by value 7,15.
159        call "scr$set_cursor" using by value 7,32.
160        accept trans-inv-no.
161        move trans-inv-no to mast-num.
162        read masterfile invalid key
163            call "scr$set_cursor" using by value 22,30
164            display "RECORD NOT FOUND - PRESS <RET>"
                    with no advancing
165            accept crt-response
166            go to 600-end-change.
167        call "scr$put_screen" using by descriptor inventory-line-two
168                    by value 10,5.
169        call "scr$put_screen" using by descriptor
170            inventory-line-three by value 13,20.
171        if add-amount
172            call "scr$set_cursor" using by value 10,14
173            accept trans-quan
174            add trans-quan to mast-quan
175            rewrite mastrec invalid key display "CHANGE NOT POSSIBLE"
176        else
177          if sub-amount
178            call "scr$set_cursor" using by value 10,14
179            accept trans-quan
180              if trans-quan > mast-quan
181                perform 700-back-order-routine
182                go to 600-end-change
183              else
184                subtract trans-quan from mast-quan
185                rewrite mastrec invalid key
                    display "CHANGE NOT POSSIBLE"
186          else
187            if change-price
188                call "scr$set_cursor" using by value 10,34
189                accept trans-dollars
190                call "scr$set_cursor" using by value 10,38
191                accept trans-cents
192                move trans-price to mast-price
193                rewrite mastrec invalid key display "CHANGE NOT POSSIBLE"
194            else
195              if change-desc
196                call "scr$set_cursor" using by value 13,32
197                accept trans-desc
198                move trans-desc to mast-desc
199                rewrite mastrec invalid key display
                    "CHANGE NOT POSSIBLE".
200        call "scr$set_cursor" using by value 22,30.
201        display "CHANGE COMPLETED - PRESS <RET>" with no advancing.
202        accept crt-response.
203    600-end-change.
204        exit.
205    700-BACK-ORDER-ROUTINE.
206        CALL "SCR$SET_CURSOR" USING BY VALUE 22,30.
```

```
207        DISPLAY "not enough in stock - press <RET> to continue"
                   WITH NO ADVANCING.
208        ACCEPT CRT-RESPONSE.
209    900-LAST-PART.
210        CLOSE MASTERFILE.
211        EXIT PROGRAM.
```

The UPDATER program has just doubled in size. One can see the expansion of the delete, add, and change modules. Let us examine these modules one by one:

DELETE (lines 88–125)

1. When this module is entered, the screen is cleared (line 89).

2. A screen is produced (Figure 18–5) that allows the user to enter an inventory number (lines 90–94).

3. If a record cannot be found, then a message is displayed on the bottom of the screen (Figure 18–6) and the module is exited (lines 95–100).

4. If a record is found, the entire inventory screen is displayed along with the contents of that particular record and a message is also displayed at the bottom asking the user whether or not a deletion should take place (lines 101–114).

5. If the user responds affirmatively, then the record is deleted along with a message stating so; otherwise a message states that the record is not deleted (lines 115–123).

6. The paragraph (400–end-delete) is necessary to bypass the deletion process if there is an invalid key (lines 124–125).

ADD (lines 126–154)

1. When this module is entered, the entire screen is displayed (lines 127–134).

2, As with the delete module, the cursor is positioned to the right of where "INVENTORY NUMBER:" is displayed. After the user enters a legitimate number (no provision was made for erroneous input) and hits the ⟨ret⟩ key, the cursor is positioned to the right of where "QUANTITY:" is displayed. For the price, the user must enter dollars, including left zeros, hit the ⟨ret⟩ key, and enter cents. No provision was made for invalid quantities or prices, or for enabling the user to enter one number which would be automatically filled with zeros to the left. For example, if a stock item should have six units, then the user should enter "0006" not "6", for quantity. Of course, more detailed code would enhance this program so that the user need not left-zero any quantity or price. Any description greater than 10 characters is truncated

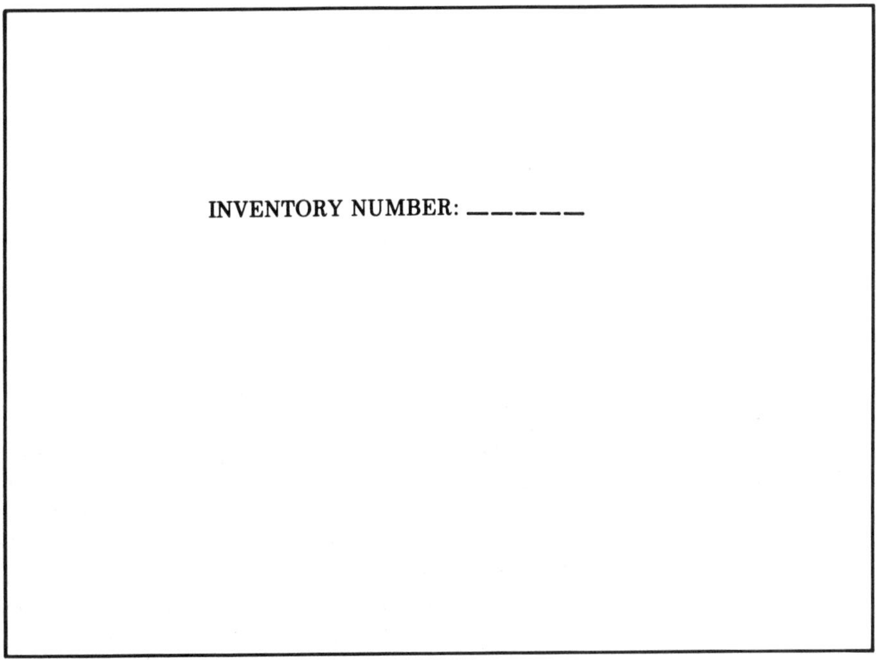

INVENTORY NUMBER: _____

Figure 18-5

INVENTORY NUMBER: _____

RECORD NOT FOUND – PRESS <RET>

Figure 18-6

on the right. Although lines 135–143 allow for movement of the cursor and user input of specific fields, the next statement either writes the record to the indexed file or displays an error message if it (the record) already exists (lines 144–149).

3. An appropriate message is displayed informing the user that the addition to the file took place and that the ⟨ret⟩ key should be pressed to continue processing (lines 150–152).

CHANGE (lines 155–208)

1. This module is, by far, the largest. The screen is cleared as before and the "INVENTORY NUMBER:" is displayed. The user must enter a number. Upon pressing the ⟨ret⟩ key, this number is moved to the record key area and the record is read. If no record exists an error message is displayed, "RECORD NOT FOUND—PRESS ⟨RET⟩", and the module is exited (lines 155–166 and lines 203–204). The function of the GO TO statement (line 166) is to bypass, unconditionally, the rest of the statements in the paragraph (600–CHANGE-ROUTINE). To avoid any stack dumps the unconditional branch is to the very next paragraph (600–END-CHANGE) which only contains the EXIT statement. All paragraphs should be entered by a PERFORM statement. These paragraphs should only be exited by the normal sequence of instructions within the paragraph or by an unconditional branch to an adjacent (lower) paragraph that contains only an EXIT statement.

2. If the record exists, then the rest of the screen is displayed. The cursor is moved to the appropriate areas depending on the type of change operation (lines 167–202).

3. If the user enters an amount to be subtracted that is greater than the amount or quantity found in the master file, a module is entered that displays a message stating that there in not enough in stock (lines 180–181 and lines 205–208). In any case the user is required to press the ⟨ret⟩ key to continue processing.

Why should the user press the ⟨ret⟩ key after certain operations? If this is not done, i.e., "ACCEPT CRT-RESPONSE" is not present, the messages come across the screen too fast. One cannot be sure, then, if a deletion, addition, or change actually took place. One would have to exit the program and examine the master file or generate a report, which is cumbersome.

B.

```
1    IDENTIFICATION DIVISION.
2    PROGRAM-ID. UPDATER.
3    AUTHOR. STEVE SAMUELS.
4    ENVIRONMENT DIVISION.
5    CONFIGURATION SECTION.
```

```
 6      SOURCE-COMPUTER. VAX-750.
 7      OBJECT-COMPUTER. VAX-750.
 8      INPUT-OUTPUT SECTION.
 9      FILE-CONTROL.
10          SELECT MASTERFILE ASSIGN TO MASTER
11              ORGANIZATION IS INDEXED
12              ACCESS IS RANDOM
13              RECORD KEY IS MAST-NUM.
14      DATA DIVISION.
15      FILE SECTION.
16      FD  MASTERFILE
17          DATA RECORD IS MASTREC.
18      01  MASTREC.
19          02 MAST-NUM        PIC X(5).
20          02 MAST-QUAN       PIC 9999.
21          02 mast-price      pic 999v99.
22          02 MAST-DESC       PIC X(10).
23      WORKING-STORAGE SECTION.
24      01  UPDATE-CHOICE      PIC 9.
25          88 DELETE-REC      VALUE 1.
26          88 ADD-REC         VALUE 2.
27          88 ADD-AMOUNT      VALUE 3.
28          88 SUB-AMOUNT      VALUE 4.
29          88 CHANGE-PRICE    VALUE 5.
30          88 CHANGE-DESC     VALUE 6.
31      01  CRT-RESPONSE       PIC X.
32      01  inventory-line-one.
33          02 filler     pic x(22) value "INVENTORY NUMBER:_____".
34      01  inventory-line-two.
35          02 filler     pic x(13) value "QUANTITY:____".
36          02 filler     pic x(10) value spaces.
37          02 filler     pic x(12) value "PRICE:_____".
38      01  inventory-line-three.
39          02 filler     pic x(22) value "DESCRIPTION:_____".
40      01  LINE-1 PIC X(11) VALUE "UPDATE MENU".
41      01  LINE-2 PIC X(17) VALUE " 1. DELETE RECORD".
42      01  LINE-3 PIC X(14) VALUE " 2. ADD RECORD".
43      01  LINE-4 PIC X(32) VALUE " 3. CHANGE RECORD (ADD AMOUNT)".
44      01  LINE-5 PIC X(35) VALUE " 4. CHANGE RECORD (SUBTRACT AMOUNT)".
45      01  LINE-6 PIC X(16) VALUE " 5. CHANGE PRICE".
46      01  LINE-7 PIC X(22) VALUE " 6. CHANGE DESCRIPTION".
47      01  LINE-8 PIC X(23) VALUE " 7. RETURN TO MAIN MENU".
48      01  LINE-9 PIC X(14) VALUE " enter choice".
49      01  edit-price         pic zz9.99.
50      01  transrec.
51          02 trans-inv-no    pic x(5).
52          02 trans-quan      pic 9999.
53          02 trans-price     pic 999v99.
54          02 trans-desc      pic x(10).
55      PROCEDURE DIVISION.
56      BEGIN.
57          PERFORM 100-FIRST-PART.
58          PERFORM 200-LOOPS UNTIL UPDATE-CHOICE = 7.
59          PERFORM 900-LAST-PART.
60      100-FIRST-PART.
61          OPEN I-O MASTERFILE.
62          PERFORM 300-UPDATE-MENU.
63      200-LOOPS.
64          EVALUATE UPDATE-CHOICE
65              WHEN 1 PERFORM 400-DELETE-ROUTINE thru 400-end-delete
66              WHEN 2 PERFORM 500-ADD-ROUTINE thru 500-end-add
```

```
67              WHEN 3 THRU 6 PERFORM 600-CHANGE-ROUTINE
68                  thru 600-end-change
69              WHEN 7 GO TO 200-LOOPS-END.
70          PERFORM 300-UPDATE-MENU.
71      200-LOOPS-END.
72          EXIT.
73      300-UPDATE-MENU.
74          display "" at line 1 column 1 erase to end of screen.
75          display line-1 at line 5 column 28.
76          display line-2 at line 8 column 25.
77          display line-3 at line 9 column 25.
78          display line-4 at line 10 column 25.
79          display line-5 at line 11 column 25
80          display line-6 at line 12 column 25.
81          display line-7 at line 13 column 25.
82          display line-8 at line 14 column 25.
83          display line-9 at line 20 column 30.
84          accept update-choice from line 20 column 44.
85      400-DELETE-ROUTINE.
86          display "" at line 1 column 1 erase to end of screen.
87          display inventory-line-one at line 7 column 15.
88          accept trans-inv-no from line 7 column 32.
89          move trans-inv-no to mast-num.
90          read masterfile invalid key
91              display "RECORD NOT FOUND - PRESS <RET>"
92              at line 22 column 30
93              accept crt-response
94              go to 400-end-delete.
95          display inventory-line-two at line 10 column 5.
96          display mast-quan at line 10 column 14.
97          move mast-price to edit-price.
98          display edit-price at line 10 column 34.
99          display inventory-line-three at line 13 column 20.
100         display mast-desc at line 13 column 32.
101         display "DO YOU WANT TO DELETE THIS RECORD - (Y/N)?"
102             at line 20 column 30
103         accept crt-response.
104         if crt-response = "Y" delete masterfile invalid key
105             go to 400-end-delete.
106         if crt-response = "Y"
107             display "RECORD DELETED - PRESS <RET>"
108                 at line 22 column 30
109         else
110             display "RECORD NOT DELETED - PRESS <RET>"
111                 at line 22 column 30.
112         accept crt-response.
113     400-end-delete.
114         exit.
115     500-ADD-ROUTINE.
116         display "" at line 1 column 1 erase to end of screen.
117         display inventory-line-one at line 7 column 15.
118         display inventory-line-two at line 10 column 5.
119         display inventory-line-three at line 13 column 20.
120         accept trans-inv-no from line 7 column 32.
121         accept trans-quan with conversion from line 10 column 14.
122         display trans-quan at line 10 column 14.
123         accept trans-price with conversion from line 10 column 34.
124         accept trans-desc from line 13 column 32.
125         write mastrec from transrec invalid key
126             display "RECORD ALREADY EXISTS - PRESS <RET>"
127                 at line 22 column 30
```

```
128              accept crt-response from line 22 column 65
129              go to 500-end-add.
130          display "RECORD ADDED - PRESS <RET>"
131                  at line 22 column 30.
132          accept crt-response.
133      500-end-add.
134          exit.
135      600-CHANGE-ROUTINE.
136          display "" at line 1 column 1 erase to end of screen.
137          display inventory-line-one at line 7 column 15.
138          accept trans-inv-no from line 7 column 32.
139          move trans-inv-no to mast-num.
140          read masterfile invalid key
141              display "RECORD NOT FOUND - PRESS <RET>"
142                  at line 22 column 30
143              accept crt-response
144              go to 600-end-change.
145          display inventory-line-two at line 10 column 5.
146          display inventory-line-three at line 13 column 20.
147          if add-amount
148              accept trans-quan with conversion from line 10 column 14
149              add trans-quan to mast-quan
150              rewrite mastrec invalid key display "CHANGE NOT POSSIBLE"
151          else
152            if sub-amount
153              accept trans-quan with conversion from line 10 column 14
154                  if trans-quan > mast-quan
155                      perform 700-back-order-routine
156                      go to 600-end-change
157                  else
158                      subtract trans-quan from mast-quan
159                      rewrite mastrec invalid key display
160                          "CHANGE NOT POSSIBLE"
161            else
162              if change-price
163                accept trans-price with conversion from line 10 column 34
164                move trans-price to mast-price
165                rewrite mastrec invalid key display "CHANGE NOT POSSIBLE"
166              else
167                if change-desc
168                  accept trans-desc from line 13 column 32
169                  move trans-desc to mast-desc
170                  rewrite mastrec invalid key display
171                      "CHANGE NOT POSSIBLE".
172          display "CHANGE COMPLETED - PRESS <RET>"
173                  at line 22 column 30.
174          accept crt-response.
175      600-end-change.
176          exit.
177      700-BACK-ORDER-ROUTINE.
178          DISPLAY "not enough in stock - press <RET> to continue"
179                  AT LINE 22 COLUMN 30.
180          ACCEPT CRT-RESPONSE.
181      900-LAST-PART.
182          CLOSE MASTERFILE.
183          EXIT PROGRAM.
```

If you are fortunate enough to be able to use these extensions, the resultant code is reduced (183 lines for program B versus 211 lines for program A). Both programs do exactly the same thing.

Again, it is easier to use the extensions than direct calls to RTL routines because:

1. There is no reason to break down the TRANS-PRICE field into dollars and cents because one can enter an edited price, and this price will be converted, with the use of WITH CONVERSION extension, to a non-edited number (lines 123 and 163). In other words, the user can enter 7.00 and it will be converted to 00700.

2. One does not need to enter leading zeros for TRANS-QUAN because the WITH CONVERSION extension will convert, let's say 15, to 0015 (lines 121, 148, and 153). To prove this point, TRAN-QUAN is displayed after it is entered by the user (line 122).

3. The WITH NO ADVANCING option can be removed since one can "accept" from any line and column.

SUMMARY

Random updating is an "on-line" process much of the time. It is possible to create "user-friendly" screens in order to facilitate terminal input of data. To do this on VAX the programmer needs to know additional RTL functions that can be called by a COBOL program. The RTL functions used in this chapter are:

a. SCR$SET_CURSOR

b. SCR$ERASE_PAGE

c. SCR$PUT_SCREEN

It is important to note, however, that errors in the spelling of these functions or the invalid use of descriptors and/or values will become apparent during the $LINK, and not the $COB job step!

An easier method of screen cursor movement programming involves extensions of the ACCEPT and DISPLAY statements. To avoid warning errors during linking, one should use the /NOSYSSHR option of the $LINK command. This easier method can only be accomplished if you have Version 3 of VAX COBOL installed and your RTL library has been updated.

The EVALUATE statement was discussed and was shown to provide an alternative to the use of multiple or compound IF statements.

PROGRAMMING PROBLEMS

1. As was stated above, no provision was made for invalid input of data. The user might enter 89G32 instead of 89432. Invalid input may occur for

quantity or price. What happens if one attempts to press 8 when the update menu is displayed? What happens if one attempts to press 4 or H when the main menu is displayed? What happens when "y" is pressed rather than "Y"? You should modify the above program to handle these and other possible sources of erroneous input.

2. Robbem State Bank is experiencing growing pains. For many years, Robbem was simply a small community bank with one centrally located banking facility. In keeping with its small-town spirit, Robbem had refused to automate any of its bookkeeping functions.

This year, some things changed at the bank. Robbem opened two new branch banks bringing to three the total number of banks in the Robbem State Bank chain. The "fathers" at Robbem are considering buying a computer and hiring a consultant (you!?) to write a system to computerize several of the banking functions currently executed manually. Your task is to convince the founding fathers at Robbem to invest in a computer system (a VAX perhaps!) and to hire you as the house programmer/analyst.

Each branch contains data about certificates of deposit. There are six types of certificates. The last number of the account number denotes the type of certificate.

Examine the input record specification below:

Field	Columns	Data Class
last name	1–10	
first name	11–20	
account number	21–26	alphnumeric
amount deposited	28–34	assumed decimal
branch number	36–37	

The input data for each branch is listed below:

file 1:	JONES	JOHN	1342–3	0098078	01
	CLAUS	SANTA	3425–2	0000783	01
	DARROW	CLARENCE	6493–4	0004612	01
	PAN	PETER	8512–5	0000413	01
	FARMER	FANNIE	9248–1	0003976	01
	SAMUELS	SAMMIE	3028–5	0241583	01
	FROG	KERMIT	7014–6	0083183	01
	VADER	DARTH	3075–2	0000034	01
	TANNIE	VIC	3920–3	0000385	01
	SUNSHINE	MARY	8993–6	0003902	01
	BURNED	JANE	6200–1	0030184	01
	KRAFT	DARTON	7390–4	0029017	01
	SAMPLER	SIMON	4910–5	0000013	01
	BOSS	BRUCE	8302–3	0083491	01

	BINGO	RICH	4710–1	0000348	01
	BONZO	BRAD	8201–1	0006829	01
	ALLEN	ETHAN	9137–1	0038001	01
	GATES	GONZO	6666–2	0002519	01
	DIMPLES	DENNIS	7836–6	0000568	01
	DOLITTLE	DANNY	3719–3	0003581	01
	GOLD	PENNEY	7100–4	9999999	01
	PEACHES	GEORGIA	6628–4	0008461	01
	BEACHES	FLO	4418–2	0057194	01
file 2:	DIEGO	SANDRA	8739–3	0023618	02
	DURAN	DAN	3891–4	0000283	02
	BAILY	BOOM-BOOM	2900–1	0002947	02
	FEZZO	FRED	1039–5	0000281	02
	CARTER	SMILEY	8104–6	0927419	02
	CROOKS	U.S.	7651–6	0001351	02
	VAX	VIC	4610–1	0000281	02
	GRAUER	ROBERT	8108–1	0831450	02
	TYLER	TOBY	5027–4	0037193	02
	NIXON	TRIXIE	5024–6	0103820	02
	HANA	BENNY	8201–2	0000291	02
	ABEL	CAIN	1582–2	0029482	02
	FRANGO	MARSHALL	1372–4	0284104	02
	BUCK	CHUCK	7310–1	0003810	02
	BERRY	MARY	8203–2	0381938	02
	JUNGLES	JIM	3918–3	1238294	02
	ROBBINS	BASKIN	8103–4	0018362	02
	INTHESUN	BASKIN	2290–5	0200681	02
	INTHERAIN	SINGIN	4444–5	0058193	02
	SPUMONI	TONI	3388–6	0020938	02
file 3:	ON	CARRIE	9371–2	8927418	03
	CANIT	BEE	8301–3	0029385	03
	CANUSEE	JOSE	4482–4	0000281	03
	CRAWFORD	JOE	8382–6	0039510	03
	ZUPPA	ANGELO	7730–1	0003920	03
	ONASSIS	JACKIE	6672–1	9939290	03
	ROSS	RANDALL	8362–2	0063812	03
	FILE	RANKIN	3317–2	8937263	03
	SMEDLEY	DUDLEY	5573–3	0283174	03
	LACOSTE	IZOD	2999–4	0308201	03
	GONER	AL	1111–5	0084289	03
	GOMEZ	MARIA	8329–6	0381038	03
	MAX	T. J.	4710–5	0382910	03

BONDO	JAMES	9835-1	0038417	03
BENATAR	PATRICK	4820-2	0005739	03
CRANDALL	RANDALL	2222-3	0048297	03
MALPH	RALPH	6663-5	0003826	03
STAT	RHEA	7736-1	0381274	03
STAT	THELMA	3028-3	0938472	03
SOCIETY	HI	2847-1	0003821	03
WATERS	MUDDY	5549-2	0372184	03
LATER	C. U.	6392-6	0027410	03

You should do the following first:

 a. Merge these three files.
 b. Sort the resulting file in ascending order of account number and create an indexed file with this number as the primary key.
 [Using subprograms is a very good idea!!]

3. Now you should be able to show the "founding fathers" how you can randomly update this indexed file with data entered at a terminal. If successful, you may become director of a newly created Management Information System. If you are not successful . . .
 An example of a run of a typical program of this type would be as follows. A menu would appear asking for the following choices:

MENU ONE
1. Report
2. Update
3. Exit program
 Which?__

If the user chooses #3, the program terminates.

If the user chooses #1, some sort of report should be produced which includes header lines, detail lines, and maybe a total line.

If the user chooses #2, a new menu should appear:

MENU TWO
1. Add
2. Delete
3. Change (add to amount)
4. Change (subtract from amount)
5. Exit
 Which?__

If the user chooses 1-4, a screen is displayed like this:

ACCOUNT NUMBER_____

NAME_____

BRANCH NUMBER_____

AMOUNT_____

If #1, then the cursor would move to all fields (eventually) and a record would be added. Then the second menu would be displayed.

If #2, then the cursor would move to only the account number and return to the second menu after the first return or enter. A delete should also occur. (It would be a good idea, however, to display the whole record before deletion—although this is recommended, it is optional.)

If #3 or #4, then the cursor would move to the account number and then to the amount area after the return or enter. You would go back to the second menu after entering the amount. Of course that particular record should be changed!

If #5, the update process ceases and the first menu should be displayed.

4. Finally, no programming assignment in COBOL would be complete if a fancy report could not be produced. You should use the Report Writer feature to produce this report showing subtotals of amounts deposited for each type of certificate, subtotals for amounts deposited in each branch, and a final total showing the total amount deposited. This means that the master file has to be sorted by certificate type within branch number creating a sequential file to be used by the Report Writer program. [Again, the use of subprograms is encouraged.]

## 19

Advanced File Processing and Cursor Movement Techniques

In this final chapter some advanced features of COBOL programming on VAX can be demonstrated:

a. The ability to begin processing records sequentially from a place other than the beginning of a file.

b. The ability to access records using another (alternate) key field.

c. The ability to use additional RTL functions to control handling of cursor and screen displays. [A program using ACCEPT and DISPLAY extensions in place of calls to RTL functions is presented in the last section of this chapter.]

d. The ability to let the system indicate the status of a particular input/output operation.

19.1 SERIAL ACCESS

Suppose one would want to access a particular record, somewhere in the middle of the file, and access each record after that sequentially. It is possible to do this if you use additional syntax:

1) ACCESS IS DYNAMIC

This mode allows one to examine or update records at random or sequentially within the scope of the same OPEN statement (OPEN I-O filename).

2) START

This procedure division statement provides the capability to start sequential processing for a file whose ORGANIZATION IS SEQUENTIAL or whose ORGANIZATION IS INDEXED along with ACCESS IS DYNAMIC. With the the START statement, sequential processing can begin at any record within the file. It has the following format:

START filename

```
        ( EQUAL TO        )
[KEY IS ( GREATER THAN )  data-name]
        ( NOT LESS THAN )
[INVALID KEY imperative statement].
```

When the ORGANIZATION IS INDEXED the data-name must be either the RECORD KEY field or the ALTERNATE RECORD KEY field.

3) READ filename NEXT RECORD [INTO identifier] AT END imperative statement.

This allows one to retrieve the next record in sequence after a data pointer is positioned to the current record through the use of the START statement.

The following program illustrates the use of all three items above. After the listing will come a complete explanation of the new syntax employed and results of the execution:

```
1     IDENTIFICATION DIVISION.
2     PROGRAM-ID. finder-serially.

3     AUTHOR. STEVE SAMUELS.
4     ENVIRONMENT DIVISION.
5     CONFIGURATION SECTION.
6     SOURCE-COMPUTER. VAX-750.
7     OBJECT-COMPUTER. VAX-750.
8     INPUT-OUTPUT SECTION.
9     FILE-CONTROL.
10        SELECT MASTERFILE ASSIGN TO MASTER
11            ORGANIZATION IS INDEXED
12            access is dynamic
13            RECORD KEY IS MAST-NUM.
14        select infile assign to menu.
15    DATA DIVISION.
16    FILE SECTION.
17    FD  MASTERFILE
18        DATA RECORD IS MASTREC.
```

```
19    01   MASTREC.
20         02 MAST-NUM            PIC X(5).
21         02 MAST-QUAN           PIC 9999.
22         02 MAST-PRICE.
23            03 MAST-DOLLARS     PIC 999.
24            03 MAST-CENTS       PIC v99.
25         02 MAST-DESC           PIC X(10).
26    fd  infile
27         data record is inrec.
28    01  inrec                   pic x(60).
29    WORKING-STORAGE SECTION.
30    01  CRT-RESPONSE            PIC X.
31    01  initial-message.
32         02 messanger    occurs 10 times   indexed by m-ind.
33            03 line-coordinate    pic 99.
34            03 column-coordinate  pic 99.
35            03 message-line       pic x(46).
36    01  line-val     pic S9(5) comp value 0.
37    01  col-val      pic S9(5) comp value 0.
38    01  switch       pic xxx value spaces.
39    01  INVENTORY-LINE-ONE.
40         02 FILLER      PIC X(22) VALUE "INVENTORY NUMBER:_____".
41    01  INVENTORY-LINE-TWO.
42         02 FILLER      PIC X(13) VALUE "QUANTITY:____".
43         02 FILLER      PIC X(10) VALUE SPACES.
44         02 FILLER      PIC X(12) VALUE "PRICE:___.__".
45         02 FILLER      PIC X(30) VALUE "    (dollars-<ret>-cents)".
46    01  INVENTORY-LINE-THREE.
47         02 FILLER      PIC X(22) VALUE "DESCRIPTION:_____".
48    01  trans-inv-no   pic x(5).
49    PROCEDURE DIVISION.
50    BEGIN.
51         PERFORM 100-FIRST-PART.
52         perform 200-loops until switch = "YES".
53         PERFORM 900-LAST-PART.
54    100-FIRST-PART.
55         open input infile i-o masterfile.
56         perform 300-load-menu1-routine varying m-ind from 1 by 1
                    until m-ind > 10.
57         call "scr$erase_page" using by value 1,1.
58         perform 400-display-menu1 varying m-ind from 1 by 1
                    until m-ind > 10.
59         call "scr$set_cursor" using by value 22,24.
60         display "press <ret> to continue - control_Z to stop".

61         accept crt-response at end move "YES" to switch.
62         if switch = "YES" perform 900-last-part
63           else perform 500-inventory-screen-display.
64    200-LOOPS.
65         accept crt-response.
66         if crt-response = "Y" perform 600-next-show-routine
67           else perform 500-inventory-screen-display.
68    300-load-menu1-routine.
69         read infile at end move "yes" to switch.
70         move inrec to messanger (m-ind).
71    400-display-menu1.
72         compute line-val = line-coordinate (m-ind).
73         compute col-val = column-coordinate (m-ind).
74         call "lib$put_screen" using by descriptor
75             message-line (m-ind)  by reference line-val, col-val.
76    500-inventory-screen-display.
```

```
77       call "scr$erase_page" using by value 1,1.
78       call "scr$put_screen" using by descriptor inventory-line-one
79              by value 7,15.
80       call "scr$set_cursor" using by value 7,32.
81       accept trans-inv-no at end perform 900-last-part.
82       move trans-inv-no to mast-num.
83       start masterfile key not less than mast-num
84           invalid key call "scr$set_cursor" using by value 22,30
85            display "RECORD NOT FOUND - PRESS <RET>"
86                with no advancing
87            accept crt-response
88            go to 500-endit.
89       call "scr$put_screen" using by descriptor inventory-line-two
90              by value 10,5.
91       call "scr$put_screen" using by descriptor inventory-line-three
92              by value 13,20.
93       read masterfile next record at end move "YES" to sw
94       perform 600-next-show-routine.
95       call "scr$set_cursor" using by value 20,16.
96       display "DO YOU WANT TO SEE ANOTHER RECORD - (Y/N)?"
97            with no advancing.
98   500-endit.
99       exit.
100  600-next-show-routine.
101      call "scr$put_screen" using by descriptor mast-num
              by value 7,32.
102      call "scr$put_screen" using by descriptor mast-quan
              by value 10,14.
103      call "scr$put_screen" using by descriptor mast-dollars
              by value 10,34.
104      call "scr$put_screen" using by descriptor mast-cents
              by value 10,38.
105      call "scr$put_screen" using by descriptor mast-desc
              by value 13,32.
106      read masterfile next record at end move "YES" to switch.
107      call "scr$set_cursor" using by value 20,58.
108  900-last-part.
109      close infile masterfile.
110      stop run.
```

There is some new and interesting syntax present in the above program. Line 56 and lines 68–70 load a menu into a table in Working-Storage (lines 31–35) from an input file (line 14 and lines 26–8).

Examine this input file:

```
0515THIS PROGRAM WILL ALLOW YOU TO ENTER AN
0615INVENTORY NUMBER. UPON ENTERING THIS NUMBER
0715THE REST OF THE RECORD IS DISPLAYED.
0918YOU ARE THEN ASKED IF YOU WANT TO EXAMINE
1018THE RECORDS THAT FOLLOW THE FIRST RECORD
1118THAT YOU EXAMINED ONE BY ONE.
1321UPON ENTERING A CONTROL_Z CHARACTER IN
1422PLACE OF THE INVENTORY NUMBER THE PROGRAM
1522          STOPS.
1824     GOOD LUCK!!
```

Notice that each record (line) contains a 4 digit number. This number is actually two numbers—a line number and column number. Line 58 and lines 71–75 put this table on the screen. Each line number and column number must be converted to binary (lines 36–37 and lines 72–73) so that the BY REFERENCE clause of the new RTL function ("LIB$PUT_SCREEN") can be used. **This has very important implications in the fact that text files containing menus can be updated, changed, etc., producing different screen outputs without changing a program.** In other words, another data file with 10 lines but with different line and column values could be read into the same table in the same way producing a different output screen.

When executed, the above data file is put on the screen (see Figure 19-1). If the ⟨ret⟩ is then entered, a second screen is displayed (Figure 19-2). This is the result of lines 77–80. Upon entering an inventory number, a data pointer is set to the appropriate record by the use of the START statement (lines 83–88). Lines 89–97 and lines 100–106 display the rest of the screen along with the current fields of that particular record. If one answers affirmatively to the question asking to see the next record (lines 96–97) then the next record is shown. Notice the NEXT RECORD clause of the READ statement to allow records to be viewed in sequence. If one answers negatively, then Figure 19-2 is displayed again. Entering a different inventory number starts processing somewhere else (unless an invalid inventory number is entered). The program allows one to exit with the use of the CONTROL_Z character. Notice the AT END option of the ACCEPT statements in lines 61 and 81. CONTROL_Z satisfies the AT END clause.

19.2 ACCESS BY ALTERNATE KEY

Suppose one wanted to access a record by another, or alternate key. This would be done if the latter is more accessible or easier to remember. It would be easier to access a record, let's say, by last name instead of social security number, unless the social security number was available. There may be, however, more than one last name that is the same. Alternate keys that may be duplicates are allowed. The primary or record key **must be unique**. The following program allows for alternate key entries and provides some additional syntax in case the information entered is larger than the field itself:

```
1    IDENTIFICATION DIVISION.
2    PROGRAM-ID. finder-serially.
3    AUTHOR. STEVE SAMUELS.
4    ENVIRONMENT DIVISION.
5    CONFIGURATION SECTION.
6    SOURCE-COMPUTER. VAX-750.
7    OBJECT-COMPUTER. VAX-750.
8    INPUT-OUTPUT SECTION.
9    FILE-CONTROL.
```

```
THIS PROGRAM WILL ALLOW YOU TO ENTER AN
INVENTORY NUMBER. UPON ENTERING THIS NUMBER
THE REST OF THE RECORD IS DISPLAYED.

YOU ARE THEN ASKED IF YOU WANT TO EXAMINE
THE RECORDS THAT FOLLOW THE FIRST RECORD
THAT YOU EXAMINED ONE BY ONE.

UPON ENTERING A CONTROL _ Z CHARACTER IN
PLACE OF THE INVENTORY NUMBER THE PROGRAM
STOPS


GOOD LUCK!!
```

Figure 19–1

```
INVENTORY NUMBER: _ _ _ _ _ _
```

Figure 19–2

```
10          SELECT MASTERFILE ASSIGN TO MASTER
11              ORGANIZATION IS INDEXED
12              ACCESS IS DYNAMIC
13              RECORD KEY IS MAST-NUM
14              alternate record key is mast-desc with duplicates.
15          SELECT INFILE ASSIGN TO MENU.
16      DATA DIVISION.
17      FILE SECTION.
18      FD  MASTERFILE
19          DATA RECORD IS MASTREC.
20      01  MASTREC.
21          02 MAST-NUM            PIC X(5).
22          02 MAST-QUAN           PIC 9999.
23          02 MAST-PRICE.
24              03 MAST-DOLLARS    PIC 999.
25              03 MAST-CENTS      PIC v99.
26          02 MAST-DESC           PIC X(10).
27      FD  iNFILE
28          DATA RECORD IS INREC.
29      01  INREC                  pic x(60).
30      WORKING-STORAGE SECTION.
31      01  CRT-RESPONSE           PIC X.
32      01  INITIAL-MESSAGE.
33          02 MESSANGER    OCCURS 10 TIMES   INDEXED BY M-IND.
34              03 LINE-COORDINATE    PIC 99.
35              03 COLUMN-COORDINATE  PIC 99.
36              03 MESSAGE-LINE       PIC X(46).
37      01  LINE-VAL     PIC S9(5) COMP VALUE 0.
38      01  COL-VAL      PIC S9(5) COMP VALUE 0.
39      01  SWITCH       PIC XXX VALUE SPACES.
40      01  INVENTORY-LINE-ONE.
41          02 FILLER     PIC X(22) VALUE "INVENTORY NUMBER:_____".
42      01  INVENTORY-LINE-TWO.
43          02 FILLER     PIC X(13) VALUE "QUANTITY:____".
44          02 FILLER     PIC X(10) VALUE SPACES.
45          02 FILLER     PIC X(12) VALUE "PRICE:___.__".
46          02 FILLER     PIC X(30) VALUE "  (dollars-(ret)-cents)".
47      01  INVENTORY-LINE-THREE.
48          02 FILLER     PIC X(22) VALUE "DESCRIPTION:_____".
49      01  TRANS-INV-NO   PIC X(5).
50      01  trans-desc     pic x(10).
51      PROCEDURE DIVISION.
52      BEGIN.
53          PERFORM 100-FIRST-PART.
54          PERFORM 200-LOOPS UNTIL SWITCH = "YES".
55          PERFORM 900-LAST-PART.
56      100-FIRST-PART.
57          OPEN INPUT INFILE I-O MASTERFILE.
58          PERFORM 300-LOAD-MENU1-ROUTINE VARYING M-IND FROM 1 BY 1
                        UNTIL M-IND > 10.
59          perform 250-initialize.

60      200-LOOPS.
61          ACCEPT CRT-RESPONSE.
62          IF CRT-RESPONSE = "Y" PERFORM 800-NEXT-SHOW-ROUTINE
63              else perform 250-initialize.
64      250-initialize.
65          CALL "SCR$ERASE_PAGE" USING BY VALUE 1,1.
66          PERFORM 400-DISPLAY-MENU1 VARYING M-IND FROM 1 BY 1
                        UNTIL M-IND > 10.
67          CALL "SCR$SET_CURSOR" USING BY VALUE 22,2.
```

```
68              display "access by name (N), inventory number (I), or
                    CONTROL_Z to stop?"
69                  with no advancing.
70          accept crt-response at end move "YES" to switch.
71          IF SWITCH = "YES" PERFORM 900-LAST-PART.
72          If crt-response = "I"
73            perform 500-inventory-screen-display thru 500-endit
74          else
75            perform 700-description-screen-display thru 700-endit.
76      300-LOAD-MENU1-ROUTINE.
77          READ INFILE AT END MOVE "YES" TO SWITCH.
78          MOVE INREC TO MESSANGER (M-IND).
79      400-DISPLAY-MENU1.
80          COMPUTE LINE-VAL = LINE-COORDINATE (M-IND).
81          COMPUTE COL-VAL = COLUMN-COORDINATE (M-IND).
82          CALL "LIB$PUT_SCREEN" USING BY DESCRIPTOR
83              MESSAGE-LINE (M-IND)  BY REFERENCE LINE-VAL, COL-VAL.
84      500-INVENTORY-SCREEN-DISPLAY.
85          CALL "SCR$ERASE_PAGE" USING BY VALUE 1,1.
86          CALL "SCR$PUT_SCREEN" USING BY DESCRIPTOR INVENTORY-LINE-ONE
87                  BY VALUE 7,15.
88          CALL "SCR$SET_CURSOR" USING BY VALUE 7,32.
89          ACCEPT TRANS-INV-NO AT END PERFORM 900-LAST-PART.
90          MOVE TRANS-INV-NO TO MAST-NUM.
91          START MASTERFILE KEY NOT LESS THAN MAST-NUM
92              INVALID KEY CALL "SCR$SET_CURSOR" USING BY VALUE 22,30
93              DISPLAY "RECORD NOT FOUND - PRESS <RET>"
94              WITH NO ADVANCING
95              ACCEPT CRT-RESPONSE
96              move "YES" to switch
97              GO TO 500-ENDIT.
98          CALL "SCR$PUT_SCREEN" USING BY DESCRIPTOR INVENTORY-LINE-TWO
99                  BY VALUE 10,5.
100         CALL "SCR$PUT_SCREEN" USING BY DESCRIPTOR
101             INVENTORY-LINE-THREE BY VALUE 13,20.
102         READ MASTERFILE NEXT RECORD AT END MOVE "YES" TO SWITCH.
103         PERFORM 800-NEXT-SHOW-ROUTINE.
104         CALL "SCR$SET_CURSOR" USING BY VALUE 20,16.
105         DISPLAY "DO YOU WANT TO SEE ANOTHER RECORD - (Y/N)?"
106             WITH NO ADVANCING.
107     500-ENDIT.
108         EXIT.
109     700-description-screen-display.
110         call "scr$erase_page" using by value 1,1.
111         call "scr$put_screen" using by descriptor inventory-line-three
112                 by value 13,20.
113         call "scr$set_cursor" using by value 13,32.
114         accept trans-desc at end perform 900-last-part.
115         move trans-desc to mast-desc.

116         start masterfile key not less than mast-desc
117             invalid key call "scr$set_cursor" using by value 22,30
118             display "RECORD NOT FOUND - PRESS <RET>"
119             with no advancing
120             accept crt-response
121
122             move "YES" to switch
123             go to 700-endit.
124         call "scr$put_screen" using by descriptor inventory-line-one
125                 by value 7,15.
126         call "scr$put_screen" using by descriptor inventory-line-two
```

```
127                       by value 10,5.
128         read masterfile next record at end move "YES" to switch.
129         perform 800-next-show-routine.
130         call "scr$set_cursor" using by value 20,16.
131         display "DO YOU WANT TO SEE ANOTHER RECORD - (Y/N)?"
132             with no advancing.
133     700-endit.
134         exit.
135     800-NEXT-SHOW-ROUTINE.
136         CALL "SCR$PUT_SCREEN" USING BY DESCRIPTOR MAST-NUM
                            BY VALUE 7,32.
137         CALL "SCR$PUT_SCREEN" USING BY DESCRIPTOR MAST-QUAN
                            BY VALUE 10,14.
138         CALL "SCR$PUT_SCREEN" USING BY DESCRIPTOR MAST-DOLLARS
                            BY VALUE 10,34.
139         CALL "SCR$PUT_SCREEN" USING BY DESCRIPTOR MAST-CENTS
                            BY VALUE 10,38.
140         CALL "SCR$PUT_SCREEN" USING BY DESCRIPTOR MAST-DESC
                            BY VALUE 13,32.
141         READ MASTERFILE NEXT RECORD AT END MOVE "YES" TO SWITCH.
142         CALL "SCR$SET_CURSOR" USING BY VALUE 20,58.
143     900-LAST-PART.
144         call "scr$set_cursor" using by value 23,2.
145         display "R U N    T E R M I N A T E D" with no advancing.
146         CLOSE INFILE MASTERFILE.
147         STOP RUN.
```

It is now possible to access a record by either the inventory number or description. Line 14 provides for the alternate key field. There can be more than one alternate key field. Upon execution a menu of lines is put on the screen (Figure 19–3). Notice that it is a little different from Figure 19–1. The MENU.DAT file was changed slightly, but the program still loaded this modified file into the same table area. This time the user is able to access by description (by entering an "N") or inventory number (by entering an "I"). Lines 68–69 cause the "choice" line to be displayed on the screen. Line 75 and lines 109–134 provide for alternate key access. If "N" is entered, then Figure 19–4 is displayed. Upon entering a description, the rest of the record is displayed on the screen. If the user wants to see additional records, **they are displayed in ascending sequence by description**, and not by ascending sequence according to inventory number. When 800–next-show-routine is entered (originally 600–next-show-routine), line 128 (READ MASTERFILE NEXT RECORD. . . . . .) "searches" for the next higher description. The entire module, 800–next-show-routine, was moved by the use of the "move" edit command.

Another important point needs to be considered. With the use of the NOT LESS THAN option of the START statement (line 91 and line 116), the exact inventory number or exact description need not be entered. The record or data pointer is positioned to a record not less than the number entered!! The same thing happens with entering a description. If "BLADES" is entered, "BLOWERS" will be displayed, since the field "BLOWERS" is not less than "BLADES". If "21000" is entered for an inventory number, then "21111" will be displayed.

THIS PROGRAM WILL ALLOW YOU TO ENTER AN
INVENTORY NUMBER. UPON ENTERING THIS NUMBER
THE REST OF THE RECORD IS DISPLAYED.

YOU ARE THEN ASKED IF YOU WANT TO EXAMINE
THE RECORDS THAT FOLLOW THE FIRST RECORD
THAT YOU EXAMINED ONE BY ONE.

UPON ENTERING A CONTROL _ Z CHARACTER
INSTEAD OF "N" (DESCRIPTION) OR "I"
(INVENTORY NUMBER) THE PROGRAM STOPS.

GOOD LUCK!!

access by name (N), inventory number (I), or CONTROL _ Z to stop?

Figure 19-3

DESCRIPTION: _____

Figure 19-4

Finally, the program has been somewhat enhanced to exit properly if an invalid inventory number is entered (#H85T for example) or an invalid description is entered (lower case, for example). One even sees "R U N T E R M I N A T E D" before the "$" prompt is displayed.

19.3   FILE STATUS AND ADDITIONAL RTL FUNCTIONS

What happens when the user enters information longer than the length of the receiving field? Is there a method by which he/she could be informed that the string of characters entered was too long? Is there a way to erase a line of information entered without clearing the whole screen? Is there a method of automatically recording the status of an I/O operation? These questions can be answered by observing two updated versions of the above program. The first program (A) uses calls to RTL functions and program B uses extensions of ACCEPT and DISPLAY. [As always, additional code in lower case.]

A.

```
 1      IDENTIFICATION DIVISION.
 2      PROGRAM-ID. finder-serially.
 3      AUTHOR. STEVE SAMUELS.
 4      ENVIRONMENT DIVISION.
 5      CONFIGURATION SECTION.
 6      SOURCE-COMPUTER. VAX-750.
 7      OBJECT-COMPUTER. VAX-750.
 8      INPUT-OUTPUT SECTION.
 9      FILE-CONTROL.
10          SELECT MASTERFILE ASSIGN TO MASTER
11              ORGANIZATION IS INDEXED
12              ACCESS IS DYNAMIC
13              RECORD KEY IS MAST-NUM
14          ALTERNATE RECORD KEY IS MAST-DESC WITH DUPLICATES
15          file status is ws-file-status-flag.
16          SELECT INFILE ASSIGN TO MENU.
17      DATA DIVISION.
18      FILE SECTION.
19      FD  MASTERFILE
20          DATA RECORD IS MASTREC.
21      01  MASTREC.
22          02 MAST-NUM            PIC X(5).
23          02 MAST-QUAN           PIC 9999.
24          02 MAST-PRICE.
25              03 MAST-DOLLARS     PIC 999.
26              03 MAST-CENTS       PIC v99.
27          02 MAST-DESC           PIC X(10).
28      FD  INFILE
29          DATA RECORD IS INREC.
30      01  INREC               pic x(60).
31      WORKING-STORAGE SECTION.
32      01  ws-file-status-flag         pic xx         value spaces.
33          88  successful-completion            value "00".
```

```
34      88  duplicate-alternate-key          value "02".
35      88  end-of-file                      value "10".
36      88  sequence-error                   value "21".
37      88  duplicate-key                    value "22".
38      88  no-record-found                  value "23".
39      88  boundary-violation-ind-rel       value "24".
40      88  permanent-i-o-data-error         value "30".
41      88  boundary-violation-seq           value "34".
42      88  implementor-defined-error        value "9 ".

43  01  CRT-RESPONSE                PIC X.
44  01  INITIAL-MESSAGE.
45      02 MESSANGER     OCCURS 10 TIMES    INDEXED BY M-IND.
46         03 LINE-COORDINATE      PIC 99.
47         03 COLUMN-COORDINATE    PIC 99.
48         03 MESSAGE-LINE          PIC X(46).
49  01  LINE-VAL       PIC S9(5) COMP VALUE 0.
50  01  COL-VAL        PIC S9(5) COMP VALUE 0.
51  01  SWITCH         PIC XXX VALUE SPACES.
52  01  INVENTORY-LINE-ONE.
53      02 FILLER       PIC X(22) VALUE "INVENTORY NUMBER:_____".
54  01  INVENTORY-LINE-TWO.
55      02 FILLER       PIC X(13) VALUE "QUANTITY:____".
56      02 FILLER       PIC X(10) VALUE SPACES.
57      02 FILLER       PIC X(12) VALUE "PRICE:___.__".
58      02 FILLER       PIC X(30) VALUE "   (dollars-<ret>-cents)".
59  01  INVENTORY-LINE-THREE.
60      02 FILLER       PIC X(22) VALUE "DESCRIPTION:_____".
61  01  TRANS-INV-NO   PIC X(5).
62  01  TRANS-DESC     PIC x(10).
63  01  call-status    pic s9(9) comp value 0.
64      88 ok             value external SS$_NORMAL.
65      88 too-long       value external LIB$_INPSTRTRU.
66  PROCEDURE DIVISION.
67  BEGIN.
68      PERFORM 100-FIRST-PART.
69      PERFORM 200-LOOPS UNTIL SWITCH = "YES".
70      PERFORM 900-LAST-PART.
71  100-FIRST-PART.
72      OPEN INPUT INFILE I-O MASTERFILE.
73      PERFORM 300-LOAD-MENU1-ROUTINE VARYING M-IND FROM 1 BY 1
                    UNTIL M-IND > 10.
74      PERFORM 250-INITIALIZE.
75  200-LOOPS.
76      ACCEPT CRT-RESPONSE.
77      IF CRT-RESPONSE = "Y" PERFORM 800-NEXT-SHOW-ROUTINE
78          ELSE PERFORM 250-INITIALIZE.
79  250-INITIALIZE.
80      CALL "SCR$ERASE_PAGE" USING BY VALUE 1,1.
81      PERFORM 400-DISPLAY-MENU1 VARYING M-IND FROM 1 BY 1
                    UNTIL M-IND > 10.
82      CALL "SCR$SET_CURSOR" USING BY VALUE 22,2.
83      DISPLAY "access by name (N), inventory number (I),
                    or CONTROL_Z to stop?"
84                  WITH NO ADVANCING.
85      ACCEPT CRT-RESPONSE AT END MOVE "YES" TO SWITCH.
86      IF SWITCH = "YES" PERFORM 900-LAST-PART.
87      IF CRT-RESPONSE = "I"
88          PERFORM 500-INVENTORY-SCREEN-DISPLAY THRU 500-ENDIT
89      ELSE
90          PERFORM 700-DESCRIPTION-SCREEN-DISPLAY THRU 700-ENDIT.
```

```
91      300-LOAD-MENU1-ROUTINE.
92          READ INFILE AT END MOVE "YES" TO SWITCH.
93          MOVE INREC TO MESSANGER (M-IND).
94      400-DISPLAY-MENU1.
95          COMPUTE LINE-VAL = LINE-COORDINATE (M-IND).
96          COMPUTE COL-VAL = COLUMN-COORDINATE (M-IND).
97          CALL "LIB$PUT_SCREEN" USING BY DESCRIPTOR
98              MESSAGE-LINE (M-IND) BY REFERENCE LINE-VAL, COL-VAL.

99      500-INVENTORY-SCREEN-DISPLAY.
100         CALL "SCR$ERASE_PAGE" USING BY VALUE 1,1.
101         CALL "SCR$PUT_SCREEN" USING BY DESCRIPTOR INVENTORY-LINE-ONE
102                     BY VALUE 7,15.
103         CALL "SCR$SET_CURSOR" USING BY VALUE 7,32.
104         ACCEPT TRANS-INV-NO.
105         MOVE TRANS-INV-NO TO MAST-NUM.
106         START MASTERFILE KEY = MAST-NUM
107             INVALID KEY CALL "SCR$SET_CURSOR" USING BY VALUE 22,30
108             DISPLAY "RECORD NOT FOUND - PRESS <RET>"
109             WITH NO ADVANCING
110             ACCEPT CRT-RESPONSE.
111         if no-record-found move "YES" to switch
112             GO TO 500-ENDIT.
113         CALL "SCR$PUT_SCREEN" USING BY DESCRIPTOR INVENTORY-LINE-TWO
114                     BY VALUE 10,5.
115         CALL "SCR$PUT_SCREEN" USING BY DESCRIPTOR
116              INVENTORY-LINE-THREE BY VALUE 13,20.
117         READ MASTERFILE NEXT RECORD AT END MOVE "YES" TO SWITCH.
118         PERFORM 800-NEXT-SHOW-ROUTINE.
119         CALL "SCR$SET_CURSOR" USING BY VALUE 20,16.
120         DISPLAY "DO YOU WANT TO SEE ANOTHER RECORD - (Y/N)?"
121             WITH NO ADVANCING.
122     500-ENDIT.
123         EXIT.
124     700-DESCRIPTION-SCREEN-DISPLAY.
125         CALL "SCR$ERASE_PAGE" USING BY VALUE  ,1.
126         CALL "SCR$PUT_SCREEN" USING BY DESCRIPTOR
127              INVENTORY-LINE-THREE BY VALUE 13,20.
128         CALL "SCR$SET_CURSOR" USING BY VALUE 13,32.
129         perform 750-checkforlength until ok.
130         MOVE TRANS-DESC TO MAST-DESC.
131         START MASTERFILE KEY NOT LESS THAN MAST-DESC
132             INVALID KEY CALL "SCR$SET_CURSOR" USING BY VALUE 22,30
133             DISPLAY "RECORD NOT FOUND - PRESS <RET>"
134             WITH NO ADVANCING
135             ACCEPT CRT-RESPONSE
136             MOVE "YES" TO SWITCH
137             GO TO 700-ENDIT.
138         move 0 to call-status.
139         call "scr$erase_line" using by value 16,20.
140         CALL "SCR$PUT_SCREEN" USING BY DESCRIPTOR INVENTORY-LINE-ONE
141                     BY VALUE 7,15.
142         CALL "SCR$PUT_SCREEN" USING BY DESCRIPTOR INVENTORY-LINE-TWO
143                     BY VALUE 10,5.
144         READ MASTERFILE NEXT' RECORD AT END MOVE "YES" TO SWITCH.
145         PERFORM 800-NEXT-SHOW-ROUTINE.
146         CALL "SCR$SET_CURSOR" USING BY VALUE 20,16.
147         DISPLAY "DO YOU WANT TO SEE ANOTHER RECORD - (Y/N)?"
148             WITH NO ADVANCING.
149     700-ENDIT.
150         EXIT.
```

```
151     750-checkforlength.
152         call "scr$get_screen" using by descriptor trans-desc
                giving call-status.
153         if too-long
154             call "scr$erase_line" using by value 13,32
155             call "scr$set_cursor" using by value 16,20
156             display "TOO LONG - TRY AGAIN" with no advancing
157             call "scr$set_cursor" using by value 13,32.

158     800-NEXT-SHOW-ROUTINE.
159         CALL "SCR$PUT_SCREEN" USING BY DESCRIPTOR MAST-NUM
                BY VALUE 7,32.
160         CALL "SCR$PUT_SCREEN" USING BY DESCRIPTOR MAST-QUAN
                BY VALUE 10,14.
161         CALL "SCR$PUT_SCREEN" USING BY DESCRIPTOR MAST-DOLLARS
                BY VALUE 10,34.
162         CALL "SCR$PUT_SCREEN" USING BY DESCRIPTOR MAST-CENTS
                BY VALUE 10,38.
163         CALL "SCR$PUT_SCREEN" USING BY DESCRIPTOR MAST-DESC
                BY VALUE 13,32.
164         READ MASTERFILE NEXT RECORD AT END MOVE "YES" TO SWITCH.
165         CALL "SCR$SET_CURSOR" USING BY VALUE 20,58.
166     900-LAST-PART.
167         CALL "SCR$SET_CURSOR" USING BY VALUE 23,2.
168         DISPLAY "R U N    T E R M I N A T E D" WITH NO ADVANCING.
169         CLOSE INFILE MASTERFILE.
170         STOP RUN.
```

Some of the questions asked before the listing of this program can now be answered. Examine lines 129, 151–157, and 63–65. All this syntax serves the sole purpose of informing the user that the description he/she entered was too long (if over 10 characters were entered).

a. SCR$GET_SCREEN (line 152) acts the same as the ACCEPT verb except that a value can be put into CALL-STATUS. If the string is longer than 10 characters, it is truncated, but the RTL function, LIB$_INPSTRTUR is invoked (VALUE EXTERNAL). A binary value is returned that satisfies the conditional name, TOO-LONG.

b. Hence, if the string is truncated, then it is "TOO-LONG" and the area that the string was originally entered into is erased using another RTL function, SCR$ERASE_LINE (line 154). Notice that the user must enter another string. OK is satisfied when the user decides to enter a string less than 11 characters. The SCR$ERASE LINE is a nice feature, for without it, extra characters from a long previous description entry remain on the screen—it doesn't look professional!! When OK is satisfied, the module 750-CHECK-FORLENGTH is exited.

c. Notice the use of the FILE STATUS option of the SELECT statement. This clause, in conjunction with lines 32–42, allows the program to satisfy a condition by returning a number corresponding to the status of a particular input-output operation. If, for example, a READ is attempted and the end-of-file mark is reached, then "10" is returned to WS-FILE-STATUS-FLAG.

Then the conditional name, END-OF-FILE is satisfied. If a WRITE is attempted on an indexed file, and the record key already exists, the INVALID KEY option is invoked and, in addition, the number "22" is returned which satisfies DUPLICATE-KEY. I have attempted to show what happens when an invalid inventory number is entered. Notice line 111. If the user enters an invalid inventory number then NO-RECORD-FOUND is satisfied because of the use of the FILE STATUS option and related identifier WS-FILE-STATUS-FLAG in Working-Storage. The user must enter the correct number because the START statement includes the "=" condition, not the NOT LESS THAN condition (line 106). [See Appendix E for a complete set of File Status codes.]

B.

```
1        IDENTIFICATION DIVISION.
2        PROGRAM-ID. finder-serially.
3        AUTHOR. STEVE SAMUELS.
4        ENVIRONMENT DIVISION.
5        CONFIGURATION SECTION.
6        SOURCE-COMPUTER. VAX-750.
7        OBJECT-COMPUTER. VAX-750.
8        INPUT-OUTPUT SECTION.
9        FILE-CONTROL.
10           SELECT MASTERFILE ASSIGN TO MASTER
11               ORGANIZATION IS INDEXED
12               ACCESS IS DYNAMIC
13               RECORD KEY IS MAST-NUM
14             ALTERNATE RECORD KEY IS MAST-DESC WITH DUPLICATES
15             file status is ws-file-status-flag.
16           SELECT INFILE ASSIGN TO MENU.
17       DATA DIVISION.
18       FILE SECTION.
19       FD  MASTERFILE
20           DATA RECORD IS MASTREC.
21       01  MASTREC.
22           02 MAST-NUM          PIC X(5).
23           02 MAST-QUAN         PIC 9999.
24           02 MAST-PRICE        PIC 999v99.
25           02 MAST-DESC         PIC X(10).
26       FD  INFILE
27           DATA RECORD IS INREC.
28       01  INREC              pic x(60).
29       WORKING-STORAGE SECTION.
30       01  ws-file-status-flag              pic xx        value spaces.
31               88  successful-completion          value "00".
32               88  duplicate-alternate-key        value "02".
33               88  end-of-file                    value "10".
34               88  sequence-error                 value "21".
35               88  duplicate-key                  value "22".
36               88  no-record-found                value "23".
37               88  boundary-violation-ind-rel     value "24".
38               88  permanent-i-o-data-error       value "30".
39               88  boundary-violation-seq         value "34".
40               88  implementor-defined-error      value "9 ".
41       01  CRT-RESPONSE              PIC X.
42       01  INITIAL-MESSAGE.
```

```
43          02 MESSANGER     OCCURS 10 TIMES    INDEXED BY M-IND.
44              03 LINE-COORDINATE        PIC 99.
45              03 COLUMN-COORDINATE      PIC 99.
46              03 MESSAGE-LINE           PIC X(46).
47      01  LINE-VAL              PIC S9(5) COMP VALUE 0.
48      01  COL-VAL               PIC S9(5) COMP VALUE 0.
49      01  SWITCH                PIC XXX VALUE SPACES.
50      01  INVENTORY-LINE-ONE.
51          02 FILLER     PIC X(22) VALUE "INVENTORY NUMBER:_____".
52      01  INVENTORY-LINE-TWO.
53          02 FILLER     PIC X(13) VALUE "QUANTITY:____".
54          02 FILLER     PIC X(10) VALUE SPACES.
55          02 FILLER     PIC X(12) VALUE "PRICE:_____".
56      01  INVENTORY-LINE-THREE.
57          02 FILLER     PIC X(22) VALUE "DESCRIPTION:_____".
58      01  TRANS-INV-NO    PIC X(5).
59      01  TRANS-DESC      PIC X(10).
60      PROCEDURE DIVISION.
61      BEGIN.
62          PERFORM 100-FIRST-PART.
63          PERFORM 200-LOOPS UNTIL SWITCH = "YES".
64          PERFORM 900-LAST-PART.
65      100-FIRST-PART.
66          OPEN INPUT INFILE I-O MASTERFILE.
67          PERFORM 300-LOAD-MENU1-ROUTINE
68              VARYING M-IND FROM 1 BY 1 UNTIL M-IND > 10.
69          PERFORM 250-INITIALIZE.
70      200-LOOPS.
71          ACCEPT CRT-RESPONSE
72              protected size 1 with bell from line 20 column 58.
73          IF CRT-RESPONSE = "Y" PERFORM 800-NEXT-SHOW-ROUTINE
74              ELSE PERFORM 250-INITIALIZE.
75      250-INITIALIZE.
76          Display "" erase screen.
77          PERFORM 400-DISPLAY-MENU1
78              VARYING M-IND FROM 1 BY 1 UNTIL M-IND > 10.
79          DISPLAY
80              "access by name (N), inventory number (I),
81              or CONTROL_Z to stop?" at line 22 column 22.
82          accept crt-response protected size 1 from line 22 column 68
83              at end perform 900-last-part.
84          IF SWITCH = "YES" PERFORM 900-LAST-PART.
85          IF CRT-RESPONSE = "I"
86              PERFORM 500-INVENTORY-SCREEN-DISPLAY THRU 500-ENDIT
87          ELSE
88              PERFORM 700-DESCRIPTION-SCREEN-DISPLAY THRU 700-ENDIT.
89      300-LOAD-MENU1-ROUTINE.
90          READ INFILE AT END MOVE "YES" TO SWITCH.
91          MOVE INREC TO MESSANGER (M-IND).
92      400-DISPLAY-MENU1.
93          display message-line (m-ind) at
94              line line-coordinate (m-ind)
95              column column-coordinate (m-ind).
96
97      500-INVENTORY-SCREEN-DISPLAY.
98          display "" erase screen.
99          display inventory-line-one at line 7 column 15.
100         ACCEPT TRANS-INV-NO protected size 5 from line 7 column 32.
101         MOVE TRANS-INV-NO TO MAST-NUM.
102         START MASTERFILE KEY = MAST-NUM
103             INVALID KEY display "RECORD NOT FOUND - PRESS <RET>"
```

```
104                reversed at line 22 column 30.
105           if no-record-found move "YES" to switch
106               GO TO 500-ENDIT.
107           display inventory-line-two at line 10 column 5.
108           display inventory-line-three at line 13 column 22.
109           READ MASTERFILE NEXT RECORD AT END MOVE "YES" TO SWITCH.
110           PERFORM 800-NEXT-SHOW-ROUTINE.
111           DISPLAY "DO YOU WANT TO SEE ANOTHER RECORD - (Y/N)?"
112               blinking at line 20 column 16.
113       500-ENDIT.
114           EXIT.
115       700-DESCRIPTION-SCREEN-DISPLAY.
116           display "" erase screen.
117           display inventory-line-three at line 13 column 22.
118           accept trans-desc protected size 10 from line 13 column 34.
119           MOVE TRANS-DESC TO MAST-DESC.
120           START MASTERFILE KEY NOT LESS THAN MAST-DESC
121               INVALID KEY display "RECORD NOT FOUND - PRESS <RET>"
122               reversed at line 22 column 30
123               ACCEPT CRT-RESPONSE
124               MOVE "YES" TO SWITCH
125               GO TO 700-ENDIT.
126           display inventory-line-one at line 7 column 15.
127           display inventory-line-two at line 10 column 5.
128           READ MASTERFILE NEXT RECORD AT END MOVE "YES" TO SWITCH.
129           PERFORM 800-NEXT-SHOW-ROUTINE.
130           DISPLAY "DO YOU WANT TO SEE ANOTHER RECORD - (Y/N)?"
131               blinking at line 20 column 16.
132       700-ENDIT.
133           EXIT.
134       800-NEXT-SHOW-ROUTINE.
135           display mast-num at line 7 column 32.
136           display mast-quan with conversion at line 10 column 14.
137           display mast-price with conversion at line 10 column 34.
138           display mast-desc at line 13 column 34.
139           READ MASTERFILE NEXT RECORD AT END MOVE "YES" TO SWITCH.
140       900-LAST-PART.
141           DISPLAY "R U N   T E R M I N A T E D" at line 23 column 2.
142           CLOSE INFILE MASTERFILE.
143           STOP RUN.
```

Once again, the extensions of ACCEPT and DISPLAY make screen displays fancier and easier to handle. The entire check for length logic can be minimized with the PROTECTED SIZE extension (lines 82, 100, and 118). If, for example, PROTECTED SIZE 5 is used, one can enter no more than 5 characters. When an attempt is made to enter a 6th character, the bell sounds and the cursor remains in the same place. The CALL-STATUS identifiers in Working-Storage are noticeably absent along with an entire module (750–CHECK-FOR-LENGTH). Also, the screens can be made fancier quite easily by the use of BLINKING, REVERSED, and BOLD extensions.

The CONVERSION option also works with DISPLAY (lines 136–137). The picture clause for MAST-PRICE is 999v99. The WITH CONVERSION option automatically edits this price with left zero suppression and inclusion of a decimal point! The zero suppression also occurs with MAST-QUAN. If a data item was negative and a picture clause was, let's say, S999, a negative value would be displayed if the WITH CONVERSION option was used in the DISPLAY statement.

SUMMARY

Additional syntax was provided for random access and serial access with the use of an alternate key. In addition, text files were read into a table and "screen displayed." This enabled the programmer to change a screen format without changing the program. A new RTL function was used to check for truncation during terminal entry. Finally, the FILE–STATUS function was used to clarify certain conditions resulting from an input-output operation.

The AT END option of the ACCEPT verb was added to make exiting from an input function easier and standardized.

The extensions of ACCEPT and DISPLAY are able to reduce code and make it easier for screen cursor movement programming. The PROTECTED SIZE option was used to limit the amount of user input on a given field, and there were more examples of the WITH CONVERSION extension.

PROGRAMMING PROBLEMS

1. Provide additional code (modules) in the above to handle invalid terminal entry such as:
   a. Incorrect answers to questions (i.e, enter another letter besides "Y" or "N" to the question. "DO YOU WANT TO SEE ANOTHER RECORD—(Y/N)?").
   b. An error routine to handle invalid inventory number entry rather than just program termination.

2. Incorporate many of the advanced features into the program you developed (hopefully) to answer problem 3 in the previous chapter. Include the following:
   a. Menus loaded into tables from external text files.
   b. Additional RTL functions.
   c. File status techniques (employ more than one I/O condition).
   d. Create proper error routines and files (use additional subprograms—impress someone!!).

Appendix A

VAX Debugger Facility

Programmers rarely write programs that compile correctly the first time. Even after successful compilation, there are usually errors in the $LINK and/or the $RUN phase. There is a facility that can aid one to find and correct errors in executable COBOL programs. This appendix not only introduces you to the VAX-11 Symbolic Debugger, but also provides two sample Debugger sessions.

In chapter 9, a control break program was shown that produced a report containing subtotals for salesman, branch, and region. It would be a good idea to refer back to the last listing in chapter 9 at this time. Suppose, for example, that the program compiles correctly, but produces a "symbolic stack dump" upon execution (see arrow 1 of Sample Debugger Session—A).

To invoke the VAX-11 Symbolic Debugger, you need to include the /DEBUG option on the compile ($COB) and link ($LINK) steps. It is not necessary to include it on $RUN. When in execution, the Debugger takes control and presents you with the following command:

DBG⟩

The first DBG command used (see arrow 2) (lower case) is SET TRACE %LINE 265.

[******Note: all user commands are presented in lower case on both Debugger sessions. ********]

The SET TRACE allows one to monitor the sequential flow of a program. It has the following general format:

DBG)SET TRACE %LINE #

To execute the program in the debug made, you need the GO command. The general format for this command is:

DBG)GO [location]

where "location" is some starting point other than the beginning of the program. If no line number is used, then execution begins at the beginning of the program. An example of starting at line 80 of a program is:

DBG)go %line 80

where "%" = "at." After the GO command is used the first time (see arrow 3) line 265 is executed twice and then the following message appears:

%COB-F-INVEDECDAT, invalid decimal data

Something caused this to happen. It is possible to examine the data-name used in line 265 by the use of the EXAMINE statement. It has the general format:

DBG)EXAMINE data-name

When this is done, we find that WS-COMMISS-RATE = 7. The problem must be somewhere else. When IN-REC is examined, all data-names are accounted for except PRICE-IN. Apparently, there is invalid decimal (non-numeric) data in one of the input records. We can put new (numeric) data into that data-name with the use of the DEPOSIT command. It has the following general form:

DBG)DEPOSIT data-name=value

When 22.00 is deposited into PRICE-IN, the invalid contents are moved out; hence, execution can continue with the GO command. Execution is, however, interrupted again by invalid decimal data (see arrow 4). Upon examining IN-REC, non-numeric data is present in QUANTITY-IN. Depositing 35 in QUANTITY-IN allows us to complete execution of this program in the debug mode. Notice the "%SYSTEM-S-NORMAL, normal successful completion" message at the end of this section (see arrow 5).

It is possible to monitor values in one or more data names during execution with the SET BREAK command. The general format of this command is as follows:

DBG)SET BREAK %LINE # DO(DEBUG commands)

A break is set at line 269 and the contents of WS-TOT-BRANCH-COMMISSIONS is examined during execution (see arrow 6). Notice that the EXAMINE command is separated by the GO command with a semicolon. As expected, this total increases until there is a branch break and then the total is reinitialized to 0 (see arrow 7). The Debugger facility is exited with the use of the EXIT command (see arrow 8).

Additional Debugger commands can be used when this facility is invoked with subprograms. To aid you in understanding how to use the Debugger facility with subprograms, it is imperative that you refer back to the programs listed in chapter 15 (SUBPROGRAMMING). Debugger Session B will be more easily understood.

At the beginning of Sample Debugger Session—B the "MAIN" or driver program is executed after the Debug option is used on the compile step for each program and on the link step. A new command, SHOW MODULE, is entered (see arrow 9) and the Debugger facility responds by showing nine modules, the first five of which were compiled and linked into one executable module. You need not concern yourself with the "Image" modules. Only those symbols (data-names or identifiers) present in DRIVER are in the symbol table. This is significant, since one cannot set break points and examine contents of data-names unless they are in the symbol table! In order to get those symbols into the table, the SET MODULE command is used. If no module is SET then only the first program will display "yes" for symbols.

Notice that a break point is attempted at line 49 (see arrow 10) that results in an error message explaining that "%line 49 is not in the symbol table." The command SET MODULE UNSTRING-IT allows us to SET BREAK %LINE 49 DO (EXAMINE PRICE-OUT;GO). SET MODULE SORTER puts the SORTER program into the symbol table, a break point is set at line 110, and the contents of MAST-PRICE are to be examined during execution. Incidentally, if there was a line 110 in the UNSTRING program, there would be a conflict when a break point at this line was attempted because of an ambiguity. An attempt is made to break at line 70 of reporter (see arrow 11) which results in an error message. The SORTER module is removed from the symbol table with the CANCEL MODULE command and the SET MODULE REPORTER command is entered (see arrow 12). A break point can now be entered at line 70 of the REPORTER module.

All the break points are shown with the SHOW BREAK command. The break at line 70 of the REPORTER program shows that two data-names are to be examined, MAST PRICE and AMOUNT. The break point at SORTER shows that the break occurs in the REPORT-N-MASTER section, and line

110 specifically occurs in 200-LOOPDELOOP paragraph of this section.

An attempt is made to execute with the GO statement but an error, "%DEBUG-W-NOSYMBOL, symbol 'PRICE-OUT' is not in the table," is displayed. To execute the entire executable module, the SET MODULE/ALL must be used. Then, SHOW MODULE confirms that all COBOL modules are in the symbol table. SHOW CALLS is a command that displays what modules are being executed after the GO statement is used. If there was a normal completion message, then all modules would have been shown; however, since execution was interrupted with the error pointing to UN-STRING-IT, only two modules are shown in execution.

Since all modules are now in the symbol table, the GO command is entered and the Debugger facility displays the contents of the various data-names mentioned in the break points. It appears as if execution terminated normally (see arrow 13).

In examining the output from the Debugger facility during execution, there are more breaks for SORTER and REPORTER (nineteen in each) than UNSTRING-IT (seven). With the original data set presented in chapter 15, there are nine records containing nineteen subrecords. The nineteen breaks in SORTER and REPORTER can be accounted for, but only seven breaks occur in UNSTRING-IT.

The explanation for this discrepancy is determined by where the break point was set in UNSTRING-IT and the first attempt at execution that produced an error (see arrow 12). The break point is set in a paragraph that only executes as many times as there are records, not subrecords. The first attempt at execution caused the Debugger facility to state that PRICE-OUT was not in the symbol table. By that time, the second record had already been read; therefore, only the last seven executions are shown after the Debugger error was fixed (SET MODULE/ALL). As expected, only the last PRICE-OUT of each record is shown.

The other Debugger commands not shown in the sample sessions are as follows:

1. DBG)SET LANGUAGE language-name

2. DBG)SET SCOPE

3. DBG)SET WATCH

4. DBG)STEP

The SET LANGUAGE allows one to debug an executable image containing modules that were written in more than one language. The default is the language specified with the Debug option used with the $LINK or the program's main language.

The SET SCOPE command controls the defaults the Debugger facility uses to resolve references to symbols. If one uses the EXAMINE statement without specifying the module name, the Debugger uses the default name. This command is similar to the SET MODULE command. You can also use CANCEL SCOPE and SHOW SCOPE.

The SET WATCH command suspends execution if the contents of the associated identifier is changed. This command is particularly useful when one needs to know whether or not a particular identifier is being inadvertently changed. The CANCEL WATCH and SHOW WATCH commands are also available.

The STEP command continues execution at the current location for a specified number of steps ([n]).

The only way to fully understand the VAX-11 Symbolic Debugger (DEBUG) is to use it. You must experiment with it on many different types of programming assignments in order to appreciate its capability to help you resolve those "stack dump" errors in less time than it would take using other methods, such as use of "DISPLAY" statements in paragraphs.

SAMPLE DEBUGGER SESSION—A

```
      $ run prac09c
1 →   %COB-F-INVDECDAT, invalid decimal data
      %TRACE-F-TRACEBACK, symbolic stack dump follows
      module name    routine name              line    rel PC     abs PC
      FIFTH          FIFTH                     265    000002C9   000014C9


      $ cob/debug prac09c
      $ link/debug prac09c
      $ run prac09c


      VAX-11 DEBUG Version X3B-8


      %DEBUG-I-INITIAL, language is COBOL, module set to 'FIFTH'
2 →   DBG)set trace %line 265
3 →   DBG)go
      trace at FIFTH\300-MAIN-LOOP\%LINE 265
         265:                    ELSE MOVE 10 TO WS-COMMISS-RATE.
      trace at FIFTH\300-MAIN-LOOP\%LINE 265
         265:                    ELSE MOVE 10 TO WS-COMMISS-RATE.
      %COB-F-INVDECDAT, invalid decimal data
      DBG)examine ws-commiss-rate
      WS-COMMISS-RATE of FIFTH\WS-CALCULATION-REGISTERS:      7
      DBG)examine in-rec
      FIFTH\IN-REC
         REGION-IN:   "01"
         BRANCH-IN:   "11"
         SMAN-NUMBER-IN:      "14"
         PROD-NUMBER-IN:      "958492"
         QUANTITY-IN:         300
         COMMISSION-TYPE-IN: "B"
```

%DEBUG-E-DECROPRAND, illegal packed or decimal string value (Reserved Operand fault occurred during conversion)
DBG)deposit price-in=22.00
DBG)go
trace at FIFTH\300-MAIN-LOOP\%LINE 265
   265:                    ELSE MOVE 10 TO WS-COMMISS-RATE.
trace at FIFTH\300-MAIN-LOOP\%LINE 265
   265:                    ELSE MOVE 10 TO WS-COMMISS-RATE.
trace at FIFTH\300-MAIN-LOOP\%LINE 265
   265:                    ELSE MOVE 10 TO WS-COMMISS-RATE.
trace at FIFTH\300-MAIN-LOOP\%LINE 265
   265:                    ELSE MOVE 10 TO WS-COMMISS-RATE.
trace at FIFTH\300-MAIN-LOOP\%LINE 265
   265:                    ELSE MOVE 10 TO WS-COMMISS-RATE.
trace at FIFTH\300-MAIN-LOOP\%LINE 265
   265:                    ELSE MOVE 10 TO WS-COMMISS-RATE.
trace at FIFTH\300-MAIN-LOOP\%LINE 265
   265:                    ELSE MOVE 10 TO WS-COMMISS-RATE.
trace at FIFTH\300-MAIN-LOOP\%LINE 265
   265:                    ELSE MOVE 10 TO WS-COMMISS-RATE.
trace at FIFTH\300-MAIN-LOOP\%LINE 265
   265:                    ELSE MOVE 10 TO WS-COMMISS-RATE.
trace at FIFTH\300-MAIN-LOOP\%LINE 265
   265:                    ELSE MOVE 10 TO WS-COMMISS-RATE.
trace at FIFTH\300-MAIN-LOOP\%LINE 265
   265:                    ELSE MOVE 10 TO WS-COMMISS-RATE.
trace at FIFTH\300-MAIN-LOOP\%LINE 265
   265:                    ELSE MOVE 10 TO WS-COMMISS-RATE.
trace at FIFTH\300-MAIN-LOOP\%LINE 265
   265:                    ELSE MOVE 10 TO WS-COMMISS-RATE.
trace at FIFTH\300-MAIN-LOOP\%LINE 265
   265:                    ELSE MOVE 10 TO WS-COMMISS-RATE.
4 →   %COB-F-INVDECDAT, invalid decimal data
DBG)examine in-rec
FIFTH\IN-REC
    REGION-IN: "66"
    BRANCH-IN: "97"
    SMAN-NUMBER-IN: "43"
    PROD-NUMBER-IN: "294652"
%DEBUG-E-DECROPRAND, illegal packed or decimal string value (Reserved Operand fault occurred during conversion)
DBG)deposit quantity-in=35
DBG)go
trace at FIFTH\300-MAIN-LOOP\%LINE 265
   265:                    ELSE MOVE 10 TO WS-COMMISS-RATE.
trace at FIFTH\300-MAIN-LOOP\%LINE 265
   265:                    ELSE MOVE 10 TO WS-COMMISS-RATE.
trace at FIFTH\300-MAIN-LOOP\%LINE 265
   265:                    ELSE MOVE 10 TO WS-COMMISS-RATE.
5 →   %DEBUG-I-EXITSTATUS, is '%SYSTEM-S-NORMAL, normal successful completion'
DBG)exit

$ run prac09c

VAX-11 DEBUG Version X3B-8

%DEBUG-I-INITIAL, language is COBOL, module set to 'FIFTH'

6 →   DBG)set break %line 269 do(examine ws-branch-tot-commissions;go)

DBG)go

break at FIFTH\300-MAIN-LOOP\%LINE 269

    269:     ADD WS-COMMISSION TO WS-TOTAL-COMMISSIONS

WS-BRANCH-TOT-COMMISSIONS of FIFTH\WS-CALCULATION-REGISTERS: 0.00

break at FIFTH\300-MAIN-LOOP\%LINE 269

    269:     ADD WS-COMMISSION TO WS-TOTAL-COMMISSIONS

WS-BRANCH-TOT-COMMISSIONS of FIFTH\WS-CALCULATION-REGISTERS: 300.00

break at FIFTH\300-MAIN-LOOP\%LINE 269

    269:     ADD WS-COMMISSION TO WS-TOTAL-COMMISSIONS

WS-BRANCH-TOT-COMMISSIONS of FIFTH\WS-CALCULATION-REGISTERS: 405.00

break at FIFTH\300-MAIN-LOOP\%LINE 269

    269:     ADD WS-COMMISSION TO WS-TOTAL-COMMISSIONS

WS-BRANCH-TOT-COMMISSIONS of FIFTH\WS-CALCULATION-REGISTERS: 655.00

break at FIFTH\300-MAIN-LOOP\%LINE 269

    269:     ADD WS-COMMISSION TO WS-TOTAL-COMMISSIONS

WS-BRANCH-TOT-COMMISSIONS of FIFTH\WS-CALCULATION-REGISTERS: 1055.00

break at FIFTH\300-MAIN-LOOP\%LINE 269

    269:     ADD WS-COMMISSION TO WS-TOTAL-COMMISSIONS

WS-BRANCH-TOT-COMMISSIONS of FIFTH\WS-CALCULATION-REGISTERS: 1077.50

break at FIFTH\300-MAIN-LOOP\%LINE 269

    269:     ADD WS-COMMISSION TO WS-TOTAL-COMMISSIONS

7 → WS-BRANCH-TOT-COMMISSIONS of FIFTH\WS-CALCULATION-REGISTERS: 0.00

break at FIFTH\300-MAIN-LOOP\%LINE 269

    269:     ADD WS-COMMISSION TO WS-TOTAL-COMMISSIONS

WS-BRANCH-TOT-COMMISSIONS of FIFTH\WS-CALCULATION-REGISTERS: 168.00

break at FIFTH\300-MAIN-LOOP\%LINE 269

    269:     ADD WS-COMMISSION TO WS-TOTAL-COMMISSIONS

WS-BRANCH-TOT-COMMISSIONS of FIFTH\WS-CALCULATION-REGISTERS: 1168.00

break at FIFTH\300-MAIN-LOOP\%LINE 269

    269:     ADD WS-COMMISSION TO WS-TOTAL-COMMISSIONS

WS-BRANCH-TOT-COMMISSIONS of FIFTH\WS-CALCULATION-REGISTERS: 0.00

break at FIFTH\300-MAIN-LOOP\%LINE 269

    269:     ADD WS-COMMISSION TO WS-TOTAL-COMMISSIONS

WS-BRANCH-TOT-COMMISSIONS of FIFTH\WS-CALCULATION-REGISTERS: 2.56

break at FIFTH\300-MAIN-LOOP\%LINE 269

    269:     ADD WS-COMMISSION TO WS-TOTAL-COMMISSIONS

WS-BRANCH-TOT-COMMISSIONS of FIFTH\WS-CALCULATION-REGISTERS: 1429.23

break at FIFTH\300-MAIN-LOOP\%LINE 269

    269:     ADD WS-COMMISSION TO WS-TOTAL-COMMISSIONS

WS-BRANCH-TOT-COMMISSIONS of FIFTH\WS-CALCULATION-REGISTERS: 1491.56

break at FIFTH\300-MAIN-LOOP\%LINE 269

    269:     ADD WS-COMMISSION TO WS-TOTAL-COMMISSIONS

WS-BRANCH-TOT-COMMISSIONS of FIFTH\WS-CALCULATION-REGISTERS: 1579.51

break at FIFTH\300-MAIN-LOOP\%LINE 269

    269:     ADD WS-COMMISSION TO WS-TOTAL-COMMISSIONS

WS-BRANCH-TOT-COMMISSIONS of FIFTH\WS-CALCULATION-REGISTERS: 1762.53

break at FIFTH\300-MAIN-LOOP\%LINE 269

269:     ADD WS-COMMISSION TO WS-TOTAL-COMMISSIONS
WS-BRANCH-TOT-COMMISSIONS of FIFTH\WS-CALCULATION-REGISTERS: 2070.87
break at FIFTH\300-MAIN-LOOP\%LINE 269
269:     ADD WS-COMMISSION TO WS-TOTAL-COMMISSIONS
WS-BRANCH-TOT-COMMISSIONS of FIFTH\WS-CALCULATION-REGISTERS: 2238.65
break at FIFTH\300-MAIN-LOOP\%LINE 269
269:     ADD WS-COMMISSION TO WS-TOTAL-COMMISSIONS
WS-BRANCH-TOT-COMMISSIONS of FIFTH\WS-CALCULATION-REGISTERS: 24939.71
break at FIFTH\300-MAIN-LOOP\%LINE 269
269:     ADD WS-COMMISSION TO WS-TOTAL-COMMISSIONS
WS-BRANCH-TOT-COMMISSIONS of FIFTH\WS-CALCULATION-REGISTERS: 25765.78
break at FIFTH\300-MAIN-LOOP\%LINE 269
269:     ADD WS-COMMISSION TO WS-TOTAL-COMMISSIONS
WS-BRANCH-TOT-COMMISSIONS of FIFTH\WS-CALCULATION-REGISTERS: 25765.82
break at FIFTH\300-MAIN-LOOP\%LINE 269
269:     ADD WS-COMMISSION TO WS-TOTAL-COMMISSIONS
WS-BRANCH-TOT-COMMISSIONS of FIFTH\WS-CALCULATION-REGISTERS: 25828.23
break at FIFTH\300-MAIN-LOOP\%LINE 269
269:     ADD WS-COMMISSION TO WS-TOTAL-COMMISSIONS
WS-BRANCH-TOT-COMMISSIONS of FIFTH\WS-CALCULATION-REGISTERS: 0.00
break at FIFTH\300-MAIN-LOOP\%LINE 269
269:     ADD WS-COMMISSION TO WS-TOTAL-COMMISSIONS
WS-BRANCH-TOT-COMMISSIONS of FIFTH\WS-CALCULATION-REGISTERS: 2199.36
break at FIFTH\300-MAIN-LOOP\%LINE 269
269:     ADD WS-COMMISSION TO WS-TOTAL-COMMISSIONS
WS-BRANCH-TOT-COMMISSIONS of FIFTH\WS-CALCULATION-REGISTERS: 2263.54
break at FIFTH\300-MAIN-LOOP\%LINE 269
269:     ADD WS-COMMISSION TO WS-TOTAL-COMMISSIONS
WS-BRANCH-TOT-COMMISSIONS of FIFTH\WS-CALCULATION-REGISTERS: 17915.34
break at FIFTH\300-MAIN-LOOP\%LINE 269
269:     ADD WS-COMMISSION TO WS-TOTAL-COMMISSIONS
WS-BRANCH-TOT-COMMISSIONS of FIFTH\WS-CALCULATION-REGISTERS: 17962.34
break at FIFTH\300-MAIN-LOOP\%LINE 269
269:     ADD WS-COMMISSION TO WS-TOTAL-COMMISSIONS
WS-BRANCH-TOT-COMMISSIONS of FIFTH\WS-CALCULATION-REGISTERS: 517907.34
break at FIFTH\300-MAIN-LOOP\%LINE 269
269:     ADD WS-COMMISSION TO WS-TOTAL-COMMISSIONS
WS-BRANCH-TOT-COMMISSIONS of FIFTH\WS-CALCULATION-REGISTERS: 517917.26
break at FIFTH\300-MAIN-LOOP\%LINE 269
269:     ADD WS-COMMISSION TO WS-TOTAL-COMMISSIONS
WS-BRANCH-TOT-COMMISSIONS of FIFTH\WS-CALCULATION-REGISTERS: 517925.19
break at FIFTH\300-MAIN-LOOP\%LINE 269
269:     ADD WS-COMMISSION TO WS-TOTAL-COMMISSIONS
WS-BRANCH-TOT-COMMISSIONS of FIFTH\WS-CALCULATION-REGISTERS: 0.00
break at FIFTH\300-MAIN-LOOP\%LINE 269
269:     ADD WS-COMMISSION TO WS-TOTAL-COMMISSIONS
WS-BRANCH-TOT-COMMISSIONS of FIFTH\WS-CALCULATION-REGISTERS: 7719.43
break at FIFTH\300-MAIN-LOOP\%LINE 269
269:     ADD WS-COMMISSION TO WS-TOTAL-COMMISSIONS
WS-BRANCH-TOT-COMMISSIONS of FIFTH\WS-CALCULATION-REGISTERS: 7778.41
break at FIFTH\300-MAIN-LOOP\%LINE 269
269:     ADD WS-COMMISSION TO WS-TOTAL-COMMISSIONS

WS-BRANCH-TOT-COMMISSIONS of FIFTH\WS-CALCULATION-REGISTERS: 7807.61
break at FIFTH\300-MAIN-LOOP\%LINE 269
    269:    ADD WS-COMMISSION TO WS-TOTAL-COMMISSIONS
WS-BRANCH-TOT-COMMISSIONS of FIFTH\WS-CALCULATION-REGISTERS: 9000.51
break at FIFTH\300-MAIN-LOOP\%LINE 269
    269:    ADD WS-COMMISSION TO WS-TOTAL-COMMISSIONS
WS-BRANCH-TOT-COMMISSIONS of FIFTH\WS-CALCULATION-REGISTERS: 9031.15
break at FIFTH\300-MAIN-LOOP\%LINE 269
    269:    ADD WS-COMMISSION TO WS-TOTAL-COMMISSIONS
WS-BRANCH-TOT-COMMISSIONS of FIFTH\WS-CALCULATION-REGISTERS: 9031.18
break at FIFTH\300-MAIN-LOOP\%LINE 269
    269:    ADD WS-COMMISSION TO WS-TOTAL-COMMISSIONS
WS-BRANCH-TOT-COMMISSIONS of FIFTH\WS-CALCULATION-REGISTERS: 9208.69
break at FIFTH\300-MAIN-LOOP\%LINE 269
    269:    ADD WS-COMMISSION TO WS-TOTAL-COMMISSIONS
WS-BRANCH-TOT-COMMISSIONS of FIFTH\WS-CALCULATION-REGISTERS: 12053.41
break at FIFTH\300-MAIN-LOOP\%LINE 269
    269:    ADD WS-COMMISSION TO WS-TOTAL-COMMISSIONS
WS-BRANCH-TOT-COMMISSIONS of FIFTH\WS-CALCULATION-REGISTERS: 12055.76
break at FIFTH\300-MAIN-LOOP\%LINE 269
    269:    ADD WS-COMMISSION TO WS-TOTAL-COMMISSIONS
WS-BRANCH-TOT-COMMISSIONS of FIFTH\WS-CALCULATION-REGISTERS: 12093.50
break at FIFTH\300-MAIN-LOOP\%LINE 269
    269:    ADD WS-COMMISSION TO WS-TOTAL-COMMISSIONS
WS-BRANCH-TOT-COMMISSIONS of FIFTH\WS-CALCULATION-REGISTERS: 0.00
break at FIFTH\300-MAIN-LOOP\%LINE 269
    269:    ADD WS-COMMISSION TO WS-TOTAL-COMMISSIONS
WS-BRANCH-TOT-COMMISSIONS of FIFTH\WS-CALCULATION-REGISTERS: 3.20
break at FIFTH\300-MAIN-LOOP\%LINE 269
    269:    ADD WS-COMMISSION TO WS-TOTAL-COMMISSIONS
WS-BRANCH-TOT-COMMISSIONS of FIFTH\WS-CALCULATION-REGISTERS: 5183.95
break at FIFTH\300-MAIN-LOOP\%LINE 269
    269:    ADD WS-COMMISSION TO WS-TOTAL-COMMISSIONS
WS-BRANCH-TOT-COMMISSIONS of FIFTH\WS-CALCULATION-REGISTERS: 5240.41
break at FIFTH\300-MAIN-LOOP\%LINE 269
    269:    ADD WS-COMMISSION TO WS-TOTAL-COMMISSIONS
WS-BRANCH-TOT-COMMISSIONS of FIFTH\WS-CALCULATION-REGISTERS: 504860.44
break at FIFTH\300-MAIN-LOOP\%LINE 269
    269:    ADD WS-COMMISSION TO WS-TOTAL-COMMISSIONS
WS-BRANCH-TOT-COMMISSIONS of FIFTH\WS-CALCULATION-REGISTERS: 1199708.95
break at FIFTH\300-MAIN-LOOP\%LINE 269
    269:    ADD WS-COMMISSION TO WS-TOTAL-COMMISSIONS
WS-BRANCH-TOT-COMMISSIONS of FIFTH\WS-CALCULATION-REGISTERS: 0.00
break at FIFTH\300-MAIN-LOOP\%LINE 269
    269:    ADD WS-COMMISSION TO WS-TOTAL-COMMISSIONS
WS-BRANCH-TOT-COMMISSIONS of FIFTH\WS-CALCULATION-REGISTERS: 0.07
break at FIFTH\300-MAIN-LOOP\%LINE 269
    269:    ADD WS-COMMISSION TO WS-TOTAL-COMMISSIONS
WS-BRANCH-TOT-COMMISSIONS of FIFTH\WS-CALCULATION-REGISTERS: 0.07
break at FIFTH\300-MAIN-LOOP\%LINE 269
    269:    ADD WS-COMMISSION TO WS-TOTAL-COMMISSIONS
WS-BRANCH-TOT-COMMISSIONS of FIFTH\WS-CALCULATION-REGISTERS: 547.96

```
break at FIFTH\300-MAIN-LOOP\%LINE 269
    269:      ADD WS-COMMISSION TO WS-TOTAL-COMMISSIONS
WS-BRANCH-TOT-COMMISSIONS of FIFTH\WS-CALCULATION-REGISTERS:          548.20
break at FIFTH\300-MAIN-LOOP\%LINE 269
    269:      ADD WS-COMMISSION TO WS-TOTAL-COMMISSIONS
WS-BRANCH-TOT-COMMISSIONS of FIFTH\WS-CALCULATION-REGISTERS:          26227.75
break at FIFTH\300-MAIN-LOOP\%LINE 269
    269:      ADD WS-COMMISSION TO WS-TOTAL-COMMISSIONS
WS-BRANCH-TOT-COMMISSIONS of FIFTH\WS-CALCULATION-REGISTERS:          26323.72
break at FIFTH\300-MAIN-LOOP\%LINE 269
    269:      ADD WS-COMMISSION TO WS-TOTAL-COMMISSIONS
WS-BRANCH-TOT-COMMISSIONS of FIFTH\WS-CALCULATION-REGISTERS:          26326.13
break at FIFTH\300-MAIN-LOOP\%LINE 269
    269:      ADD WS-COMMISSION TO WS-TOTAL-COMMISSIONS
WS-BRANCH-TOT-COMMISSIONS of FIFTH\WS-CALCULATION-REGISTERS:          26488.41
break at FIFTH\300-MAIN-LOOP\%LINE 269
    269:      ADD WS-COMMISSION TO WS-TOTAL-COMMISSIONS
WS-BRANCH-TOT-COMMISSIONS of FIFTH\WS-CALCULATION-REGISTERS:          0.00
break at FIFTH\300-MAIN-LOOP\%LINE 269
    269:      ADD WS-COMMISSION TO WS-TOTAL-COMMISSIONS
WS-BRANCH-TOT-COMMISSIONS of FIFTH\WS-CALCULATION-REGISTERS:          49.64
break at FIFTH\300-MAIN-LOOP\%LINE 269
    269:      ADD WS-COMMISSION TO WS-TOTAL-COMMISSIONS
WS-BRANCH-TOT-COMMISSIONS of FIFTH\WS-CALCULATION-REGISTERS:          150.34
break at FIFTH\300-MAIN-LOOP\%LINE 269
    269:      ADD WS-COMMISSION TO WS-TOTAL-COMMISSIONS
WS-BRANCH-TOT-COMMISSIONS of FIFTH\WS-CALCULATION-REGISTERS:          3079.01
break at FIFTH\300-MAIN-LOOP\%LINE 269
    269:      ADD WS-COMMISSION TO WS-TOTAL-COMMISSIONS
WS-BRANCH-TOT-COMMISSIONS of FIFTH\WS-CALCULATION-REGISTERS:          3757.02
break at FIFTH\300-MAIN-LOOP\%LINE 269
    269:      ADD WS-COMMISSION TO WS-TOTAL-COMMISSIONS
WS-BRANCH-TOT-COMMISSIONS of FIFTH\WS-CALCULATION-REGISTERS:          3827.44
break at FIFTH\300-MAIN-LOOP\%LINE 269
    269:      ADD WS-COMMISSION TO WS-TOTAL-COMMISSIONS
WS-BRANCH-TOT-COMMISSIONS of FIFTH\WS-CALCULATION-REGISTERS:          3831.14
break at FIFTH\300-MAIN-LOOP\%LINE 269
    269:      ADD WS-COMMISSION TO WS-TOTAL-COMMISSIONS
WS-BRANCH-TOT-COMMISSIONS of FIFTH\WS-CALCULATION-REGISTERS:          3841.18
break at FIFTH\300-MAIN-LOOP\%LINE 269
    269:      ADD WS-COMMISSION TO WS-TOTAL-COMMISSIONS
WS-BRANCH-TOT-COMMISSIONS of FIFTH\WS-CALCULATION-REGISTERS:          5278.40
break at FIFTH\300-MAIN-LOOP\%LINE 269
    269:      ADD WS-COMMISSION TO WS-TOTAL-COMMISSIONS
WS-BRANCH-TOT-COMMISSIONS of FIFTH\WS-CALCULATION-REGISTERS:          930069.87
break at FIFTH\300-MAIN-LOOP\%LINE 269
    269:      ADD WS-COMMISSION TO WS-TOTAL-COMMISSIONS
WS-BRANCH-TOT-COMMISSIONS of FIFTH\WS-CALCULATION-REGISTERS:          931425.90
%DEBUG-I-EXITSTATUS, is '%SYSTEM-S-NORMAL, normal successful completion'
8 →  DBG)exit
     $
```

SAMPLE DEBUGGER SESSION—B

$ run main
VAX-11 DEBUG Version X3B-8
%DEBUG-I-INITIAL, language is COBOL, module set to 'DRIVER'

9 → DBG)show module

module name	symbols	language	size
DRIVER	yes	COBOL	132
UNSTRING-IT	no	COBOL	960
SORTER	no	COBOL	2048
REPORTER	no	COBOL	844
DATE-GETTER	no	COBOL	868
SHARE$VMSRTL	no	Image	0
SHARE$DEBUG	no	Image	0
SHARE$LBRSHR	no	Image	0
SHARE$PLIRTL	no	Image	0

total modules: 9.   remaining size: 54724.

10 → DBG)set break %line 49 do(examine price-out;go)
%DEBUG-I-LINEINFO, no line 49, previous line is 12
%DEBUG-W-NOSYMBOL, symbol '%LINE 49' is not in the symbol table
DBG)set module unstring-it
DBG)show module

module name	symbols	language	size
DRIVER	yes	COBOL	132
UNSTRING-IT	yes	COBOL	960
SORTER	no	COBOL	2048
REPORTER	no	COBOL	844
DATE-GETTER	no	COBOL	868
SHARE$VMSRTL	no	Image	0
SHARE$DEBUG	no	Image	0
SHARE$LBRSHR	no	Image	0
SHARE$PLIRTL	no	Image	0

total modules: 9.   remaining size: 53636.
DBG)set break %line 49 do(examine price-out;go)
DBG)cancel module unstring-it
DBG)set module sorter
DBG)set break %line 110 do(examine mast-price;go)
DBG)show module

module name	symbols	language	size
DRIVER	yes	COBOL	132
UNSTRING-IT	no	COBOL	960

SORTER	yes	COBOL	2048
REPORTER	no	COBOL	844
DATE-GETTER	no	COBOL	868
SHARE$VMSRTL	no	Image	0
SHARE$DEBUG	no	Image	0
SHARE$LBRSHR	no	Image	0
SHARE$PLIRTL	no	Image	0

total modules: 9.   remaining size: 51880.

11 →   DBG)set break %line 70 do(examine mast-price; examine amount;go)
%DEBUG-I-LINEINFO, no line 70, previous line is 12
%DEBUG-W-NOSYMBOL, symbol '%LINE 70' is not in the symbol table
12 →   DBG)cancel module sorter
DBG)set module reporter
DBG)st break %line 70 do(examine mast-price; examine amount;go)
DBG)show break
breakpoint at UNSTRING-IT\200-LOOPER\%LINE 49
   do (EXAMINE PRICE-OUT;go)
breakpoint at SORTER\REPORT-N-MASTER\200-LOOPDELOOP\%LINE 110
   do (EXAMINE MAST-PRICE;go)
breakpoint at REPORTER\200-LOOPS\%LINE 70
   do (EXAMINE MAST-PRICE; examine amount;go)

DBG)go
break at UNSTRING__IT+513
%DEBUG-W-NOSYMBOL, symbol 'PRICE-OUT' is not in the symbol table

DBG)set module/all

DBG)show module
module name	symbols	language	size
DRIVER	yes	COBOL	132
UNSTRING-IT	yes	COBOL	960
SORTER	yes	COBOL	2048
REPORTER	yes	COBOL	844
DATE-GETTER	yes	COBOL	868
SHARE$VMSRTL	no	Image	0
SHARE$DEBUG	no	Image	0
SHARE$LBRSHR	no	Image	0
SHARE$PLIRTL	no	Image	0

total modules: 9.   remaining size: 48276.
DBG)show calls

module name	routine name	line	rel PC	abs PC
*UNSTRING-IT	UNSTRING-IT	49	00000201	00002C31
*DRIVER	DRIVER	9	00000012	00002A12

DBG〉go
break at UNSTRING-IT\200-LOOPER\%LINE 49
   49:      MOVE 1 TO XPOINT.
PRICE-OUT of UNSTRING-IT\OUTREC: "   .50"
break at UNSTRING-IT\200-LOOPER\%LINE 49
   49:      MOVE 1 TO XPOINT.
PRICE-OUT of UNSTRING-IT\OUTREC: " 12.00"
break at UNSTRING-IT\200-LOOPER\%LINE 49
   49:      MOVE 1 TO XPOINT.
PRICE-OUT of UNSTRING-IT\OUTREC: " 80.00"
break at UNSTRING-IT\200-LOOPER\%LINE 49
   49:      MOVE 1 TO XPOINT.
PRICE-OUT of UNSTRING-IT\OUTREC: " 6.50"
break at UNSTRING-IT\200-LOOPER\%LINE 49
   49:      MOVE 1 TO XPOINT.
PRICE-OUT of UNSTRING-IT\OUTREC: " 1.50"
break at UNSTRING-IT\200-LOOPER\%LINE 49
   49:      MOVE 1 TO XPOINT.
PRICE-OUT of UNSTRING-IT\OUTREC: "140.00"
break at UNSTRING-IT\200-LOOPER\%LINE 49
   49:      MOVE 1 TO XPOINT.
PRICE-OUT of UNSTRING-IT\OUTREC: "650.00"
break at SORTER\REPORT-N-MASTER\200-LOOPDELOOP\%LINE 110
   110:      MOVE SORT-DESC   TO MAST-DESC
MAST-PRICE of SORTER\WORK-MAST-REC: 130.00
break at SORTER\REPORT-N-MASTER\200-LOOPDELOOP\%LINE 110
   110:      MOVE SORT-DESC   TO MAST-DESC
MAST-PRICE of SORTER\WORK-MAST-REC: 45.00
break at SORTER\REPORT-N-MASTER\200-LOOPDELOOP\%LINE 110
   110:      MOVE SORT-DESC   TO MAST-DESC
MAST-PRICE of SORTER\WORK-MAST-REC: 15.50
break at SORTER\REPORT-N-MASTER\200-LOOPDELOOP\%LINE 110
   110:      MOVE SORT-DESC   TO MAST-DESC
MAST-PRICE of SORTER\WORK-MAST-REC: 650.00
break at SORTER\REPORT-N-MASTER\200-LOOPDELOOP\%LINE 110
   110:      MOVE SORT-DESC   TO MAST-DESC
MAST-PRICE of SORTER\WORK-MAST-REC: 146.20
break at SORTER\REPORT-N-MASTER\200-LOOPDELOOP\%LINE 110
   110:      MOVE SORT-DESC   TO MAST-DESC
MAST-PRICE of SORTER\WORK-MAST-REC: 10.50
break at SORTER\REPORT-N-MASTER\200-LOOPDELOOP\%LINE 110
   110:      MOVE SORT-DESC   TO MAST-DESC
MAST-PRICE of SORTER\WORK-MAST-REC: 20.00
break at SORTER\REPORT-N-MASTER\200-LOOPDELOOP\%LINE 110
   110:      MOVE SORT-DESC   TO MAST-DESC
MAST-PRICE of SORTER\WORK-MAST-REC: 10.50

```
break at SORTER\REPORT-N-MASTER\200-LOOPDELOOP\%LINE 110
    110:        MOVE SORT-DESC    TO MAST-DESC
MAST-PRICE of SORTER\WORK-MAST-REC:      2.00
break at SORTER\REPORT-N-MASTER\200-LOOPDELOOP\%LINE 110
    110:        MOVE SORT-DESC    TO MAST-DESC
MAST-PRICE of SORTER\WORK-MAST-REC:      17.20
break at SORTER\REPORT-N-MASTER\200-LOOPDELOOP\%LINE 110
    110:        MOVE SORT-DESC    TO MAST-DESC
MAST-PRICE of SORTER\WORK-MAST-REC:      8.60
break at SORTER\REPORT-N-MASTER\200-LOOPDELOOP\%LINE 110
    110:        MOVE SORT-DESC    TO MAST-DESC
MAST-PRICE of SORTER\WORK-MAST-REC:      0.50
break at SORTER\REPORT-N-MASTER\200-LOOPDELOOP\%LINE 110
    110:        MOVE SORT-DESC    TO MAST-DESC
MAST-PRICE of SORTER\WORK-MAST-REC:      4.50
break at SORTER\REPORT-N-MASTER\200-LOOPDELOOP\%LINE 110
    110:        MOVE SORT-DESC    TO MAST-DESC
MAST-PRICE of SORTER\WORK-MAST-REC:      140.00
break at SORTER\REPORT-N-MASTER\200-LOOPDELOOP\%LINE 110
    110:        MOVE SORT-DESC    TO MAST-DESC
MAST-PRICE of SORTER\WORK-MAST-REC:      6.50
break at SORTER\REPORT-N-MASTER\200-LOOPDELOOP\%LINE 110
    110:        MOVE SORT-DESC    TO MAST-DESC
MAST-PRICE of SORTER\WORK-MAST-REC:      4.60
break at SORTER\REPORT-N-MASTER\200-LOOPDELOOP\%LINE 110
    110:        MOVE SORT-DESC    TO MAST-DESC
MAST-PRICE of SORTER\WORK-MAST-REC:      1.50
break at SORTER\REPORT-N-MASTER\200-LOOPDELOOP\%LINE 110
    110:        MOVE SORT-DESC    TO MAST-DESC
MAST-PRICE of SORTER\WORK-MAST-REC:      1.50
break at SORTER\REPORT-N-MASTER\200-LOOPDELOOP\%LINE 110
    110:        MOVE SORT-DESC    TO MAST-DESC
MAST-PRICE of SORTER\WORK-MAST-REC:      80.00
break at REPORTER\200-LOOPS\%LINE 70
    70:      READ INFILE AT END MOVE "YES" TO SWITCH.
MAST-PRICE of REPORTER\INREC: 130.00
REPORTER\AMOUNT:       1300.00
break at REPORTER\200-LOOPS\%LINE 70
    70:      READ INFILE AT END MOVE "YES" TO SWITCH.
MAST-PRICE of REPORTER\INREC: 45.00
REPORTER\AMOUNT:       360.00
break at REPORTER\200-LOOPS\%LINE 70
    70:      READ INFILE AT END MOVE "YES" TO SWITCH.
MAST-PRICE of REPORTER\INREC: 15.50
REPORTER\AMOUNT:       155.00
```

break at REPORTER\200-LOOPS\%LINE 70
   70:     READ INFILE AT END MOVE "YES" TO SWITCH.
MAST-PRICE of REPORTER\INREC: 650.00
REPORTER\AMOUNT: 650.00
break at REPORTER\200-LOOPS\%LINE 70
   70:     READ INFILE AT END MOVE "YES" TO SWITCH.
MAST-PRICE of REPORTER\INREC: 146.20
REPORTER\AMOUNT: 292.40
break at REPORTER\200-LOOPS\%LINE 70
   70:     READ INFILE AT END MOVE "YES" TO SWITCH.
MAST-PRICE of REPORTER\INREC: 10.50
REPORTER\AMOUNT: 157.50
break at REPORTER\200-LOOPS\%LINE 70
   70:     READ INFILE AT END MOVE "YES" TO SWITCH.
MAST-PRICE of REPORTER\INREC: 20.00
REPORTER\AMOUNT: 100.00
break at REPORTER\200-LOOPS\%LINE 70
   70:     READ INFILE AT END MOVE "YES" TO SWITCH.
MAST-PRICE of REPORTER\INREC: 10.50
REPORTER\AMOUNT: 157.50
break at REPORTER\200-LOOPS\%LINE 70
   70:     READ INFILE AT END MOVE "YES" TO SWITCH.
MAST-PRICE of REPORTER\INREC: 2.00
REPORTER\AMOUNT: 200.00
break at REPORTER\200-LOOPS\%LINE 70
   70:     READ INFILE AT END MOVE "YES" TO SWITCH.
MAST-PRICE of REPORTER\INREC: 17.20
REPORTER\AMOUNT: 172.00
break at REPORTER\200-LOOPS\%LINE 70
   70:     READ INFILE AT END MOVE "YES" TO SWITCH.
MAST-PRICE of REPORTER\INREC: 8.60
REPORTER\AMOUNT: 86.00
break at REPORTER\200-LOOPS\%LINE 70
   70:     READ INFILE AT END MOVE "YES" TO SWITCH.
MAST-PRICE of REPORTER\INREC: 0.50
REPORTER\AMOUNT: 25.00
break at REPORTER\200-LOOPS\%LINE 70
   70:     READ INFILE AT END MOVE "YES" TO SWITCH.
MAST-PRICE of REPORTER\INREC: 4.50
REPORTER\AMOUNT: 450.00
break at REPORTER\200-LOOPS\%LINE 70
   70:     READ INFILE AT END MOVE "YES" TO SWITCH.
MAST-PRICE of REPORTER\INREC: 140.00
REPORTER\AMOUNT: 840.00
break at REPORTER\200-LOOPS\%LINE 70

```
        70:      READ INFILE AT END MOVE "YES" TO SWITCH.
MAST-PRICE of REPORTER\INREC: 6.50
REPORTER\AMOUNT:       1495.00
break at REPORTER\200-LOOPS\%LINE 70
        70:      READ INFILE AT END MOVE "YES" TO SWITCH.
MAST-PRICE of REPORTER\INREC: 4.60
REPORTER\AMOUNT:         46.00
break at REPORTER\200-LOOPS\%LINE 70
        70:      READ INFILE AT END MOVE "YES" TO SWITCH.
MAST-PRICE of REPORTER\INREC: 1.50
REPORTER\AMOUNT:         18.00
break at REPORTER\200-LOOPS\%LINE 70
        70:      READ INFILE AT END MOVE "YES" TO SWITCH.
MAST-PRICE of REPORTER\INREC: 1.50
REPORTER\AMOUNT:        150.00
break at REPORTER\200-LOOPS\%LINE 70
        70:      READ INFILE AT END MOVE "YES" TO SWITCH.
MAST-PRICE of REPORTER\INREC: 80.00
REPORTER\AMOUNT:        400.00
```

13 → %DEBUG-I-EXITSTATUS, is '%SYSTEM-S-NORMAL, normal successful completion'

DBG)exit

Appendix B

Magnetic Disk
File Concepts

The two most common types of auxiliary storage (secondary storage) devices in use today are magnetic tapes and magnetic disks. Magnetic tape storage is quite similar to audio/video tape storage. Each consists of the unit itself and the tape for recording or playing. Magnetic disk storage devices are more complex. A magnetic disk unit usually consists of more than one disk separated from another as shown in Figure B-1.

In contrast to tape units that have only one area to write and/or read, these disk units allow for access to the top and bottom of all recording surfaces. Although magnetic tape devices are cheaper, only one kind of file structure can be used: sequential files. In contrast, magnetic disk storage units allow for sequential, relative, and indexed files. This appendix will concentrate on files stored on magnetic disk units.

The efficient and flexible storage, retrieval, and modification of files on magnetic disk (and other storage units) are the result of a subsystem of the VAX/VMS operating system called VAX-11 RMS (Record Management Services). With RMS, the VAX/VMS file system implements the disk structure and provides access control to the files located on the disk.

A block, 512 8-bit bytes (characters), is the smallest addressable unit of information on a disk. Blocks are organized into clusters. The cluster size, which can range from 1 to over 65,535, is determined by the system manager

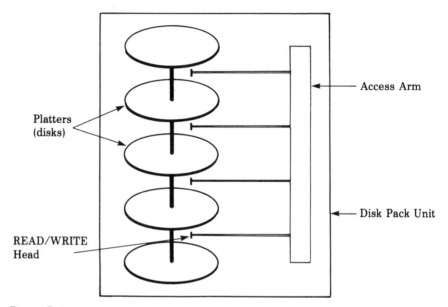

Figure B-1

or operator. A file allocated to contiguous clusters is called an extent. Some-times the file is small enough for one extent, or the file can be divided into two or more parts, each part with its own extent. A typical hierarchy of blocks, clusters, extents, and files is shown in Figure B-2.

The disk structure itself consists of tracks and cylinders. A track is a collection of blocks at a single radius on one recording surface, and a cylin-der consists of all tracks at the same radius on all recording surfaces of a disk. If there are, for example, 100 tracks per recording surface and 10 surfaces, then there are 100 cylinders of 10 tracks each. It is advantageous to keep re-lated data blocks, clusters, on the same cylinder so that movement of read/write heads is kept at a minimum.

A common disk drive unit, the RM05, contains 20 recording surfaces with 823 tracks per surface. Each track contains 32 sectors, and each sector contains 512 bytes. More than 256 million characters can be stored on this disk unit.

A file is made up of records. Each record can be less than, same as, or more than a block. These records, making up the file, can be organized into three physical arrangements: sequential, relative, or indexed.

In sequential file organization, records are arranged one after the other and appear in the order in which they were originally written to this file.

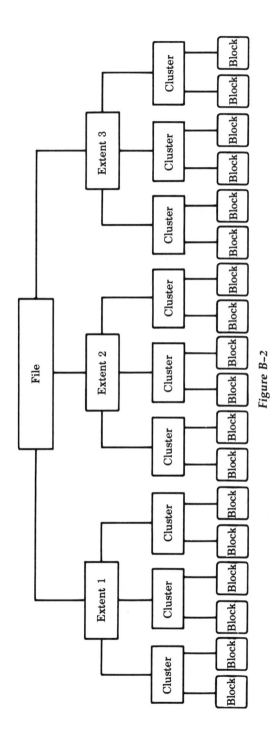

Figure B-2

With this type of organization you can only add records at the current end of the file. To access (read) a particular record in a sequential file, one must open the file and read one record after another. You cannot back up during sequential access; rather the file has to be closed and reopened, and record after record read again.

A second method of file organization is called relative file organization. It consists of a series of fixed-length positions (cells) that are numbered consecutively from 1 to n. A record's position RELATIVE to the beginning of the file is the relative record number. If the third record is written in the seventh cell, it would have a relative record number 7. Empty cells may be available for the addition of other records. When records are deleted these positions are opened. The cells are of fixed length although the records themselves can be variable in size. To randomly access these records one needs to provide the relative record number. An easy method of keeping track of each record's cell is to store records using a numeric value within the record, for example, making an employee number equivalent to the relative record number. Since these fixed-length cells let VAX-11 RMS calculate the record's actual position, records do not have to be read serially until the particular record in question is found; hence, this type of organization can only be present on disks.

Sequential and relative file organizations are represented schematically in Figures B-3 and B-4.

Indexed file organization is the third and final type of file organization and is only available on disk devices. This type of organization allows you to store records in predefined orders of sorting. The sorting of records within

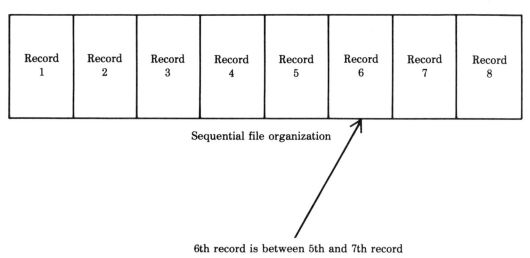

Sequential file organization

6th record is between 5th and 7th record

Figure B-3

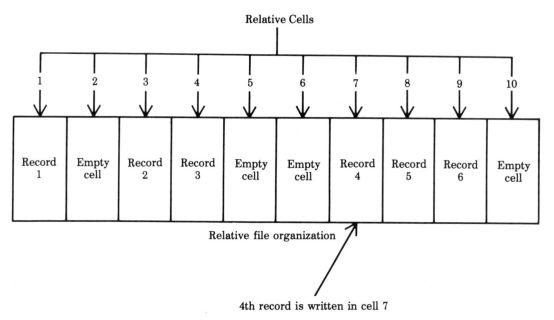

Figure B-4

the file is on certain keys, which are specific fields within each record. Each indexed file must have at least one key (primary) on sort order. Additional (alternate) keys need not be in sort order within the file. The primary keys must be unique. Typical primary keys may be numeric (account number or social security number, for example) or alphanumeric (full name or some type of code). Alternate keys, however, can have duplicate values. VAX-11 RMS builds and maintains a separate index for each key that is defined for the file, and each index is stored in the file. An example of an indexed file with only a primary key is diagrammed in Figure B-5, followed by a diagram depicting an indexed file with one alternate key, Figure B-6.

Notice that the index records are placed in groups called buckets. The amount of records placed in a bucket depends on the size of the bucket and the size of the records. The last record in the bucket has the highest key value. This highest key value, along with a pointer to the data bucket, is copied to an index record on the next level of the index structure. If all key values can fit into this higher level, then this level is known as the Root Level for that index structure.

Suppose one wanted to access a record with a primary key equal to 27. Using random access, the search would begin at the start of the Root Level until a value was found that was greater than 27. A pointer at that value directs the search to the appropriate bucket. The search would continue at the

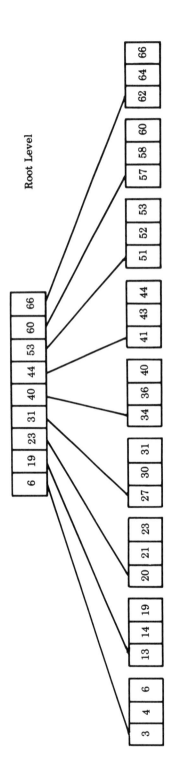

A Primary Index Structure

Figure B-5

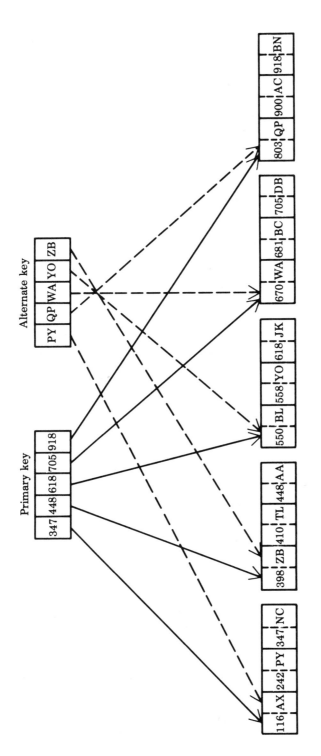

Figure B-6

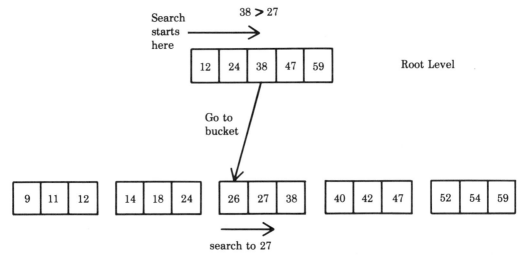

Figure B-7

bucket (lower level) until the record was found. Records can be updated and rewritten to the same bucket.

If one wanted to add records to an indexed file and a particular bucket was full, a bucket split would occur with half the records remaining in one bucket and the other half going to the new bucket. The Root Level would change also.

Diagrams depicting a search for record 27 and the addition of record 46 are shown in Figures B-7 and B-8.

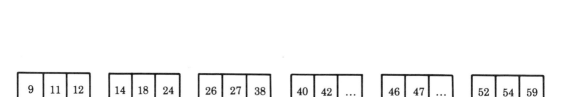

Figure B-8

Appendix C

COBOL Reserved Words

ACCEPT	ASSIGN	COLLATING
ACCESS	AT	COLUMN
ADD	AUTHOR	COMMA
ADVANCING	BEFORE	COMMIT
AFTER	BLANK	COMMON
ALL	BLOCK	COMMUNICATION
ALLOWING	BOOLEAN	COMP
ALPHABET	BOTTOM	COMP-1
ALPHABETIC	BY	COMP-2
ALPHANUMERIC	CALL	COMP-3
ALPHANUMERIC-EDITED	CANCEL	COMP-4
ALSO	CD	COMP-5
ALTER	CF	COMP-6
ALTERNATE	CH	COMPUTATIONAL
AND	CHARACTER	COMPUTATIONAL-1
ANY	CHARACTERS	COMPUTATIONAL-2
APPLY	CLOCK-UNITS	COMPUTATIONAL-3
ARE	CLOSE	COMPUTATIONAL-4
AREA	COBOL	COMPUTATIONAL-5
AREAS	CODE	COMPUTATIONAL-6
ASCENDING	CODE-SET	COMPUTE

Reprinted by permission of Digital Equipment Corporation, *VAX-11 COBOL Pocket Guide,* August 1980.

CONFIGURATION	DELETE	ENVIRONMENT
CONNECT	DELIMITER	EOP
CONTAINS	DEPENDING	EQUAL
CONTENT	DESCENDING	ERASE
CONTINUE	DESCRIPTOR	ERROR
CONTROL	DESTINATION	ESI
CONTROLS	DETAIL	EVALUATE
CONVERSION	DISABLE	EVERY
CONVERTING	DISCONNECT	EXCEPTION
COPY	DISPLAY	EXCLUSIVE
CORR	DISPLAY-6	EXIT
CORRESPONDING	DISPLAY-7	EXOR
COUNT	DISPLAY-9	EXTEND
CURRENCY	DIVIDE	EXTERNAL
CURRENT	DIVISION	FILE
DATA	DOWN	FILE-CONTROL
DATE	DUPLICATE	FILLER
DATE-COMPILED	DUPLICATES	FINAL
DATE-WRITTEN	DYNAMIC	FIND
DAY	EGI	FINISH
DAY-OF-WEEK	ELSE	FIRST
DB	EMI	FOOTING
DB-ACCESS-CONTROL-KEY	EMPTY	FOR
DB-EXCEPTION	ENABLE	FREE
DB-RECORD-NAME	END	FROM
DB-SET-NAME	END-ADD	GENERATE
DB-STATUS	END-CALL	GET
DE	END-COMPUTE	GIVING
DEBUG-CONTENTS	END-DELETE	GLOBAL
DEBUG-ITEM	END-DIVIDE	GO
DEBUG-LENGTH	END-IF	GREATER
DEBUG-LINE	END-MULTIPLY	GROUP
DEBUG-NAME	END-OF-PAGE	HEADING
DEBUG-NUMERIC-CONTENTS	END-PERFORM	HIGH-VALUE
DEBUG-SIZE	END-READ	HIGH-VALUES
DEBUG-START	END-RECEIVE	I-O
DEBUG-SUB	END-RETURN	I-O-CONTROL
DEBUG-SUB-ITEM	END-REWRITE	IDENTIFICATION
DEBUG-SUB-N	END-SEARCH	IF
DEBUG-SUB-1	END-START	IN
DEBUG-SUB-2	END-STRING	INCLUDING
DEBUG-SUB-3	END-SUBTRACT	INDEX
DEBUGGING	END-UNSTRING	INDEXED
DECIMAL-POINT	END-WRITE	INITIAL
DECLARATIVES	ENTER	INITIALIZE

INITIATE
INPUT
INPUT-OUTPUT
INSPECT
INSTALLATION
INTO
INVALID
IS
JUST
JUSTIFIED
KEEP
KEY
LABEL
LAST
LD
LEADING
LEFT
LENGTH
LESS
LIMIT
LIMITS
LINAGE
LINAGE-COUNTER
LINE
LINE-COUNTER
LINES
LINKAGE
LOCK
LOW-VALUE
LOW-VALUES
MEMBER
MEMBERSHIP
MEMORY
MERGE
MESSAGE
MODE
MODIFY
MODULES
MOVE
MULTIPLE
MULTIPLY
NATIVE
NEGATIVE
NEXT
NO

NOT
NULL
NUMBER
NUMERIC
NUMERIC-EDITED
OBJECT-COMPUTER
OCCURS
OF
OFF
OMITTED
ON
ONLY
OPEN
OPTIONAL
OR
ORDER
ORGANIZATION
OTHER
OTHERS
OUTPUT
OVERFLOW
OWNER
PADDING
PAGE
PAGE-COUNTER
PERFORM
PF
PH
PIC
PICTURE
PLUS
POINTER
POSITION
POSITIVE
PRINTING
PRIOR
PROCEDURE
PROCEDURES
PROCEED
PROGRAM
PROGRAM-ID
PROTECTED
PURGE
QUEUE
QUOTE

QUOTES
RANDOM
RD
READ
READERS
READY
REALM
REALMS
RECEIVE
RECORD
RECORD-NAME
RECORDS
REDEFINES
REEL
REFERENCE
REFERENCE-MODIFIER
REFERENCES
RELATIVE
RELEASE
REMAINDER
REMOVAL
RENAMES
REPLACE
REPLACING
REPORT
REPORTING
REPORTS
RERUN
RESERVE
RESET
RETAINING
RETRIEVAL
RETURN
REVERSED
REWIND
REWRITE
RF
RH
RIGHT
ROLLBACK
ROUNDED
RUN
SAME
SD
SEARCH

SECTION
SECURITY
SEGMENT
SEGMENT-LIMIT
SELECT
SEND
SENTENCE
SEPARATE
SEQUENCE
SEQUENTIAL
SET
SIGN
SIZE
SORT
SORT-MERGE
SOURCE
SOURCE-COMPUTER
SPACE
SPACES
SPECIAL-NAMES
STANDARD
STANDARD-1
STANDARD-2
START
STATUS
STOP
STORE
STRING
SUB-QUEUE-1

SUB-QUEUE-2
SUB-QUEUE-3
SUB-SCHEMA
SUBTRACT
SUM
SUPPRESS
SYMBOLIC
SYNC
SYNCHRONIZED
TABLE
TALLYING
TENANT
TERMINAL
TERMINATE
TEST
TEXT
THAN
THEN
THROUGH
THRU
TIME
TIMES
TO
TOP
TRAILING
TRUE
TYPE
UNIT
UNSTRING

UNTIL
UP
UPDATE
UPDATERS
UPON
USAGE
USAGE-MODE
USE
USING
VALUE
VALUES
WHEN
WITH
WITHIN
WORDS
WORKING-STORAGE
WRITE
WRITERS
ZERO
ZEROES
ZEROS
+
−
*
/
**
>
<
=

COBOL Language Formats for VAX-11

COBOL META-LANGUAGE ELEMENTS

Underlined uppercase words are key or required words.

Uppercase words not underlined are optional words.

Lowercase words are generic terms supplied by the programmer.

Brackets [ ] enclose an optional part of a general format. When they enclose vertically stacked entries, brackets indicate that only one entry can be selected.

Braces { } indicate that you must select one (but no more than one) of the enclosed entries.

Choice indicators {| |} enclose part of a general format. One or more of the enclosed entries must be selected; however, none can be used more than once.

Reprinted by permission of Digital Equipment Corporation, *VAX-11 COBOL Pocket Guide*, August, 1980.

Ellipses...allow repetition of a part of the format.

Commas and semicolons indicate optional punctuation.

Periods are required where shown in the format.

COBOL GENERAL FORMATS

IDENTIFICATION DIVISION.
PROGRAM-ID. program-name [IS INITIAL PROGRAM].
[AUTHOR. [comment-entry] ...]
[INSTALLATION. [comment-entry] ...]
[DATE-WRITTEN. [comment-entry] ...]
[DATE-COMPILED. [comment-entry] ...]
[SECURITY. [comment-entry] ...]
[ENVIRONMENT DIVISION.

 [CONFIGURATION SECTION.

    [SOURCE-COMPUTER. [source-computer-entry .]]

    [OBJECT-COMPUTER. [object-computer-entry]]

    [SPECIAL-NAMES. [special-names-entry]]]

[INPUT-OUTPUT SECTION.

    FILE-CONTROL. { file-control-entry } ...

       [I-O-CONTROL. [input-output-control-entry]]]]

SOURCE-COMPUTER. $\begin{bmatrix} \begin{Bmatrix} \text{VAX-11} \\ \text{computer-type} \end{Bmatrix} \end{bmatrix}$

OBJECT-COMPUTER. $\begin{bmatrix} \begin{Bmatrix} \text{VAX-11} \\ \text{computer-type} \end{Bmatrix} \end{bmatrix}$

$\begin{bmatrix} \text{MEMORY SIZE integer } \begin{Bmatrix} \text{WORDS} \\ \text{CHARACTERS} \\ \text{MODULES} \end{Bmatrix} \end{bmatrix}$

$\begin{bmatrix} \text{PROGRAM COLLATING SEQUENCE IS alphabet-name} \\ \begin{bmatrix} \text{SEGMENT-LIMIT IS segment-number} \end{bmatrix} \end{bmatrix}$

SPECIAL-NAMES.

$$\left\{\begin{array}{l} \text{CARD-READER} \\ \text{PAPER-TAPE-READER} \\ \text{CONSOLE} \\ \text{LINE-PRINTER} \\ \text{PAPER-TAPE-PUNCH} \\ \underline{\text{C01}} \end{array}\right\} \text{IS device-name}$$

SWITCH switch-num
$$\left\{\begin{array}{l} \text{IS switch-name [} \underline{\text{ON}} \text{ STATUS IS cond-name] [} \underline{\text{OFF}} \text{ STATUS IS cond-name]} \\ \text{IS switch-name [} \underline{\text{OFF}} \text{ STATUS IS cond-name] [} \underline{\text{ON}} \text{ STATUS IS cond-name]} \\ \underline{\text{ON}} \text{ STATUS IS cond-name [} \underline{\text{OFF}} \text{ STATUS IS cond-name]} \\ \underline{\text{OFF}} \text{ STATUS IS cond-name [} \underline{\text{ON}} \text{ STATUS IS cond-name]} \end{array}\right\} \dots$$

OBJECT-COMPUTER.
$$\left\{\begin{array}{l} \text{VAX-11} \\ \text{computer-type} \end{array}\right\}$$

[MEMORY SIZE integer $\left\{\begin{array}{l} \text{WORDS} \\ \text{CHARACTERS} \\ \text{MODULES} \end{array}\right\}$]

[PROGRAM COLLATING SEQUENCE IS alphabet-name]

[SEGMENT-LIMIT IS segment-number]

SPECIAL-NAMES.

$$\left\{\begin{array}{l} \text{CARD-READER} \\ \text{PAPER-TAPE-READER} \\ \text{CONSOLE} \\ \text{LINE-PRINTER} \\ \text{PAPER-TAPE-PUNCH} \\ \underline{\text{C01}} \end{array}\right\} \text{IS device-name}$$

SWITCH switch-num
$$\left\{\begin{array}{l} \text{IS switch-name [} \underline{\text{ON}} \text{ STATUS IS cond-name] [} \underline{\text{OFF}} \text{ STATUS IS cond-name]} \\ \text{IS switch-name [} \underline{\text{OFF}} \text{ STATUS IS cond-name] [} \underline{\text{ON}} \text{ STATUS IS cond-name]} \\ \underline{\text{ON}} \text{ STATUS IS cond-name [} \underline{\text{OFF}} \text{ STATUS IS cond-name]} \\ \underline{\text{OFF}} \text{ STATUS IS cond-name [} \underline{\text{ON}} \text{ STATUS IS cond-name]} \end{array}\right\} \dots$$

$$
\text{ALPHABET alphabet-name IS}
\left\{
\begin{array}{l}
\left\{
\begin{array}{l}
\underline{\text{ASCII}} \\
\underline{\text{STANDARD-1}} \\
\underline{\text{STANDARD-2}} \\
\underline{\text{NATIVE}} \\
\underline{\text{EBCDIC}}
\end{array}
\right\} \\
\\
\left[
\left\{
\text{first-literal}
\left[
\left\{
\begin{array}{l}
\underline{\text{THRU}} \\
\underline{\text{THROUGH}}
\end{array}
\right\}
\text{last-literal}
\right]
\cdots
\atop
\{\underline{\text{ALSO}}\ \text{lit}\}\ \cdots
\right]
\right\}
\cdots
\right]
\end{array}
\right\}
\cdots
$$

$$
\underline{\text{SYMBOLIC}}\ \text{CHARACTERS}\ \{\ \text{symbolic-char}\ \}\ \cdots
\left\{
\begin{array}{l}
\text{IS} \\
\text{ARE}
\end{array}
\right\}
\{\ \text{char-val}\ \}\ \cdots
$$

[<u>CURRENCY</u> SIGN IS char]

[<u>DECIMAL-POINT</u> IS <u>COMMA</u>] .

<u>FILE-CONTROL</u>.

<u>SELECT</u> [<u>OPTIONAL</u>] file-name

    <u>ASSIGN</u> TO file-spec

$$
\left[
\underline{\text{RESERVE}}\ \text{reserve-num}
\left[
\begin{array}{l}
\text{AREA} \\
\text{AREAS}
\end{array}
\right]
\right]
$$

$$
\left[
[\ \underline{\text{ORGANIZATION}}\ \text{IS}\ ]
\left\{
\begin{array}{l}
\underline{\text{SEQUENTIAL}} \\
\underline{\text{RELATIVE}} \\
\underline{\text{INDEXED}}
\end{array}
\right\}
\right]
$$

$$
\left[
\underline{\text{BLOCK}}\ \text{CONTAINS}\ [\ \text{smallest-block}\ \underline{\text{TO}}\ ]\ \text{blocksize}
\left\{
\begin{array}{l}
\underline{\text{RECORDS}} \\
\text{CHARACTERS}
\end{array}
\right\}
\right]
$$

[<u>CODE-SET</u> IS alphabet-name]

[FILE <u>STATUS</u> IS file-stat]

[<u>ACCESS</u> MODE IS] <u>SEQUENTIAL</u>

$$
[\ \underline{\text{ACCESS}}\ \text{MODE IS}\ ]
\left\{
\begin{array}{l}
\underline{\text{SEQUENTIAL}}\ [\ \underline{\text{RELATIVE}}\ \text{KEY IS}\ \text{rel-key}\ ] \\
\left\{
\begin{array}{l}
\text{RANDOM} \\
\underline{\text{DYNAMIC}}
\end{array}
\right\}
\underline{\text{RELATIVE}}\ \text{KEY IS}\ \text{rel-key}
\end{array}
\right\}
$$

[ACCESS MODE IS] $\left\{ \begin{array}{l} \text{SEQUENTIAL} \\ \text{RANDOM} \\ \text{DYNAMIC} \end{array} \right\}$

[RECORD KEY IS rec-key]

$\left[\text{ALTERNATE RECORD KEY IS alt-key [WITH DUPLICATES]} \right]$ ... $\left.\begin{array}{l}\\\\\end{array}\right\}$ ...

[PADDING CHARACTER IS pad-char]

I-O-CONTROL. $\Big[$

$\left[\text{APPLY} \quad \left\{ \begin{array}{l} \left| \begin{array}{l} \text{DEFERRED-WRITE} \\ \text{EXTENSION extend-amt} \\ \text{FILL-SIZE} \\ \text{MASS-INSERT} \\ \left[\begin{array}{l} \text{CONTIGUOUS} \\ \\ \text{CONTIGUOUS-BEST-TRY} \end{array} \right] \text{PREALLOCATION preall-amt} \\ \text{PRINT-CONTROL} \\ \text{WINDOW window-ptrs} \end{array} \right. \\ \quad \underline{\text{ON}} \{ \text{ file-name } \} \text{ ...} \end{array} \right\} \text{ ...} \right]$

$\left[\text{SAME} \quad \left[\begin{array}{l} \text{RECORD} \\ \text{SORT} \\ \text{SORT-MERGE} \end{array} \right] \text{AREA FOR} \{ \text{ same-area-file } \} \text{ ...} \right]$ ...

$\left[\text{RERUN} \quad [\underline{\text{ON}} \text{ file-name}] \right.$

$\text{EVERY} \left\{ \begin{array}{l} \left\{ \begin{array}{l} [\underline{\text{END}} \text{ OF}] \\ \text{integer } \underline{\text{RECORDS}} \end{array} \right\} \left\{ \begin{array}{l} \underline{\text{REEL}} \\ \underline{\text{UNIT}} \end{array} \right\} \text{OF file-name} \\ \text{integer } \underline{\text{CLOCK-UNITS}} \\ \text{condition-name} \end{array} \right\} \left.\begin{array}{l}\\\\\end{array}\right] \text{ ...} \right]$

$\left[\underline{\text{MULTIPLE FILE}} \text{ TAPE CONTAINS} \left\{ \text{file-name [} \underline{\text{POSITION}} \text{ integer]} \right\} \text{...} \right] \text{ ...} \right]$

$\left[\text{DATA DIVISION.} \right.$

$\left[\text{FILE SECTION.} \right.$

[file-description-entry { record-description-entry } ...] ... $\Big]$

$\left[\underline{\text{WORKING-STORAGE SECTION.}} \right.$

[record-description-entry] ... $\Big]$

$$\begin{bmatrix} \text{LINKAGE SECTION.} \\ \quad [\text{ record-description-entry }] \ \dots \end{bmatrix} \ \end{bmatrix}$$

File description entry:

Format 1

FD file-name

$$\left[\text{ BLOCK CONTAINS } [\text{ smallest-block } \underline{\text{TO}} \text{] blocksize } \backsim \begin{Bmatrix} \underline{\text{RECORDS}} \\ \text{CHARACTERS} \end{Bmatrix} \right]$$

[CODE-SET IS alphabet-name]

$$\left[\underline{\text{RECORD}} \begin{Bmatrix} \text{CONTAINS} \quad [\text{ shortest-rec } \underline{\text{TO}} \text{] } \text{ longest-rec CHARACTERS} \\ \text{IS } \underline{\text{VARYING}} \text{ IN SIZE} \quad \left[[\text{ FROM shortest-rec }] [\underline{\text{TO}} \text{ longest-rec }] \text{ CHARACTERS} \right] \\ [\underline{\text{DEPENDING}} \text{ ON depending-item }] \end{Bmatrix} \right]$$

$$\left[\text{LABEL} \begin{bmatrix} \underline{\text{RECORDS}} \text{ ARE} \\ \text{RECORD IS} \end{bmatrix} \begin{Bmatrix} \underline{\text{STANDARD}} \\ \underline{\text{OMITTED}} \end{Bmatrix} \right]$$

[VALUE OF ID IS file-spec]

$$\left[\underline{\text{DATA}} \begin{bmatrix} \underline{\text{RECORDS}} \text{ ARE} \\ \text{RECORD IS} \end{bmatrix} \{ \text{ rec-name } \} \ \dots \right]$$

[FILE STATUS IS file-stat]

$$\left[[\underline{\text{ACCESS}} \text{ MODE IS }] \underline{\text{SEQUENTIAL}} \right]$$

$$\left[\underline{\text{LINAGE}} \text{ IS } \{ \text{ page-size } \} \text{ LINES } [\text{ WITH } \underline{\text{FOOTING}} \text{ AT footing-line }] \right.$$

$$\left. [\text{ LINES AT } \underline{\text{TOP}} \text{ top-lines }] [\text{ LINES AT } \underline{\text{BOTTOM}} \text{ bottom-lines }] \right] .$$

Format 2

FD   file-name

$$\left[\underline{\text{BLOCK}} \text{ CONTAINS } [\text{ smallest-block } \underline{\text{TO}} \text{] blocksize } \begin{Bmatrix} \underline{\text{RECORDS}} \\ \text{CHARACTERS} \end{Bmatrix} \right]$$

[CODE-SET IS alphabet-name]

$$
\left[\text{RECORD} \left\{ \begin{array}{l} \text{CONTAINS} \quad [\text{ shortest-rec } \underline{\text{TO}} \text{] } \quad \text{longest-rec CHARACTERS} \\ \text{IS } \underline{\text{VARYING}} \text{ IN SIZE} \quad \left[[\text{ FROM shortest-rec] } [\underline{\text{TO}} \text{ longest-rec] CHARACTERS} \right] \\ [\underline{\text{DEPENDING}} \text{ ON depending-item] } \end{array} \right\} \right]
$$

$$
\left[\underline{\text{LABEL}} \left[\begin{array}{l} \underline{\text{RECORDS}} \text{ ARE} \\ \underline{\text{RECORD}} \text{ IS} \end{array} \right] \left\{ \begin{array}{l} \underline{\text{STANDARD}} \\ \underline{\text{OMITTED}} \end{array} \right\} \right]
$$

[VALUE OF ID IS file-spec]

$$
\left[\underline{\text{DATA}} \left[\begin{array}{l} \underline{\text{RECORDS}} \text{ ARE} \\ \underline{\text{RECORD}} \text{ IS} \end{array} \right] \quad \{ \text{ rec-name } \} \ \dots \right]
$$

[FILE STATUS IS file-stat]

$$
\left[[\underline{\text{ACCESS}} \text{ MODE IS] } \left\{ \begin{array}{l} \underline{\text{SEQUENTIAL}} \\ \left\{ \begin{array}{l} \text{RANDOM} \\ \text{DYNAMIC} \end{array} \right\} \end{array} \right. \left\{ \begin{array}{l} [\underline{\text{RELATIVE}} \text{ KEY IS rel-key] } \\ \underline{\text{RELATIVE}} \text{ KEY IS rel-key} \end{array} \right\} \right]
$$

Format 3

<u>FD</u>   file-name

$$
\left[\underline{\text{BLOCK}} \text{ CONTAINS } [\text{ smallest-block } \underline{\text{TO}} \text{] blocksize } \left\{ \begin{array}{l} \underline{\text{RECORDS}} \\ \text{CHARACTERS} \end{array} \right\} \right]
$$

[<u>CODE-SET</u> IS alphabet-name]

$$
\left[\underline{\text{RECORD}} \left\{ \begin{array}{l} \text{CONTAINS} \quad [\text{ shortes-rec } \underline{\text{TO}} \text{] } \quad \text{longest-rec CHARACTERS} \\ \text{IS } \underline{\text{VARYING}} \text{ IN SIZE} \quad \left[[\text{ FROM shortest-rec] } [\underline{\text{TO}} \text{ longest-rec] CHARACTERS} \right] \\ [\underline{\text{DEPENDING}} \text{ ON depending-item] } \end{array} \right\} \right]
$$

$$
\left[\underline{\text{LABEL}} \left[\begin{array}{l} \underline{\text{RECORDS}} \text{ ARE} \\ \underline{\text{RECORD}} \text{ IS} \end{array} \right] \left\{ \begin{array}{l} \underline{\text{STANDARD}} \\ \underline{\text{OMITTED}} \end{array} \right\} \right]
$$

[VALUE OF ID IS file-spec].

$$\left[\text{DATE} \begin{bmatrix} \text{RECORDS ARE} \\ \text{RECORD IS} \end{bmatrix} \{ \text{rec-name} \} \, ... \right]$$

[FILE STATUS IS file-stat]

$$\left[[\text{ACCESS MODE IS}] \begin{Bmatrix} \text{SEQUENTIAL} \\ \text{RANDOM} \\ \text{DYNAMIC} \end{Bmatrix} \right]$$

RECORD KEY IS rec-key

$$\left[\text{ALTERNATE RECORD KEY IS alt-key [WITH DUPLICATES]} \right] \, ...$$

Format 4

SD   file-name

$$\left[\text{RECORD} \begin{Bmatrix} \text{CONTAINS} \quad [\text{shortest-rec TO}] \quad \text{longest-rec CHARACTERS} \\ \text{IS VARYING IN SIZE} \quad \left[[\text{FROM shortest-rec] [TO longest-rec] CHARACTERS} \right] \\ [\text{DEPENDING ON depending-item}] \end{Bmatrix} \right]$$

$$\left[\text{DATA} \begin{bmatrix} \text{RECORDS ARE} \\ \text{RECORD IS} \end{bmatrix} \{ \text{rec-name} \} \, ... \right] .$$

Data description entry:

Format 1

level-number $\begin{bmatrix} \text{data-name} \\ \text{FILLER} \end{bmatrix}$

[REDEFINES other-data-item]

[IS EXTERNAL]

$$\left[\left\{ \begin{array}{l} \underline{PICTURE} \\ \underline{PIC} \end{array} \right\} \text{IS character-string} \right]$$

$$\left[[\underline{USAGE} \text{ IS }] \left\{ \begin{array}{l} \underline{COMPUTATIONAL} \\ \underline{COMP} \\ \underline{COMPUTATIONAL-1} \\ \underline{COMP-1} \\ \underline{COMPUTATIONAL-2} \\ \underline{COMP-2} \\ \underline{COMPUTATIONAL-3} \\ \underline{COMP-3} \\ \underline{DISPLAY} \\ \underline{INDEX} \end{array} \right\} \right]$$

$$\left[[\underline{SIGN} \text{ IS }] \left\{ \begin{array}{l} \underline{LEADING} \\ \underline{TRAILING} \end{array} \right\} [\underline{SEPARATE} \text{ CHARACTER }] \right]$$

$$\left[\begin{array}{l} \underline{OCCURS} \text{ table-size TIMES} \\[4pt] \left[\left\{ \begin{array}{l} \underline{ASCENDING} \\ \underline{DESCENDING} \end{array} \right\} \text{ KEY IS } \{ \text{ key-name } \} \text{ ... } \right] \text{ ... } \\[8pt] [\underline{INDEXED} \text{ BY } \{ \text{ ind-name } \} \text{ ... } \\[8pt] \underline{OCCURS} \text{ min-times } \underline{TO} \text{ max-times TIMES } \underline{DEPENDING} \text{ ON depending-item} \\[4pt] \left[\left\{ \begin{array}{l} \underline{ASCENDING} \\ \underline{DESCENDING} \end{array} \right\} \text{ KEY IS } \{ \text{ key-name } \} \text{ ... } \right] \text{ ... } \\[8pt] [\underline{INDEXED} \text{ BY } \{ \text{ ind-name } \} \text{ ... } \end{array} \right]$$

$$\left[\left\{ \begin{array}{l} \underline{SYNCHRONIZED} \\ \underline{SYNC} \end{array} \right\} \left[\begin{array}{l} \underline{LEFT} \\ \underline{RIGHT} \end{array} \right] \right]$$

$$\left[\left\{ \begin{array}{l} \underline{JUSTIFIED} \\ \underline{JUST} \end{array} \right\} \text{ RIGHT} \right]$$

[BLANK WHEN ZERO]

[VALUE IS lit]

Format 2

66 new-name RENAMES rename-start $\left[\left\{ \begin{array}{l} \underline{THRU} \\ \underline{THROUGH} \end{array} \right\} \text{ rename-end} \right]$

Format 3

88 condition-name

$$\begin{Bmatrix} \underline{VALUE} \text{ IS} \\ \underline{VALUES} \text{ ARE} \end{Bmatrix} \begin{Bmatrix} \text{low-val} \begin{bmatrix} \begin{Bmatrix} \underline{THRU} \\ \underline{THROUGH} \end{Bmatrix} \text{high-val} \end{bmatrix} \end{Bmatrix} \dots \ .$$

Format 1

$\Big[$ <u>PROCEDURE DIVISION</u> [<u>USING</u> { data-name } ...]

    [<u>GIVING</u> identifier]

[<u>DECLARATIVES</u>.

    { section-name <u>SECTION</u> [segment-number]. declarative-sentence

    [paragraph-name. [sentence] ...] ... } ...

    { section-name <u>SECTION</u> [segment-number].

    [paragraph-name. [sentence] ...] ... } ... $\Big]$

Format 2

$\Big[$ <u>PROCEDURE DIVISION</u> [<u>USING</u> { data-name } ...]

    [<u>GIVING</u> identifier].

    [paragraph-name. [sentence] ...] ... $\Big]$

Format 1

<u>ACCEPT</u> dest-item [<u>FROM</u> input-source]

Format 2

$$\underline{ACCEPT} \text{ dest-item } \underline{FROM} \begin{Bmatrix} \text{DATE} \\ \text{DAY} \\ \text{DAY-OF-WEEK} \\ \text{TIME} \end{Bmatrix}$$

Format 1

<u>ADD</u> { num } ... <u>TO</u> { rsult [<u>ROUNDED</u>] } ...

    [ON <u>SIZE</u> <u>ERROR</u> stment [<u>END-ADD</u>]]

Format 2

ADD { num } { num } ... GIVING { rsult [ROUNDED] } ...

[ON SIZE ERROR stment [END-ADD]]

Format 3

$$\text{ADD} \left\{ \begin{array}{l} \underline{\text{CORRESPONDING}} \\ \underline{\text{CORR}} \end{array} \right\} \text{grp-1} \underline{\text{TO}} \text{ grp-2 [} \underline{\text{ROUNDED}} \text{]}$$

[ON SIZE ERROR stment [END-ADD]]

ALTER { proc TO [PROCEED TO] new-proc } ...

CALL prog-name

$$\left[\quad \underline{\text{USING}} \quad \left\{ \left\{ \begin{array}{l} [\text{ BY } \underline{\text{REFERENCE}} \text{]} \\ \text{BY } \underline{\text{VALUE}} \\ \text{BY } \underline{\text{DESCRIPTOR}} \end{array} \right\} \{ \text{ arg } \} ... \right\} \right.$$

$$\left. \left[\left\{ \begin{array}{l} \text{BY } \underline{\text{REFERENCE}} \\ \text{BY } \underline{\text{VALUE}} \\ \text{BY } \underline{\text{DESCRIPTOR}} \end{array} \right\} \{ \text{ arg } \} ... \right] \quad ... \right]$$

[GIVING function-res]

$$\left[\quad \text{ON} \quad \left\{ \begin{array}{l} \underline{\text{EXCEPTION}} \\ \underline{\text{OVERFLOW}} \end{array} \right\} \quad \text{stment} \quad [\underline{\text{END-CALL}}] \right]$$

CANCEL { prog-name } ...

$$\underline{\text{CLOSE}} \left\{ \text{file-name} \left[\begin{array}{l} \left\{ \begin{array}{l} \underline{\text{REEL}} \\ \underline{\text{UNIT}} \end{array} \right\} \left[\begin{array}{l} \text{FOR } \underline{\text{REMOVAL}} \\ \text{WITH } \underline{\text{NO REWIND}} \end{array} \right] \\ \text{WITH} \left\{ \begin{array}{l} \underline{\text{NO REWIND}} \\ \underline{\text{LOCK}} \end{array} \right\} \end{array} \right] \right\} ...$$

COMPUTE { rsult [ROUNDED] } ... = arithmetic-expression

[ON SIZE ERROR stment [END-COMPUTE]]

<u>CONTINUE</u>

<u>DELETE</u> file-name RECORD $\left[\text{INVALID KEY stment [\underline{END-DELETE}]} \right]$

<u>DISPLAY</u> { src-item } ... [<u>UPON</u> output-dest]

[WITH <u>NO</u> ADVANCING]

Format 1

<u>DIVIDE</u> srcnum INTO { rsult [<u>ROUNDED</u>] } ...

$\left[\text{ON \underline{SIZE} \underline{ERROR} stment [\underline{END-DIVIDE}]} \right]$

Format 2

<u>DIVIDE</u> srcnum <u>INTO</u> srcnum
   <u>GIVING</u> { rsult [<u>ROUNDED</u>] } ...

$\left[\text{ON \underline{SIZE} \underline{ERROR} stment [\underline{END-DIVIDE}]} \right]$

Format 3

<u>DIVIDE</u> srcnum BY srcnum
   <u>GIVING</u> { rsult [<u>ROUNDED</u>] } ...

$\left[\text{ON \underline{SIZE} \underline{ERROR} stment [\underline{END-DIVIDE}]} \right]$

Format 4

<u>DIVIDE</u> srcnum <u>INTO</u> srcnum
   <u>GIVING</u> { rsult [<u>ROUNDED</u>] } ...
   <u>REMAINDER</u> remaind

$\left[\text{ON \underline{SIZE} \underline{ERROR} stment [\underline{END-DIVIDE}]} \right]$

Format 5

<u>DIVIDE</u> srcnum BY srcnum
   <u>GIVING</u> { rsult [<u>ROUNDED</u>] } ...
   <u>REMAINDER</u> remaind

$\left[\text{ON \underline{SIZE} \underline{ERROR} stment [\underline{END-DIVIDE}]} \right]$

<u>EXIT</u> [<u>PROGRAM</u>]

Format 1

GO TO [proc-name]

Format 2

GO TO { proc-name } ...
 DEPENDING ON num

IF condition THEN $\left\{ \begin{array}{l} \text{\{ stment-1 \}...} \\ \text{NEXT SENTENCE} \end{array} \right\}$

$\left[\begin{array}{l} \text{ELSE \{ stment-2 \}... [END-IF]} \\ \text{ELSE NEXT SENTENCE} \\ \text{END-IF} \end{array} \right]$

INITIALIZE $\left\{ \text{fld-name} \right\}$ ...

$\left[\text{REPLACING} \left\{ \begin{array}{l} \text{ALPHABETIC} \\ \text{ALPHANUMERIC} \\ \text{NUMERIC} \\ \text{ALPHANUMERIC-EDITED} \\ \text{NUMERIC-EDITED} \end{array} \right\} \text{DATA BY   val} \right]$

Format 1

INSPECT src-string TALLYING

$\left\{ \text{tally-ctr FOR} \left\{ \left\{ \begin{array}{l} \left\{ \begin{array}{l} \text{ALL} \\ \text{LEADING} \end{array} \right\} \text{compare-val} \\ \text{CHARACTERS} \end{array} \left[\left\{ \begin{array}{l} \text{BEFORE} \\ \text{AFTER} \end{array} \right\} \text{INITIAL delim-val} \right] \text{...} \right\} \text{...} \right\} \text{...} \right\}$

Format 2

INSPECT src-string REPLACING

$\left\{ \begin{array}{l} \text{CHARACTERS BY replace-char} \left[\left\{ \begin{array}{l} \text{BEFORE} \\ \text{AFTER} \end{array} \right\} \text{INITIAL delim-val} \right] \text{...} \\ \\ \left\{ \begin{array}{l} \text{ALL} \\ \text{LEADING} \\ \text{FIRST} \end{array} \right\} \left\{ \text{compare-val BY replace-val} \left[\left\{ \begin{array}{l} \text{BEFORE} \\ \text{AFTER} \end{array} \right\} \text{INITIAL delim-val} \right] \text{...} \right\} \text{...} \end{array} \right\} \text{...}$

Format 3

INSPECT src-string TALLYING

$$\left\{ \text{tally-ctr } \underline{\text{FOR}} \left\{ \left\{ \begin{array}{l} \text{ALL} \\ \underline{\text{LEADING}} \\ \text{CHARACTERS} \end{array} \right\} \text{compare-val} \right\} \left[\left\{ \begin{array}{l} \underline{\text{BEFORE}} \\ \underline{\text{AFTER}} \end{array} \right\} \text{INITIAL delim-val} \right] \quad \dots \right\} \dots \right\} \dots$$

<u>REPLACING</u>

$$\left\{ \begin{array}{l} \underline{\text{CHARACTERS}} \ \underline{\text{BY}} \ \text{replace-char} \qquad \left[\left\{ \begin{array}{l} \underline{\text{BEFORE}} \\ \underline{\text{AFTER}} \end{array} \right\} \text{INITIAL delim-val} \right] \quad \dots \\[2em] \left\{ \begin{array}{l} \underline{\text{ALL}} \\ \underline{\text{LEADING}} \\ \underline{\text{FIRST}} \end{array} \right\} \left\{ \text{compare-val } \underline{\text{BY}} \text{ replace-val} \quad \left[\left\{ \begin{array}{l} \underline{\text{BEFORE}} \\ \underline{\text{AFTER}} \end{array} \right\} \text{INITIAL delim-val} \right] \quad \dots \right\} \dots \end{array} \right\} \dots$$

Format 4

INSPECT src-string <u>CONVERTING</u> compare-chars <u>TO</u> convert-chars

$$\left[\left\{ \begin{array}{l} \underline{\text{BEFORE}} \\ \underline{\text{AFTER}} \end{array} \right\} \text{INITIAL delim-val} \right] \quad \dots$$

$$\underline{\text{MERGE}} \text{ mergefile} \left\{ \text{ON} \left\{ \begin{array}{l} \underline{\text{DESCENDING}} \\ \underline{\text{ASCENDING}} \end{array} \right\} \underline{\text{KEY}} \left\{ \text{ mergekey } \right\} \ \dots \right\} \dots$$

$$[\ \text{COLLATING } \underline{\text{SEQUENCE}} \text{ IS alpha} \ ]$$

$$\underline{\text{USING}} \left\{ \text{ infile } \right\} \left\{ \text{ infile } \right\} \ \dots$$

$$\left\{ \begin{array}{l} \underline{\text{OUTPUT}} \ \underline{\text{PROCEDURE}} \text{ IS first-proc} \quad \left[\left\{ \begin{array}{l} \underline{\text{THRU}} \\ \underline{\text{THROUGH}} \end{array} \right\} \text{end-proc} \right] \\[2em] \underline{\text{GIVING}} \left\{ \text{ outfile } \right\} \ \dots \end{array} \right\}$$

$$\underline{\text{MOVE}} \left\{ \begin{array}{l} \left[\begin{array}{l} \underline{\text{CORRESPONDING}} \\ \underline{\text{CORR}} \end{array} \right] \text{src-item} \\[2em] \text{lit} \end{array} \right\} \underline{\text{TO}} \left\{ \text{ dest-item } \right\} \ \dots$$

Format 1

MULTIPLY srcnum <u>BY</u> {   rsult [<u>ROUNDED</u>] }   ...

$\left[\text{ON } \underline{\text{SIZE}} \ \underline{\text{ERROR}} \text{ stment } [\ \underline{\text{END-MULTIPLY}} \ ] \right]$

Format 2

MULTIPLY srcnum <u>BY</u>   srcnum
   <u>GIVING</u> {   rsult [<u>ROUNDED</u>] }   ...

$\left[\text{ON } \underline{\text{SIZE}} \ \underline{\text{ERROR}} \text{ stment } [\ \underline{\text{END-MULTIPLY}} \ ] \right]$

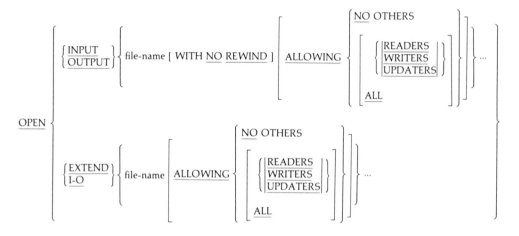

Format 1

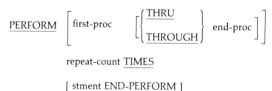

PERFORM $\left[\text{first-proc} \quad \left[\left\{ \begin{array}{c} \underline{\text{THRU}} \\ \underline{\text{THROUGH}} \end{array} \right\} \ \text{end-proc} \right] \right]$

    [stment <u>END-PERFORM</u>]

Format 2

PERFORM $\left[\text{first-proc} \quad \left[\left\{ \begin{array}{c} \underline{\text{THRU}} \\ \underline{\text{THROUGH}} \end{array} \right\} \ \text{end-proc} \right] \right]$

    repeat-count <u>TIMES</u>

    [stment <u>END-PERFORM</u>]

Format 3

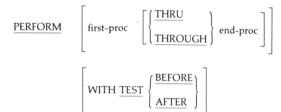

$$\text{PERFORM} \left[\text{first-proc} \left[\left\{ \begin{array}{c} \text{THRU} \\ \text{THROUGH} \end{array} \right\} \text{end-proc} \right] \right]$$

$$\left[\text{WITH TEST} \left\{ \begin{array}{c} \text{BEFORE} \\ \text{AFTER} \end{array} \right\} \right] \text{UNTIL cond}$$

Format 4

$$\text{PERFORM} \left[\text{first-proc} \left[\left\{ \begin{array}{c} \text{THRU} \\ \text{THROUGH} \end{array} \right\} \text{end-proc} \right] \right]$$

$$\left[\text{WITH TEST} \left\{ \begin{array}{c} \text{BEFORE} \\ \text{AFTER} \end{array} \right\} \right]$$

VARYING var FROM init BY increm UNTIL cond

[AFTER var FROM init BY increm UNTIL cond] ...

[stment END-PERFORM]

Format 1

READ file-name [NEXT] RECORD [INTO dest-item]

$$\left[\text{AT END stment [END-READ]} \right]$$

Format 2

READ file-name RECORD [INTO dest-item]

[KEY IS key-name]

$$\left[\text{INVALID KEY stment [END-READ]} \right]$$

RELEASE rec [FROM src-area]

RETURN smrg-file RECORD [INTO dest-area]

AT END stment

[END-RETURN]

REWRITE rec-name [FROM src-item]

$$\left[\text{INVALID KEY stment [END-REWRITE] }\right]$$

Format 1

SEARCH src-table [VARYING pointr]

  [AT END stment]

$$\left\{ \text{WHEN cond} \quad \left\{ \begin{array}{l} \text{stment} \\ \text{NEXT SENTENCE} \end{array} \right\} \right\} \text{ ... [END-SEARCH]}$$

Format 2

SEARCH ALL src-table [AT END stment]

$$\text{WHEN} \left\{ \begin{array}{l} \text{elemnt} \quad \left\{ \begin{array}{l} \text{IS EQUAL TO} \\ \text{IS =} \end{array} \right\} \text{ arg} \\ \\ \text{cond-name} \end{array} \right\}$$

$$\left[\text{AND} \left\{ \begin{array}{l} \text{elemnt} \quad \left\{ \begin{array}{l} \text{IS EQUAL TO} \\ \text{IS =} \end{array} \right\} \text{ arg} \\ \\ \text{cond-name} \end{array} \right\} \right] \text{ ...}$$

$$\left\{ \begin{array}{l} \text{stment} \\ \text{NEXT SENTENCE} \end{array} \right\} \text{ [END-SEARCH]}$$

Format 1

SET { rsult } ... TO val

Format 2

$$\text{SET \{ indx \} ...} \left\{ \begin{array}{l} \text{UP BY} \\ \text{DOWN BY} \end{array} \right\} \text{ increm}$$

Format 3

<u>SET</u> { cond-name } ... <u>TO</u> <u>TRUE</u>

Format 4

$$\underline{SET} \left\{ \{ \text{ switch-name } \} \text{ ... } \underline{TO} \left\{ \begin{array}{c} \underline{ON} \\ \underline{OFF} \end{array} \right\} \right\} \text{ ...}$$

$$\underline{SORT} \text{ sortfile} \left\{ ON \left\{ \begin{array}{c} \underline{DESCENDING} \\ \underline{ASCENDING} \end{array} \right\} \underline{KEY} \{ \text{ sortkey } \} \text{ ...} \right\} \text{ ...}$$

[WITH <u>DUPLICATES</u> IN ORDER]

$$\left\{ \begin{array}{l} \underline{INPUT} \ \underline{PROCEDURE} \ IS \ \text{first-proc} \ \left[\left\{ \begin{array}{c} \underline{THRU} \\ \underline{THROUGH} \end{array} \right\} \text{end-proc} \right] \\ \underline{USING} \ \{ \ \text{infile} \ \} \ \text{...} \end{array} \right\}$$

$$\left\{ \begin{array}{l} \underline{OUTPUT} \ \underline{PROCEDURE} \ IS \ \text{first-proc} \ \left[\left\{ \begin{array}{c} \underline{THRU} \\ \underline{THROUGH} \end{array} \right\} \text{end-proc} \right] \\ \underline{GIVING} \ \{ \ \text{outfile} \ \} \ \text{...} \end{array} \right\}$$

$$\underline{START} \ \text{file-name} \ \left[\underline{KEY} \left\{ \begin{array}{l} IS \ \underline{EQUAL} \ TO \\ IS = \\ IS \ \underline{GREATER} \ THAN \\ IS > \\ IS \ \underline{NOT} \ \underline{LESS} \ THAN \\ IS \ \underline{NOT} < \end{array} \right\} \text{key-data} \right]$$

$$\left[\underline{INVALID} \ KEY \ \text{stment} \quad [\ \underline{END\text{-}START} \ ] \right]$$

$$\underline{STOP} \left\{ \begin{array}{c} \underline{RUN} \\ \text{disp} \end{array} \right\}$$

$$\underline{STRING} \left\{ \{ \ \text{src-string} \}... \ \underline{DELIMITED} \ BY \left\{ \begin{array}{c} \text{delim} \\ \underline{SIZE} \end{array} \right\} \right\} \text{ ...}$$

<u>INTO</u> dest-string [WITH <u>POINTER</u> pointr]

$$\left[ON \ \underline{OVERFLOW} \ \text{stment} \ [\ \underline{END\text{-}STRING} \ ] \right]$$

Format 1

SUBTRACT { num } ... FROM { rsult [ROUNDED] } ...

$\left[\text{[ON SIZE ERROR stment [END-SUBTRACT]}\right]$

Format 2

SUBTRACT { num } ... FROM num
GIVING { rsult [ROUNDED] } ...

$\left[\text{ON SIZE ERROR stment [END-SUBTRACT]}\right]$

Format 3

SUBTRACT $\left\{\begin{array}{c}\text{CORRESPONDING} \\ \text{CORR}\end{array}\right\}$ grp-1 FROM grp-2 [ROUNDED]

$\left[\text{ON SIZE ERROR stment [END-SUBTRACT]}\right]$

CREATING src-string

$\left[\text{DELIMITED BY [ALL] delim } \left[\text{OR [ALL] delim}\right] ...\right]$

INTO $\left\{\text{dest-string [DELIMINTER IN delim-dest] [COUNT IN countr]}\right\}$ ...

[WITH POINTER pointr]

[TALLYING IN tally-ctr]

$\left[\text{ON OVERFLOW stment [END-UNSTRING]}\right]$

USE AFTER STANDARD $\left\{\begin{array}{c}\text{EXCEPTION} \\ \text{ERROR}\end{array}\right\}$ PROCEDURE ON $\left\{\begin{array}{l}\text{file-name ...} \\ \text{INPUT} \\ \text{OUTPUT} \\ \text{I-O} \\ \text{EXTEND}\end{array}\right\}$

Format 1

WRITE rec-name [FROM src-item]

$$\left[\left\{ \begin{array}{l} \text{BEFORE} \\ \text{AFTER} \end{array} \right\} \text{ADVANCING} \left\{ \begin{array}{l} \left\{ \text{advance-num} \left[\begin{array}{l} \underline{\text{LINE}} \\ \text{LINES} \end{array} \right] \right\} \\ \left\{ \begin{array}{l} \text{top-name} \\ \underline{\text{PAGE}} \end{array} \right\} \end{array} \right\} \right]$$

$$\left[\text{AT} \left\{ \begin{array}{l} \text{END-OF-PAGE} \\ \underline{\text{EOP}} \end{array} \right\} \text{stment} \quad [\underline{\text{END-WRITE}}] \right]$$

Format 2

<u>WRITE</u> rec-name [<u>FROM</u> src-item]

$$\left[\underline{\text{INVALID}} \text{ KEY stment } [\underline{\text{END-WRITE}}] \right]$$

REFERENCING FORMATS.

Qualification:

Format 1

$$\left\{ \begin{array}{l} \text{data-name-1} \\ \text{condition-name} \end{array} \right\} \left\{ \begin{array}{l} \left\{ \left\{ \begin{array}{l} \underline{\text{IN}} \\ \text{OF} \end{array} \right\} \text{data-name-2} \right\} \cdots \left[\left\{ \begin{array}{l} \underline{\text{IN}} \\ \text{OF} \end{array} \right\} \text{file-name} \right] \\ \left\{ \begin{array}{l} \underline{\text{IN}} \\ \text{OF} \end{array} \right\} \text{file-name} \end{array} \right\}$$

Format 2

$$\text{paragraph-name} \left\{ \begin{array}{l} \underline{\text{IN}} \\ \text{OF} \end{array} \right\} \text{section-name}$$

Format 3

$$\text{text-name} \quad \left\{ \begin{array}{l} \underline{\text{IN}} \\ \text{OF} \end{array} \right\} \text{library-name}$$

Format 4

$$\text{LINAGE-COUNTER} \begin{Bmatrix} \underline{\text{IN}} \\ \underline{\text{OF}} \end{Bmatrix} \text{file-name}$$

Subscripting:

$$\begin{Bmatrix} \text{data-name} \\ \text{condition-name} \end{Bmatrix} (\{ \text{ arithmetic-expression } \} \dots)$$

Indexing

$$\begin{Bmatrix} \text{data-name} \\ \text{condition-name} \end{Bmatrix} \left(\begin{Bmatrix} \text{, index-name} \begin{bmatrix} \begin{Bmatrix} + \\ - \end{Bmatrix} \text{ literal-2} \end{bmatrix} \\ \text{, literal-1} \end{Bmatrix} \dots \right)$$

Reference Modification:

data-name (leftmost-character-position : [length])

Identifier:

Format 1

data-name [qualification] [subscripting] [reference modification]

Format 2

data-name [qualification] [indexing] [reference modification]

GENERAL FORMAT

Format 1

ACCEPT dest-item [FROM input-source]   [AT END stment [END-ACCEPT]]

Format 2

$$\text{\underline{ACCEPT} dest-item \underline{FROM}} \begin{Bmatrix} \text{DATE} \\ \text{DAY} \\ \text{DAY-OF-WEEK} \\ \text{TIME} \end{Bmatrix}$$

Format 3

ACCEPT dest-item

$$\left\{ \begin{array}{l} \text{FROM \underline{LINE} NUMBER} \begin{Bmatrix} \text{line-num} \\ \text{line-id} \quad \left[\text{\underline{PLUS} [plus-num]} \right] \\ \text{\underline{PLUS} [plus-num]} \end{Bmatrix} \\[2em] \text{FROM \underline{COLUMN} NUMBER} \begin{Bmatrix} \text{column-num} \\ \text{column-id} \quad \left[\text{\underline{PLUS} [plus-num]} \right] \\ \text{\underline{PLUS} [plus-num]} \end{Bmatrix} \\[2em] \text{\underline{ERASE} [TO \underline{END} OF]} \begin{Bmatrix} \text{\underline{SCREEN}} \\ \text{\underline{LINE}} \end{Bmatrix} \\[1em] \text{WITH \underline{BELL}} \\ \text{\underline{UNDERLINED}} \\ \text{\underline{BOLD}} \\ \text{WITH \underline{BLINKING}} \\ \text{\underline{PROTECTED} [\underline{SIZE} protect-length]} \\ \text{with \underline{CONVERSION}} \\ \text{\underline{REVERSED}} \\ \text{WITH \underline{NO} \underline{ECHO}} \\ \text{\underline{DEFAULT} IS} \begin{Bmatrix} \text{def-src-lit} \\ \text{def-src-item} \end{Bmatrix} \\ \text{CONTROL \underline{KEY} IN key-dest-item} \end{array} \right\}$$

$$\left[\begin{Bmatrix} \text{ON \underline{EXCEPTION} stment} \\ \text{AT \underline{END} stment} \end{Bmatrix} \text{[\underline{END-ACCEPT}]} \right]$$

Format 4

ACCEPT CONTROL KEY IN key-dest-item

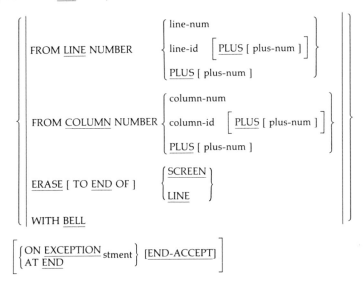

$$
\left\{
\begin{array}{l}
\left|
\begin{array}{l}
\text{FROM \underline{LINE} NUMBER} \left\{
\begin{array}{l}
\text{line-num} \\
\text{line-id} \left[\underline{PLUS}\;[\;\text{plus-num}\;]\right] \\
\underline{PLUS}\;[\;\text{plus-num}\;]
\end{array}
\right\} \\
\text{FROM \underline{COLUMN} NUMBER} \left\{
\begin{array}{l}
\text{column-num} \\
\text{column-id} \left[\underline{PLUS}\;[\;\text{plus-num}\;]\right] \\
\underline{PLUS}\;[\;\text{plus-num}\;]
\end{array}
\right\} \\
\underline{ERASE}\;[\;\text{TO \underline{END} OF}\;] \left\{
\begin{array}{l}
\underline{SCREEN} \\
\underline{LINE}
\end{array}
\right\} \\
\text{WITH \underline{BELL}}
\end{array}
\right|
\end{array}
\right\}
$$

$$
\left[
\left\{
\begin{array}{l}
\text{ON \underline{EXCEPTION}} \\
\text{AT \underline{END}}
\end{array}
\right\}
\text{stment}\;[\text{END-ACCEPT}]
\right]
$$

Format 1

DISPLAY { src-item } ... [UPON output-dest] [WITH NO ADVANCING]

Format 2

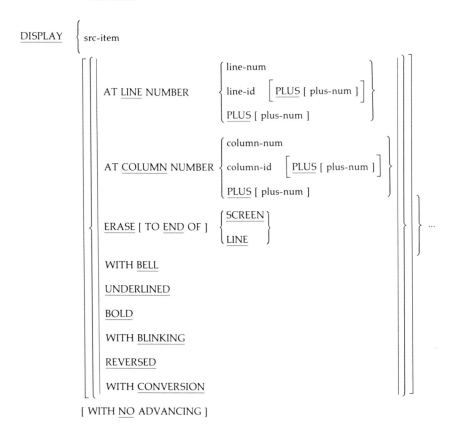

[WITH NO ADVANCING]

Appendix E

File Status Codes

File Status	Input–Output Statements	File Organization	Access Method	Meaning
00	All	All	All	Successful
02	REWRITE WRITE	Ind	All	Created duplicate Alternate Key
05	OPEN	All	All	Optional file not present
13	READ	All	Seq	No next logical record (at end)
15	READ	All	Seq	Optional file not present (at end)
16	READ	All	Seq	No valid next record (at end)
21	REWRITE	Ind	Seq	Primary key changed after READ or START (invalid key)
21	WRITE	Ind	Seq	Attempted non-ascending key value (invalid key)
22	REWRITE	Ind	All	Duplicate Alternate Key (invalid key)
22	WRITE	Ind. Rel	All	Duplicate key (invalid key)
23	DELETE READ REWRITE START	Ind. Rel	Ran	Record not in file (invalid key)
24	WRITE	Ind. Rel	All	Boundary violation (invalid key)
25	READ START	Ind. Rel	Ran	Optional file not present (invalid key)
30	All	All	All	All other permanent errors
34	WRITE	Seq	Seq	Boundary violation
90	READ	All	All	Record locked by another user; record is available in record area
91	OPEN	All	All	File locked by another program; record is not available
92	DELETE READ REWRITE START WRITE	All	All	Record locked by another program
93	DELETE REWRITE	All	Seq	No previous READ or START
94	CLOSE	All	All	File never opened or already closed
94	OPEN	All	All	File already open, or closed with lock
94	DELETE READ REWRITE START WRITE	All	All	File not open, or incompatible open mode
95	OPEN	All	All	No file space on device
97	OPEN	All	All	File not found
98	CLOSE	All	All	Any other CLOSE error

Reprinted by permission of Digital Equipment Corporation, *VAX-11 COBOL Pocket Guide*, August, 1980.

Index